THE COMPLE   OK OF
GARDEN PESTS
AND DISE
AND HOW TO GET RII

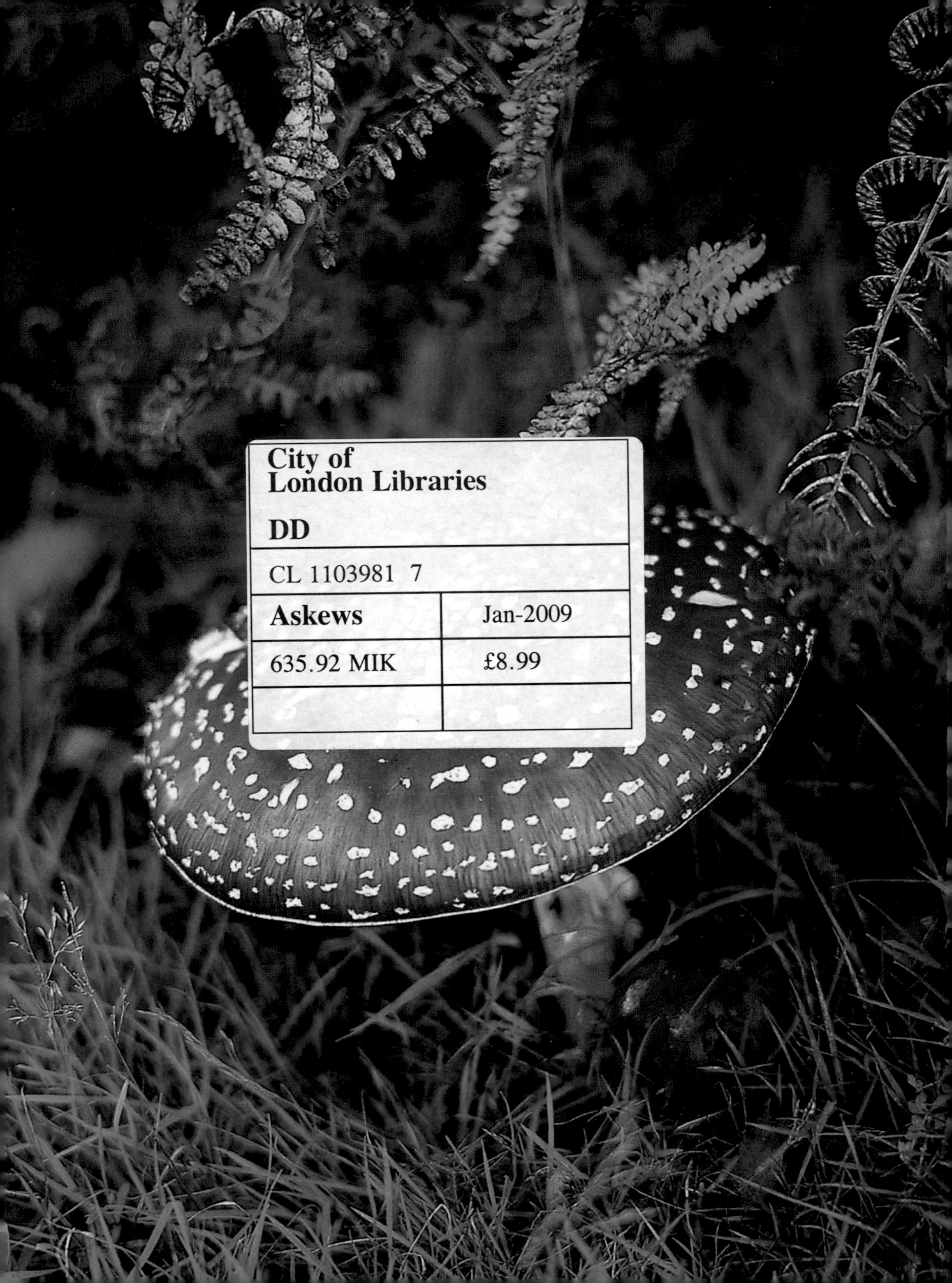

THE COMPLETE ILLUSTRATED HANDBOOK OF
GARDEN PESTS AND DISEASES
AND HOW TO GET RID OF THEM

A COMPREHENSIVE GUIDE TO OVER 800 GARDEN PROBLEMS AND HOW TO IDENTIFY, CONTROL AND TREAT THEM SUCCESSFULLY

ANDREW MIKOLAJSKI

southwater

This edition is published by Southwater,
an imprint of Anness Publishing Ltd
Hermes House, 88–89 Blackfriars Road,
London SE1 8HA
tel. 020 7401 2077; fax 020 7633 9499

www.southwaterbooks.com; www.annesspublishing.com

If you like the images in this book and would like
to investigate using them for publishing, promotions
or advertising, please visit our website
www.practicalpictures.com for more information.

UK agent: The Manning Partnership Ltd;
tel. 01225 478444; fax 01225 478440;
sales@manning-partnership.co.uk
UK distributor: Grantham Book Services Ltd;
tel. 01476 541080; fax 01476 541061;
orders@gbs.tbs-ltd.co.uk
North American agent/distributor: National Book Network;
tel. 301 459 3366; fax 301 429 5746; www.nbnbooks.com
Australian agent/distributor: Pan Macmillan Australia;
tel. 1300 135 113; fax 1300 135 103;
customer.service@macmillan.com.au
New Zealand agent/distributor: David Bateman Ltd;
tel. (09) 415 7664; fax (09) 415 8892

Publisher: Joanna Lorenz
Editorial Directors: Judith Simons and Helen Sudell
Executive Editor: Caroline Davison
Project Editor: Simona Hill
Copy Editor: Alison Bolus
Designer: Nigel Partridge
Editorial Reader: Penelope Goodare
Production Controller: Wendy Lawson

ETHICAL TRADING POLICY
Because of our ongoing ecological investment programme,
you, as our customer, can have the pleasure and reassurance
of knowing that a tree is being cultivated on your behalf
to naturally replace the materials used to make
the book you are holding. For further information about
this scheme, go to www.annesspublishing.com/trees

Previously published as *The Practical Encyclopedia
of Garden Pests and Diseases*

Contents

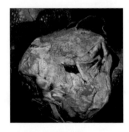

Introduction

This is a book for gardeners who want to grow and nurture robust and healthy plants, whether in the ornamental flower garden, orchard or vegetable plot. Understanding how plants are affected by their environment, and recognizing which plants are susceptible to specific pests and diseases, will help keep you one step ahead of any potential problem.

Plant pathology, the study of plant abnormalities, is a large and complex subject that rightly is the focus of academic research. As far as insect pests go, the average gardener can

Below: Wild flower or weed? Attitudes towards gardening will dictate how you choose to deal with garden problems.

be easily baffled by the complexities of the animal kingdom. Many insects look similar, even though the damage they create can vary dramatically. Learning to recognize a beneficial insect from a pest is one of the first stages in learning to improve the health of your garden. In this book, pests are described with reference to the plants that they attack; therefore this book cannot function as a field guide to insects and other invertebrates.

Fungi are a major cause of gardeners problems. They are more primitive organisms than plants, and many are microscopic. Bacteria, another potential problem group, are never seen, and usually function within plant tissue. Many are beneficial, and play an

Above: Petal blight is caused by a fungus that attacks susceptible plants in damp weather.

important part in breaking down dead plant material in soil in order to return valuable nutrients to growing plants. Those that cause problems for gardeners are discussed here.

The scope of the book is international. The simple fact is that at a time of increased global warming and climate change, and the development of global markets in fresh foods, pests and diseases can, potentially at least, be transmitted around the world at an alarming rate.

A case in point is the recent outbreak of sudden oak death, a problem that has decimated tracts of oak woodland in California. The disease spread rapidly to neighbouring Oregon (where it has been successfully contained), and has now appeared in Europe, introduced – we can only assume – on plant material exported from America. European oak species are apparently immune; the disease can affect viburnums and rhododendrons in gardens (possibly introduced via nursery stock), but, more worryingly, has the potential to strike beech, a common European forestry tree. The disease is potentially as destructive as Dutch elm was 30 years ago, and all those involved in forest management are rightly concerned.

Invertebrate pests can all too easily cross from country to country – despite stringent quarantine laws – in fruits and root crops (and even on cut flowers), sometimes at the egg stage. Many moths and larger flighted insects are capable of flying vast distances, and, if blown off course, can easily turn up far from

Above: Downy mildew is a common garden problem that is caused by a fungus.

Right: An unsightly abnormal growth in a woody plant would take time to reach this size.

their native land. If local conditions suit them, even if only in the short term, they can multiply and cause unforeseen damage. A recent scare was the appearance in Europe of Australian and New Zealand flatworms, leech-like creatures that devour earthworms and thus have a detrimental effect on soil structure, and hence on plant health.

Gardeners play an important part in containing the spread of certain potentially damaging pests and diseases. In some areas, the appearance or outbreak of a particular pest or disease (usually those that have the potential to strike commercial crops) must be reported to the local agriculture department.

Most gardeners manage to control, or live with, a whole host of pests and diseases. Being able to produce strong and healthy plants, regardless of the myriad garden problems is what gardening is about.

How to use this book

This book is intended as a practical guide to garden problems and how to deal with them. Chapter 1, *Diagnosing and Controlling Problems*, shows you how to look for the early warning signs that a problem might be present in the garden. It defines what we understand as pests, such as mammals and birds – including domestic pets – as well as insects and other invertebrates. It describes the pathogens that cause various plant diseases. Physiological disorders (problems caused by the growing environment) are also defined. Problems specific to lawns and ponds are discussed here, and there is also a section on weeds and weed control – an important aspect of good garden management. Ways in which garden problems can be tackled are suggested throughout. Some management techniques, such as crop rotation, are still an excellent strategy for keeping a whole host of problems at bay, or at least limiting their impact.

This chapter also discusses how to attract beneficial wildlife into the garden to help in the control of certain insect and invertebrate pests. It looks at the importance of good pruning practices to keep woody plants healthy and productive. Hygiene in the greenhouse is also included. The various methods available to the amateur gardener to control pests and diseases are assessed, as are the safe use and storage of garden chemicals.

Chapter 2, the *Plant Problem Identifier*, functions as an index to the encyclopedia that follows. This chapter contains three lists. The first, shorter list, on pages 48–49 *The common name plant index*, is a list of plants by common name. The page number indicated at the right-hand side of each entry, will lead you to an entry within the following *Botanical name plant list*. This second list, on pages 50–99, contains the name and a brief description of every pest, disease and disorder that might attack a specific plant. Some entries such as tomatoes and potatoes have extensive lists. To help you narrow down the search, a brief description of the causes of damage is included.

Some pests such as slugs, for example, eat a range of plants and it would be unwieldy to include them under each plant entry. For a fuller description, turn to the relevant page reference in chapters 3, 4 and 5. This chapter concludes with a list of general problems, *Plant list by general plant group*, on pages 100–109.

Botanical name plant list

Once you have the botanical name of your plant, find it in the following list. Following the plant name is the name of each pest, disease or problem that may affect it. To find a description of each turn to the page reference indicated.

PLANT	PROBLEM	SYMPTOMS/DESCRIPTION	PAGE
A			
Abies	woolly adelgid	*Some yellowing of foliage.*	113
fir	witches' brooms	*Broom-like mass of erect shoots.*	195
	cracking of bark	*Long, vertical cracks in bark.*	240
Acacia	wattle leafminer	*Pink blisters on leaves; brown flaking.*	112
wattle	California red scale, red scale	*Orange-pink scale; die-back; leaves shed.*	116
	oleander scale, ivy scale	*White-brownish circular scales.*	117
	large auger beetle	*White larvae tunnel through wood.*	118
	moth borer	*Large larvae tunnel into wood. Serious weakening.*	126
	wasp gall	*Galls on leaves.*	132
	gumtree hopper	*Various insects. Honeydew, sooty mould.*	135
	gall wasps	*Galls on leaves.*	135
	loopers and semi-looper	*Holes are chewed in leaves. Flowers can be damaged.*	136
	cottony cushion scale	*Brown scale. Honeydew, sooty mould.*	140
	fruit-tree borerturni	*White moth. Larvae tunnel into wood.*	145
	wattle mealybug	*Purple-black scales. Honeydew, sooty mould.*	146
	crusader bug	*Brown bug, yellow cross. Yellow dots on nymph. Plants wilt.*	146
	bag-shelter moth	*Yellow eggs; hairy larvae. "Bags" in trees; leaves eaten.*	149
	acacia spotting bug	*Slender, brown bug. Leaves spotted.*	160
	green treehopper	*Green, horned insect. Die-back; slits in twigs for eggs.*	162
	painted apple moth	*Black-tufted caterpillars chew leaves.*	165
	stem gall, Dingley branch gall	*Small, cushion-like galls on branches.*	176
	sooty blotch	*Dark, circular, cloudy enlarging patches on fruit skins.*	192
	fly speck	*Small, circular specks on fruit skins; taste unaffected.*	196
	rust gall	*Large, woody, red-brown galls; distorted "broom" growths.*	218
Acer	acer pimple gall mite, acer gall mite	*Red pimples on leaves.*	116
maple	gall mites, rust mite	*Galls on leaves/stems.*	133
	leopard moth	*White/black-spotted moth. Black-spotted larvae tunnel into wood.*	169
	coral spot	*Die-back; pink-red, cushion-like pustules.*	198
	scorch	*Leaves turn brown at edges and curl.*	239
Agave	pineapple scale	*Yellow spots on leaves.*	129
agave			
Ageratum	chrysanthemum stunt viroid	*Stunting, brittle stems. Yellow spots on leaves; distortion.*	223
floss flower			

Abies   Acacia   Ageratum

Left: The *Botanical name plant list* is a comprehensive list of the most common plants grown by gardeners. Every plant is listed in botanical name alphabetical order. This index provides a complete listing of every common problem that affects specific plants.

You can only use this list if you know the botanical name of your affected plant. If you know just the common name of your plant, for example, "daffodil", then you must refer to the *Common name plant index* on page 48–49 to locate the botanical name. The *Common name plant index* will tell you that the botanical name for daffodil is *Narcissus*. Now turn back to the Botanical name plant list. You will find the entry for Narcissus on page 75.

Some of the lists of pests that affect specific plants are quite long. Read the brief descriptions. at the side of each pest, disease or physiological problem to see if you can narrow down the potential cause of the problem. You can do this by identifying the pest by type and size, or by the type of damage caused. The list refers you to specific entries in the encyclopedia that follows. The page reference for each entry appears on the right of the page.

Right: The encyclopedia is arranged into chapters according to type of problem. Chapter 3 includes all the insect and invertebrate pests. Chapter 4 includes fungal and bacterial problems, and Chapter 5 includes all the physiological problems – those that are caused by weather, soil or nutritional problems.

The entries within each chapter of the encyclopedia are arranged according to Latin name alphabetical order of the problem, and not according to plant host. If three or four entries on the same page have the same common or Latin name, for speed of identification, we have included the names of the plant hosts in brackets after the common name of the problem.

The entries in the encyclopedia provide information to help identify and eradicate, if necessary, a specific problem. Look first at the geographical area where the problem is known to exist and disregard any that are not specific to your location.

If you suspect your plant is manifesting a particular problem that you know the common name of, refer to the index at the back of the book to locate the correct page reference.

124 INSECTS AND OTHER INVERTEBRATES

Above: This adult turnip flea beetle is feeding on an oilseed rape plant.

be killed outright, though older plants generally recover.
Plants affected: Brassicas; sweet corn, aubergines (eggplants) and sweet potatoes; fuchsias (*Fuchsia*). Weeds can harbour the pests.
Prevention and control: *Chemical*: Treat with derris or bifenthrin, lindane or pirimiphos-methyl. *Non-chemical/organic*: Substitute pyrethrum. Protect seedlings with a floating mulch. Keep a weed-free vegetable garden.

BEET LEAFHOPPER
Circulifer tenellus
Range: North America, Europe, Asia.
Description: The adult is a pale green to brown insect, to 3mm (1/8in) long, capable of rapid hopping and flying. Nymphs are pale green and lack wings. Both adults and nymphs are vectors of a number of plant diseases, including beet curly top (Western yellow blight). There are one to three generations per year.
Damage: Adults and nymphs suck sap from plants. This generally causes little damage in itself, but can result in harmful viral infections.
Plants affected: Beans, beets, carrots, aubergines (eggplants), spinach and tomatoes; also delphiniums (*Delphinium*), carnations (*Dianthus*), petunias (*Petunia*) and zinnias (*Zinnia*); and weeds.
Prevention and control: *Chemical*: Spray with dimethoate, malathion, permethrin or pirimiphos-methyl. *Non-chemical/organic*: Protect vulnerable crops with a floating mulch when the pests are active. Clear the garden of weeds that can harbour the pest.

SOFT SCALES
Coccidae
Range: Cosmopolitan.
Description: Soft scales are sap-sucking insects, which have a tough outer skin, or cover themselves with wax. Many species have no males. Females lay eggs that hatch into crawlers, which wander about until they find a suitable resting place. Their feeding activities cause little direct harm, but the honeydew they excrete is damaging.
Damage: Honeydew excreted by the scales attracts *sooty mould*.
Plants affected: A wide range; some species have specific hosts.
Prevention and control: *Chemical*: Spray with dimethoate or insecticidal soap. *Non-chemical/organic*: Brush off scales by hand. Control ants, which deter the scales' natural predators.

Above: Scale insects have excreted honeydew on to this leaf.

COCCID GALLS (eucalyptus)
Coccoidea
Range: Widely distributed.
Description: A number of sap-sucking insects can cause galls to appear on eucalyptus. The size and shape of the galls vary according to the species of pest and its sex.
Damage: Unsightly galls appear on the stems and leaves of eucalyptus.
Plants affected: Eucalyptus (*Eucalyptus*), especially young plants.
Prevention and control: *Non-chemical/organic*: Prune affected growth if necessary; feed and water the plant well.

SOFT SCALE, Brown Soft Scale, Soft Brown Scale
Coccus hesperidum
Range: Europe, North America, Australia and New Zealand.
Description: This scale is a sap-sucking insect that is capable of breeding throughout the year in favourable conditions. Scales are yellow-brown and roughly oval, to 4mm (1/6in) long, and are usually found on the undersides

Above: These overturned leaves are infested with young scale insects.

of leaves. The honeydew they excrete drips down and forms sticky areas on the upper sides of leaves lower down the plant. Infestations are worse in hot, dry climates.
Damage: Honeydew attracts *sooty mould*.
Plants affected: Many plants commonly grown under glass, including citrus, grapes, figs, passion fruit, peaches and pears; also ornamental plants such as ferns, ivies (*Hedera*), *Ficus* and *Schefflera*.
Prevention and control: *Chemical*: Spray with malathion. *Non-chemical/organic*: The parasitic wasp *Metaphycus helvolus* provides some control. *Ferns*: Cut back affected growth. Heavily infested specimens are best discarded.

SPRINGTAILS
Collembola
Range: Cosmopolitan.
Description: Springtails are small, white insects that feed on moist, decaying organic matter. The most commonly seen species are less than 2mm (1/12in) long. They are found in compost heaps, and sometimes

Below: A shiny, black cabbage stem flea beetle.

Below: White soft scale insects on some new laurel growth.

Below: This coffee leaf has been heavily infested with soft scales.

Below: A large colony of brown scale insects lives on this grapevine.

Chapter 3, *Insects and Other Invertebrates,* functions as a directory of garden invertebrate pests. Pests are listed alphabetically by Latin name. Their common names are also given, as these are the ones most likely to be familiar to the average gardener (to locate a pest by common name, consult the index). In some cases, an individual species is described (for example, the apple blossom weevil, *Anthonomus pomorum*) but other pests (for example, ants, which comprise a wide range of different species) have generic entries. Some pests have entries of both types; for instance, soft scales have a general entry under Coccidae, but individual species that cause problems specific to certain plants also have their own entries.

Range indicates the geographical range of the pest. *Description* provides a description of the pest together with its feeding activities and any other factors (such as its excrement or eggs) that help in identifying it. *Damage* describes the damage caused (in some cases, the use of italics, e.g. *sooty mould*, indicates that there is a further entry on this secondary problem elsewhere). *Plants affected* lists the plants that are likely to suffer attack, with kitchen garden plants listed first. (Some pests have a wide host range, and it would be impractical to list all vulnerable plants: nearly all plants are susceptible to slug damage at the seedling stage, for instance). *Prevention and control* suggests some of the ways the pest can be controlled. Where relevant, both *chemical* and *non-chemical/organic* methods are discussed. (Note that this is not designed as a book for organic gardeners, and no judgement has been made as to the environment-friendliness or otherwise of any control method suggested.)

Chapter 4, *Fungal, Bacterial and Other Problems,* is a directory of fungal, bacterial and viral diseases. These are also ordered by Latin name (apart from the viruses, which, owing to their ability to mutate, are difficult to classify: these have their own subsection). If you know the common name of a certain disease, but not the name of the pathogen, use the index to locate the entry. Some similar problems that can be caused by a range of pathogens, for example, leaf spots, are grouped together. Host-specific pathogens, or those that affect only a limited range of plants, have their own entries. The *Definition* indicates the type of the disease (e.g. fungal, bacterial or other), and under what conditions it is likely to strike. *Symptoms and damage* describes how the plant is likely to suffer. *Plants affected* lists vulnerable plants. *Prevention and control* suggests ways of combating the problem, often a matter of good garden management.

Chapter 5, *Physiological Problems,* is a directory of problems caused by environment. These are grouped according to what factor (for example, cold, drought) causes the problem. *How to identify* describes the symptoms. *Damage* indicates in what way the plant is likely to suffer. *Cause* clarifies the cause of the problem. *Plants affected* lists plants that are likely to be vulnerable to the problem. *Prevention and control* suggests ways of reducing the problem.

Diagnosing and Controlling Problems

Recognizing that a pest or disease exists in the garden is the first stage in learning how to eradicate or control it. The damage created by insects, often microscopic, can be infuriating, particularly if you are a gardener who enjoys watching the plants blossom and have put hours of work into creating a thriving garden. Once you establish which plants are being attacked and recognize the conditions in which a pest thrives, you can take steps to remove it.

Left: Painted lady butterfly on a thistle.

What is a pest?

Pests come in all guises. A pest is any living creature that causes damage to garden plants and pond life. Pests include mammals, birds and insects. Some are highly visible and easily recognized, while others are microscopic, live underground or only come out at night.

Mammals that are pests, such as rabbits, squirrels and mice are clearly visible and often cause considerable damage. Other pests, such as insects, are often much less visible to the naked eye. These may be microscopic and they are not always easy to identify. The damage they cause can devastate garden crops and cause unsightly conditions that raise the risk of infection in vulnerable plants.

Invertebrate pests

The pests among the invertebrates (animals without backbones) are the most troublesome, and include mainly insects, such as beetles, aphids, grubs, bugs, butterflies, moths and

Above: Aphid-eating ladybirds are small beetles, and are welcome visitors in any garden.

Above: Snails, though often attractive to look at, are invertebrates that can leave a trail of destruction as they feed on plant leaves.

weevils, also molluscs such as slugs and snails, as well as a host of other creatures such as mites. Not only are the majority of invertebrates tiny and well camouflaged (often their presence goes undetected until the damage they have caused is all too apparent), but in favourable conditions they are able to reproduce very quickly, and huge populations (referred to as plagues in severe cases) can appear, seemingly, almost overnight.

Butterflies and moths perform a valuable function as pollinators: they are the means by which plants set seed. However, their caterpillars can create problems. Ladybirds are a positive benefit because they feed on aphids (a large group of troublesome insects) and will significantly control their numbers.

The life cycle of an insect

Understanding the life cycle of an insect pest gives some clues as to methods and timing of control. Once you have identified a culprit, you need to be aware of the conditions that favour it in order to steal a march on the pest in the future.

All insects hatch from eggs. The immature insect, which is wingless, is referred to as a larva (pl. larvae). (Note that moth and butterfly caterpillars are also called larvae.) Adults are often winged, though in some species only the males have wings. Some winged insects are strong fliers, while others capable of flying only short distances. Most insects are short-lived, but several are capable of producing two or more generations per season.

The process by which the larva becomes an adult, capable of reproduction, is called metamorphosis. There are two different types of metamorphosis: incomplete, or simple, and complete metamorphosis.

Incomplete metamorphosis

Insects that have a life cycle involving incomplete metamorphosis show three basic phases: egg, larva and adult.

The larvae (also commonly called nymphs) more or less resemble the adults but do not have wings or reproductive organs. They

Below: Fuller's rose weevil is one insect that feeds at night.

undergo a series of moults until they reach the adult stage, with or without wings, depending on the species. Both nymphs and adults tend to appear together on the same plants, eating the same food.

Common insects of this type include aphids, crickets, grasshoppers, mantids, scale insects, thrips and whiteflies.

Complete metamorphosis

Insects that undergo complete metamorphosis pass through four distinct stages: egg, larva, pupa (pl. pupae) and adult.

The emerging larvae differ radically from the adults, most being soft grubs, maggots or caterpillars. They can have many legs or be legless; some are hairy or spiny, while others are hairless. As they grow, they moult, but without the external characteristics changing.

As they approach the final moult, the larvae turn into pupae. During this phase, feeding stops and the pupae remain immobile. Some larvae spin a cocoon or web around themselves (the chrysalis), while others roll a leaf around themselves. This is the most dramatic stage in the insect's development. Its tissues break down completely and are rebuilt in the form of a sexually mature adult with a segmented body, legs and, in many cases, wings.

Adults have a different diet to larvae. Typically, they suck nectar from flowers (hence their value as pollinators), whereas larvae eat leaves or flowers or prey on other insects. Almost invariably it is the larvae that cause damage, and the activities of the adult are relatively benign.

Common insects of this type include bees, wasps, butterflies, moths and flies.

Insect behaviour and feeding patterns

Most insects are adapted to feed on only one type of food: the cabbage root fly, for instance, feeds only on cabbages, and related plants. Identifying these "related plants" can be a

Below: At the nymph stage, the cricket does not yet have its adult wings.

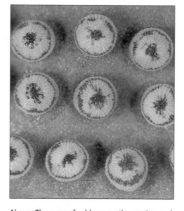
Above: The eggs of cabbage moths are tiny, and barely visible to the human eye.

Above: A tightly-wrapped cocoon is the third stage of a moth or butterfly's development.

Above: It is at the larva stage that most damage is done in the garden.

Above: When the adult moth or butterfly emerges, it has been completely transformed.

significant factor in controlling pests. Certain weeds that are related to ornamental and crop plants will attract pests that then migrate to the cultivated plants. This demonstrates the importance of weed control in the garden.

Insects usually either suck sap from plants or have jaws that are capable of chewing plant leaves and other soft tissue or tearing them to shreds.

A very common scenario runs as follows: adult insects that have undergone complete metamorphosis emerge from their cocoons during warm, still weather and look for a mate. Females lay their eggs on appropriate plant material (often the emerging flower of a fruiting plant), which is almost invariably soft, young growth. The egg hatches in favourable conditions, and the larva begins to feed on the plant, often causing considerable damage, though not necessarily resulting in the death

of the plant. (This would be counterproductive, since it would cut off the larva's own food supply.) The activities of the larva are often undetected, and unless you inspect each plant closely, it is possible to be unaware of a problem until harvest time, when large grubs are to be found in the body of fruits.

Control measures therefore tend to be directed during the times when the activities of the pest are most easily discernible.

Insect populations vary from year to year and from area to area, depending on the climate, the season and the presence (or absence) of their natural predators. Freak weather conditions often result in "plagues" of particular insects, causing havoc to certain plants, although such occurrences are infrequent. Some very successful pests can have two, or even more, generations per year, if the conditions suit them.

Mammals and birds

A number of mammals and birds – domestic pets as well as uninvited guests, whether agricultural or wild – can cause damage in gardens. Whether your garden suffers from scratching cats, digging and urinating dogs, marauding starlings, invading livestock or rabbits and deer, which can strip trees and shrubs, dealing with the problems they create is often a matter of management rather than control. Killing such animals is not a serious proposition, and it may even be illegal, so in most cases deterrence is the most appropriate, or indeed the only possible, control.

Birds

Many gardeners have an ambivalent attitude to birds. On the plus side, they eat slugs and many insect pests. On the debit side, they eat fruits (especially soft fruits) and the buds of certain plants. These are best protected with netting (many gardeners grow their soft fruit inside a dedicated fruit cage). The netting should be of a small enough gauge to prevent flying birds from becoming trapped in it, but should allow access to pollinating insects and not shade out the sun. On trees, individual fruits (or fruit trusses) can be protected with netted bags.

Troublesome birds include blackbirds, bullfinches and starlings.

Cats

Domestic cats can scratch in borders and on newly dug areas, disturbing any seeds or small plants, and on gravel and bark mulches. They also sharpen their claws on tree bark – an

Below: Birds are a mixed blessing. They eat insects but can peck at fruits.

activity that can expose vulnerable tissue to pests and diseases. They also have the disadvantage of deterring birds, which are the natural predators of a range of insect pests. Although cats can catch birds, snakes, frogs, mice, rabbits and voles, they are generally inefficient hunters.

Cats have territories, which they are not always successful in defending. Even if you own a cat, and your garden is its territory, you can expect visits from neighbours' cats. There are certain cat-repellent sprays that can be used in gardens, but their effect is temporary. Placing stems of berberis or other thorny shrubs on recently dug borders may help to deter cats.

Dogs

Some dogs dig in borders and will chase birds and smaller, fast-moving animals such as rabbits (and cats). They may also eat plants and even the small branches of some shrubs. At the least, they may flatten plants as they run across borders. Unless your garden is very large, they will need to be exercised elsewhere. Male dogs will urinate on plants and against tree trunks; any green growth will rapidly turn yellow. Treat vulnerable plants with a repellent spray. Bitches frequently urinate on lawns, turning patches of grass yellow.

Bats

These are mainly beneficial creatures, attacking a range of nocturnal insects and molluscs. In many areas, bat species are protected and control measures are illegal, so do not attempt to get rid of a bat colony without consulting the relevant authority.

Fruit bats (*Dobsonia* spp. and *Pteropus* spp.) occur in tropical and subtropical climates. They feed on fruit, and can cause considerable damage to bananas, mangoes, guavas and lychees. Control is difficult. High-frequency sound and strong-smelling substances such as naphthalene can deter them. Netting, however, is unsuitable, since the animals can become trapped.

Rats

Common in most areas, particularly in towns and cities, rats are a serious pest. Besides the damage they cause, they are also carriers of disease. They are usually attracted by fruits, root crops and dormant bulbs in storage, but will also feed on growing root crops in the vegetable garden. Rats sometimes nest in compost heaps. To avoid this, keep the compost free of cooked foods, meat and dairy products such as milk, butter and cheese, all of which

Above: A cat's sharp claws can damage garden plants in a variety of ways.

Below: Rabbits can leave a trail of devastation behind them.

can attract rats. (Such material can, however, be safely composted in an enclosed wormery.)

In the case of an infestation, contact your local authority in the first instance. Rats can also be controlled with traps (both sprung and humane) and poisoned baits, though all poisons should be kept away from other animals and children, and used in accordance with the manufacturer's instructions.

Mice, voles and squirrels

Small rodents such as mice and voles dig up and eat bulbs (especially those that have been recently planted), as well as the fleshy roots of certain perennials, such as peonies. They will also eat plant material in storage, such as root vegetable crops, fruit and the dormant bulbs of such plants as tulips and dahlias.

Below: Mice nibble vegetable crops and flowering bulbs and will steal berries.

Above: Where one sheep ventures, others are sure to follow, grazing as they go.

Voles will also gnaw the bark of young trees and shrubs. A range of traps are available for catching mice (most are also effective on voles), but a pet cat will generally deter smaller pests from spending too long in the garden or near the house.

Squirrels are more troublesome, being faster moving and capable of climbing trees. Besides inflicting similar damage to that caused by mice and voles, they eat flower buds, the soft young growth of plants and fruits and nuts, and can strip bark from trees (in some cases causing serious harm). They also steal food put out for birds. Protect vulnerable plants with wire (not plastic) netting,

Below: Fruit cages are an effective way of protecting crops from birds.

use squirrel-proof bird feeders, and cover plantings of bulbs, particularly those in pots with chicken wire.

Agricultural livestock

If your garden backs on to fields that are grazed by sheep or cows, you need to make sure they are kept out of the garden. Sheep will eat a variety of vegetation and crush plants. Cows will also cause havoc by trampling through borders.

If you need to create a boundary between your property and grazing land, do not plant a yew hedge, since all parts of this are toxic to cattle. A fence or wall of sufficient height is likely to provide the best protection to your garden while causing no harm to the animals. Make sure that any gates you have in the boundary wall are kept firmly closed and will not blow open in the wind, so that the animals stay on the right side of the boundary.

Rabbits and deer

Mainly prevalent in rural areas, rabbits and deer are troublesome pests that can cause large-scale damage to plants. Deer will browse at head height and will tug or bite off branches from trees and shrubs. Rabbits will eat virtually all garden plants, especially when these are in the early stages of growth, and hence soft and tender; they also gnaw tree bark, especially in winter, when other sources of food may be scarce.

To keep rabbits out of gardens, erect a boundary fence at least 1.2m (4ft) high. In addition, to guard against their burrowing, sink a length of strong corrugated plastic or metal along the fence, to a depth of about 45cm (18in). A taller fence, say to 2m (6ft) high, is needed to deter deer.

The bark of young trees can be protected with proprietary guards placed around the base of the trunk.

Moles

While not actually harming plants, moles cause problems on lawns: when burrowing, they throw up heaps of soil (mole hills), which spoil the appearance of the lawn. Humane methods of controlling moles are as follows. They can be trapped with special mole traps, which usually have to be inserted in one of the animal's tunnels. They can also be controlled by the use of smoke, which is also placed in the tunnels. Electronic devices that give off high-pitched noises are also available. These are said to deter moles.

Below: A dog may dig holes in borders, eat plants and urinate on plants or lawns.

What is a disease?

Some plant diseases are easily identified, while others become apparent only once serious damage has already occurred. Diseases are caused by parasitic organisms known as pathogens. Most plant diseases are caused by fungi; although bacteria and viruses can also cause problems.

What is a fungus?

A fungus (pl. fungi) is an organism that lacks chlorophyll – the green colouring matter that many plants use to make food. Fungi cannot make their own food and so instead have adapted methods to enable them to absorb food from their surroundings.

Fungi are found almost everywhere on land and in water. Some are parasites that feed on living plants (and animals). Others, called saprophytes, live on decaying matter. Fungi survive and grow by taking carbohydrates, proteins and other nutrients from their host. Some fungi also live with the roots of plants in a symbiotic (mutually beneficial) relationship known as a mycorrhiza. The fungus takes carbohydrates from the plant but supplies the plant in turn with water and certain important minerals. Most species of trees, shrubs and herbs have mycorrhizal relationships with fungi.

Above: Mildew has a velvety pile that is raised above the surface of the leaf. It is a fungus that feeds on living plant material.

There are more than 100,000 species of fungi. Most can be seen with the naked eye; among the most common are mildews, moulds, mushrooms and plant rusts. All differ dramatically in appearance.

Generally, the main part of a fungus consists of thousands of thread-like cells called hyphae. These tiny branching cells form a tangled mass called a mycelium. Often, the mycelium will grow beneath the surface of the material on which the organism is feeding. For example, the mycelium of a mushroom often grows just beneath the surface of the soil, and so is invisible to the eye.

Below: Saprophytic fungi are feeding and growing on this dead tree stump.

Below: Plant rust is recognizable by its rusty-orange colour and raised markings.

Below: The fruiting bodies of fungi can be easy to identify and attractive in their own right.

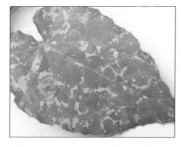

Above: A plant virus may infect just one leaf or a whole plant.

Above: Mycoplasmas can cause conditions such as big bud. They are spread by leafhoppers and should be removed on first sighting.

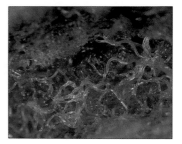

Above: Nematodes are tiny organisms that are visible only with the aid of a microscope.

The umbrella-shaped growth that we know as a mushroom is actually the fruiting body of the fungus. The fruiting body produces cells called spores, which are smaller and simpler than the seeds of plants and develop into new hyphae. Many spores are scattered by the wind, while others may be transported by water or by animals. Mushrooms and some other fungi forcefully discharge their spores. A spore that lands in a favourable location germinates and eventually produces a new mycelium.

Some fungi are microscopic and, without the aid of a microscope, can be identified only by the symptoms they cause.

The majority of fungi live on decaying animal and plant matter, which they break down into simple compounds. This process of decomposition enriches the soil and makes essential substances available to plants in a form that they can use. Through decomposition, fungi also return carbon dioxide to the atmosphere, which trees, plants and shrubs reuse to make food. A minority, however, are capable of taking their food from living plant material, and it is these that cause disease.

What are bacteria?

Bacteria are small and are incapable of breaking down the protective layer that plant cells possess. They can enter plants through wounds or the plant's natural openings.

What is a virus?

A virus is a primitive, microscopic organism that lives in a cell of another living thing. They are a major cause of disease in all living things, and are difficult to classify because of their ability to mutate. By itself, a virus is a lifeless particle that cannot reproduce. But inside a living cell, a virus becomes an active organism that can multiply hundreds of times. As new viruses are produced, they are released from the cell and go on to infect other cells, thus spreading the infection (though viruses sometimes live in cells without harming them).

Viruses infect all kinds of plants, often causing serious damage. Plant cells have tough walls that a virus cannot penetrate, but insects penetrate the cell walls while feeding on a plant and thus enable viruses to enter. Plant viruses may infect one or two leaves or an entire plant. They produce billions of viruses, which are then carried to other plants by insects or air currents. Common diseases that are caused by plant viruses include tobacco mosaic and turnip yellows mosaic. These can be devastating to the agricultural industry.

Certain viruses cause fatal diseases in insects. Virologists are seeking ways to use these viruses to kill insects that damage plants. The use of such viruses may one day replace insecticides, which do kill their intended victims but may also harm plants and other animals, as well as leaving harmful residues on edible crops and contaminating the soil.

Mycoplasmas

These are among the smallest of bacterial organisms. Mycoplasmas are parasites, and their toxic by-products accumulate in the host's tissues, causing damage that can be spread to other plants by leafhoppers.

Nematodes

Also called roundworms, nematodes are slender worms. Many species live in soil and water. Some are microscopic and live as parasites in plants, causing disease. They are not capable of moving great distances and so are often localized. They can therefore be conveniently considered alongside other disease-producing organisms rather than among the other invertebrates.

Below: Keep a look out for the early signs that a pest, disease or disorder may be present. Small-scale scarring or discoloured leaves could be an indicator.

What is a physiological problem?

A sudden mild or cold spell, strong winds, rain or snow or drought conditions can all cause damage, and even death, to plants. So too can a lack of good garden management.

Plants respond to their environment. Most of the time, the cycle of the seasons, rainfall, periods of hot and cold, and the composition of the soil promote plant growth, allowing for periods of dormancy when conditions for growth are not favourable. Dormancy allows plants to rest, ensuring a good performance the following year. A sudden change in the environment, or inappropriate growing conditions, can result in a range of symptoms, and in severe cases can cause the death of a plant.

Recognizing physiological problems

Outwardly, many problems caused by physiological factors resemble those caused by pests and diseases. Discoloured leaves, lack of even growth, aborted flowers or failure of crop set can be caused just as readily by an environmental factor as by some external agent. However, a physiological problem is likely to strike a range of plants growing in the same locality. On the other hand, many pests and diseases are host-specific and can occur on pockets of susceptible plants in the garden.

Below: Check foliage regularly for signs of plant sickness.

A plant suffering from a physiological problem will be vulnerable to pest and disease attack, since the plant's natural immunity will be weakened. It is important, therefore, to take action as soon as possible. But physiological problems often occur when plants are sited in the wrong place, and often the cure lies simply in substituting different plants for the ailing ones.

Climate and the weather

Plants are adapted to withstand certain degrees of hot and cold. Many bulbs, for instance, disappear underground completely in summer and winter, emerging to flower or put out leaves only in spring or autumn when the weather is milder. Herbaceous perennials also disappear below ground in winter. Deciduous trees and shrubs shed all their leaves in order to survive freezing winter temperatures.

It is often overlooked that the majority of plants are dormant in summer as well as winter: above a certain temperature, plant growth above ground stops. Deciduous trees and shrubs often respond to a prolonged hot, dry spell by shedding some (or even all) of their leaves. Cacti and succulents, however, are adapted to survive prolonged periods of drought, storing moisture in their swollen, fleshy leaves or stems.

A sudden change in the weather can cause plant problems. For instance, a mild, damp

Above: Mediterranean gardens can be damaged by too much water.

spell in winter persuades plants that spring has arrived, and they respond by putting out leaves. A sudden drop in temperature can spell disaster, since the soft new growth has not been sufficiently ripened by warm, dry weather to withstand freezing temperatures.

Plants are also sensitive to light levels. They need sunlight in order to manufacture food (by photosynthesis). Too much direct sunlight, however, can scorch soft leaves. Plants under glass are doubly at risk, since the glass raises the temperature still higher.

Wind and rain

Severe weather can cause physical damage to plants. Strong winds can have a drying effect on leaves, and affected plants show a scorched appearance. All young evergreen plants are vulnerable, especially conifers. Gales can strip branches and stems or even fell tall trees, particularly in exposed sites. Such plants are also susceptible to lightning strikes, which usually spell the death of a tree.

Snowfall can cause problems if a pile of snow is allowed to collect on the crown of a tree or on the top of a conifer. The sheer weight of the snow can cause the tree to split. Hailstones can cause damage to plants with large, soft leaves, such as hostas or the Indian bean tree (*Catalpa bignonioides*). Holes will be ripped in the leaves, and even though hailstorms are usually brief, affected plants present a sorry appearance afterwards.

Know your soil

Plants derive most of their nutrients from the soil they are growing in. The most important nutrients for plant growth are the elements nitrogen (N), potassium (K) and phosphorus (P). Nitrogen promotes lush, leafy growth, potassium is necessary for flowering and fruiting, while phosphorus aids good root development. Most soils contain a reasonable balance of all three, but a deficiency can cause problems. Some plants definitely perform best with a boost of one or the other nutrients at certain points during the growth cycle. Tomato fertilizers, for instance, are high in potassium to stimulate good flowering and fruit set, and they should be applied when the plants are in active growth for the best results.

A trace element (or micronutrient) is a chemical element that plants need only in tiny amounts (exact needs vary, depending on the species). Commonly required trace elements are copper (Cu), boron (B), zinc (Zn), manganese (Mn) and molybdenum (Mo). They are present in adequate amounts in most garden soils, but a shortage can cause certain plants to present specific symptoms.

The acidity or alkalinity of soil can also affect plant growth. Soil acidity/alkalinity is expressed in terms of the pH scale, 1–14, in which numbers below 7 indicate acidity while those above 7 indicate alkalinity (7 itself is neutral). A reading between 6.5 and 8.5 is normal. While the majority of plants are indifferent to soil pH, some are very sensitive. Rhododendrons, camellias and some heathers (*Erica*) will not grow in alkaline soil, developing a degree of chlorosis or yellowing of the leaves. Some plants, while known to tolerate alkaline soils, prefer acid conditions, and may not be at their best in lime or chalk soils. Skimmias provide a good example: in alkaline soils, the leaves show a distinct yellow cast; on acid soils they are a lustrous green. A few plants, such as carnations and pinks (*Dianthus*) and ivies (*Hedera*), seem to prefer alkaline conditions.

If you are in doubt as to the pH of your soil, test it with a simple chemical test (sold at garden centres) or take a look at what is growing in the locality. The presence of healthy heathers and rhododendrons growing in abundance would suggest that the soil is acid, while birches (*Betula*), elder (*Sambucus*) and ivies would imply alkalinity. It is possible for pockets of alkaline soil to occur on predominantly acid sites, and vice versa. For this and other reasons, soil assessment is often a case of trial and error.

Above: Shady areas of the garden can give rise to a range of physiological problems.

Water

The correct amount of water – neither too little nor too much – is vital for successful plant growth. In the ornamental garden, many plants will tolerate temporary drought, but an excess of water, especially on heavy soils that are prone to waterlogging, often causes problems. Most fruit and vegetable plants need regular applications of water to keep them growing evenly. Lack of sufficient water at critical times (for instance when fruits are forming) can result in poor cropping and can cause leafy vegetables to "bolt" (put out flowering stems rather than more leaves), especially during hot weather.

Below: A soil-testing kit will identify the level of acidity/alkalinity of your soil.

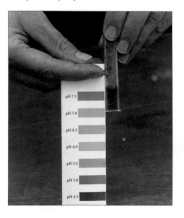

Accidental damage

Gardeners themselves are often the perpetrators of plant damage.

Inappropriate pruning cuts (or pruning at the wrong time of year) can cause dieback and/or render a plant vulnerable to disease. Damage can also be caused by careless use of a lawnmower, as when border plants at the edge of a lawn are cut through.

Weedkillers and pesticides applied during windy weather can drift on to other plants and impair growth. Excessive applications of fertilizer can also have negative effects. Plants that are overfed are often "soft": the growth is not firm enough to withstand sudden drops in temperature, and can be vulnerable to disease as well as being highly palatable to pests.

Below: Apply fertilizers judiciously to benefit plant growth.

Lawn problems

Lawns have a practical as well as aesthetic function. While we want our lawns to look beautiful, they must also stand up to a lot of wear and tear. Among other things, a lawn is a recreation area and because of this we treat lawns differently to other planted areas of the garden. Lawns can be affected by pests and diseases, as well as physiological problems. Keeping it looking good will enhance your pleasure in its use. Even if it is not your intention to produce an even grassy sward, a lawn needs regular mowing and a certain amount of attention to keep it looking good. If the lawn is neglected, coarser grasses will proliferate, choking out the finer ones.

Some pests and fungal diseases are specific to lawns – they do not harm other plants. Some mammals (including domestic pets) also commonly cause problems on lawns. You can save yourself work by choosing the grass variety that best suits your needs. Grass seed companies regularly bring out new varieties. Certain varieties have been bred for even colour, disease resistance, tolerance of wear and tear and compact growth.

Lawn mowers

There are various types of mower available, each of which gives different results. Cylinder mowers (powered or manual) are ideal for producing a tight, even cut on a flat lawn, but are often heavy to use. Electric hover mowers are light to handle and are good for cutting uneven surfaces or banks. The rotating cutting blade is either metal or plastic and should be periodically replaced. Powered rotary mowers, also with a rotating blade, are usually petrol driven. They are ideal for mowing large tracts of grass, including rough and long

Below: Raking out moss helps the grass roots to spread underground.

grass. When using powered lawn mowers, pay attention to any health and safety procedures detailed by the manufacturer (including the safe storage of flammable fuels).

To keep them functioning well, mowers should be regularly cleaned, according to the manufacturer's instructions. Petrol or diesel powered mowers should be taken to a garage periodically for servicing.

Mowing

All lawns need regular mowing. Cutting the grass stimulates it to grow and produce a dense, even sward.

Do not mow during hot, dry periods or periods of intense cold, when the grass will not be growing. It is difficult to cut grass immediately after a heavy shower of rain: the wet grass tends to stick to the mower blades and clog the mechanism. Wait until the grass has dried. If you are planning to mow early in the morning and there is a heavy dew on the lawn, brushing this off with a stiff broom will make the job considerably easier.

If you have missed a few mowings, do not cut the grass too short initially. Set the blades higher than normal, then cut again a week or so later to the desired length.

Watering

Established lawns, whatever their condition, stand up to drought well. Even if they turn brown and appear to wilt, they will soon recover with the first drop of rain. Fine lawns can be watered with a rotating sprinkler

Above: Lawns need a certain amount of attention to keep them looking good.

(usually powered by the pressure of the water), which distributes drops of water evenly over the surface.

Feeding

Nearly all plants respond well to appropriate feeding, and lawn grasses are no exception. It is best to use a special lawn fertilizer, which has the necessary blend of nutrients. Many lawn fertilizers contain iron, which darkens the grass, making it look more lush.

Lawn fertilizers should be applied evenly across the lawn, or growth will be uneven. Take care not to apply too much fertilizer, which can kill the grass. Some lawn fertilizers also contain weedkillers that act on lawn weeds and moss killers that kill moss.

Below: Aerating the grass each year in the autumn will have beneficial results. Brushing fine sand into the holes will improve drainage.

INSECTS AND OTHER INVERTEBRATES

A number of invertebrates cause problems on lawns, even those that are otherwise considered to be beneficial creatures. Some are specific pests of lawn grasses, while others can also attack other garden plants.

EARTHWORMS

Allolobophora spp.
Range: Widely distributed.
Description: Invertebrates, up to 20cm (8in) long, that spend their lives underground. Their casts (piles of muddy excrement) spoil the appearance of fine lawns. They are most likely to cause problems during warm, wet weather in spring and autumn. Earthworms are vital to the health of the soil, however, so controlling their numbers is not desirable.
Damage: Worm casts can become smeared in patches on the surfaces of lawns, allowing lawn weeds to take a hold.
Prevention and control: *Non-chemical/organic:* Brush casts away with a stiff broom. Avoid walking on lawns during wet weather, which can compact any casts.

BLACKHEADED PASTURE COCKCHAFER

Aphodius tasmaniae
Range: Parts of Australia and New Zealand, especially coastal areas.
Description: The larva of a beetle that lays its eggs in soil in summer. Older larvae emerge from tunnels to feed at night

Below: Blackheaded pasture cockchafer grubs leave tell-tale mounds of earth.

on grasses (especially rye) at ground level. They are active from summer and through winter. A mound of dry soil at the entrance to their tunnels can betray their presence.
Damage: Lawns show bare patches.
Prevention and control: *Chemical:* Spray with carbaryl. *Non-chemical/organic:* Collect and dispose of adults and larvae.

GRASS-CROWN MEALYBUG, Felted Grass Coccid

Antonina graminis
Range: Tropical and subtropical regions.
Description: An insect that sucks the sap from many warm-season grasses. It develops a waxy coat.
Damage: Grasses lose vigour and show bare patches.
Prevention and control: *Chemical:* Spray with dimethoate (effective only before the insect's waxy covering has developed). *Non-chemical/organic:* Spray with insecticidal soap or oil.

CHINCH BUGS

Blissus spp.
Range: Throughout North America, including southern Canada, particularly central and eastern regions.
Description: The adult is a black bug, about 5mm (⅕in)

long, with white forewings, that lays its eggs among grass roots. Nymphs are red with a white stripe across their backs, then turn black with white spots. They chew roots; adults also suck sap from stems.
Damage: Dry patches appear.
Prevention and control: *Non-chemical/organic:* Rake off excess thatch and spike lawns on compacted soil. The fungus *Beauvaria bassiana* can help to control the pest; an insecticidal soap can also be used. Plant grasses known to be resistant to chinch bugs.

COUCHTIP MAGGOT

Delia urbana
Range: Eastern Australia (native).
Description: The larva of a fly that lays its eggs at the growing points of couch grasses. The larvae eat the growing tip of the grass, but without killing it.
Damage: Grasses fail to develop runners that cover the ground.
Prevention and control: *Chemical:* Spray with

Above: Although earthworms are beneficial creatures, and their appearance in the garden shows the soil is healthy, earthworm casts can be a problem.

dimethoate. *Non-chemical/organic:* Feed and water to keep the grasses growing strongly.

COUCHGRASS MITES

Dolichotetranychus australianus, other species
Range: Eastern Australia.
Description: Mites that cause the condition known as "witches' brooms" – a shortening of the internodes on grasses, leading to a bunched appearance. Couchgrass mites are most likely to be found in dry areas, and often damage a lawn where it meets a wall.
Damage: Affected areas turn straw-coloured.
Prevention and control: *Chemical:* Spray with difocol. *Non-chemical/organic:* Keep areas of lawns that are prone to drying out well watered. Mites can also be treated with sulphur.

Above: An adult mole cricket.

Above: An African black beetle.

MOLE CRICKETS
Gryllotalpa spp.
Range: Africa, Eurasia and North America; some species also occur in Australia.
Description: Mole crickets spend most of their time underground, eating plant roots and other invertebrates. Besides eating grass roots, they can also damage vegetables and ornamentals and can dislodge seedlings with their burrowings.
Damage: Grass is killed.
Prevention and control:
Chemical: Treat with diazinon or fenthion.

AFRICAN BLACK BEETLE
Heteronychus arator
Range: Southern Africa (native); also occurring in Australia and New Zealand.
Description: The adult is a black beetle, 1.2cm (½in) long, active from spring to summer. The larvae are white curl grubs, 2.5cm (1in) long; older larvae

feed on grass roots.
Damage: Brown patches appear on lawns.
Prevention and control:
Chemical: Apply fenamiphos in spring, while the larvae are still young and near the soil surface.

ARGENTINE STEM WEEVIL
Listronotus bonariensis, syn. *Hyperodes bonariensis*
Range: S. America, Australia, New Zealand.
Description: The adult is 3mm (⅛in) long, dark greyish-brown. Adults and larvae feed on grass, severing leaves. Weevils are active from spring to summer; the number of generations per year depends on the climate.
Damage: Patches of lawn appear dry.
Prevention and control:

Below: An Argentine stem weevil.

Chemical: Spray with diazinon.
Non-chemical/organic: In areas where the pest is common, choose a lawn grass variety that is less attractive to it.

CHAFER GRUB
Phyllopertha horticola, Hoplia philanthus
Range: Europe.
Description: The larvae of a beetle that feed on grass roots, causing considerable damage to lawns. They are fat, white grubs, with brown heads, around 2cm (⅝in) long, depending on the species. They also attract foxes, badgers, magpies and crows, which cause more damage as they scratch or peck at the lawn in search of the grubs. *Hoplia philanthus* (the Welsh chafer) prefers sandy soils.
Damage: Yellow patches appear on lawns. More damage is caused by predatory wildlife.
Prevention and control:
Chemical: Treat with lindane or pirimiphos-methyl in midsummer (effective only on young larvae). *Non-chemical/organic:* A pathogenic nematode, *Steinernema carpocapsae,* can provide some control.

JUNE BEETLES, MAY BEETLES
Phyllophaga spp., including *P. decemliniata*
Range: North America.
Description: The adult is a red-brown or black beetle, up to 2.5cm (1in) long, that lays its eggs in the soil in spring. The larvae, which cause most dam-

age, are fat, grey-white grubs, up to 3.8cm (1½in) long, with brown heads. They feed on grass roots.
Damage: Areas of lawn die back.
Prevention and control:
Chemical: Treat with fenamiphos.
Non-chemical/organic: Apply the parasitic nematodes *Heterorhabdits bacteriophora* and *Steinernema glaseri* or the fungus *Beauveria bassiana.*

JAPANESE BEETLE
Popillia japonica
Range: Eastern USA and southern Canada.
Description: The adult is a blue or black beetle, 1.2cm (½in) long, that lays its eggs in the soil around grasses in late summer. The larvae, which grow to 2cm (⅝in), are fleshy and greyish-white. They feed on grass roots.
Damage: Patches of dead grass appear in the lawn.
Prevention and control:
Chemical: Treat with fenamiphos.
Non-chemical/organic: Allow lawns to dry out in summer to kill larvae. The parasitic nematodes *Heterohabditis bacteriophora* and *Steinernema glaseri* can also be used to control the larvae.

LAWN ARMYWORM
Spodoptera mauritia
Range: Widely distributed.
Description: A greenish-brown, brown or black moth caterpillar, up to 4.5cm (1¼in) long, with stripes along its body. Lawn armyworms feed on

Below: A chafer grub.

Above: Japanese beetles cause widespread damage to lawns.

Above: Be vigilant for shiny metallic click beetles. Their larvae, the false wireworms, can cause unsightly damage to lawns.

Above: June beetles are shield beetles that can damage other garden plants.

lawn and other grasses (also weeds and cereals), attacking leaves, stems and seedheads. They can occur in large numbers. Only Queensland blue couch grass is unpalatable.
Damage: Large areas of lawn can be left bare after an attack.
Prevention and control:
Chemical: Spray with carbaryl, chlorpyrifos, diazinon or cyfluthrin. *Non-chemical/organic:* Rake up and dispose of the caterpillars.

FALSE WIREWORMS
Tenebrionidae
Range: Cosmopolitan.
Description: Wireworms are the larvae of certain beetles (some of which are referred to as click beetles). They are 2–3.5cm (⅘–1⅖in) long and can be yellow or brown. They feed on plant tissue underground, chewing at grass roots.
Damage: Patches of grass die back.
Prevention and control:
Chemical: Apply fenamiphos, and water in.

LEATHERJACKETS
Tipula spp., *Nephrotoma* spp.
Range: Widely distributed.
Description: The larvae of craneflies (better known as daddy-long-legs). Eggs are laid in soil in late summer. The grey-brown larvae grow to 4.5cm (1¾in) and feed on grass roots. Leatherjackets can also cause problems in the kitchen and ornamental garden, if they eat the roots of small plants and seedlings.
Damage: Areas of lawn turn

yellow-brown in midsummer.
Prevention and control:
Chemical: Control young larvae with lindane or pirimiphos-methyl. *Non-chemical/organic:* Older larvae can be controlled with the pathogenic nematode *Steinernema carpocapsae.* Alternatively, cover areas of lawn with black plastic over night (preferably after rain). During the night, the leatherjackets come to the surface, and they can then be removed by hand and disposed of the following day.

FUNGAL AND OTHER DISEASES

Diseases often take a hold on lawns where growing conditions are inappropriate, such as, if there is too much shade in the garden or a lack of nutrients in the soil. It is usually easy to restore the lawn to a lush, even green.

FAIRY RINGS
Agaricus spp., *Lycoperdon* spp., *Marasmius oreades*, other species
Definition: Fairy rings are gradually expanding rings of brown toadstools, up to 10cm (4in) high, that appear on lawns in summer/autumn (usually in wet weather). To either side of the toadstool rings are zones of lush-growing grass. Dense mats of fungal growth develop underground.
Symptoms and damage: In between the zones of lush grass, the grass turns brown or dies back to leave bare soil. Death of grass in the central

area is due to drought, since the fungus underground forms a water-repellent mat.
Prevention and control:
Eradicating fairy rings is difficult. Brush or rake off any toadstools, to prevent spores spreading further. Mow affected areas separately and burn all mowings to prevent the fungus spreading. Treat the blades of the mower with a garden fungicide. For complete control, dig up the affected area to a depth of at least 30cm (1ft), extending the hole to 30cm (1ft) beyond the outermost toadstool ring. Dispose of the soil and turf so as to avoid reinfection.

Replace with fresh topsoil and reseed.

RED THREAD, Turf Red Thread
Corticium fuciforme, syn. *Laetisaria fuciformis*
Definition: A fungal disease that predominantly affects fine grasses such as fescue, rye grass and annual meadow grass. It is often a problem in a year following a hot, dry summer and usually occurs between late spring and early autumn.

Right: Fairy rings have areas of dense grass around them caused by excess nitrogen.

Symptoms and damage: Pink or reddish mottled areas, up to 8cm (3¼in) across, appear. Individual blades bear jelly-like, pale red or pink growths, which later become pale pink and fluffy.

Prevention and control: *Chemical*: Treat affected areas with carbendazim or other lawn fungicide, followed by a nitrogen-high lawn fertilizer. Spike to improve aeration.

LEAF SPOTS
Drechslera spp.

Definition: A fungal disease of predominantly warm-climate grasses. It occurs mostly during hot, humid weather in mid- to late summer.

Symptoms and damage: Areas of turf, up to 15cm (6in) across, turn black, then brown and grey. The discoloration can persist for some time.

Prevention and control: *Chemical*: Spray with mancozeb. Also, boost grass growth with a nitrogen-high fertilizer.

OPHIOBOLUS PATCH
Gaeumannomyces graminis var. *avenae*, syn. *Ophiobolus graminis* var. *avenae*

Definition: A fungus that affects bent grasses. Outbreaks are most likely to occur on soils low in organic matter, or where nutrients are unbalanced, and will be most severe on alkaline soils (or following applications of lime). The fungus strikes during cool weather, but symptoms are often not evident until the return of warm weather.

Symptoms and damage: Circular areas of browning, then yellowing, which can be 3m (10ft) or more across, appear on lawns. The edges of the circles are orange. The grass in the middle recovers poorly, allowing lawn weeds to take a hold.

Prevention and control: *Non-chemical/organic*: On alkaline soils, add an acidifier to lower

Above: Low nitrogen levels encourage red thread to grow.

the pH. Improve drainage and apply lawn fertilizers to boost recovery.

TURF NEMATODE, Cyst Nematode
Heterodera graminis

Definition: A nematode that damages warm-climate grasses (especially couch grasses). It may be confined to specific areas.

Symptoms and damage: Roots are stunted and become prone to fungal infections and water stress.

Prevention and control: *Chemical*: In cases of severe infestation, control the nematode with fenamiphos. Keep lawns well fed and watered to maintain strong growth.

SPRING DEAD SPOT
Leptosphaeria narmari, L. korrae

Definition: A fungus that attacks the roots of grasses. It damages roots in late summer and autumn, and affected grass fails to grow during the following spring. Couch grass (*Cynodon dactylon*) and South African couch grass (*Cynodon transvaalensis*) are the grasses most commonly affected.

Symptoms and damage: Dead, circular patches of grass, up to 50cm (20in) in diameter, appear in spring.

Prevention and control: *Non-chemical/organic*: In areas where this is a common problem, resow the whole lawn, if necessary, with disease resistant varieties.

SNOW MOULD, Fusarium Patch, Fusarium Wilt
Monographella nivalis, syn. *Fusarium nivale*

Definition: A fungal disease of grass that can appear at any time of year, but usually occurs under snow cover, especially if the ground is compacted, or during mild weather in winter and spring. It spreads rapidly during damp, cool weather, but slows down if the grass warms up and dries out. It is spread by mowing and is more likely to occur on lawns that have been fed excess nitrogen.

Symptoms and damage: Grass dies back in patches. Initially, they are yellow, turning brown. A white or pinkish fungus can appear on the patches.

Prevention and control: *Chemical*: Treat areas with a fungicide such as carbendazim or triadimefon. Spike lawns and brush off heavy dews. Apply a high-potash fertilizer in autumn.

LICHENS and ALGAE
Peltigera canina, other species

Definition: Lichens and algae can appear on the lawn surface, usually indicating poor drainage, though they can also occur where water drips, for instance from an overhanging tree or leaking guttering. They may form a gelatinous patch.

Symptoms and damage: The lawn's appearance is spoilt.

Prevention and control: *Non-chemical/organic*: Repair guttering or cut back overhanging branches. Where lichens and algae appear on an open area of lawn, spike the lawn and topdress with lawn sand to improve drainage.

DAMPING OFF
Pythium spp.

Definition: All lawn grasses are susceptible to damping off, particularly at the seedling stage, or where bare patches

have been oversown. Damping off can also affect established lawns during warm, humid weather, especially where the soil is excessively moist.

Symptoms and damage: Grass turns pale; in severe cases, circular areas up to 10cm (4in) across show signs of dying back. Seedlings appear wrinkled or distorted, and the roots are stunted and brown.

Prevention and control: *Non-chemical/organic*: Provide seedling grasses with sufficient irrigation to keep them growing strongly without saturating the soil. Fertilize with a high-phosphorus fertilizer. Improve drainage on soils that tend to hold excessive moisture.

RUSTS
Puccinia spp., *Uromyces* spp.

Definition: Some rusts affect lawn grasses, and can cause serious problems owing to the speed with which they can be spread. Rye grass, Kentucky blue grass, fescues, winter grass and kikuyus are particularly vulnerable (kikuyu and rye especially during warm, humid weather).

Symptoms and damage: Individual blades are covered with orange pustules, which darken as they age. Large areas of lawn can turn orange-red.

Prevention and control: *Non-chemical/organic*: Apply a high-nitrogen fertilizer to keep the grass growing strongly.

BROWN PATCHES
Rhizoctonia spp.

Definition: This fungal disease has a number of strains, and can affect all types of grasses. Symptoms vary depending on the season and climate. Brown patch is most commonly a problem during warm, humid weather, but it can also occur in cool conditions. Damage tends to be most severe on cool-climate grasses.

Symptoms and damage:

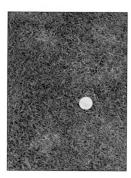

Left: Yellowing patches are an indication of dollar spot.

Circular areas, up to 1m (3ft) across, appear in lawns, often with a darker edge. The grass thins out in the affected areas. In cool climates, the edges of circles are depressed. In warm climates, algae can take a hold where growth has thinned.
Prevention and control:
Chemical: Spray with chlorothalonil. Withhold nitrogen-high fertilizers.
Non-chemical/organic: Improve the drainage on soils that tend to hold excessive amounts of moisture.

DOLLAR SPOT

Sclerotinia homeocarpa, other species
Definition: A disease that can be caused by a number of different fungi. It tends to occur where heavy dews are common, especially in spring and autumn (also in summer in humid climates) and where lawns have become compacted. Fescues are particularly susceptible to the disease.
Symptoms and damage: Spots of dead grass, about 5cm (2in) across, appear on the lawn. (The spots can be bigger if the grass is not cut short.) A white, fluffy fungal growth can sometimes be observed on the grass in early morning.
Prevention and control:
Chemical: Spray with triadimefon or carbendazim. Spike the lawn to improve drainage, if necessary. Boost recovery with a nitrogen-high fertilizer.

KIKUYU YELLOWS

Verrucalvus flavofaciens
Definition: A fungal disease of kikuyu grass that is favoured by wet soil conditions during spells of hot weather.
Symptoms and damage: Grass roots rot and turf turns yellow (initially in circles, then in sheets). The grass thins and dies out, leaving bare areas that are then rapidly colonized by weeds.
Prevention and control: *Non-chemical/organic*: Improve drainage on wet soils.

OTHER LAWN PROBLEMS

Lawns can be large expanses of land that are made up of a variety of different grasses. Position, aspect and local weather conditions can all have an impact on how they grow.

DRY PATCH

Definition: A condition that can affect any lawn grass, though short-rooted species are most at risk. It occurs mainly on established lawns that have been neglected, and damage is most severe on sandy soils.
Symptoms and damage: Thatch accumulated among the blades is subject to fungal infection. Chemicals produced leach down to form a water-proof layer in the soil, resulting in a lack of moisture available to the grass roots. Roughly circular patches of dead grass appear in the lawn.
Prevention and control: *Non-chemical/organic*: Rake the lawn regularly to remove thatch. Spike lawns to improve drainage and take-up of water. Feed and water lawns well.

SLIME MOULDS

Definition: Slime moulds are intermediate between bacteria and fungi. Grey, yellow, whitish or orange, jelly-like blobs appear clustered on grass blades. They usually occur in damp, shady places, and can also appear on dead leaves and logs. *Diachea leucopoda* can sometimes be seen on strawberries.
Symptoms and damage: Slime moulds cause no major problems, since they are non-parasitic.
Prevention and control: *Non-chemical/organic*: If necessary, wash off slime moulds with a water jet.

TOADSTOOLS

Definition: Toadstools, which commonly appear in autumn, are the fruiting bodies of various underground fungi. They feed not on grass directly but on organic material in the soil (including the tree and shrub roots growing under turf).
Symptoms and damage: Toadstools appear in random patches or in straight lines on lawns. The grass continues to grow normally.
Prevention and control: *Non-chemical/organic*: Brush off toadstools with a stiff broom before any spores are released. If necessary, dig up areas of lawn and cut back any tree or shrub roots or remove any woody material on which the fungus is feeding.

Below: Dry patch can be removed by cutting out affected areas of lawn.

Right: Slime moulds look unpleasant, but do no long-term damage.

Below: Removing toadstools before they release spores may slow their spread.

Pond problems

Water features pose few problems for the gardener. A reasonably large pond that is well stocked with a range of water plants will attract a host of wildlife and be largely self-regulating. However, a few problems may occur from time to time. Garden chemicals such as fertilizers, weedkillers, pesticides and fungicides should not be used in the vicinity of a pond. Contaminated water could spell disaster for much of the wildlife it supports.

Water clarity and filtration

The water in a large, well-stocked pool will usually be crystal clear. What turns pond water green is the presence of algae – microscopic non-flowering plants that thrive in wet conditions. Excessive algal growth can occur during hot weather, especially if the surface of the water is not adequately covered by the floating leaves of aquatics such as waterlilies, which help regulate water temperature.

To keep the water cool enough to keep algae in check, 50 to 70 per cent of the water surface should be covered during summer. To lower the temperature and raise the oxygen level (which discourages algal growth), top up the water each evening using a hose. Do not plunge the nozzle into the water but position it just above the surface: water splash increases the amount of oxygen that will be introduced into the water. If you have a fountain in the pond, switch it on at dusk to achieve the same effect.

The temperature of water in a small pool is likely to exceed that in a large pool, and algal growth will be more of a problem.

Water can be kept clear by means of a filter (not to be confused with the strainer on a pump, which merely prevents larger debris from clogging it up). A mechanical filter involves the use of a submersible pump, which draws the water through plastic foam, gravel or some other medium in which algae and other matter are collected. The pump usually feeds a fountain or waterfall. A biological filter is sited outside the pond, and water is pumped through it. The water passes through a range of media that contain bacteria, which purify the water before it returns to the pool. Both types of filter should be regularly cleaned according to the manufacturer's instructions if they are to remain effective.

If the above methods fail to kill off all algae, an ultra-violet (UV) clarifier can be used in conjunction with a filter. A UV clarifier consists of a unit that contains an ultra-violet light, which will kill algae (as well as any other harmful bacteria).

Water clarity can also be affected if dead leaves (from deciduous trees and shrubs) are allowed to fall in the water in autumn. These produce noxious gases as they break down. To prevent leaves accumulating, net the surface of the pond in autumn and remove any dead leaves and other plant debris regularly, or use a rake to clear them from the surface.

A pool that is strictly ornamental and contains no plants can be kept clear by having chlorine added to the water.

Water pH

The pH (degree of acidity/alkalinity) of the water is an important contributor to plant health and rates of growth. Water pH can fluctuate, depending on the amount of rainfall. Rain tends to be acid, so topping up the pool with tap water during a period of drought tends to increase the alkalinity. While most plants – and indeed fish – can tolerate a range of pH values, fluctuations cause stress, increasing vulnerability of both to certain diseases and disorders.

You can test the pH of the water in a pool with a simple chemical tester (available at aquatic centres and larger garden centres) in the same way as for soil.

Alkaline water can damage the mucous coating of fish. Very alkaline water can kill fish outright. Very acid water is uncommon. You can regulate the pH by means of a partial water change.

Pond weeds

Two troublesome weeds frequently appear in ponds and can spoil the appearance of the water features.

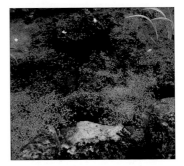

Above: Duckweed (*Lemna* spp.) consists of tiny plants that float on the water surface. Although the plants are very small, they often occur in sufficient quantities to cover a large area. Duckweed is best removed with a net.

Above: Blanketweed (*Spirogyra* spp.) is a type of algae that forms hairlike strands just below the water surface. To remove it, insert a cane into a dense area of growth and twist it, wrapping the weed around like candy-floss.

Left: The ideal pond environment will support a wide range of plant and animal life, with water that is kept clean and well oxygenated.

WATER PLANT PESTS

Since aquatic plants have a constant supply of the water they need to grow, they are generally vigorous and healthy. Usually a pond supports predators in sufficient quantities to keep pests under control.

WATER SNAILS
Mollusca
Water snails cause little damage, since they usually feed on plant material that is already decaying. If they appear to be feeding on young growth, trap them by floating a lettuce or cabbage leaf on the surface of the water overnight. Remove the leaf the following morning and dispose of any snails found clinging to the lower surface.

IRIS SAWFLY
Rhadinoceraea micans
The adult is a black sawfly that shelters among water irises (especially *Iris pseudacorus*) in late spring to early summer. The grey-brown larvae, up to 1.5cm (⅗in) long, eat notches from the edges of iris leaves in early to midsummer. In severe cases, plants are completely defoliated. Pick off the larvae by hand and destroy them.

Right: Water snails are usually beneficial to a garden pond.

WATERLILY PROBLEMS

Waterlilies – the most highly bred among commonly grown water plants – are subject to a number of pests and diseases. Chemical control is inappropriate, because of the risk of contamination to the water. Besides the specific problems listed below, waterlilies are also subject to crown rot (*Pythium* and *Phytophthora* spp.), which affects a range of other garden plants.

BROWN CHINA-MARK MOTH, Beautiful China-mark Moth
Elophila nymphaeata, *Nymphula stagnata*
Larvae, up to 2.5cm (1in) long, of these European moths mine waterlily leaves from midsummer to autumn, creating large holes in leaves. There can be two generations per year. The damage caused is rarely serious.

Below: Waterlilies are good providers of shade for pondlife.

WATERLILY BEETLE
Galerucella nymphaeae
The adult is a yellow-brown beetle, 7mm (¼in) long, that eats irregular holes in waterlily leaves. The yellow and black larvae, up to 8mm (⅜in) long, eat leaves from midsummer. (Adults also feed on flowers.) There can be two generations per year. To control them, pick them off by hand.

The waterlily beetle prefers to live on large expanses of water, and is seldom a wide-spread pest in small ponds. It overwinters among the dead topgrowth of marginals, so this should be cut back and destroyed if the pest has caused problems.

WATERLILY APHID
Rhopalosiphum nymphaeae
This aphid is olive green or brown. Colonies appear on leaves, stems and flower buds in summer, especially during hot, dry periods, resulting in poor growth. (The waterlily aphid can also attack other water plants with floating leaves.) In autumn, the pest leaves the water to lay its eggs and over-winter on its secondary host – members of *Prunus*. To control the pest, wash the aphids from leaves with a hose or spray (using plain water). Avoid planting *Prunus* near the pond.

WATERLILY LEAF SPOT
Ramularia nymphaerum
A fungal disease that occurs during warm, damp weather. Spots, initially red but turning black, appear at the edges of leaves, on upper and lower surfaces. Affected areas rot, resulting in holes. Cut off and destroy affected leaves.

Below: The characteristic spots of waterlily leaf spot appear all over the leaf surface.

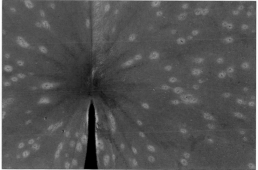

Weeds and weed control

A weed may or may not have intrinsic beauty – what makes it a weed is the fact that it is growing where it is not wanted, and competing with plants the gardener has chosen to grow. At its simplest, a weed is any plant in the wrong place. The presence of weeds in an uncultivated site is not necessarily a bad thing: it indicates that the ground is fertile.

Many weeds are cosmopolitan: they are found throughout the world, or across large areas. They are usually tolerant of a variety of conditions, growing in sun or shade, in dry or damp soil. Often, seemingly, they grow in no soil at all, as when they seed in the cracks in paving or appear on the tops of walls, growing out of the mortar.

In a cultivated bed, weeds compete with garden plants for soil moisture and nutrients. They tend to be more vigorous than cultivated plants, overshadowing them and reducing air circulation. Their unchecked growth causes air to stagnate around plants, creating the ideal breeding conditions for a number of common fungal infections, notably mildew.

Many weeds are also a food source for certain insect pests, and once this food source

Above: Many popular and attractive plants may be thought of as weeds.

has been exhausted, the insects will then move on to cultivated plants. Weeds can suffer from fungal and bacterial infections to the same extent as cultivated plants. The plant families Solanaceae (which includes the nightshades) and Cruciferae (including the brassicas) encompass several pernicious weeds as well as some vegetable crops, and it is particularly important to remove these from the vegetable garden, since their presence can undermine crop rotation.

Weeds can be annual or perennial. Many annual weeds are capable of producing two or more generations per year, and so can multiply rapidly. Weeds with seeds that are dispersed on the wind, such as dandelions, are particularly widespread. Many perennial weeds are capable of spreading far and wide underground, and can be difficult to eradicate, since they can regenerate from the tiniest amount of root left in the ground.

Some widely grown garden plants can also be considered to be weeds: Lady's mantle (*Alchemilla mollis*) will seed itself indiscriminately around the garden; snow-in-summer (*Cerastium tomentosum*) will spread underground and rapidly colonize a large area; and mile-a-minute plant (*Fallopia baldschuanica*) is a rampant climber that is capable of choking all other vegetation it meets in its path.

While weeds have a part to play in the ecological garden, providing shelter and a food source for a range of beneficial garden creatures, some measure of control is necessary in other parts of the garden.

Below: Bindweed (left) travels rapidly underground and can regenerate from a tiny piece of root. Taproots (right) grow deep into the ground and are difficult to eradicate once established.

Below: *Rhododendron ponticum* has "escaped" from gardens and covers large uncultivated areas of Ireland and Britain.

Above: A young elder growing in an inappropriate place is effectively a weed.

Above: Many lawns are marred by the presence of dandelions.

Above: Daisies either spoil or enhance a lawn, depending on how you see them.

Right: Weed or wild flower? Foxgloves colonize large areas of ground quickly, but attract many pollinating insects.

Taprooted weeds

These weeds can be either annual or perennial. They are particularly difficult to remove, because of the length of their root. Taproots are often brittle and can easily snap off as they are removed from the ground. Any portion of root left in the soil will continue to grow. Common taprooted weeds include dandelions (*Taraxacum officinale*).

Weeds with rhizomes or creeping underground roots include couch grass (*Elymus repens*) and willowherb (*Epilobium* spp.).

Woody weeds

Trees and shrubs can be weeds. Among the commonest are brambles (the wild ancestor of cultivated soft fruits such as blackberries), which are capable of colonizing ground by tip-layering (in which arching stems take root where they touch the soil). The European elder (*Sambucus nigra*) often appears in gardens where the soil is alkaline. Woody weeds can be difficult to eradicate if they are established and have a deep root system.

Lawn weeds

Typically low-growing and tough, lawn weeds stand up to the wear and tear to which a lawn is usually subjected. Left untreated, they tend to dominate and crowd out the finer-leaved grasses. Clovers (*Trifolium*) and plantains

(*Plantago*) commonly appear. Some weeds, such as daisies (*Bellis perennis*), can be an ornament to a lawn and others are themselves grasses.

Mosses

These are primitive, ground-hugging plants that thrive in damp places. The presence of moss in the garden is usually an indicator of poor drainage in the land. The excess moisture provides the perfect growing conditions for the moss, which then thrives at the expense of the grass.

Above right: Tough lawn weeds such as this plantain can appear among the grass.

Right: Moss quickly ruins the appearance of a lawn, especially on damp ground.

Methods of weed control

There are several methods of weed control that you can use. The method which you choose will depend on the size of plot, the state of its cultivation, the plants being grown, and whether you are gardening organically.

Hand-weeding

The most eco-friendly, satisfying and effective, but potentially time-consuming, method of controlling weeds is hand-weeding. If weeds cover an area of uncultivated ground, fork the ground over to expose the roots. These can then be picked off and removed by hand. For complete control, all traces of roots belonging to perennial weeds must be removed from the soil.

If weeds are growing among other plants, such as in a border or in the vegetable plot, the best way of eradicating them is with a hand fork or hoe. Small weed seedlings can easily be cut with a hoe. In spring, the weeds can be left on the soil surface, where they will quickly break down and return nutrients to the soil. Older, larger and stronger weeds need to be dug up individually. Special tools known as grubbers are available for lifting taprooted weeds such as dandelions. Some care is generally needed, since the act of disturbing soil can damage vulnerable roots of other plants and dislodge seedlings growing close by. A certain amount of topsoil will cling to the roots of the weed, and so some plant nutrients will be lost from the soil in the weeding process.

Below: Gently forking out a large weed may be the best method of removal, particularly if it is growing among prized flowers or vegetables.

Above: Special tools designed to make weeding easier are available.

Below: For tap-rooted weeds special tools anchor around the root.

Isolated weeds can be tackled with a special flame gun. This is a useful method for disposing of plants in paving or in gravel, where the flame will not damage other plants.

On lawns, regular mowing helps to keep down weeds, since the seed-producing parts of the plant will be continually cut off. Deep-rooted weeds will regenerate for a while, but will gradually be weakened and die back.

Woody weeds should be chopped down with an axe in the first instance. Grub out the trunks and roots with a mattock.

Above: Weedkiller can be applied to specific plants by painting it directly on to the leaves.

Below: Liquid weedkillers can be dispensed with a tool that can be attached to a watering can.

Weedkillers

Herbicides or weedkillers work in a variety of ways. Contact weedkillers usually have to be painted or sprayed on to leaves by hand and kill only the part of the plant with which they are in contact. They are useful where isolated weeds have to be removed from among other plants and hand-weeding is inappropriate, but can also be applied over a wider area. Contact weedkillers usually kill annual weeds outright. Two or more applications may be needed to kill perennial weeds. This method of weeding is laborious and time-consuming.

Systemic, or translocating, weedkillers enter the plant's system, and so kill the roots as well. They are usually most effective when applied when the weeds are growing strongly. To increase the effectiveness of both contact and systemic weedkillers, bruise the leaves of the weeds before treatment to maximize take-up of the product.

Pre-emergent or soil-acting weedkillers can be applied to bare soil before the weeds emerge. These are then absorbed by the weeds as they grow. However, the poison can persist in the soil for up to a year or more, so you need to choose carefully the crop that will grow in the plot. Check the manufacturer's recommendations before replanting a treated area. Pre-emergent weedkillers are useful for clearing an area that is not going to be planted, such as a patio area, path or driveway.

Other methods

Where weeds effectively carpet the ground (as, for instance, in the case of ground elder), it is possible to kill them off through regular shearing or mowing, as for a lawn. Cut the weeds to the ground as new growth begins to appear in spring. Provided you cut back all the new growth on a regular basis (say every week), it is possible to eradicate many weeds, which are then deprived of the possibility of photosynthesizing.

It is possible to eradicate weeds from areas of the garden that are yet to be cultivated by covering the ground with a material that blocks out the light, so preventing weeds from growing and also stopping any weed seed from coming into contact with the soil. Special plastic sheeting is available for the purpose. Some types have perforations that allow rainwater to permeate through to the soil. Most need to be left in situ for two years or more to be effective. Many pernicious perennial weeds are able to survive, however, and the use of a membrane may not be enough, unless used in conjunction with a weedkiller. It is the usual practice to lay such a membrane before paving or decking an area, but here too the ground must already have been cleared of weeds. Old carpet can be used instead of a proprietary weed-suppressing membrane, but weeds will be capable of growing through any threadbare patches.

Membranes can be used on weed-free soil in the ornamental and kitchen garden to help control weeds. Spread the membrane over the ground, then cut holes in the fabric for your chosen plants. The membrane can then be covered with a bark or grit mulch. With this method of gardening, an organic mulch cannot break down and enter the soil in the normal way, so plants are best fed with a foliar feed or root drench applied to the base.

Mulches, if thick enough (say to a depth of at least 10cm (4in)), can also be used to suppress weeds, though they are less effective than membranes. A mulch will not prevent perennial weeds from pushing through, but these weeds will be weakened and easy to pull up. A mulch can prevent weed seeds from germinating, since they will not receive any light.

Above: Annual weeds can be composted effectively although garden refuse containing perennial weeds needs to reach a high temperature to kill the weeds.

Shredded bark or wood chips make an effective mulch, but they will need to be replaced after two or three years as they break down. In the process of breaking down, they will also use up nitrogen in the soil. Hence it is usually advisable to feed plants with a nitrogen-high fertilizer to replace any nitrogen lost and avoid the plants' suffering from a nitrogen deficiency.

Inert mulches include gravel, pebbles and builder's rubble. These do not break down, but will gradually be washed down into the soil by rain. If there is some compaction of the soil underneath, water can collect on the surface, allowing algae, lichens and mosses to take a hold, which will need treatment.

Disposing of weeds

Annual weeds can be composted, provided they are not in the process of setting seed. Cut off any seedheads before adding to the compost. (The seed will remain dormant in the compost heap and can germinate once this is added to soil as a mulch; the heat produced in the composting process is usually not enough to kill weed seeds.) Most perennial weeds do not compost successfully, and can survive in the compost heap. In periods of hot weather, they can be spread out in the sun to dry and added to the compost once they have completely shrivelled. Alternatively, rot them in a bucket of water, or add the topgrowth only (removing any seeds).

Woody weeds such as elder (*Sambucus*) and brambles (*Rubus*) can be shredded for use as a mulch. Otherwise, woody material should be burnt. Ashes from garden bonfires (a good source of potash) can be added to the compost heap or used as a dressing for plants. Any plant material treated with a weedkiller should not be composted.

Above and below: A carpet spread over soil will suppress weeds, but can be unsightly. It takes a few years for carpets to kill weeds totally, so this method is good for any ground that is out of sight.

Above: Weed-suppressing membrane is effective for years.

Below: Bark chippings make an effective mulch that can suppress weeds.

Preventing problems

Rather than wait for a pest or disease to strike, it is best to adopt a general policy of garden management that will positively help to prevent their occurrence.

To maintain effective control over garden pests and diseases, it is necessary to employ a range of strategies. Increasingly, many gardeners favour an organic approach to controlling garden pests and diseases. Such an approach is perceived as less harmful to the environment, including wildlife, than chemical methods. Organic methods are not necessarily more effective, or indeed less damaging, than conventional ones, however, and an integrated approach involving both chemical and organic products is often the most successful method.

Be vigilant

Most gardeners who love their plants spend a lot of time looking for signs of new growth, flower buds and developing fruits. Whenever you make your rounds of the garden, keep a look-out for signs of pest and disease attack and anything else that suggests poor growth. If a whole group of unrelated plants suddenly wilts, the problem is almost certain to be lack of water; but if one plant among a group of healthy specimens suddenly shows signs of failing, there is probably some other cause.

Exact diagnosis can be tricky. In many cases, the outward signs of damage by a pest, disease or physiological problem are very similar: leaves turning yellow could indicate any one of a number of problems, and you may not arrive at the correct diagnosis straight away. Some insects are difficult to spot if they are fast-moving, microscopic, well camouflaged or hidden under leaves. In certain cases they can be identified only by the damage they cause, or else by their excreta ("frass"). Sometimes their actions are relatively benign, but the wounds they open up on plants provide an entry point for fungal and other diseases. The effects of some diseases are noticeable only when the damage has already been done (to root crops, for example).

Both pests and diseases seem to occur in waves. In other words, the local conditions (which can change from year to year) and the season (wet or dry) will tend to favour certain pests and diseases, which can then proliferate alarmingly. Hence the desirability of getting on top of problems at as early a stage as possible, and of taking preventive measures in the first place to stop them taking hold.

There are a number of strategies that will save you headaches and keep garden problems at arm's length. Should a problem occur, swift action will keep potential damage to the absolute minimum.

Good cultivation

Keeping the soil in good heart will make plants grow strongly. Healthy plants will recover faster from any pest or disease attack than those that are weak-growing.

Prior to planting, improve the soil by digging in organic matter in the form of garden compost, well-rotted farmyard manure or other soil improver. This will both increase the fertility of light soils and help to open up heavy clay soils. If the soil is very heavy and prone to waterlogging, dig in grit to improve the drainage. Soil fertility is especially important in the vegetable garden, but improvements to the soil structure are beneficial to all types of plants.

Feeding plants with an appropriate fertilizer keeps them growing strongly and can improve their resistance to disease. If a plant does succumb to disease or pest attack, a boost with a foliar feed can help it on the way to recovery. Beware, however, of overfeeding plants, which can result in too much soft growth, which will itself be vulnerable.

Avoid plant stress

Plants are as vulnerable to stress as we are. Without adequate supplies of light, water and nutrients, and with temperatures that are too hot or too cold, growth is uneven and plants will be susceptible to disease.

To avoid excess stress to plants, make sure they are sited in a position in the garden that suits them, and that they are not overcrowded. Water new plantings well to help them establish. Be sure to keep weed numbers down: weeds compete with plants for valuable moisture and nutrients.

Propagation for plant health

Certain perennials benefit from division every few years. Left to their own devices, they can become congested, or woody towards the centre of the clump. Such plants tend to lose vigour and become prone to a range of

Below: Careful inspection of these leaves reveals some macadamia cup moths.

Below: Dividing a congested plant rejuvenates it and provides new plants.

diseases. Splitting the clumps, in spring or autumn, refreshes the plant. Replant pieces from the edge of the clump (which are younger) and discard the older section, usually at the centre. Many perennials, such as hardy geraniums and lady's mantle (*Alchemilla mollis*), can be pulled apart by hand. To divide tougher plants, such as hostas, drive two garden forks held back to back into the centre of the clump and prize them apart to divide the clump, or cut them apart with a sharp garden knife.

Many bulbs form offsets, and these can crowd each other underground. Congested bulbs will fail to reach their full size and will tend to produce leaves only, with no flowers. Lift clumps of bulbs after any flowers have been produced, and before the leaves die down, split them up, then space them at the distance recommended for the species.

Good garden hygiene

Practising good hygiene means keeping the garden as free as possible of any material that will encourage pests and diseases.

Avoid introducing diseased material into the garden, which can pass on problems to existing plants. Buy only strong-growing plants that are free of pests and diseases (check them over for tell-tale signs of infestation before parting with any money). If possible, slide containerized plants from their pots to check over the root system to see if they are healthy. Bulbs should be guaranteed virus-free. Seeds of vegetables that are vulnerable to seed-borne diseases should also be guaranteed disease-free.

In the garden, cut off any diseased or damaged material from plants as soon as you spot it. Such material should be burnt or thrown away, not composted. Some plants present the gardener with a dilemma at the end of the season. Dead, twiggy stems on some perennials (for instance fuchsias) can provide shelter for overwintering pests, but they also protect the plant's resting crown from frost damage. Whether you cut back the dead stems before the onset of winter depends on which you consider to be the greater risk. However, decaying leaves on herbaceous perennials such as hostas should be cut back and composted. If left around the plant, they can rot.

Choose disease-resistant varieties

Certain varieties of plant have been bred for their resistance to disease. This is particularly true of many fruit and vegetable crops but also applies to certain extensively hybridized ornamentals such as roses.

Above: A healthy garden begins with the soil.

It makes sense to look for disease-resistant varieties, especially if you have experienced problems with certain crops before. However, disease-resistance is not the same as immunity: there is always the possibility of disease striking. When growing a "resistant" variety it is important to practise the preventive measures outlined to ensure the plant stays healthy.

Lawns

Neglected lawns easily become threadbare, and this is when certain pernicious weeds can take a hold. A neglected lawn that is heavily used will also be subject to waterlogging, since the ground will become compacted and water will not drain through.

Below: Early morning and evening is the best time to water the garden in hot weather.

To keep a lawn in good condition, rake it regularly to remove any thatch. In spring, spike the lawn with a spiker (the best of which actually remove plugs of soil, which can be added to the compost heap or spread around the garden) or use a garden fork. Topdress the lawn with lawn sand, peat (or an alternative) and a general lawn fertilizer. If the grass is wearing thin, add some lawn seed.

Water

Wildlife pools are largely self-regulating. Problems tend to occur when the water in the pool heats up in summer and the water level drops. Keep pools regularly topped up during hot, dry spells, allowing the water to run into the pond from a hose. It is seldom necessary to replace all the water in a pool.

Below: Clean tools regularly to ensure that disease is not spread on them.

Attracting wildlife

Besides being a place for plants, a garden can also be a haven for a variety of wildlife, from small mammals, birds and reptiles to a range of beneficial insects and other invertebrates.

A good balance of predators helps immeasurably in the control of a range of creatures that cause harm to plants. To ensure good crops on many fruit and vegetable plants, it is essential to encourage pollinating insects into the garden.

Keeping the garden well stocked with as wide a range of plants as possible will ensure that the widest range of wildlife will visit. (A planting that relies on one type of plant only – known as a monoculture – has the adverse effect of providing ideal conditions for certain pests and diseases, which can then proliferate.)

If possible, try to make sure that you have plants in flower throughout the year to attract pollinating insects. This is easy to manage in spring and summer (and, to a lesser extent, autumn), but it is still possible in winter if you look to some of the many winter-flowering shrubs, such as *Viburnum tinus*, *Sarcococca humilis*, and also to early bulbs such as *Crocus tommasinianus* and snowdrops (*Galanthus*).

Keep an area of the garden uncultivated, and allow native weeds to seed themselves there. Many are a valuable food source for insects. A pile of logs left to rot in a corner will also be a refuge for invertebrates, as well as offering shelter to hedgehogs and other small mammals.

Birds

On the whole, birds are to be welcomed into gardens. They feed on many insects and will also pick off slugs and snails. At a time when their numbers appear to be declining, it is all the more important that gardeners do what they can to promote their survival.

Broadly speaking, birds prefer to keep to the trees. There they are safer from predatory mammals such as foxes, and take-off is easier: they simply have to drop from a branch. Take-off from ground level involves more effort. Hence, birds descend to feed at ground level only in rare circumstances. There should be room for at least one tree in all but the smallest gardens, but you should also make sure there is an adequate expanse of lawn or other flat surface to act as a landing and take-off strip. Where space is limited, a bird table that is raised out of reach of any cats will tempt birds into the garden. Bird baths are also appreciated, especially during a winter freeze.

To attract birds, plant as many berrying shrubs and trees as possible. Not only do birds feed on the berries, but they will also look for insects that live in the bark. Trees and shrubs popular with birds include rowans (*Sorbus*), cotoneasters, pyracanthas and hollies (*Ilex*). Evergreens will provide them with cover in winter. Birds will often nest in tall trees, but to give them a start, try fixing a few bird boxes to the trunks. Different sizes and styles will attract different birds.

Turning over bare soil in the vegetable garden during winter will bring earthworms and a host of other invertebrates to the surface, which will attract birds to ground level.

Bats

Nocturnal pests such as moths, gnats and other flying insects are eaten by bats; some bat species can pick off non-flying invertebrates, such as woodlice, from tree bark. Bat boxes will provide them with a place to roost, but bats often take up residence in attics (assuming they can gain entry) or hollow trees, either singly or in large colonies. They hibernate in winter in cold climates. Bats include many protected species.

Hedgehogs

Gardeners love hedgehogs, since they eat slugs and snails, which are among the most troublesome of garden pests. You can attract hedgehogs by piling logs in an area of long grass or other quiet part of the garden. If you know there is a hedgehog in the vicinity, resist the temptation to put out saucers of milk to

Below: Some logs in your garden may attract a hedgehog or two.

Below: Sunflowers will attract birds to a garden in search of their seeds.

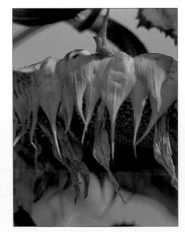

Below: Many flowers attract pollinating bees.

Above: A butterfly house is a good idea if you want to cultivate a wildlife garden.

Above: Providing a designated home for overwintering beneficial insects is good practice.

enter the water usually only to breed. Be sure to place some large stones near a wildlife pool (and, if possible, elsewhere in the garden) among which they can take shelter and keep cool in summer. If frogs fail to find the pond of their own accord, ask a friend with a pond for some spawn (it is illegal to remove frog spawn from the wild). If you intend the pool to be a home to frogs, do not introduce fish into it, since the fish will eat the tadpoles.

A pool for wildlife

The best attractant for wildlife that you can make in your garden is a wildlife pool. The water in a new pool rapidly matures to form a vibrant eco-system, but if you feel you must accelerate the process, introduce a bucketful of water from a garden pond that is already teeming with wildlife. The eggs of many pond creatures will be introduced into the garden on the feet of birds.

To one side, create a beach that slopes gently into the water. This will encourage smaller birds to bathe, and will help any small mammal that falls into the pond to get out again.

Insects

Certain plants are known to attract bees. Bees prefer plants with single flowers because the pollen grains are more accessible. Good bee plants include sedum, lavender (*Lavandula*) and many annuals. Butterflies are attracted to nectar-rich flowers such as those of buddleias, *Verbena bonariensis* and valerian (*Centranthus*).

Leaving a few windfall apples or pears on the ground to rot will attract wasps into the garden to pollinate flowers.

attract it. Besides diverting it from seeking its own food, cow's milk is not good for any animal. Hedgehogs will eat dog or cat food, and it is possible to buy food specially formulated for them, but bear in mind that any food put out to attract hedgehogs can also attract unwelcome visitors such as rats and neighbours' cats.

Frogs and toads

These amphibians prey on a range of insects and – usefully for the gardener – slugs and snails. The presence of water in a garden attracts frogs and toads, though the latter will

Above: Frogs and toads will naturally find a garden pond.

Below: Rotting fruit attracts insects and grubs – a feast for any passing bird.

Below: Attract butterflies into the garden with highly scented flowers.

Pruning for health

Pruning is an effective method of keeping woody plants (including fruiting bushes and trees) in good health. Climbers especially can accumulate a lot of congested, unproductive growth in time. Removing old or diseased wood helps to keep plants healthy. A good pruning regime will greatly enhance the productivity of a range of woody plants

The aim of pruning is to refresh the plant. In essence, the removal of older material stimulates the plant to replace it with new growth, which is always more vigorous and resistant to disease than old wood.

Keep your pruning tools sharp and clean: a ragged cut from a blunt tool exposes too much soft tissue, and it is often through such wounds that diseases enter a plant. Sharp tools make clean cuts that heal most quickly.

As a matter of routine, cut back all dead, diseased and damaged growth from woody plants. Such material can begin to rot, and infection can then spread to the rest of the plant. Cut back to firm, healthy growth.

Remove any crossing branches (where they rub against each other, the outer layer of bark is damaged, and provides an entry point for disease). Always favour young, healthy growth over older material: older wood is sometimes best cut back to ground level. Prune out twiggy growth in the centre of a shrub to relieve congestion. Air can stagnate in a dense plant, providing the ideal environment for mildew and other fungal diseases to take hold.

After you have pruned a plant, feed it well to boost recovery. A foliar feed is often the best type to apply if you have had to cut back a lot of diseased material, because the nutrients are immediately available to the plant. Water well, then mulch around the plant to conserve soil moisture.

Healthy prunings can be shredded for use as a mulch. Diseased or damaged material should be burnt or thrown away, but not composted.

Renewal pruning

Overgrown or neglected plants can be given a new lease of life by renewal, or renovative, pruning. It is particularly effective on climbers, which tend to be naturally vigorous, and a host of shrubs. In some cases (for example some late-flowering hybrid clematis and buddleias) annual renewal pruning is a matter of routine

Above: Sharp tools make clean cuts, which help the plant heal more quickly.

maintenance, without which the plants will become ragged and straggly.

Renewal pruning is best done when the plant is dormant in winter or just as it is coming into growth in early spring. Cut all the growth hard back to leave a "hat rack" of stems that are 30–45cm (12–18in) long. Very old wood can be taken out at ground level. If you are at all nervous (if the plant is very old, for instance), cut back only a third of the stems initially. If recovery is good, cut back the remaining two-thirds in the following two years. If the plant fails to put on vigorous new growth, dig up and destroy it.

Making the cuts

New growth will always appear from the growth bud nearest to the cut. You need to cut as close to the bud as possible without damaging it, and not cut too far above it, leaving a long length of wood that will die back. This length of wood could itself be vulnerable to disease.

It is often suggested that on plants on which growth buds lie alternately on the stem (such as on a rose), pruning cuts should be angled away from the bud to allow any rainwater to run away from the bud (rather than into it), but this is largely a matter of judgement. Cutting straight across exposes a smaller

Above: Prune roses just above a growth bud.

area of tissue, so such wounds will heal more rapidly. The wetness of the climate may well dictate which strategy you adopt.

Trees

The pruning of large, established trees is best left to a tree surgeon, who will have the appropriate level of expertise, tools and safety equipment. However, you may sometimes need to remove a single dead, diseased or damaged branch from a tree. Any such branch should be cut back flush with the trunk.

To minimize damage to the trunk, use a pruning saw to make a shallow upward cut on the underside of the branch about 10cm (4in) from the trunk. Cut downwards at the same distance to sever the branch. The initial undercut prevents the bark on the trunk tearing as the branch is removed. Finally, shorten the stub. (It is not necessary to paint the wound with a wound paint or dressing. If the tree is healthy, the wound will callus over.)

Some trees, especially those trained as pollards, tend to throw out green shoots (epicormic or water shoots) from the trunk. These should be removed, either by rubbing them out with finger and thumb or by using secateurs (pruners). Besides spoiling the appearance of the tree, such shoots tend to harbour insect pests.

Crop rotation

Growing different plants in an area each year helps to prevent the build-up of diseases in the soil. While not normally practical in the ornamental garden, it is a perfect system for a vegetable plot.

Crop rotation is a sound horticultural practice based on tried and tested principles. In the vegetable garden, growing the same (or related) crops in the same ground year after year can lead to problems. Soil-borne diseases specific to one type of crop can build up, and various soil nutrients will be depleted. It is good practice to divide up the vegetable plot and in each section to grow a crop from a different family each year to prevent diseases from building up to a damaging level.

Some diseases may still persist – clubroot (which affects brassicas) and onion white rot can survive in the soil for much longer than four years – but many problems will be minimized or avoided.

The same principle also applies in the ornamental garden, especially in areas given over to annual bedding schemes. In this case, planting different bedding plants each year will reduce the likelihood of disease building up in the soil.

A four-year rotation scheme might run according to the sequence illustrated below; plot 5 is for permanent plantings.

Below: Decide on the vegetables you want to grow and divide them into the five groups. Draw a plan to indicate which group of crops goes where. Next year, move the crops in each group on to the next plot.

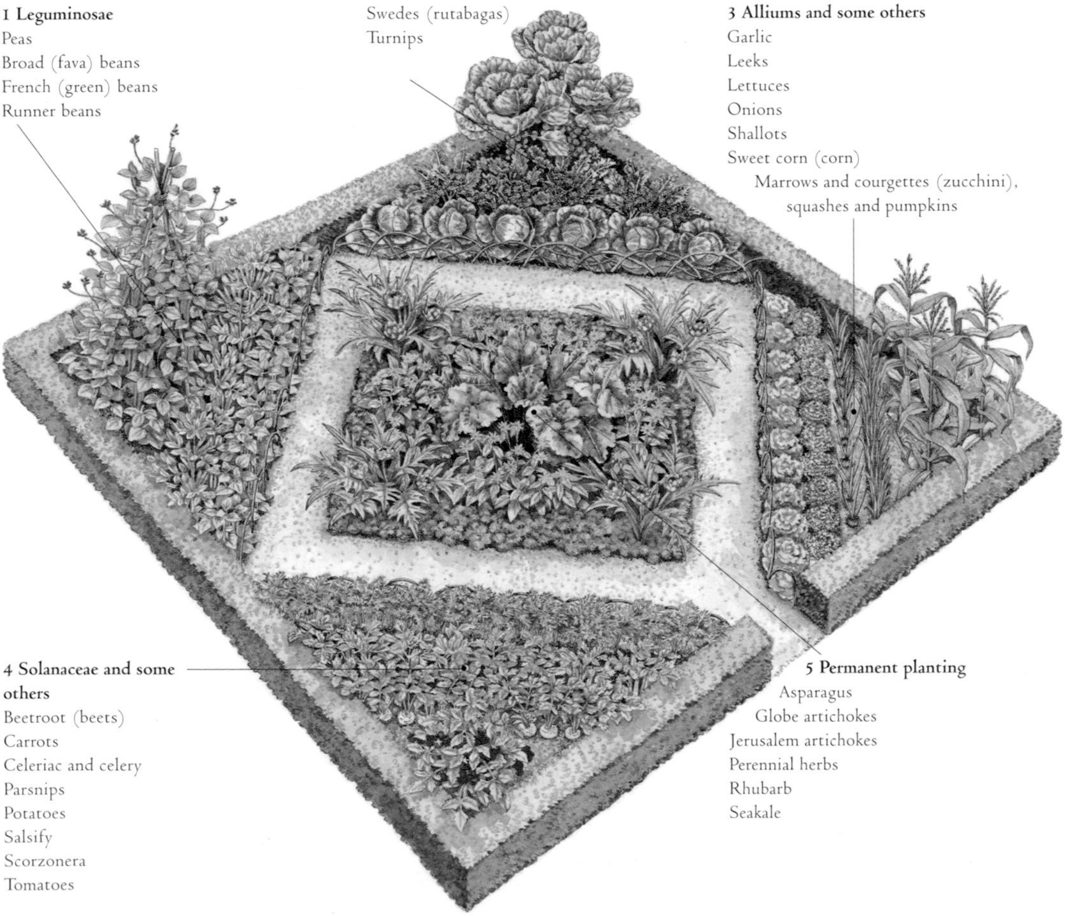

1 Leguminosae
Peas
Broad (fava) beans
French (green) beans
Runner beans

2 Brassicas and crucifers
Broccoli
Brussels sprouts
Cabbages
Calabrese (Italian sprouting broccoli)
Cauliflowers
Radishes
Swedes (rutabagas)
Turnips

3 Alliums and some others
Garlic
Leeks
Lettuces
Onions
Shallots
Sweet corn (corn)
 Marrows and courgettes (zucchini), squashes and pumpkins

4 Solanaceae and some others
Beetroot (beets)
Carrots
Celeriac and celery
Parsnips
Potatoes
Salsify
Scorzonera
Tomatoes

5 Permanent planting
Asparagus
Globe artichokes
Jerusalem artichokes
Perennial herbs
Rhubarb
Seakale

Greenhouse hygiene

The enclosed world of the greenhouse, with its own microclimate, can be an ideal breeding ground for many pests and diseases. Practising good hygiene is your best defence against them. A greenhouse presents the gardener with particular problems. It is an enclosed environment, so there is not the range of wildlife (invertebrates, as well as mammals and birds) that helps to control pests in the open garden. With few if any natural predators, pests in the greenhouse can proliferate. Further, gardeners tend to grow a restricted range of plants (for instance, fruiting crops such as tomatoes, chillies and cucumbers), so the insect population itself is less diverse.

There is a natural tendency to crowd plants in a greenhouse to get the maximum use of the, usually limited, space available. The overcrowding makes for high humidity levels – precisely the conditions that favour a large number of fungal diseases. As if that were not enough, there are attendant (potential) physiological problems. Many plants in greenhouses (in some cases all plants) are grown in containers, and these are prone to dry out, especially in summer. An irregular water supply leads to uneven growth. Furthermore, the temperature can fluctuate widely within the

Below: A well-maintained greenhouse will provide many healthy crops.

Above: Shading mesh helps to protect greenhouse crops from the summer heat.

confines of a greenhouse. The glass can intensify the heat of the sun to a stifling level in summer, unless you take care to keep the temperature down.

Hygiene

Good greenhouse hygiene is critical if fungal and other diseases are to be kept at bay. Keep a close watch on your plants. Cut off any dead or decaying leaves and flowers and remove dead plant material from the compost (soil mix) surface, from the greenhouse staging and the floor. Not only can they harbour fungal spores and rots, but they can also provide nesting sites for a whole host of insect pests.

Clean all pots after use. Store them in a shed or garage, rather than under the staging, where they can shelter slugs and snails.

On sunny days in summer, stand all the plants outside, on staging, as far as is practical, to expose them to insect predators outdoors. Warm days in late summer/autumn provide a good opportunity to give the greenhouse a thorough clean. Remove the plants temporarily, then sweep and wash down all the staging and the floor with a household disinfectant cleaner. Wash the glass, being sure to remove all the algal deposits that tend to build up where the panes overlap. A metal paint scraper is useful for this purpose and will not scratch the glass.

Controlling the temperature

Plants in a greenhouse are vulnerable to fluctuations of temperature (such as when bright sunny days are followed by clear, cold nights). A maximum–minimum thermometer will help you to judge the temperature range at any given time.

Greenhouses can be insulated in winter with bubble-wrap plastic taped to the inside of the glass. This can keep the temperature above freezing in an unheated greenhouse, and will help to keep running costs down if used in conjunction with a heating system. Bubble-wrap does, however, have the disadvantage of lowering the light levels.

Below: A maximum-minimum thermometer will help you monitor the greenhouse temperature.

Above: Bubble-wrap can provide insulation for tender plants in the winter greenhouse.

Above: Heating a greenhouse enables you to grow cold-sensitive plants in winter.

Various heating systems can be used to raise the temperature in winter, if you are growing plants that are vulnerable to the cold. Some sophisticated systems monitor the temperature, turn on heating elements and open vents as necessary.

Paraffin and some gas heaters release fumes that are toxic to plants, and the greenhouse must be adequately ventilated when they are in use.

Good ventilation is essential to the greenhouse environment, even in winter, to prevent a build-up of stuffy air in which bacteria can thrive. Open the vents as necessary to keep the temperature down and improve air quality. It may sometimes be necessary to open the door as well. In this case, you may need to net the aperture to prevent birds, small mammals, frogs and toads from finding their way into the greenhouse.

Controlling the light level

Light intensity varies throughout the year and glass magnifies the intensity of sunlight. To prevent the leaves of plants from scorching in summer, make sure that they do not touch the glass. Move the plant away from the glass, or, if this is not possible, trim back any growth that touches the glass. Turn pot plants as necessary to keep them growing evenly.

Some crops need additional light in winter, and the available natural light can be supplemented with special growing lamps.

In summer, it will almost certainly be necessary to shade the glass, both to lower the light level and to help keep the temperature down. Plants can be shaded by applying a special wash to the outside of the glass at the start of summer (the wash is then wiped or washed off in autumn). Alternatively, blinds can be installed on the outside of the greenhouse roof (some powered versions can be linked to a thermostat so that they are automatically lowered when the temperature rises above a certain point). Special fabric meshes are also available that can be fixed to the outside of the glass.

Controlling the humidity

Most plants thrive within a range of 40 to 60 per cent humidity. (Rainforest plants need up to 85 per cent, while desert plants, such as cacti, need as little as 15 per cent.)

As the temperature rises in summer, the air dries out. Plants lose excess water from their leaves and can scorch; the growing medium dries out, leading to wilting.

To maintain adequate humidity levels, hose down the hard surfaces on hot days during the evening and early morning (water will evaporate too quickly during the heat of the day). This also lowers the temperature.

Below: A biological control, released from a sachet, can help in pest management.

Pest control

Many insect pests thrive in the enclosed, sheltered environment of a greenhouse, making them difficult to control. On the other hand, certain control measures are more effective here than in the open garden.

Most of the biological controls are highly successful in greenhouses. Sticky traps for whitefly and other small flying insects give good results. Insect pests can also be controlled by the use of insecticidal smokes. For these to be effective, all vents should be closed. Take care not to inhale the smoke. Some smokes also have a fungicidal action and are useful for maintaining the appropriate hygiene level.

Above: Algae can grow where water collects.

Below: Clean greenhouse windows thoroughly using a disinfectant.

Controlling garden problems

Pests can be controlled in a number of ways. They can be killed outright, trapped or merely deterred from entering the garden. The gardener has a range of choices for keeping pests out of the garden, including a variety of methods to keep down insect populations. One of the most effective is, in fact, the simplest and the most environmentally friendly: where possible, simply pick the insects off by hand. This may be easier at the larval stage, when most are slow-moving. Some insects, however, have a defence mechanism. Hairy caterpillars, for instance, can irritate the skin, so take care and wear gloves if necessary.

If they are conspicuous, remove eggs when you know the adults are active (and if these are too swift-moving to trap). It is sometimes possible to scrape off light infestations of scale insects with a sharp knife, but be careful not to damage the tissue of the host plant. Sometimes a strong jet of water from a hose or spray can displace pests, so long as this is not strong enough to damage plant tissue.

You will need to patrol the garden at night to eradicate certain pests by hand (especially slugs and snails, but also moths).

Below: Slugs and snails can be controlled to an extent by using a water trap. It will not stop pests travelling below ground.

Above: Spraying shrubs and plants with a blast of water can dislodge many insect pests, although you will need to remain vigilant.

Pests and diseases can also be controlled, with varying success, by the use of certain proprietary garden chemicals.

Organic versus inorganic

Gardeners are increasingly wary of using chemicals in the garden because of the perceived damage to the environment. In addition, recent legislation is directed towards safety in the garden, so only chemicals that are safe to use are given a licence for distribution within the garden-centre trade. (Note that laws regarding the acceptability of certain chemicals differ between countries, so keep abreast of changing regulations where you live.)

Above: Some pests, such as this lily beetle, are large enough to be easily detected and can be removed by hand.

"Organic" pesticides are derived from plants and other naturally occurring materials. They include derris, fatty acids and soft soaps, nicotine, pyrethrum, sulphur and various vegetable oils.

Products such as pyrethrins are not organic as such, but are based on natural products derived from plant material. (Pyrethrum is an insecticide derived from the dried flowers of certain cultivated chrysanthemums.) Sunlight renders them inactive, therefore they should be applied directly to the pest at dusk.

Below: A scarecrow is an age-old method of pest control designed to frighten away birds.

Right: Horticultural fleece spread over young plants can provide a physical barrier to insects.

Conveniently, this is a time of day when beneficial butterflies and bees are not active, so they escape unharmed.

It must be noted, however, that many products sold as "organic" are no safer in use than chemical controls, and are in any case subject to the same legislation. The ideal is a range of products that can be used without the benefit of protective clothing: typically eye goggles and/or gloves.

Organic, or no-chemical, methods of pest control are arguably no more humane than other methods. If you pick off adult insects or their eggs or larvae by hand, they still have to be disposed of somehow.

Most insects have a sense of taste that guides them in their choice of food. Certain crop sprays are designed not to kill insects, but to cause a subtle change in the smell or taste of the plant to render it unattractive to the pest. This is the method by which the fatty acids/soft soaps and vegetable oils work, both of which are sprayed on to plants when the pests are known to be active.

How pesticides work

Insecticides – chemicals that kill insects – work in one of two ways, and this determines when and how you use the product.(Chemicals that cause the death of slugs and snails are technically molluscides.) Contact insecticides kill insects on contact, while systemic insecticides are absorbed into the plant and kill the insect when it sucks sap or eats the leaves. Obviously, a systemic insecticide can be applied before the pests become active, while for a contact pesticide to be effective, the pest has to be clearly visible. In both cases, repeated applications may be necessary. Insecticides include certain tar acids and tar oil.

Insects can rapidly develop immunity to pesticides, particularly those that breed very fast and can produce several generations per season. It is sensible, therefore, to change the chemicals you use each year by using a product with a different active ingredient. If a particular pesticide fails to give the desired result, try another one.

Always check the label of any pesticide to see what the active ingredients are. Be aware that liquid and powdered products sold under the same brand name (and often in similar packaging) can have different active ingredients and work in different ways.

There are some gaps in the chemical armoury: in other words, there are certain pests against which available chemical controls are ineffective. These include some lawn pests, some other soil pests, chrysanthemum leaf miner (and other leaf miners) and

Below: Covering young crops with plastic tunnels will prevent flying insects from settling on the plants.

Below: A compact disc hanging from string may frighten birds away when it blows in the wind.

Below: String wrapped with kitchen foil is an effective and harmless deterrent to birds when placed over crops.

certain kitchen garden pests that attack fruits such as plums, gooseberries and currants, and such vegetables as onions, artichokes and spinach.

Biological controls

Most biological controls rely on introducing into the environment an organism that is a natural predator or parasite of the pest you wish to control. They are usually effective only within a confined area, such as in a greenhouse, though some are available for more general use in the garden.

Barrier methods

So-called barrier methods can be highly effective means of avoiding damage by insect pests to certain crops. Unlike other methods, they do not kill the pest outright, or even harm it, but involve the use of a physical barrier that keeps the pest off the plants, in the same way that a fence can be used to keep rabbits out of a garden.

Copper strips can be placed around certain vulnerable plants to deter slugs and snails. On making contact with the metal, the molluscs experience an electric shock that discourages further progress. Sticky bands wrapped around tree trunks (usually in winter) can deter certain flightless female moths that climb up the trunks to lay their eggs near next season's flower buds. Sometimes, simply spreading a length of horticultural fleece over vulnerable plants as a short-term measure is sufficient to protect them from pest attack, especially in the vegetable garden.

Below: Companion planting is an age-old method of pest control.

Above: A sticky trap will attract flying insects, which then stick to the surface.

Right: Set traps filled with stale beer in and among tender plants to catch slugs and snails.

Traps

Some pests can be caught in traps. Their effectiveness as a method of control is limited, since their use is localized; but they can serve as a useful indicator of the presence of a particular pest, and further steps can then be taken.

Most traps contain a sticky substance to which the pests adhere. Sticky yellow cards (the colour seems to attract certain insects) can be used to trap whiteflies, aphids, thrips, leafhoppers and other small flying insects.

Pheromone traps contain chemicals that mimic the scent of fertile females and attract males. Hung from tree branches, they can be useful to indicate the activities of codling moths in orchards.

Earwigs can be trapped by filling pots with straw. Invert these on canes and place around susceptible plants (such as dahlias, clematis and chrysanthemums). The insects will shelter in the straw by night and can be removed and disposed of each morning.

Companion planting

Certain plants have been found to reduce pest problems on a different plant growing nearby, and using these combinations is known as companion planting. It can either involve interplanting plants susceptible to particular pests with others that attract their natural predators; or the vulnerable crop is interplanted with another that gives off a scent that deters the relevant pests.

To give some examples, French marigolds (*Tagetes patula*) can be planted among plants that are susceptible to aphid attack. The marigolds will attract hoverflies, which prey on the aphids. Rows of cabbages, broccoli or other brassicas can be alternated with rows of onions. The strong smell of the onions seems to confuse many brassica pests that are guided

BIOLOGICAL CONTROLS

Adalia 2-punctata	aphid predator
Amblyseius spp.	thrips predator (in glasshouses)
Aphidius spp./*Praon* spp.	aphid parasites
Aphidoletes aphidimyza	aphid predator
Bacillus thuringiensis	caterpillar bacterium
Chrysopa carnea	aphid predator
Cryptolaemus montrouzieri	mealybug predator
Delphastus catalinae	glasshouse whitefly predator
Encarsia formosa	glasshouse whitefly parasite
Heterorhabditis megidis	pathogenic nematode for vine weevil grubs/ chafer grubs
Hypoaspis miles	fungus gnat/sciarid fly larvae predator
Metaphycus helvolus	soft scale parasite
Phasmarhabditis hermaphrodita	pathogenic nematode for slugs
Phytoseiulus persimilis	glasshouse red spider mite predator
Steinernema feltiae	pathogenic nematode for leatherjackets and fungus gnat larvae

by scent. Tomato plants also appear to deter caterpillars from cabbages, and growing leeks next to carrots can repel carrot flies.

Controlling diseases

Correct diagnosis of fungal diseases is not always easy, since many symptoms are similar, especially those that result merely in the debility of a previously healthily growing plant. Diseases that are soil-borne and affect the roots of plants are particularly difficult to spot. You may not be aware of a problem until the plant keels over.

Much will depend on the weather. Some fungal diseases will be more troublesome during wet summers, for instance; but many are associated with poor garden hygiene. Breeders try to develop plants resistant to fungal attacks, and it makes sense to look for such varieties if you know a particular problem is likely to occur in your area.

Outbreaks can usually be controlled by the use of a garden fungicide. More than one application of a fungicide may be necessary to check the outbreak of a disease, however, so be prepared to repeat doses.

Regular use of fungicides is not recommended, since tolerant strains of fungus can build up, meaning that the fungicide ceases to be effective. Spores of grey mould (*Botrytis cinerea*), for instance, are always in the air and are often seen on dying weeds – hence the importance of keeping the garden (especially the fruit garden) weed free. It can also be present in thick straw mulches, so you need to

Above: Slug pellets are a quick and easy way of dispensing with slugs and snails, but can be harmful to hedgehogs or birds, which may eat the slugs.

be aware of this potential risk if you wish to use this material in the garden.

Preventive methods are often the best solution. Practising crop rotation and appropriate pruning greatly improve the health of plants. You should also take care not to overcrowd plants, not only in the kitchen garden, but also in the ornamental garden. Overcrowding creates the stagnant air in which fungal spores can proliferate. Besides, overcrowded plants tend to show distorted and/or weak growth, which is more vulnerable to disease than healthy growth.

Many plant diseases are spread by aphids and other insect pests, so you need to be active on all fronts if you are to prevent potential problems.

Hot water treatments

Certain nematodes, especially a few that live in bulb tissue, can be controlled by immersing the dormant plant in hot water for a certain length of time. The water has to be kept at a constant temperature (too hot, and the plant is damaged; too cool, and the nematode can survive), so the technique is largely practised only by nurserymen, who own the specialist baths required.

To control narcissus eelworm, the required water temperature is 44.5°C (112°F) for three hours; for the chrysanthemum eelworm, dormant stools need to be plunged into water kept at 46°C (115°F) for five minutes.

Below: Stuffing a plastic plant pot with straw and turning it upside down over an upright cane makes an effective earwig trap.

Below: Plastic bottles covering young plants can provide some protection from pests, particularly those that fly, as well as sheltering them from the cold.

Below: Plastic or wire fencing will stop larger mammals nibbling tender plants.

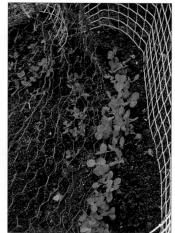

Using chemical controls

Chemical methods of pest control are subject to changing legislation. Legislation covers which chemicals may be sold, and how they may be stored and disposed of.

The manufacture and sale – and indeed use – of garden chemicals are subject to strict legislation that is constantly under review.

An increasing number of garden chemicals that our parents used freely are being delisted. This means that not only are they being withdrawn from sale but it is illegal for gardeners to stockpile them and continue to use them beyond a certain date.

Legislation varies from country to country. In the UK, for instance, since 2003, no manufacturer has been able to legally sell any of the organochlorines or organophosphates. These groups include such chemicals as dicofol, fenitrothion, malathion and pirimiphos-methyl. This will make it necessary to look at alternative methods of control.

Below: Avoid spraying on open flowers, or you may poison any pollinating insects.

Effects of legislation

Generally, it is not in the manufacturer's economic interests to develop safe alternatives to any product based on a chemical that has been delisted. The costs of research and development are high, and the market share occupied by garden chemicals, as opposed to agricultural chemicals (to which different rules apply), is actually very small. Further costs are incurred in testing and gaining the necessary licences for distribution and sale.

Gardeners are therefore increasingly reliant on alternative, eco-friendly methods of controlling pests and diseases. This does not in itself imply that you should look exclusively to organic methods, since organic products are also subject to the same legislation as inorganic ones.

Use of chemicals

Chemicals should be used in the garden only when absolutely necessary. You can control many pests by practising good cultivation techniques such as crop rotation, destruction

of crop residues or hand removal of pests. Encouraging their natural predators, possibly combined with the use of biological controls, will reduce the need for spraying. Make sure you identify the pest correctly to be sure of applying the correct control measures. Ideally, buy only enough of any one product to meet your immediate needs; garden chemicals should be used within two years of purchase. Do not buy a new product if you already have a different one that will achieve the same result. Check the label carefully to see what is the active ingredient. Some contain more active ingredients than others and thus can be used to treat a range of problems. Different brands vary in the range of pests that can be treated, even though the active ingredient is the same.

Estimate the area of the garden that needs to be treated and aim to mix the exact amount of product needed. It is better to leave a small area untreated than to have an excess of any chemical to dispose of.

Select chemicals that are recommended for the purpose you have in mind, and be sure to read the label carefully before making a purchase. If the product is to be used on edible plants, check the instructions for the period of time that must be left between treatment and harvest.

Check any specific precautions, such as the need to wear protective clothing. Even if none is specified, you should wear rubber (latex) gloves when handling any product or during spraying. Follow the manufacturer's instructions, and apply the chemical at the recommended rate and in the manner described. Complying with any Statutory Conditions is a legal requirement.

Use the spray at the appropriate time and at the intervals recommended, since these are often crucial in the control of a pest.

While some products combine fungicides and insecticides, to give all-round protection on roses, for instance, it is illegal to mix different products together (unless specifically recommended by the manufacturer).

When using chemicals, avoid contact with any exposed parts of the body, the eyes especially. In the event of any splashes, wash immediately with plain water. You should also avoid inhaling any spray or dust. For optimum effectiveness, most garden chemicals are

Above: Garden centres and supermarkets sell a wide range of garden chemicals. Always follow the manufacturer's instructions with regard to use of the product, wearing protective clothing and storing safely.

best applied during dull, still weather, but it is a wise precaution to wear a mask over both nose and mouth. Make sure no children or pets are in the vicinity. Do not eat, drink or smoke while spraying.

All insecticides are dangerous to fish and other pond life. Keep all pesticides – apart from those specifically recommended for use in ponds – away from any source of water. When spraying, the aim is to wet the stems, buds and leaves thoroughly, both upper and lower surfaces, without excessive run-off or drift of the product. Do not spray on open flowers, as the chemical may be toxic to bees and other pollinating insects. Avoid spraying plants that can be damaged by the product. Ideally, check sensitivity by spraying a small area or only a small number of plants initially, and observe the results. Spray in the early morning or late afternoon or evening. Do not spray during wet or windy weather or when plants are suffering from drought.

Clean all equipment thoroughly after spraying. Ideally, keep separate equipment for pesticides and weedkillers, and do not use these for general watering.

If you miscalculate the amount needed to make up a spray, spray the excess over areas where no fruit or vegetables are to be grown for at least 12 months. Do not spray near ponds, watercourses, boggy areas, ditches or near wildlife habitats, or near to neighbouring property. Surpluses should also not be introduced into the domestic water system, so do not pour products into drains or down the lavatory.

Containers you have used to dispense the product should be rinsed at least three times, and the rinsings added to the final spray solution. Otherwise, dispose of the rinsings as recommended above. Cleaned containers can be disposed of through the usual refuse collection process, but are not suitable for recycling.

Storing chemicals

Safe use of chemicals extends to how they are stored, and how you dispose of any excess product. All products should be kept in their original containers, in a cool, dry place out of the reach of children. Ready-to-use products are stable in storage.

It is an offence to keep any product in any container other than its original one, which has a label listing the active ingredients and gives instructions on use.

Disposal of chemicals

In an ideal world, garden centres, nurseries and DIY stores – all outlets where garden chemicals are sold – would accept unused products for recycling in the same way that pharmacies accept unused medicines. The waste bin is not an option. If allowed to accumulate in landfill sites, all manner of dangerous cocktails could occur that would not only cause untold damage to the environment, but could actually be explosive.

It is illegal to dispose of chemicals down drains, sinks or lavatories, or watercourses or ditches. Contact your local waste disposal authority, who will offer advice as to which household waste sites will accept garden chemicals, or what arrangements they have – if any – for the collection and disposal of hazardous household waste. Containers should be clearly labelled to assist the disposal operator in identifying chemicals and thus choosing the appropriate method for disposal. Do not mix surplus chemicals: certain chemicals can react with each other. Waste material for disposal should be in sealed containers to prevent leakage.

Below: A barrier prevents harmful chemicals drifting on to and damaging other plants.

Plant Problem Identifier

The following chapter is designed to help in the identification of plant problems. It should be your first port of call if you spot a plant that is showing signs of distress and you wish to establish the cause. Plants are arranged alphabetically by botanical name, with a list of potential problems that can affect them. If you are unsure of the botanical name, consult the *Common name plant index* on the following two pages. You can then consult the relevant entries elsewhere in the book for further details on the cause of the problem and how to deal with it.

Left: Walnut blister mite.

Common name plant index

If you are able to identify the specific plant that is being attacked and only know the common name, use this list to find the botanical name, then locate the botanical name in the following plant list.

African violet (*Saintpaulia*) 93
Agave 50
alder (*Alnus*) 52
alfalfa (*Medicago sataiva*) 78
almond, common (*Prunus dulcis*) 87
almond, flowering (*Prunus triloba*) 88
Alyssum 52
angels' trumpets (*Brugmansia*) 58
apple (*Malus domestica*) 77
apricot (*Prunus armeniaca*) 85
arborvitae (*Thuja*) 96
arum lily (*Zantedeschia*) 99
asparagus (*Asparagus officinalis*) 54
aubergine (*Solanum melongena*) 94
Aubrieta 54
avocado (*Persea* spp.) 81
azalea (*Rhododendron*) 90

bamboo (*Nandina*) 79
banana (*Musa* spp.) 79
Banksia 54
barberry (*Berberis*) 54
bay (*Laurus nobilis*) 74
bead tree (*Melia azedarach*) 78
beech (*Fagus*) 67
beetroot (beet) (*Beta vulgaris*) 54
Begonia 54
Billbergia 55
birch (*Betula*) 55
blackberry (*Rubus fruticosus*) 92
blackcurrant (*Ribes nigrum*) 91
bluebeard (*Caryopteris*) 59
bluebell (*Hyacinthoides*) 71
blueberry (*Vaccinium corymbosum* var. *ashei*) 97
Boston ivy (*Parthenocissus tricuspidata*) 80
bottlebrush (*Callistemon*) 58
box (*Buxus*) 58
bramble (*Rubus fruticosus*) 92

Buxus

broad bean (*Vicia faba*) 97
broccoli (*Brassica oleracea*) 56
bromeliad (*Bromelia*) 58
broom (*Cytisus*) 64
brush box (*Lophostemon confertus*) 74
Brussels sprout (*Brassica oleracea*) 56
busy Lizzy (*Impatiens*) 71
butterfly bush (*Buddleia*) 58

cabbage (*Brassica oleracea*) 56
calamondin (x *Citrofortunella microcarpa*) 60
calico bush (*Kalmia latifolia*) 72
California lilac (*Ceanothus*) 59
Californian pepper-tree (*Schinus molle*) 93
Calla 58
Camellia 58
cantaloupe melon (*Cucumis melo*) 62
Cape primrose (*Streptocarpus*) 96
carnation (*Dianthus*) 66
carrot (*Daucus carota*) 65
cashew (*Anarcardia*) 52
Cassia 59
cauliflower (*Brassica oleracea*) 57
cedar (*Cedrus*) 59
celeriac (*Apium graveolens* var. *rapaceum*) 53
celery (*Apium graveolens*) 53
cherry (*Prunus avium*) 85
cherry, ornamental (*Prunus* spp.) 85
China aster (*Callistephus*) 58
chive (*Allium schoenoprasum*) 52
Chrysanthemum 60
chrysanthemum, florist's (*Dendranthema*) 66
cineraria (*Senecio*) 93
Cissus 60
Clematis 61
Clivia 61
Colchicum 59
coral flower (*Heuchera*) 71
corn (*Zea mays*) 99
Cotoneaster 62
courgette (*Cucurbita pepo*) 63
cow pea (*Vigna sinensis*) 97
crab apple (*Malus*) 76
crape myrtle (*Lagerstroemia indica*) 73

Crinum 62
Crocus 62
cucumber (*Cucumis sativus*) 63
custard apple (*Annona squamosa*) 52
Cyclamen 64
cypress (*Cupressus*) 64
cypress pine (*Callitris*) 58

daffodil (*Narcissus*) 793
Dahlia 64
Daphne 64
daylily (*Hemerocallis*) 70
Delphinium 66
dogwood (*Cornus*) 62
Douglas fir (*Pseudotsuga*) 88
dwarf apple (*Angophora hispida*) 52

eggplant (*Solanum melongena*) 94
Elaeagnus 66
elm (*Ulmus*) 97
Eucalyptus 67

false aralia (*Dizygotheca*) 66
false cypress (*Chamaecyparis*) 60
fig (*Ficus*) 67
fir (*Abies*) 50
firethorn (*Pyracantha*) 88
flame tree (*Brachychiton acerifolius*) 55
Florence fennel (*Foeniculum vulgare* var. *dulce*) 68
floss flower (*Ageratum*) 50
Forsythia 68
foxglove (*Digitalis*) 66
frangipani (*Plumeria*) 84
Freesia 69
French bean (*Phaseolus vulgaris*) 82
fritillary (*Fritillaria*) 69
Fuchsia 69

Gardenia 69
garlic (*Allium sativum*) 51
geebung (*Persoonia*) 81
gentian (*Gentiana*) 69
geranium (*Pelargonium*) 81
Gerbera 69
giant taro (*Alocasia macrorrhiza*) 52
gillyflower (*Cheiranthus*) 60
gladioli (*Gladiolus*) 69
globe artichoke (*Cynara*

carunculus) 64
globeflower (*Trollius*) 96
glory-of-the-snow (*Chionodoxa*) 60
Gloxinia 70
golden-rain tree (*Koelreuteria*) 72
gooseberry (*Ribes uva-crispa*) 91
gourd (*Lagenaria siceraria*) 73
granadilla (*Passiflora*) 80
grape (*Vitis*) 98
grape hyacinth (*Muscari*) 79
grapefruit (*Citrus paradisi*) 61
greengage (*Prunus domestica italica*) 87
Grevillea 70
guava (*Psidium*) 88
gum tree (*Eucalyptus*) 67

Hakea 70
hawthorn (*Crataegus*) 62
hazelnuts (*Corylus avellana*) 62
heather (*Erica*) 66
Hibiscus 71
hickory (*Carya*) 59
Hippeastrum 71
holly (*Ilex*) 71
hollyhock (*Alcea*) 51
honesty (*Lunaria*) 74
horehound (*Marrubium vulgare*) 78
horseradish (*Armoracia rusticana*) 54
Hosta 71
hyacinth (*Hyacinthus*) 71
Hydrangea 71

Indian hawthorn (*Raphiolepsis indica*; *R.* x *delacourii*) 90
Iris 72
ivy (*Hedera*) 70
Ixia 72

Jacaranda 72
Japanese angelica tree (*Aralia*) 53
Japanese quince (*Chaenomeles*) 60
japonica (*Chaenomeles*) 60
jasmine (*Jasminum*) 72
Jerusalem artichoke (*Helianthus tuberosus*) 70
Judas tree (*Cercis*) 59
juniper (*Juniperus*) 72

king palm (*Archontophoenix*) 53

Rosa

**Refer to the following pages for
details of problems that attack
specific groups of plants:**

Botanical name plant list

Once you have the botanical name of your plant, find it in the following list. Following the plant name is the name of each pest, disease or problem that may affect it. To find a description of each turn to the page reference indicated.

PLANT	PROBLEM	SYMPTOMS/DESCRIPTION	PAGE
A			
Abies	woolly adelgid	*Some yellowing of foliage.*	113
fir	witches' brooms	*Broom-like mass of erect shoots.*	195
	cracking of bark	*Long, vertical cracks in bark.*	240
Acacia	wattle leafminer	*Pink blisters on leaves; brown flaking.*	112
wattle	California red scale, red scale	*Orange-pink scale; die-back; leaves shed.*	116
	oleander scale, ivy scale	*White-brownish circular scales.*	117
	large auger beetle	*White larvae tunnel through wood.*	118
	moth borer	*Large larvae tunnel into wood. Serious weakening.*	126
	wasp gall	*Galls on leaves.*	132
	gumtree hopper	*Various insects. Honeydew, sooty mould.*	135
	gall wasps	*Galls on leaves.*	135
	loopers and semi-looper	*Holes are chewed in leaves. Flowers can be damaged.*	136
	cottony cushion scale	*Brown scale. Honeydew, sooty mould.*	140
	fruit-tree borerturni	*White moth. Larvae tunnel into wood.*	145
	wattle mealybug	*Purple-black scales. Honeydew, sooty mould.*	146
	crusader bug	*Brown bug, yellow cross. Yellow dots on nymph. Plants wilt.*	146
	bag-shelter moth	*Yellow eggs; hairy larvae. "Bags" in trees; leaves eaten.*	149
	acacia spotting bug	*Slender, brown bug. Leaves spotted.*	160
	green treehopper	*Green, horned insect. Die-back; slits in twigs for eggs.*	162
	painted apple moth	*Black-tufted caterpillars chew leaves.*	165
	stem gall, Dingley branch gall	*Small, cushion-like galls on branches.*	176
	sooty blotch	*Dark, circular, cloudy enlarging patches on fruit skins.*	192
	fly speck	*Small, circular specks on fruit skins; taste unaffected.*	196
	rust gall	*Large, woody, red-brown galls; distorted "broom" growths.*	218
Acer	acer pimple gall mite, acer gall mite	*Red pimples on leaves.*	116
maple	gall mites, rust mite	*Galls on leaves/stems.*	133
	leopard moth	*White/black-spotted moth. Black-spotted larvae tunnel into wood.*	169
	coral spot	*Die-back; pink-red, cushion-like pustules.*	198
	scorch	*Leaves turn brown at edges and curl.*	239
Agave	pineapple scale	*Yellow spots on leaves.*	129
agave			
Ageratum	chrysanthemum stunt viroid	*Stunting, brittle stems. Yellow spots on leaves; distortion.*	223
floss flower			

Abies

Acacia

Ageratum

PLANT	PROBLEM	SYMPTOMS/DESCRIPTION	PAGE
Albizia **mimosa**	wattle mealybug	*Purple-black scales. Honeydew, sooty mould.*	146
Alcea **hollyhock**	powdery mildew	*Grey-white powder on plants; young leaves distorted/shed.*	188
Allium **edible and ornamental onions**	onion fly maggot, onion maggot	*Bristly grey fly. Large maggots tunnel into roots.*	128
	narcissus eelworm, onion eelworm, phlox eelworm	*Nematode. Plants distorted/discoloured.*	130
	bulb and stem nematode	*New leaves distorted; raised, yellow section. Brown rings inside bulbs; brown spongy patches on outside. Streaks on stems/flowers; distortion.*	185
	allium rust	*Pustules of orange-yellow spores on leaves.*	208
	white rot	*Leaves yellow; fluffy growth at base of bulb/root. Small back sclerotia.*	211
Allium ascalonicum **shallot**	bulb and stem nematode	*New leaves distorted; raised, yellow section. Brown rings inside bulbs; brown spongy patches on outside. Streaks on stems/flowers; distortion.*	185
	downy mildew	*Leaves grey, wither; purple fungus; bulbs soften.*	199
	allium rust	*Pustules of orange-yellow spores on leaves.*	208
	white rot	*Leaves yellow; fluffy growth at base of bulb/root. Small back sclerotia.*	211
Allium cepa **onion**	lesser bulb fly	*Black fly; yellow larvae eat bulb tops.*	135
	cabbage moth	*Green-brown caterpillars eat leaves.*	144
	bulb mite	*Globular, yellow-white mite. Bulbs destroyed.*	161
	beet armyworm	*Moth. Green/yellow stripy caterpillars spin webs, eat leaves/stems/roots.*	163
	onion thrips	*Yellow-grey insect. Yellow nymph. Leaves blotched/distorted.*	167
	leaf blight, alternaria blight	*Brown spots on leaves.*	173
	black mould	*Black powder on stored bulbs.*	176
	neck rot	*Grey, furry mould on necks of stored bulbs; black resting bodies.*	176
	smudge	*Small green dots outside bulbs.*	181
	fusarium wilt	*Leaves wilt, oldest first. Yellow-brown patches. Brown-black lesions on lower stems/roots.*	190
	blue mould, soft rot	*Stored bulbs turn soft, becoming slimy, smelly; fungal growth.*	198
	downy mildew	*Leaves grey, wither; purple fungus; bulbs soften.*	199
	white rot	*Leaves yellow; fluffy growth at base of bulb/root. Small back sclerotia.*	211
	onion smut	*Blisters on new leaves, bulbs and roots; dark spores; galls.*	217
	bolting	*Crops run to seed prematurely.*	240
Allium porrum **leek**	onion thrips	*Yellow-grey insect. Yellow nymph. Leaves blotched/distorted.*	167
	bulb and stem nematode	*New leaves distorted; raised, yellow section. Brown rings inside bulbs; brown spongy patches on outside. Streaks on stems/flowers; distortion.*	185
	downy mildew	*Leaves grey, wither; purple fungus; bulbs soften.*	199
	allium rust	*Pustules of orange-yellow spores on leaves.*	208
	white rot	*Leaves yellow; fluffy growth at base of bulb/root. Small back sclerotia.*	211
	bolting	*Crops run to seed prematurely.*	240
Allium sativum **garlic**	bulb mite	*Globular, yellow-white mite. Bulbs destroyed.*	161
	onion thrips	*Yellow-grey insect. Yellow nymph. Leaves blotched/distorted.*	167

Alcea

Allium

Leeks

PLANT	PROBLEM	SYMPTOMS/DESCRIPTION	PAGE
Allium sativum **garlic**	bulb and stem nematode	*New leaves distorted; raised, yellow section. Brown rings inside bulbs; brown spongy patches on outside. Streaks on stems/flowers; distortion.*	185
	downy mildew	*Leaves grey, wither; purple fungus; bulbs soften.*	199
	allium rust	*Pustules of orange-yellow spores on leaves.*	208
Allium schoenoprasum **chive**	bulb and stem nematode	*New leaves distorted; raised, yellow section. Brown rings inside bulbs; brown spongy patches on outside. Streaks on stems/flowers; distortion.*	185
	allium rust	*Pustules of orange-yellow spores on leaves.*	208
Alnus **alder**	woolly vine scale	*Large, oval, brown scales.*	160
Alocasia macrorrhiza **giant taro**	banana rust thrips	*Grubs of black beetle cause swellings on roots.*	122
Alyssum **alyssum**	flea beetle	*Adults eat holes in leaves; larvae eat roots.*	156
	white blister, white rust	*White blisters/rings on leaves. Stunting/distortion.*	172
	mosaic	*Leaves distorted/mottled.*	225
Amaranthus **love-lies-bleeding**	beet webworm	*Moth. Cream-green caterpillars eat leaves.*	140
Amaryllidaceae	large narcissus bulb fly	*Hoverfly. Maggots tunnel into bulbs.*	146
	leaf scorch, tip burn	*Brown blotches on leaves/stalks/petals; rotting; dark red-brown spots on bulbs.*	215
Ananas comosus **pineapple**	pineapple scale	*Yellow spots on leaves.*	129
	top rot	*Heart leaves yellow-pale brown-reddish. Rotting; bad smell.*	202
	root rot	*Outer leaves die back; roots rot; fruits at base can rot.*	202
Anarcardia **cashew**	large mango tipborer	*Moth. Green/red-spotted larvae eat leaves, bore twigs.*	153
Anemone **windflower**	leaf nematode	*Yellow-brown patches on leaves.*	175
	petal blight	*Small translucent spots on outer petals.*	194
	smut	*Blisters on leaves/stems; black spores.*	217
Angophora costata **Sydney red gum** *A. hispida* **dwarf apple**	moth borer	*Large larvae tunnel into wood. Serious weakening.*	126
	cup moth	*Cup-shaped cocoons. Spiny larvae eat leaves.*	130
	shoot blight	*Shoots white/distorted; brown spots on leaves.*	210
Annona squamosa **custard apple**	pink wax scale	*Pink or grey scales; honeydew attracts sooty mould.*	122
Antirrhinum **snapdragon**	leafy gall	*Mass of abortive, distorted shoots at base.*	182
	shot hole blight	*Yellow spots on leaves/stems; holes. Scorching.*	193

Allium schoenoprasum

Anemone nemorosa

Anemone coronaria

PLANT	PROBLEM	SYMPTOMS/DESCRIPTION	PAGE
Antirrhinum **snapdragon**	damping off	*Seedlings collapse, blacken, wither.*	202
	snapdragon rust	*Pale pustules under leaves; red-brown spores.*	208
Apium graveolens **celery**	celery leaf miner	*Fly; maggots inside leaves. Discoloured patches, stunted growth.*	134
	leaf miners	*Larvae in leaves. Lines/blotches seen.*	142
	carrot weevil	*Grubs tunnel through roots/crowns.*	143
	black swallowtail butterfly, western parsleyworm, parsleyworm	*Brown-black/white, green/black larvae eat leaves.*	152
	carrot fly, carrot rust fly	*Maggots tunnel in roots.*	159
	garden symphylan	*White, many-legged soil-dweller eats roots.*	162
	cabbage looper	*Moth. Green pale-striped caterpillars eat leaves.*	168
	early blight of celery	*Small, round spots on leaves; browning. Brown lesions on stems.*	179
	heart rot	*Brown slimy mass in centre.*	188
	damping off	*Seedlings collapse; blacken, wither.*	202
	aster yellows, strawberry green petal	*Stems stunted, twisted.*	204
	sclerotinia disease, sclerotinia rot, sclerotinia wilt, white mould	*Stems rot; fluffy white growth inside; hard black fungi; flowers/buds rot.*	212
	leaf spot, late blight	*Small brown spots on leaves; black fungi.*	212
	cucumber mosaic virus	*Stunting, distortion, yellow mosaic pattern on leaves.*	224
	tobacco ring spot, bouquet disease, tomato ring spot, bud blight	*Stunting, distortion; brown-yellow, raised rings/circles on leaves/fruits.*	226
	bolting	*Crops run to seed prematurely.*	240
	boron deficiency	*Brown cracks on stems; growth stunted; leaves yellow.*	246
Apium graveolens var. *rapaceum* **celeriac**	early blight of celery	*Small, round spots on leaves; browning. Brown lesions on stems.*	179
	sclerotinia disease, sclerotinia rot, sclerotinia wilt, white mould	*Stems rot; fluffy white growth inside; hard black fungi; flowers/buds rot.*	212
Arabis **rock cress**	white blister, white rust	*White blisters/rings on leaves. Stunting/distortion.*	172
Arachis hypogaea **peanut**	wireworm	*Adults chew leaves; larvae tunnel in tuberous roots.*	114
	spotted cucumber beetle, southern corn rootworm	*Yellow/black beetle chews leaves/fruits. Long, thin larvae eat roots/corms.*	128
	sclerotium stem rot, southern blight	*Leaves yellow; watery lesions at base of plants; white growth.*	212
Aralia **Japanese angelica tree**	leaf blight	*Dark brown-black patches on leaves; distortion.*	173
Araucaria bidwillii *A. heterophylla* **Norfolk island pine**	golden mealybug	*Black, wax-coated bug. Honeydew, sooty mould.*	149
Archontophoenix **king palm**	latania scale	*Grey scales. Fruits pitted, leaves drop.*	139

Antirrhinum

Celery

Celeriac

PLANT	PROBLEM	SYMPTOMS/DESCRIPTION	PAGE
Armoracia rusticana **horseradish**	white blister, white rust	*White blisters/rings on leaves. Stunting/distortion.*	172
Asparagus officinalis **asparagus**	spotted asparagus beetle garden symphylan beet armyworm violet root rot	*Adults and grey-green larvae eat leaves/bark.* *White, many-legged soil-dweller eats roots.* *Moth. Green/yellow stripy caterpillars spin webs, eat leaves/stems/roots.* *Violet, web-like strands on roots; roots die.*	126 162 163 193
Aster **Michaelmas daisy**	Indian white wax scale white wax scale swift moth caterpillar tarsenomid mite, Michaelmas daisy mite, strawberry mite foot and root rot, black root rot Michaelmas daisy wilt aster yellows, strawberry green petal	*White scales produce honeydew; sooty mould appears.* *White scales produce honeydew.* *Large white caterpillars feed on roots.* *Mite inside buds. Scarring/distortion.* *Stem bases brown-black; leaves discoloured; die-back.* *Individual stems turn brown.* *Inner head pale.*	122 122 139 156 174 200 204
Aubrieta **aubretia**	flea beetles white blister, white rust	*Adults eat holes in leaves; larvae eat roots.* *White blisters/rings on leaves. Stunting/distortion.*	156 172
B *Banksia* **banksia**	loopers and semi-loopers grevillea looper macadamia twig-girdler	*Holes are chewed in leaves. Flowers can be damaged.* *Green caterpillars eat leaves.* *White moth. Mottled larvae spin webs, eat bark/leaves, tunnel in nuts.*	136 149 169
Begonia **begonia**	tarsenomid mites, Michaelmas daisy mite, strawberry mite cyclamen mite broad mite leaf nematode bacterial wilt	*Mite inside buds. Scarring/distortion.* *Mite inside buds, under leaves. Discoloration/distortion. Corms eaten.* *Distortion, discolouration; buds shed.* *Yellow-brown patches on leaves.* *Leaves wilt, spotted.*	156 157 158 175 219
Berberis **barberry**	Indian white wax scale white wax scale	*White scales produce honeydew; sooty mould appears.* *White scales produce honeydew.*	122 122
Beta vulgaris **beetroot (beet)** **spinach beet** **sugar beet** **Swiss chard**	beet leafhopper blister beetle beet webworm leaf miner beet leafminer vegetable weevil beet leaf miner maggot, spinach leaf miner beet armyworms cabbage looper cercospora leaf spot, leaf spot	*Green-brown adult, green nymph, spread viruses.* *Various beetles eat leaves/fruits.* *Moth. Cream-green caterpillars eat leaves.* *Larvae in leaves. Lines/blotches seen.* *Green/yellow fly. maggots in leaves. White lines seen.* *Brown beetle. Cream-green larvae. Base of plants and roots eaten.* *Fly. Maggots inside leaves; yellow-brown blotches.* *Moth. Green/yellow stripy caterpillars spin webs,* *eat leaves/stems/roots.* *Moth. Green pale-striped caterpillars eat leaves.* *Brown spots on leaves; holes.*	124 131 140 142 142 142 153 163 168 179

Armoracia rusticana

Asparagus

Aster

Beetroot

PLANT	PROBLEM	SYMPTOMS/DESCRIPTION	PAGE
Beta vulgaris **beetroot (beet)** **spinach beet** **sugar beet** **Swiss chard**	fusarium wilt	*Leaves wilt, oldest first. Yellow-brown patches. Brown-black lesions on lower stems/roots.*	190
	violet root rot	*Violet, web-like strands on roots; roots die.*	193
	damping off	*Seedlings collapse; blacken, wither.*	202
	sclerotium stem rot, southern blight	*Leaves yellow; watery lesions at base of plants; white growth.*	212
	common scab, potato scab	*Corky lesions on roots.*	215
	beet rust	*Small, red-brown spots on leaves (oldest first).*	217
	beet curly top	*Leaves crinkled; veins swollen; yellowing.*	223
	tobacco ring spot, bouquet disease, tomato ring spot, bud blight	*Stunting, distortion; brown-yellow, raised rings/circles on leaves/fruits.*	226
	bolting	*Crops run to seed prematurely.*	240
	boron deficiency	*Inside of root dry/brown; outside rots, cankers; crown sunken; leaves stunted.*	246
	manganese deficiency	*Leaves yellow/drop, oldest first.*	247
Betula **birch**	emperor gum moth	*Large green caterpillars chew leaves.*	150
	angle shades moth	*Green-brown caterpillars eat flowers/leaves.*	154
	leopard moth	*White/black-spotted moth. Black-spotted larvae tunnel into wood.*	169
	bracket fungi, wood rots	*Bracket-shaped growths on trunks/branches.*	190
Billbergia **billbergia**	pineapple scale	*Yellow spots on leaves.*	129
Brachychiton populneus **kurrajong** *B. acerifolius* **flame tree**	kurrajong leaf-tier	*Orange moth. Green larvae roll/web leaves.*	143
Brassicas	cabbage whitefly	*Tiny scales, white insects on leaves.*	114
	turnip gall weevil	*Grubs of black beetle cause swellings on roots.*	122
	flea beetle, leaf beetle, striped flea beetle	*Adults eat holes in leaves; larvae eat roots.*	123
	cabbage root fly and maggot, cabbage maggot	*Green fly. Maggots tunnel into roots and stems.*	128
	cabbage moth	*Green-brown caterpillars eat leaves.*	144
	calico back bug	*Red/black beetle. White/yellow blotched leaves; wilting.*	147
	flea beetles	*Dry areas on leaves; seedlings killed.*	156
	cabbage white butterfly, large white butterfly	*Yellow/black caterpillars eat leaves.*	157
	white blister, white rust	*White blisters/rings on leaves. Stunting/distortion.*	172
	powdery mildew	*Grey-white powder on plants; young leaves distorted/shed.*	188
	fusarium wilt	*Leaves wilt, oldest first. Yellow-brown patches. Brown-black. ...lesions on lower stems/roots.*	190
	cabbage yellows	*Leaves yellow-brown, from base up.*	191
	downy mildew	*White, mealy growth under leaves.*	199
	club root	*Stunting; leaves discoloured. Roots thickened/distorted; galls.*	204
	wirestem fungus	*Stems hard, brown, shrunken at base.*	216
	black rot	*V-shaped lesions on leaves; veins black. Leaves yellow, dry; greasy spots.*	219

Swiss chard

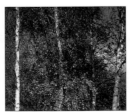

Betula

Swiss chard

Kohlrabi

PLANT	PROBLEM	SYMPTOMS/DESCRIPTION	PAGE
Brassica napus **swede (rutabaga)**	mealy cabbage aphid	*Grey aphids under leaves; yellowing leaves.*	118
	turnip gall weevil	*Grubs of black beetle cause swellings on roots.*	122
	flea beetles	*Dry areas on leaves; seedlings killed.*	156
	white blister, white rust	*White blisters/rings on leaves. Stunting/distortion.*	172
	bacterial soft rot	*Small, watery spots on leaves/roots/stored crops. Spots enlarge, slimy;* *tissue softens, liquefies.*	187
	violet root rot	*Violet, web-like strands on roots; roots die.*	193
	black leg	*Wilting, red-edged leaves, stems/roots crack. Seedlings have* *brown-black sunken area at base.*	194
	club root	*Stunting; leaves discoloured. Roots thickened/distorted; galls.*	204
	common scab, potato scab	*Corky lesions on roots.*	215
	mosaic	*Yellow rings on young leaves; green mottling; black rings.*	225
	turnip mosaic, cauliflower mosaic	*Leaves twisted/mottled/blistered; veins pale.*	227
	boron deficiency	*Grey-brown rings inside cut roots.*	246
Brassica oleracea **broccoli**	cabbage root fly and maggot, cabbage maggot	*Green fly. Maggots tunnel into roots and stems.*	128
	whitefringed weevil	*Grey/black/white adult; larvae eat roots.*	137
	small cabbage white butterfly, cabbage white butterfly, imported cabbageworm	*Green/yellow caterpillars eat leaves.*	157
	cabbage yellows	*Leaves yellow-brown, from base up.*	191
	peppery leaf spot	*Small, enlarging, purplish-brown spots on leaves; leaves yellow/* *pucker, drop.*	206
	black rot	*V-shaped lesions on leaves; veins black. Leaves yellow, dry; greasy spots.*	219
	mosaic	*Yellow rings on young leaves; green mottling; black rings.*	225
	molybdenum deficiency, whiptail	*Crops fail to develop normally.*	249
Brassica oleracea **Brussels sprout**	mealy cabbage aphid	*Grey aphids under leaves; yellowing leaves.*	118
	cabbage root fly and maggot, cabbage maggot	*Green fly. Maggots tunnel into roots and stems.*	128
	calico back bug	*Red/black beetle. White/yellow blotched leaves; wilting.*	147
	peppery leaf spot	*Small, enlarging, purplish-brown spots on leaves; leaves yellow/* *pucker, drop.*	206
Brassica oleracea **cabbage**	cabbage whitefly	*Tiny scales, white insects on leaves.*	114
	silver Y moth	*Green/white caterpillars eat flowers/leaves.*	118
	mealy cabbage aphid	*Grey aphids under leaves; yellowing leaves.*	118
	cabbage root fly and maggot, cabbage maggot	*Green fly. Maggots tunnel into roots and stems.*	128
	whitefringed weevil	*Grey-black/white adult; larvae eat roots.*	137
	corn earworm, tomato fruitworm	*Moth's larvae eat plants.*	138
	leaf miner	*Larvae in leaves. Lines/blotches seen.*	142
	vegetable weevil	*Brown beetle. Cream-green larvae. Base of plants and roots eaten.*	142
	cabbage moth	*Green-brown caterpillars eat leaves.*	144
	calico back bug	*Red/black beetle. White/yellow blotched leaves; wilting.*	147
	cabbage white butterfly, large white butterfly	*Yellow/black caterpillars eat leaves.*	157

Swedes (rutabagas)

Brocolli

Cabbages

PLANT	PROBLEM	SYMPTOMS/DESCRIPTION	PAGE
Brassica oleracea **cabbage**	small cabbage white butterfly, cabbage white butterfly, imported cabbageworm	*Green/yellow caterpillars eat leaves.*	157
	cabbage moth	*Green caterpillars tunnel through leaves; small holes.*	158
	fall armyworm	*Moth. Green-brown-black/yellow-striped caterpillars eat leaves/cobs.*	163
	false wireworms	*Beetles. Shiny brown-yellow larvae eat underground/ground-level plant parts.*	166
	cabbage looper	*Moth. Green, pale-striped caterpillars eat leaves.*	168
	cabbage yellows	*Leaves yellow-brown, from base up.*	191
	black leg	*Wilting, red-edged leaves, stems/roots crack. Seedlings have brown-black sunken area at base.*	194
	downy mildew	*White, mealy growth under leaves.*	199
	black rot	*V-shaped lesions on leaves; veins black. Leaves yellow, dry; greasy spots.*	219
	mosaic	*Yellow rings on young leaves; green mottling; black rings.*	225
Brassica oleracea **cauliflower**	mealy cabbage aphid	*Grey aphids under leaves; yellowing leaves.*	118
	cabbage root fly and maggot, cabbage maggot	*Green fly. Maggots tunnel into roots and stems.*	128
	small cabbage white butterfly, cabbage white butterfly imported cabbageworm	*Green/yellow caterpillars eat leaves.*	157
	cabbage yellows	*Leaves yellow-brown, from base up.*	191
	downy mildew	*White, mealy growth under leaves.*	199
	peppery leaf spot	*Small, enlarging, purplish-brown spots on leaves; leaves yellow/pucker, drop. Grey-brown spots on heads.*	206
	wirestem fungus	*Stems hard, brown, shrunken at base.*	216
	black rot	*V-shaped lesions on leaves; veins black. Leaves yellow, dry; greasy spots.*	219
	mosaic	*Yellow rings on young leaves; green mottling; black rings.*	225
	cauliflower mosaic	*Leaves twisted/mottled/blistered; veins pale.*	227
	molybdenum deficiency, whiptail	*Crops fail to develop normally.*	249
Brassica oleracea **kohlrabi**	calico back bug	*Red/black beetle. White/yellow blotched leaves; wilting.*	147
Brassica rapa **turnip**	turnip gall weevil	*Grubs of black beetle cause swellings on roots.*	122
	cabbage root fly and maggot, cabbage maggot	*Green fly. Maggots tunnel into roots and stems.*	128
	whitefringed weevil	*Grey/black/white adult; larvae eat roots.*	137
	calico back bug	*Red/black beetle. White/yellow blotched leaves; wilting.*	147
	flea beetles	*Dry areas on leaves; seedlings killed.*	156
	cabbage white butterfly, large white butterfly	*Yellow/black caterpillars eat leaves.*	157
	small cabbage white butterfly, cabbage white butterfly, imported cabbageworm	*Green/yellow caterpillars eat leaves.*	157
	fall armyworm	*Moth. Green-brown-black/yellow-striped caterpillars eat leaves.*	163
	white blister, white rust	*White blisters/rings on leaves. Stunting/distortion.*	172
	anthracnose	*Yellow-brown-purplish spots on leaves/stems/fruit.*	180
	bacterial soft rot	*Small, watery spots on leaves/roots/stored crops. Spots enlarge, slimy; tissue softens, liquefies.*	187
	violet root rot	*Violet, web-like strands on roots; roots die.*	193

Cauliflower

Cabbage

Turnip

PLANT	PROBLEM	SYMPTOMS/DESCRIPTION	PAGE
Brassica rapa **turnip**	black leg	*Plants wilt, leaf edges reddish, cracks on stems; wilt; seedlings die.*	194
	club root	*Stunting; leaves discoloured. Roots thickened/distorted; galls.*	204
	common scab, potato scab	*Corky lesions on roots.*	215
	mosaic	*Yellow rings on young leaves; green mottling; black rings.*	225
	turnip mosaic	*Leaves twisted/mottled/blistered; veins pale.*	227
	boron deficiency	*Grey-brown rings inside cut roots.*	246
Bromelia **bromeliad**	pineapple scale	*Yellow spots on leaves.*	129
Brugmansia **angels' trumpets**	bacterial canker	*Wilting, lower leaves upwards. Brown-black edges/leaves.*	175
Buddleia **butterfly bush**	oleander scale, ivy scale	*White-brownish circular scales.*	117
Buxus **box**	mussel scale	*Brown scale. Die-back.*	141
	box blight, cylindrocladium blight	*Leaves brown, drop. Pink-grey growths under leaves.*	207

C

Calla **calla**	grapevine hawk moth	*Large green-black caterpillars chew leaves.*	139
Callistemon **bottlebrush**	wasp gall	*Galls on leaves.*	132
	gall wasp	*Galls on leaves.*	135
	callistemon sawfly	*Green larvae eat leaves.*	143
Callistephus **China aster**	broad bean wilt	*Tips blacken; base/roots black, rotted. Leaves mottled/curled.*	223
Callitris **cypress pine**	cypress pine sawfly	*Bright green larvae eat leaves; die-back.*	169
Calluna **Scotch heather**	mussel scale	*Brown scale. Die-back.*	141
Camellia **camellia**	oleander scale, ivy scale	*White-brownish circular scales.*	117
	Fuller's rose weevil	*Grey-brown weevils eat leaves; larvae eat roots.*	117
	leaf-cutting bees	*Round holes in leaves.*	146
	broad mite	*Distortion, discoloration; buds shed*	158
	hydrangea scale	*Plants weakened.*	160
	leaf gall	*Tip leaves enlarged, thickened, dark pink-red. Later break open, shrivel.*	189
	die-back	*Fungus girdles stem. Die-back.*	192
	pestalotiopsis	*Silver-grey areas on leaves.*	200
	infectious variegation	*Yellow blotches on leaves/margins.*	224
	ringspot	*Light green rings on leaves; dark-edged spots; leaves yellow.*	227

Buddleia

Callistemon

Camellia

PLANT	PROBLEM	SYMPTOMS/DESCRIPTION	PAGE
Camellia **camellia**	oedema, dropsy splitting of stems bud drop/aborted flowers	*Pimple-like growths under leaves; later corky.* *Bark on young shoots splits/peels.* *Flower buds shrivel/drop.*	234 238 240
Capsicum **pepper**	tomato russet mite corn earworm, tomato fruitworm tomato hornworm green vegetable bug European corn borer broad mite target spot anthracnose sclerotium stem rot, southern blight bacterial spot	*Leaves grey-brown; stems brown; leaves, flowers shed.* *Moth's larvae eat plants.* *Large moth. Green/black-horned caterpillars eat leaves/fruits.* *Green-black bug, many-coloured nymph. Growth distorted, discoloured.* *Moth. Grey-pink caterpillars chew leaves.* *Distortion, discoloration; buds shed.* *Brown-black spots/rings on leaves.* *Yellow-brown-purplish spots on leaves/stems/fruit; darkening.* *Pinkish fungus* *Leaves yellow; watery lesions at base of plants; white growth.* *Small, dark, watery spots on leaves; sunken streaks on stems; small,* *growing, darkening spots on fruits.*	113 138 145 148 150 158 174 180 212 220
Carica papaya **papaya**	yellow peach moth fruitpiercing moths fruit flies yellow crinkle	*Large pink caterpillars tunnel into plants/fruits. Die-back.* *Holes in fruit.* *Eggs laid under fruit skin; larvae feed inside fruits. Cracks/spots.* *Older leaves yellow, shed; stalks bend; young leaves distorted.*	125 151 166 197
Carya **hickory**	periodical cicada	*Slits in bark for eggs.*	144
Caryopteris **bluebeard**	capsid bugs	*Green insects eat young leaves. Growth distorted.*	143
Cassia **cassia**	crusader bug	*Brown bug, yellow cross. Yellow dots on nymph. Plants wilt.*	146
Castanea sativa **sweet chestnut/** **Spanish chestnut**	oak leafminer leopard moth	*Fine lines/blisters on leaves.* *White/black-spotted moth. Black-spotted larvae tunnel into wood.*	155 169
Casuarina **she oak**	gumtree hoppers	*Various insects. Honeydew, sooty mould.*	135
Ceanothus **California lilac**	mussel scale iron deficiency, lime-induced chlorosis	*Brown scale. Die-back.* *Young leaves yellow/scorched.*	141 248
Cedrus **cedar**	phomopsis disease	*Die-back. Cankers, small black fungi.*	201
Cercis **Judas tree**	coral spot	*Die-back; pink-red, cushion-like pustules.*	198

Castanea sativa

Ceanothus

Cedrus

PLANT	PROBLEM	SYMPTOMS/DESCRIPTION	PAGE
Chaenomeles **japonica/Japanese quince**	fireblight	*Leaves brown; wither. Shoots die back and cankers appear.*	186
Chamaecyparis **false cypress**	cypress bark weevil	*Young growth eaten; tips die; larvae under bark weaken/kill tree.*	113
	cypress bark beetle (Lawson cypress)	*Brown-black adult. Larvae tunnel in wood.*	154
	cypress canker	*Bark splits; resin.*	212
Cheiranthus **wallflower/gillyflower**	flea beetles	*Dry areas on leaves; seedlings killed.*	156
	club root	*Stunting; leaves discoloured. Roots thickened/distorted galls.*	204
Chionodoxa **glory-of-the-snow**	smut	*Flowers distorted; black spores.*	218
Choisya ternata **Mexican orange blossom**	small citrus butterfly, dingy swallowtail	*Black/grey/white butterfly. Large caterpillars eat leaves.*	131
	large citrus butterfly	*Black/yellow/red male, brown/orange/blue female. Larvae like bird droppings, then fat, green/brown/white banded. Leaves eaten.*	159
Chrysanthemum **chrysanthemum**	fern eelworm, chrysanthemum eelworm	*Tiny creatures inside leaves cause browning.*	116
	Indian white wax scale	*White scales produce honeydew; sooty mould appears.*	122
	white wax scale	*White scales produce honeydew.*	122
	cineraria leafminer	*Small black fly. Larvae inside leaves cause silver lines, wilting.*	123
	earwig, European earwig	*Long, brown insect. Holes in leaves/flowers.*	135
	swift moth caterpillars	*Large white caterpillars feed on roots.*	139
	leaf miners	*Larvae in leaves. Lines/blotches seen.*	142
	capsid bugs	*Green insects eat young leaves. Growth distorted.*	143
	chrysanthemum leaf miner grub	*Fly. Maggots inside leaves; discolouration.*	156
	foot and root rot, black root rot	*Stem bases brown-black; leaves discoloured; die-back.*	174
	leaf nematodes	*Yellow-brown patches on leaves.*	175
	ray blight	*Dark pink spots on petals; brown/rotting. Stem lesions.*	183
	parsnip canker	*Cankers/horizontal cracks around roots; red-brown-black lesions.*	194
	petal blight	*Small, oval spots on outer florets; white bloom.*	194
	big bud, greening, virescence	*Unnaturally bushy growth.*	197
	chrysanthemum rust	*Blister-like swellings under leaves.*	208
	chrysanthemum leaf spot	*Yellow-brown areas on leaves.*	213
	verticillium wilt	*Wilting; leaves curl, yellow; die-back.*	218
	spotted wilt	*Brown spots on leaves; stems streaked brown.*	227
	magnesium deficiency	*Leaves yellow, oldest first, later orange-red, drop.*	249
Cissus **cissus**	painted vine moth caterpillar	*Black/orange/cream caterpillars eat holes in leaves.*	113
x *Citrofortunella* *microcarpa* **calamondin**	brown spot	*Brown spots on leaves/fruits/young stems.*	173
	citrus scab	*Brown-pink-grey scabs on leaves; fruits shed or enlarged/distorted.*	213
Citrullus vulgaris **watermelon**	anthracnose	*Round, brown-black spots on leaves/stems/fruits. Pink spores.*	181
	gummy stem blight	*Watery areas/sunken cankers on stems; black spots on leaves/fruits.*	183

Chionodoxa

Choisya ternata

Chrysanthemum

Tangelos

PLANT	PROBLEM	SYMPTOMS/DESCRIPTION	PAGE
	watermelon mosaic virus	*Leaves mottled, distorted. Fruits can have hollows, raised pattern.*	227
Citrus aurantifolia **lime**	spined citrus bug citrus scab	*Green, horned adult, yellow/black nymph; browned fruits.* *Brown-pink-grey scabs on leaves; fruits shed or enlarged/distorted.*	118 213
Citrus aurantium **sour (Seville) orange**	melanose	*Brown spots/patches on fruits; cracking, distortion.*	182
Citrus limon **lemon**	spined citrus bug citrus gall wasp citrus bud mite melanose brown rot citrus scab	*Green, horned adult, yellow/black nymph; browned fruits.* *Galls appear; plants weakened.* *Blackened buds/fruits, distorted leaves/flowers/fruits.* *Brown spots/patches on fruits; cracking, distortion.* *Yellow-brown rot on fruits.* *Brown-pink-grey scabs on leaves; fruits shed or enlarged/distorted.*	118 119 134 182 201 213
Citrus nobilis **mandarin**	spined citrus bug brown spot melanose brown rot citrus scab	*Green, horned adult, yellow/black nymph; browned fruits.* *Brown spots on leaves/fruits/young stems.* *Brown spots/patches on fruits; cracking, distortion.* *Grey-brown rot on fruits.* *Brown-pink-grey scabs on leaves; fruits shed or enlarged/distorted.*	118 173 182 201 213
Citrus paradisi **grapefruit**	citrus gall wasp brown spot	*Galls appear; plants weakened.* *Brown spots on leaves/fruits/young stems.*	119 173
Citrus sinensis **orange**	harlequin bug citrus bud mite melanose brown rot	*Large black/red bug. Frass. Plants wilt, can die.* *Blackened buds/fruits, distorted leaves/flowers/fruits.* *Brown spots/patches on fruits; cracking, distortion.* *Grey-brown rot on fruits.*	130 134 182 201
Citrus x tangelo **tangelo**	brown spot citrus scab	*Brown spots on leaves/fruits/young stems.* *Brown-pink-grey scabs on leaves; fruits shed or enlarged/distorted.*	173 213
Clematis **clematis**	earwig, European earwig clematis wilt slime fluxes, wetwood	*Long, brown insect. Holes in leaves/flowers.* *Shoots wither; lesions girdle stems; die-back.* *Orange-pink-white fluid exuded from stems.*	135 176 221
Cleome **spider flower**	small cabbage white butterfly, cabbage white butterfly, imported cabbageworm	*Green/yellow caterpillars eat leaves.*	157
Clivia **clivia**	lily caterpillar	*Red/black moth. Black/yellow caterpillars chew leaves.*	164
Colchicum **colchicum**	grey bulb rot	*Dry, grey rot from tip of corm; black fungus in soil.*	211
Compositae	English marigold rust	*Pale green-yellow spots on leaves/stems; small "cups" on leaves.*	208

Cleome

Clematis

Clematis

Colchicum

PLANT	PROBLEM	SYMPTOMS/DESCRIPTION	PAGE
Cornus **dogwood**	mussel scale	*Brown scale. Die-back.*	141
Coryllus avellana **hazel nuts**	hazelnut weevil hazel big bud mite	*Eggs laid in developing nuts; larvae eat kernels.* *Buds enlarged.*	126 156
Cotoneaster **cotoneaster**	pearleaf blister mite woolly aphid, woolly apple aphid mussel scale San Jose scale	*Discoloured blisters on leaves, spotted/distorted fruits.* *Brown aphid, white covering; soft galls.* *Brown scale. Die-back.* *Well-camouflaged scale. Rough texture; fruits damaged.*	133 134 141 160
Crambe maritima **seakale**	club root	*Stunting; leaves discoloured. Roots thickened/distorted; galls.*	204

Crataegus
hawthorn
	bryobia mite
	pear and cherry slugworm caterpillar
	    pear and cherry slug
	pearleaf blister mite
	woolly aphid, woolly apple aphid
	fruit tree red spider mite,
	    European red mite
	San Jose scale
	conifer rusts
	fireblight
		Red, then brown-grey mites; white-mottled leaves.
		Sawfly. Dark green larvae eat leaves causing vein network.
		
		Discoloured blisters on leaves, spotted/distorted fruits.
		Brown aphid, white covering; soft galls.
		Yellow-mottled leaves.
		
		Well-camouflaged scale. Rough texture; fruits damaged.
		Horn-like, gelatinous masses of orange spores on swollen shoots.
		Leaves brown; wither. Shoots die back and cankers appear.
			119
			120
			
			133
			134
			152
			
			160
			182
			186

Crinum **crinum**	leaf scorch, tip burn	*Brown blotches on leaves/stalks/petals; rotting; dark red-brown spots* *on bulbs.*	215
Crocus **crocus**	grey bulb rot core rot	*Dry, grey rot from tip of bulb; black fungus in soil* *corms in storage darken/spongy rot.*	211 211
Cucumis melo **cantaloupe melon** *see also cucurbits*	striped cucumber beetle anthracnose gummy stem blight downy mildew	*Larvae eat roots, adults eat topgrowth.* *Round, brown-black spots on leaves/stems. Can appear on fruits.* *Watery areas/sunken cankers on stems; black spots on leaves/fruits.* *Yellow spots above leaves; furry, purplish growth below.*	112 180 183 208

Cucumis melo
melon
see also cucurbits
	striped cucumber beetle
	squash bug
	green June beetle and fig beetle
	pickleworm
	
	harlequin bug
	blister beetles
	field cricket
	squash vine borer
	anthracnose
		Larvae eat roots, adults eat topgrowth.
		Brown-black bug, grey-green nymph; plants wilt/die.
		Adults eat holes in leaves/fruits. Larvae eat roots.
		Brown moth. Yellow/spotted, then green or pink larvae
		    eat buds/fruits/stems.
		Large black/red bug. Frass. Plants wilt, can die.
		Various beetles eat leaves/fruits.
		Brown-black insect chews seedlings/leaves/flowers/fruits.
		Moth. Larvae chew bases of stems.
		Yellow-brown-purplish spots on leaves/stems/fruit; darkening.
		    Pinkish fungus. Dark, sunken lesions on fruits.
			112
			115
			126
			129
			
			130
			131
			138
			146
			180

Cornus   *Crataegus*   *Crocus*   *Melons*

PLANT	PROBLEM	SYMPTOMS/DESCRIPTION	PAGE
Cucumis melo **melon**	angular leaf spot	Water-soaked spots on leaves, turn yellow then brown. Fruits shed.	206
	sclerotium stem rot, southern blight	Leaves yellow; watery lesions at base of plants; white growth.	212
Cucumis sativus **cucumber**	striped cucumber beetle	Larvae eat roots, adults eat topgrowth.	112
	greenfly	Tiny green flies on shoot tips, under leaves.	113
	wireworm	Adults chew leaves.	114
	squash bug	Brown-black bug, grey-green nymph; plants wilt/die.	115
	spotted cucumber beetle, Southern corn rootworm	Yellow/black beetle chews leaves/fruits. Long, thin larvae eat roots/crowns.	128
	pickleworm	Brown moth. Yellow/spotted, then green or pink larvae eat buds/fruits/stems.	129
	field cricket	Brown-black insect chews seedlings/leaves/flowers/fruits.	138
	glasshouse thrips, greenhouse thrips	Yellow-brown insects. Leaves/petals spotted/discoloured.	138
	squash vine borer	Moth. Larvae chew bases of stems.	146
	garden symphylan	White, many-legged soil-dweller eats roots.	162
	fruit flies	Eggs laid under fruit skin; larvae feed inside fruits. Cracks/spots.	166
	spider mites	Fine webbing. Leaves speckled/yellow-brown.	166
	glasshouse whitefly	Scale-like, pale green nymphs under leaves. Honeydew, sooty mould.	168
	anthracnose	Yellow-brown-purplish spots on leaves/stems/fruits; darkening. Pinkish fungus. Dark, sunken lesions on fruits.	180
	anthracnose	Round, brown-black spots on leaves/stems/fruits. Pink spores.	181
	gummy stem blight	Watery areas/sunken cankers on stems; black spots on leaves/fruits.	183
	bacterial wilt	Large, dull, irregular patches on leaves; die-back. White "milk" from cut stems.	188
	angular leaf spot	Water-soaked spots on leaves, turn yellow then brown. Fruits shed.	206
	downy mildew	Yellow spots above leaves; furry, purplish growth below.	208
	bacterial leaf spot	Watery area under leaves, yellow patches above. Spots on stems/fruits.	219
	withering of crop	Uneven growth; fruits wither.	237
	bitter cucumbers	Fruits taste bitter.	246
Cucurbita maxima **squash**	striped cucumber beetle	Larvae eat roots; adults eat topgrowth.	112
	squash bug	Brown-black bug, grey-green nymph; plants wilt/die.	115
	pickleworm	Brown moth. Yellow/spotted, then green or pink larvae eat buds/fruits/stems.	129
	field cricket	Brown-black insect chews seedlings/leaves/flowers/fruits.	138
	corn earworm, tomato fruitworm	Moth's larvae eat plants.	138
	squash vine borer	Moth. Larvae chew bases of stems.	146
	stink bug, earth mite	Green-brown-grey bugs, evil smell. Distorted growth/fruits.	153
	angular leaf spot	Water-soaked spots on leaves, turn yellow then brown. Fruits shed.	206
	downy mildew	Yellow spots above leaves; furry, purplish growth below.	208
	bacterial leaf spot	Watery area under leaves, yellow patches above. Spots on stems/fruits.	219
Cucurbita pepo **marrow (zucchini)**	bacterial leaf spot	Watery area under leaves, yellow patches above. Spots on stems/fruits.	219
	watermelon mosaic virus	Leaves mottled, distorted. Fruits can have hollows, raised pattern.	227

Melon

Cucumbers

Squash

Courgettes

PLANT	PROBLEM	SYMPTOMS/DESCRIPTION	PAGE
Cucurbita pepo **pumpkin**	squash bug	*Brown-black bug, grey-green nymph; plants wilt/die.*	115
	pickleworm	*Brown moth. Yellow/spotted, then green or pink larvae eat buds/fruits/stems.*	129
	squash vine borer	*Moth. Larvae chew bases of stems.*	146
	redshouldered leaf beetle	*Yellow/red beetle eats leaves/flowers/fruits.*	147
	green vegetable bug	*Green-black bug, many-coloured nymph. Growth distorted, discoloured.*	148
	gummy stem blight	*Watery areas/sunken cankers on stems; black spots on leaves/fruits.*	183
	downy mildew	*Yellow spots above leaves; furry, purplish growth below.*	208
	bacterial leaf spot	*Watery area under leaves, yellow patches above. Spots on stems/fruits.*	219
	watermelon mosaic virus	*Leaves mottled, distorted. Fruits can have hollows, raised pattern.*	227
Cupressus **cypress**	cypress bark weevil	*Young growth eaten; tips die; larvae under bark weaken/kill tree.*	113
	cypress bark beetle	*Brown-black adult. Larvae tunnel in wood.*	154
	cypress pine sawfly	*Bright green larvae eat leaves; die-back.*	169
	cypress canker	*Bark splits; resin.*	212
Cyclamen **cyclamen**	glasshouse thrips, greenhouse thrips	*Yellow-brown insects. Leaves/petals spotted/discoloured.*	138
	vine weevil, black vine weevil	*Black weevil. Grubs eat roots.*	151
	tarsenomid mite, Michaelmas daisy mite, strawberry mite	*Mite inside buds. Scarring/distortion.*	156
	cyclamen mite	*Mite inside buds, under leaves. Discoloration/distortion. Corms eaten.*	157
Cydonia oblonga **quince**	pear psylla	*Brown adult, yellow then green nymph. Spotted leaves, scarred fruit.*	120
	pear and cherry slugworm caterpillar pear and cherry slug	*Sawfly. Dark green larvae eat leaves causing vein network.*	120
	plum curculio	*Larvae tunnel into developing fruit. Fruits drop.*	125
	pearleaf blister mite	*Discoloured blisters on leaves, spotted/distorted fruits.*	133
	oriental fruit moth	*White-pink caterpillars tunnel into shoots/fruits.*	137
	fruit tree red spider mite, European red mite	*Yellow-mottled leaves.*	152
	apple curculio	*Brown-red weevil. Larvae tunnel in fruits; scarred, dropped.*	165
	quince leaf blight, fleck	*Small, irregular spots on leaves, red, then black.*	184
	powdery mildew	*Grey-white powder on plants; young leaves distorted/shed.*	188
	brown rot	*Small brown spots on petals/stems/fruits. Brown mould. Sunken brown cankers on twigs. Fruits rot; rings of grey spores.*	196
	iron deficiency, lime-induced chlorosis	*Young leaves yellow/scorched.*	248
Cynara cardunculus **globe artichoke**	blackfly	*Tiny flies on young growth; leaves curl.*	116
	root aphid	*White, waxy powder secreted on roots.*	168
	petal blight	*Round, light brown spots on young heads; browning, rotting.*	194
Cytisus **broom**	broom gall mite	*Soft green galls appear.*	112

D

Dahlia **dahlia**	metallic flea beetles	*Irregular holes in young leaves, buds.*	114
	blackfly	*Tiny flies on young growth; leaves curl.*	116

Globe artichoke

Cyclamen

Cytisus

Dahlia

PLANT	PROBLEM	SYMPTOMS/DESCRIPTION	PAGE
Dahlia **dahlia**	rose weevil	*Grey-brown weevils eat leaves; larvae eat roots.*	117
	harlequin bug	*Large black/red bug. Frass. Plants wilt, can die.*	130
	earwig, European earwig	*Long, brown insect. Holes in leaves/flowers.*	135
	African black beetle	*Adults eat stems below ground; grubs eat roots.*	139
	capsid bugs	*Green insects eat young leaves. Growth distorted.*	143
	redshouldered leaf beetle	*Yellow/red beetle eats leaves/flowers.*	147
	passionvine hopper	*Moth-like adult, green nymph. Leaves shrivel/drop.*	162
	onion thrips	*Yellow-grey insect. Yellow nymph. Leaves blotched/distorted.*	167
	leafy gall	*Mass of abortive, distorted shoots at base.*	182
	smut, leaf spot	*Brown spots/holes on leaves, from base up.*	186
	bacterial soft rot	*Small, watery spots on leaves/roots/stored tubers. Spots enlarge, slimy; tissue softens, liquefies.*	187
	petal blight	*Brown spots on petals, from outer to inner.*	194
	big bud, greening, virescence	*Unnaturally bushy growth.*	197
	sclerotium stem rot, southern blight	*Leaves yellow; watery lesions at base of plants; white growth.*	212
	verticillium wilt	*Wilting; leaves curl, yellow; die-back.*	218
	cucumber mosaic virus	*Stunting, distortion, yellow mosaic pattern on leaves.*	224
	spotted wilt	*Brown spots on leaves; stems streaked brown.*	227
	chalkiness and hardness of bulbs	*Dormant tubers in storage harden.*	243
Daphne **daphne**	oleander scale, ivy scale	*White-brownish circular scales.*	117
	crown gall	*Large galls on tree roots; small, soft galls on shrubs.*	172
Daucus carota **carrot**	wireworm	*Adults chew leaves.*	114
	beet leafhopper	*Green-brown adult, green nymph, spread viruses.*	124
	whitefringed weevil	*Grey-black/white adult; larvae eat roots.*	137
	carrot weevil	*Grubs tunnel through roots/crowns.*	143
	vegetable weevil	*Brown beetle. Cream-green larvae. Base of plants and roots eaten.*	142
	black swallowtail butterfly, western parsleyworm, parsleyworm	*Brown-black/white, green/black larvae eat leaves.*	152
	carrot fly, carrot rust fly	*Maggots tunnel in roots.*	159
	garden symphylan	*White, many-legged soil-dweller eats roots.*	162
	false wireworms	*Beetles. Shiny brown-yellow larvae eat underground/ground level plant parts.*	166
	crown gall	*Large galls on tree roots; small, soft galls on shrubs.*	172
	leaf blight, alternaria blight	*Brown/yellow-edged spots on leaf edges.*	173
	bacterial soft rot	*Small, watery spots on leaves/roots/stored crops. Spots enlarge, slimy; tissue softens, liquefies.*	187
	violet root rot	*Violet, web-like strands on roots; roots die.*	193
	blue mould, soft rot	*Stored roots soft/slimy.*	198
	aster yellows, strawberry green petal	*Stunted; leaves distorted, yellow-red-purple. Roots thin.*	204
	sclerotinia disease, sclerotinia rot, sclerotinia wilt, white mould	*Fluffy white fungal growth on stored carrots; hard black fungi.*	212
	sclerotium stem rot, southern blight	*Leaves yellow; watery lesions at base of plants; white growth.*	212
	common scab, potato scab	*Corky lesions on roots.*	215
	carrot motley dwarf disease	*Leaves yellow/pink, twisted.*	223

Dahlia

Dahlia

Daphne

Carrots

PLANT	PROBLEM	SYMPTOMS/DESCRIPTION	PAGE
Delphinium **delphinium**	beet leafhopper	*Green-brown adult, green nymph, spread viruses.*	124
	swift moth caterpillars	*Large white caterpillars feed on roots.*	139
	foot and root rot, black root rot	*Stem bases brown-black; leaves discoloured; die-back.*	174
	armillaria root rot, honey fungus	*Fan-shaped honey-coloured fungus on roots/at base.*	175
	powdery mildew	*Grey-white powder on plants; young leaves distorted/shed.*	188
	black blotch	*Black blotches on leaves/stems/flowers.*	205
	cucumber mosaic virus	*Stunting, distortion, yellow mosaic pattern on leaves.*	224
	fasciation	*Growth flattened.*	238
Dendrathema **florist's chrysanthemum**	carnation tortrix caterpillar	*Moth's green caterpillars fold and eat leaves.*	119
	chrysanthemum gall midge	*Brown fly. Larvae inside leaves; conical galls, distortion.*	161
	chrysanthemum stunt viroid	*Stunting, brittle stems. Yellow spots on leaves; distortion.*	223
Dianthus **carnations, pinks**	beet leafhopper	*Green-brown adult, green nymph, spread viruses.*	124
	budworms	*Moth's caterpillars eat holes in leaves/flowers/fruits.*	138
	gladiolus thrips	*Brown-black insect, yellow nymph. Leaves mottled, flowers flecked; stored corms attacked.*	167
	leaf and stem rot	*Pale-spotted leaves, flower buds. Rotting/damping off.*	172
	fusarium wilt (carnations)	*Leaves yellow; wilting. Brown streaks in cut stems.*	191
	sclerotium stem rot, southern blight	*Leaves yellow; watery lesions at base of plants; white growth.*	212
	carnation rust	*Grey patches on leaves/stems/sepals; dark brown spores; leaves curl/yellow.*	217
Dieffenbachia **leopard lily**	cyclamen mite	*Mite inside buds, under leaves. Discoloration/distortion. Corms eaten.*	157
Digitalis **foxglove**	glasshouse leafhopper	*Yellow adult, creamy nymph. White dots on leaves.*	138
Diospyros **persimmon**	fruitspotting bug	*Green bug, red/black nymph; fruits spotted/shed.*	115
	currant clearwing moth, currant borer moth	*Larvae feed inside stems. Small, yellow leaves; pupal cases appear.*	165
	fruit fly	*Eggs laid under fruit skin; larvae feed inside fruits. Cracks/spots.*	166
Dizygotheca **false aralia**	leaf blight	*Dark brown-black patches on leaves; distortion.*	173
E *Elaeagnus* **elaeagnus**	coral spot	*Die-back; pink-red, cushion-like pustules.*	198
Eranthis **winter aconite**	smut (winter aconites)	*Blisters on leaves/stalks; black spores.*	218
Erica **heather**	mussel scale	*Brown scale. Die-back.*	141
	foot and root rot, black root rot	*Stem bases brown-black; leaves discoloured; die-back.*	174

Delphinium

Dianthus

Digitalis

Erica

PLANT	PROBLEM	SYMPTOMS/DESCRIPTION	PAGE
Eriobotrya japonica **loquat**	quince leaf blight, fleck	*Small, irregular spots on leaves, red then black.*	184
Eriostemon myoporoides **long-leaf wax flower**	small citrus butterfly, dingy swallowtail large citrus butterfly	*Black/grey/white butterfly. Large caterpillars eat leaves.* *Black/yellow/red male, brown/orange/blue female. Larvae like* *bird droppings, then fat, green/brown/white banded. Leaves eaten.*	131 159
Eucalyptus **eucalyptus** **gum tree**	Christmas beetles large auger beetle brown basket lerp whitestemmed gum moth coccid gall moth borer cup moths wasp galls gumtree scale gumtree hopper gall wasp autumn gum moth emperor gum moth elephant weevil steelblue sawfly leafblister sawfly oak leafminer gumleaf skeletonizer leaf spot shoot blight oedema, dropsy	*Green adults eat saw-tooth holes in leaves.* *White larvae tunnel through wood.* *Insect within leaves causes red/yellow blotches, browning; can kill tree.* *Large, hairy larvae may damage bark.* *Galls on stems and leaves.* *Large larvae tunnel into wood. Serious weakening.* *Cup-shaped cocoons. Spiny larvae eat leaves.* *Galls on leaves.* *Brown scales. Honeydew, sooty mould.* *Various insects. Honeydew, sooty mould.* *Galls on leaves.* *Green-black caterpillars eat leaves, make webs.* *Large green caterpillars chew leaves.* *Grey-black adult. Larvae tunnel in trunks/roots.* *Brown larvae, yellow secretion. Leaves eaten.* *Larvae inside leaves. Blisters/lumps.* *Fine lines/blisters on leaves.* *Moth. Hairy, "horned" caterpillars eat leaves.* *Irregular brownish patches on young leaves.* *Shoots white/distorted; brown spots on leaves.* *Pimple-like growths under leaves; later corky.*	115 118 121 123 124 126 130 132 132 135 135 147 150 150 154 155 155 168 197 210 234
Euphorbia **spurge**	fasciation	*Growth flattened.*	238

F

PLANT	PROBLEM	SYMPTOMS/DESCRIPTION	PAGE
Fagus **beech**	mottled umber moth leaf miners leafhoppers oak leafminer scorch	*Brown/yellow/striped larvae eat leaves.* *Larvae in leaves. Lines/blotches seen.* *Yellow adults, white nymphs. Pale dotted leaves.* *Fine lines/blisters on leaves.* *Leaves turn brown at edges and curl.*	132 142 144 155 239
x *Fatshedera* **tree ivy**	leaf blight	*Dark brown-black patches on leaves; distortion.*	173
Ficus **fig**	pink wax scale soft scale, brown soft scale, soft brown scale green June beetle and fig beetle harlequin bug	*Pink or grey scales; honeydew attracts sooty mould.* *Yellow-brown scales under leaves. Honeydew, sooty mould.* *Adults eat holes in leaves/fruits. Larvae eat roots.* *Large black/red bug. Frass. Plants wilt, can die.*	122 124 126 130

Eucalyptus

Euphorbia

Euphorbia polychroma

Fagus

PLANT	PROBLEM	SYMPTOMS/DESCRIPTION	PAGE
Ficus **fig**	native fig moth	*White larvae eat leaves.*	141
	fruit-tree root weevil	*Adults eat young growth. Leaves folded. Larvae eat roots.*	142
	redshouldered leaf beetle	*Yellow/red beetle eats leaves/flowers/fruits.*	147
	fig psyllid	*Leaves are shed.*	147
	figleaf beetle	*Brown adults, yellow-brown-black larvae. Leaves eaten.*	158
	fruit flies	*Eggs laid under fruit skin; larvae feed inside fruits. Cracks/spots.*	166
	grey mould	*Fruits dry, not shed.*	177
	coral spot	*Die-back; pink-red, cushion-like pustules.*	198
	fig canker	*Oval cankers on bark. Tiny fungi tendrils of spores.*	200
Foeniculum vulgare var. *dulce* **Florence fennel**	black swallowtail butterfly, western parsleyworm, parsleyworm	*Brown-black/white, green/black larvae eat leaves.*	152
Forsythia **forsythia**	capsid bug	*Green insects eat young leaves. Growth distorted.*	143
	forsythia gall	*Galls on shoots.*	217
	fasciation	*Growth flattened.*	238
Fragaria x *ananassa* **strawberry**	garden webworm	*Brown moths' green-black caterpillars eat leaves, spin webs.*	112
	spittlebug	*Green nymphs hide in white froth on plants.*	121
	strawberry aphid	*Aphids on leaves.*	123
	millipedes	*Holes eaten in fruits; roots can be eaten.*	130
	whitefringed weevil	*Grey-black adult; larvae eat roots/tubers.*	137
	field cricket	*Brown-black insect chews seedlings/leaves/flowers/fruits.*	137
	strawberry seed beetles	*Black beetle eats seeds.*	137
	budworms	*Moth's caterpillars eat holes in leaves/flowers/fruits.*	138
	corn earworm	*Moth's caterpillars eat inside fruits.*	138
	redshouldered leaf beetle	*Yellow/red beetle eats leaves/flowers/fruits.*	147
	strawberry root weevil	*Brown-black adults eat leaves/stalks; larvae eat roots/crowns.*	151
	wingless weevil grub	*Roots/crowns eaten.*	151
	June beetle, May beetle	*Adults eat leaves, grubs eat roots.*	156
	tarsenomid mite, Michaelmas daisy mite, strawberry mite	*Mite inside buds. Scarring/distortion.*	156
	white curl grubs	*Beetles. Grubs eat roots.*	161
	black field cricket	*Leaves/shoots/fruits chewed.*	165
	glasshouse red spider mite, red spider mite, two-spotted mite	*Fine webbing. Mottled, pale leaves.*	166
	strawberry spider mite	*Fine webs. Leaves yellowed/shed; fruits discoloured.*	166
	plague thrips	*Tiny insect; colourless yellow nymph. Petals browned.*	167
	leaf nematode	*Yellow-brown patches on leaves.*	175
	grey mould	*Grey-brown fluff on fruits/stems/leaves.*	177
	black spot	*Round, black spots on fruits; white fungal growth.*	181
	anthracnose	*Yellow-brown-purplish spots on leaves/stems/fruits; darkening. Pinkish fungus.*	181
	strawberry leaf spot	*Small spots on leaves, red-purple, then grey-brown/red-edged.*	184
	bulb and stem nematode	*New leaves distorted; raised, yellow section.*	185

Figs

Florence fennel

Strawberries

PLANT	PROBLEM	SYMPTOMS/DESCRIPTION	PAGE
Fragaria x *ananassa* **strawberry**	powdery mildew	Grey-white powder on plants; young leaves distorted/shed. Leaves purple, curl; grey below.	188
	strawberry leaf blotch, gnomonia fruit rot	Large, brown, yellow-purple-edged blotches on leaves; leaves blacken, rot.	192
	strawberry green petal	Young leaves yellow-red, wilt, petals green.	197
	strawberry leaf blight	Red-purple, later brown, spots on leaves.	201
	red core, red stele	Wilting, stunting. Leaves discoloured.	203
	strawberry green petal	Petals green; flowers wither; new leaves redden.	204
	black eye	Flower centres turn black.	238
Freesia **freesia**	core rot	Corms in storage darken/spongy rot.	211
	bean mosaic, pea early browning virus	Leaves yellow-mottled, brown; stems streaked yellow.	222
Fritillaria **fritillary**	lily beetle, lily leaf beetle	Red adult and larvae eat leaves/flowers.	142
	grey bulb rot	Dry, grey rot from tip of bulb; black fungus in soil.	211
Fuchsia **fuchsia**	flea beetles, leaf beetles, striped flea beetles	Adults eat holes in leaves; larvae eat roots.	123
	capsid bugs	Green insects eat young leaves. Growth distorted.	143
	vine weevil, black vine weevil	Black weevil. Grubs eat roots.	151
	grapevine moth	Black/white/pink caterpillars eat under leaves.	154
	flea beetles	Dry areas on leaves; seedlings killed.	156
	cyclamen mite	Mite inside buds, under leaves. Discoloration/distortion.	157
	leaf nematodes	Yellow-brown patches on leaves.	175
	fuchsia rust	Purplish-red blotches appear on upper leaves, dry out, turn brown.	209

G

PLANT	PROBLEM	SYMPTOMS/DESCRIPTION	PAGE
Galanthus **snowdrop**	large narcissus bulb fly	Hoverfly. Maggots tunnel into bulbs.	146
	leaf scorch, tip burn	Brown blotches on leaves/stalks/petals; rotting; dark red-brown spots on bulbs.	215
Gardenia **gardenia**	Fuller's rose weevil	Grey-brown weevils eat leaves, larvae eat roots.	117
	budworms	Moth's caterpillars eat holes in leaves/flowers/fruits.	138
Gentiana **gentian**	foot and root rot, black root rot	Stem bases brown-black; leaves discoloured; die-back.	174
Gerbera **gerbera**	chrysanthemum leaf miner grub	Fly. Maggots inside leaves; discoloration.	156
	cyclamen mite	Mite inside buds, under leaves. Discoloration/distortion.	157
	broad mite	Distortion, discoloration; buds shed.	158
	white rust	White pustules under leaves, yellow blotches above.	172
	leaf spot	Brown-purple, purple-edged spots on leaves.	213
Gladiolus **gladioli**	gladiolus thrips	Brown-black insect, yellow nymph. Leaves mottled, flowers flecked; stored corms attacked.	167
	botrytis leaf and flower spot	Watery spots on petals; red-brown spots/grey mould on leaves/stems; stored corms shrivel.	178
	yellows, dry rot	Yellow stripes between leaf veins; yellowing, die-back. Corms rot.	191

Fritillaria

Fuchsia

Gladiolus

PLANT	PROBLEM	SYMPTOMS/DESCRIPTION	PAGE
Gladiolus **gladioli**	blue mould, soft rot scab grey bulb rot core rot hard rot bean mosaic, pea early browning virus	*Red-brown sunken patches on stored corms; blue mould, rotting.* *Red-brown specks on leaves; enlarge, darken. Craters on base of corm.* *Dry, grey rot from tip of corm; black fungus in soil.* *Corms in storage darken/spongy rot.* *Tiny brown spots on leaves; black fungi.* *Leaves yellow-mottled, brown; stems streaked yellow.*	198 205 211 211 213 222
Gloxinia **gloxinia**	glasshouse thrips, greenhouse thrips tarsenomid mites, Michaelmas daisy mite, strawberry mite cyclamen mite leaf nematodes	*yellow-brown insects. Leaves/petals spotted/discoloured* *Mite inside buds. Scarring/distortion.* *Mite in buds, under leaves. Discoloration/distortion. Rhizomes eaten.* *Yellow-brown patches on leaves.*	138 156 157 175
Glycine max **soya bean**	bean leaf beetle Mexican bean beetle	*Orange-yellow adults eat leaves, grubs eat roots/stems.* *Brown, spotted beetle; yellow larvae eat underside of leaves.*	122 132
Grevillea **grevillea**	macadamia flower caterpillar grevillea looper grevillea leafminer macadamia twig-girdler leaf spot	*Grey moth. Larvae feed on buds/flowers.* *Green caterpillars eat leaves.* *Moth. Larvae inside leaves; brown blisters.* *White moth. Mottled larvae spin webs, eat bark/leaves.* *Black spots on leaves.*	126 149 153 169 204

H

Hakea **hakea**	grevillea looper leaf spot	*Green caterpillars eat leaves.* *Black spots on leaves.*	149 204
Hedera **ivy**	California red scale, red scale oleander scale, ivy scale pink wax scale soft scale, brown soft scale, soft brown scale tarsenomid mite, Michaelmas daisy mite, strawberry mite cyclamen mite leaf blight leaf spot	*Orange-pink scale; die-back, leaves shed.* *White-brownish circular scales.* *Pink or grey scales; honeydew attracts sooty mould.* *Yellow-brown scales under leaves. Honeydew, sooty mould.* *Mite inside buds. Scarring/distortion.* *Mite inside buds, under leaves. Discoloration/distortion.* *Dark brown-black patches on leaves; distortion.* *Leaves yellow/drop. Brown lesions.*	116 117 122 124 156 157 173 181
Helianthus annuus **sunflower**	parsnip canker	*Cankers/horizontal cracks around roots; red-brown-black lesions.*	194
Helianthus tuberosus **Jerusalem artichoke**	root aphid sclerotinia disease, sclerotinia rot, sclerotinia wilt, white mould	*White, waxy powder secreted on roots.* *Stems rot; fluffy white growth inside; hard black fungi; flowers/buds rot.*	168 212
Hemerocallis **daylily**	bulb mite	*Globular, yellow-white mite. Bulbs destroyed.*	161

Gladiolus

Hedera

Helianthus annuus

Hedera

PLANT	PROBLEM	SYMPTOMS/DESCRIPTION	PAGE
Heuchera **coral flower**	leafy gall	*Mass of abortive, distorted shoots at base.*	182
Hibiscus **hibiscus**	hibiscus flower beetle	*Black beetle eats holes in petals.*	113
	metallic flea beetles	*Irregular holes in young leaves, buds.*	114
	cottonseed bug	*Black/grey bug. Sucks sap. Buds/flowers distorted/discoloured.*	152
	broad mite	*Distortion, discoloration; buds shed.*	158
	cotton harlequin bug	*Yellow/black female, red/blue-green male. Brown patches on leaves.*	165
	flyspeck	*Leaves yellow, shed; black spots.*	196
Hibiscus esculentus **okra**	stink bugs, earth mites	*Green-brown-grey bugs, evil smell. Distorted growth/fruits.*	153
	ascochyta blight	*Dark spots on leaves/stems.*	176
Hippeastrum **hippeastrum**	lesser bulb fly	*Black fly; yellow larvae eat bulb tops.*	135
	bulb scale mite	*Leaves curled/notched; stems stunted/distorted.*	164
	leaf scorch, tip burn	*Brown blotches on leaves/stalks/petals; rotting; dark red-brown spots on bulbs.*	215
Hosta **hosta**	snails and slugs	*Holes eaten in foliage; plants defoliated.*	135
Hyacinthoides **bluebell**	large narcissus bulb fly	*Hoverfly. Maggots tunnel into bulbs.*	146
	smut	*Flowers distorted; black spores.*	218
Hyacinthus **hyacinth**	lesser bulb fly	*Black fly; yellow larvae eat bulb tops.*	135
	bulb mite	*Globular, yellow-white mite. Bulbs destroyed.*	161
	bulb and stem nematode	*New leaves distorted; raised, yellow section. Brown rings inside bulbs; brown spongy patches. Pale streaks on stems/flowers; distortion.*	185
	grey bulb rot	*Dry, grey rot from tip of bulb; black fungus in soil.*	211
	non-rooting	*Roots fail to develop; plants stunted.*	241
	loose bud	*Stems below flower buds break.*	243
Hydrangea **hydrangea**	capsid bugs	*Green insects eat young leaves. Growth distorted.*	143
	hydrangea scale	*Plants weakened.*	160
	passionvine hopper	*Moth-like adult, green nymph. Leaves shrivel/drop.*	162
	silver leaf	*Leaves silver-brown; die-back. Mauve-white-brown brackets on dead wood.*	179
	iron deficiency, lime-induced chlorosis	*Young leaves yellow/scorched.*	248

I

Ilex **holly**	California red scale, red scale	*Orange-pink scale; die-back, leaves shed.*	116
	oleander scale, ivy scale	*White-brownish circular scales.*	117
	pink wax scale	*Pink or grey scales; honeydew attracts sooty mould.*	122
	leaf miners	*Larvae in leaves. Lines/blotches seen.*	142
Impatiens **busy Lizzy**	glasshouse thrips, greenhouse thrips	*Yellow-brown insects. Leaves/petals spotted/discoloured.*	138

Heuchera

Hippeastrum

Hyacinthus

Hydrangea

PLANT	PROBLEM	SYMPTOMS/DESCRIPTION	PAGE
Ipomoea batata **sweet potato**	metallic flea beetles	Irregular holes in young leaves, buds.	114
	flea beetles, leaf beetles, striped flea beetles	Adults eat holes in leaves; larvae eat roots.	123
	grapevine hawk moth	Large green-black caterpillars chew leaves.	139
	fall armyworm	Moth. Green-brown-black/yellow-striped caterpillars eat leaves.	163
	sclerotium stem rot, southern blight	Leaves yellow; watery lesions at base of plants; white growth.	212
Iris **iris**	lesser bulb fly	Black fly; yellow larvae eat bulb tops.	135
	gladiolus thrips	Brown-black insect, yellow nymph. Leaves mottled, flowers flecked.	167
	leaf spot	Brown-grey spots on leaves.	180
	ink disease	Black patches on bulbs; hollowing/rotting. Black patches/brown spots on leaves.	185
	rhizome rot	Rhizomes rot; yellow slime. Leaves brown.	188
	iris rust	Red, powdery spots on leaves; yellowing.	208
	sclerotium stem rot, southern blight	Leaves yellow; watery lesions at base of plants; white growth.	212
	mosaic	Streaks or mottling on leaves.	225
	phosphorus deficiency	Performance is poor.	247
	iris scorch	Leaves red-brown, curl; roots die.	249
Ixia **ixia**	grey bulb rot	Dry, grey rot from tip of bulb; black fungus in soil.	211

J

Jacaranda **jacaranda**	fruit-tree borer	White moth. Larvae tunnel into wood.	145
Jasminum **jasmine**	Australian privet hawk moth	Green/lilac/white, spined caterpillars eat leaves.	159
Juglans regia **walnut**	walnut blister mite	Leaves have oval blisters.	133
	walnut leaf blotch	Yellow-brown patches above leaves, grey-brown below. Sunken dark blotches on nuts.	193
	walnut blight, walnut black spot	Small, round, watery spots on leaves; enlarge/brown. Nuts rot.	220
	walnut soft shell	Shells thin; holes.	245
Juniperus **juniper**	juniper webber moth	Brown caterpillars eat leaves, make webs.	130
	conifer red spider mites, spruce spider mite	Green mite, red eggs. Webbing; leaves discoloured.	149
	currant clearwing moth, currant borer moth	Larvae feed inside stems. Small, yellow leaves; pupal cases appear.	165
	conifer rusts	Horn-like gelatinous masses of orange spores on swollen shoots.	182

K

Kalmia latifolia **calico bush**	petal blight	White-brown spots on petals; slimy, then dry; not shed.	198
Koelreuteria **golden-rain tree**	macadamia nutborer	Pink larvae of moths feed on seeds.	126

Iris

Jasminum

Kalmia latifolia

PLANT	PROBLEM	SYMPTOMS/DESCRIPTION	PAGE
L			
Laburnum **laburnum**	cottony cushion scale	Brown scale. Honeydew, sooty mould.	140
	leaf miners	Larvae in leaves. Lines/blotches seen.	142
Lagenaria siceraria **gourd**	squash vine borer	Moth. Larvae chew bases of stems.	146
Lagenophora **lagenophora**	English marigold rust	Pale green-yellow spots on leaves/stems; small "cups" on leaves.	208
Lagerstroemia indica **crape myrtle**	fruit-tree borer	White moth. Larvae tunnel into wood.	145
Lagunaria patersonii **Norfolk Island hibiscus**	cottonseed bug	Black/grey bug. Sucks sap. Buds/flowers distorted/discoloured.	152
Larix **larch**	woolly adelgid	Some yellowing of foliage.	113
	sirex wasp	Blue female, blue/orange male. Larvae tunnel in wood.	162
	phomopsis disease	Die-back. Cankers, small black fungi.	201
	larch canker	Large, flattened cankers on trunk/branch; orange, saucer-like fungi at edges.	217
Lathyrus odoratus **sweet pea**	leafy gall	Mass of abortive, distorted shoots at base.	189
	damping off	Seedlings collapse; blacken, wither.	202
	bacterial blight	Watery, darkening spots at stem base. Yellow lesions on leaflets; brown, papery. Dark green-brown spots on pods.	207
	broad bean wilt	Tips blacken; base/roots black, rotted. Leaves mottled/curled.	223
	bud drop/aborted flowers	Flower buds shrivel/drop.	240
	sweet pea scorch	Pale brown patches on leaves.	245
Latuca sativa **lettuce**	cineraria leafminer	Small black fly. Larvae inside leaves cause silver lines, wilting.	133
	budworms	Moth's caterpillars eat holes in leaves.	138
	vegetable weevil	Brown beetle. Cream-green larvae. Base of plants and roots eaten.	142
	lettuce aphid	Greenfly. Growth stunted.	148
	Rutherglen bug	Brown bug. Wilting; fruits pitted.	149
	lettuce root aphid	Yellow aphid feeds on roots. Waxy secretion.	153
	beet armyworm	Moth. Green/yellow stripy caterpillars spin webs, eat leaves/stems/roots.	163
	onion thrips	Yellow-grey insect. Yellow nymph. Leaves blotched/distorted.	167
	cabbage looper	Moth. Green pale-striped caterpillars eat leaves.	168
	downy mildew	Mealy-furry growths under leaves; pale green-yellow-brown above.	178
	anthracnose	Small yellow-browning, enlarging spots on leaves.	194
	big bud, greening, virescence	Unnaturally bushy growth.	197
	damping off	Seedlings collapse; blacken, wither.	202
	aster yellows, strawberry green petal	Inner head pale.	204
	wirestem fungus	Stems shrink; roots blacken.	216
	bacterial leaf spot	Translucent spots on leaves; merging.	220
	lettuce big vein	Stunting/thickening. White-yellow veins, transparent bands.	224
	lettuce necrotic yellows	Stunting; yellow, crinkled/lopsided.	225

Laburnum

Lathyrus odoratus

Lettuce

PLANT	PROBLEM	SYMPTOMS/DESCRIPTION	PAGE
Laurus nobilis **bay**	white wax scale	*White scales produce honeydew.*	122
Lens culinaris **lentil**	bean weevil	*White grubs eat holes in beans/seeds.*	112
Leptospermum **tea tree, manuka**	tea tree web moth manuka blight paperbark sawfly	*Larvae's webs disfigure trees.* *Scale. Honeydew, sooty mould.* *Larvae eat leaves, burrow into bark.*	121 133 160
Levisticum officinale	celery leaf miner black swallowtail butterfly, western parsleyworm, parsleyworm	*Fly; maggots inside leaves. Discoloured patches, stunted growth.* *Brown-black/white butterfly, green/black larvae eat leaves.*	134 152
Lewisia **lewisia**	waterlogging crown rot	*Leaves discoloured/die-back.* *Crowns soft, slimy.*	232 234
Ligustrum **privet**	privet thrips Australian privet hawk moth	*Thin, black or yellow insect. Leaves turn dull/brown.* *Green/lilac/white, spined caterpillars eat leaves.*	128 159
Lilium **lily**	lily beetle, lily leaf beetle bulb mite lily disease, leaf blight fusarium bulb rot lily viruses tulip breaking virus	*Red adults and larvae eat leaves/flowers.* *Globular, yellow-white mite. Bulbs destroyed.* *Oval spots on leaves; browning; leaves/stems rot.* *Leaves turn yellow/purple; die. Flowering impaired.* *Leaves distorted; yellow markings.* *Flowers streaked; leaves yellow-streaked, tattered.*	142 161 177 190 225 227
Litchi chinensis **lychee**	banana-spotting bug macadamia nutborer erinose mite	*Grey bug, red/black nymph; spots/patches on fruit.* *Pink larvae of moths feed on seeds.* *Leaves blistered/curled. Velvety, discoloured area.*	115 126 133
Lobelia **lobelia**	leaf and stem rot (seedlings) damping off	*Pale-spotted leaves. Rotting/damping off.* *Seedlings collapse; blacken, wither.*	172 202
Lophostemon confertus **brush box**	whitestemmed gum moth cup moths latania scale leaf spot, yellow leaf spot	*Large, hairy larvae may damage bark.* *Cup-shaped cocoons. Spiny larvae eat leaves.* *Grey scales, leaves drop.* *Dull yellowish spots on leaves.*	123 130 139 186
Lunaria **honesty**	white blister, white rust mosaic	*White blisters/rings on leaves. Stunting/distortion.* *Leaves distorted/mottled.*	172 225
Lupinus **lupin**	foot and root rot, black root rot armillaria root rot, honey fungus broad bean wilt	*Stem bases brown-black; leaves discoloured; die-back.* *Leaves wither (don't drop); die-back.* *Tips blacken; base/roots black, rotted. Leaves mottled/curled.*	174 175 223

Laurus nobilis

Levisticum officinale

Lilium

PLANT	PROBLEM	SYMPTOMS/DESCRIPTION	PAGE
Lycopersicon esculentum **tomato**	tomato russet mite	*Leaves grey-brown; stems brown; leaves, flowers shed.*	113
	driedfruit beetle	*Fruits rot.*	121
	beet leafhopper	*Green-brown adult, green nymph, spread viruses.*	124
	harlequin bug	*Large black/red bug. Frass. Plants wilt, can die.*	130
	millipedes	*Holes eaten in fruits; roots can be eaten.*	130
	leafeating ladybirds	*Yellow-spotted beetle. Spiny larvae eat below leaves.*	131
	blister beetles	*Various beetles eat leaves/fruits.*	131
	loopers and semi-loopers	*Holes are chewed in leaves. Flowers can be damaged.*	136
	potato cyst eelworms	*Cysts on roots. Leaves yellowed from base up.*	136
	whitefringed weevil	*Grey-black/white adult; larvae eat roots.*	137
	field cricket	*Brown-black insect chews seedlings/leaves/flowers/fruits.*	138
	budworms	*Moth's caterpillars eat holes in leaves/flowers/fruits.*	138
	corn earworm	*Moth's caterpillars eat inside fruits.*	138
	tomato fruitworm	*Moth's larvae eat plants.*	138
	glasshouse thrips, greenhouse thrips	*Yellow-brown insects. Leaves/petals spotted/discoloured.*	138
	African black beetle	*Adults eat stems below ground; grubs eat roots.*	139
	Colorado beetle, Colorado potato beetle	*Orange/black adults and larvae eat leaves.*	141
	tomato hornworm	*Large moth. Green/black-horned caterpillars eat leaves/fruits.*	145
	green vegetable bug	*Green-black bug, many-coloured nymph. Growth distorted, discoloured.*	148
	Rutherglen bug	*Brown bug. Wilting; fruits pitted.*	149
	European corn borer	*Moth. Grey-pink caterpillars chew leaves, enter husks/stalks.*	150
	fruitpiercing moth	*Holes in fruit.*	151
	stink bugs, earth mites	*Green-brown-grey bugs, evil smell. Distorted growth/fruits.*	153
	potato moth, potato tuberworm	*Larvae mine leaves/stems/tubers/fruits.*	155
	garden symphylan	*White, many-legged soil-dweller eats roots.*	162
	fall armyworm	*Moth. Green-brown-black/yellow-striped caterpillars eat leaves/cobs.*	163
	beet armyworms	*Moth. Green/yellow stripy caterpillars spin webs, eat leaves/stems/roots.*	163
	fruit flies	*Eggs laid under fruit skin; larvae feed inside fruits. Cracks/spots.*	166
	spider mites	*Fine webbing. Leaves speckled/yellow-brown.*	166
	onion thrips	*Yellow-grey insect. Yellow nymph. Leaves blotched/distorted.*	167
	glasshouse whitefly	*Scale-like, pale green nymphs feed under leaves. Honeydew, sooty mould.*	168
	cabbage looper	*Moth. Green pale-striped caterpillars eat leaves.*	168
	target spot	*Dark lesions at soil line; long marks on stems; dark rot on fruits.*	174
	foot and root rot, black root rot	*Stem bases brown-black; leaves discoloured; die-back.*	174
	ascochyta blight	*Dark spots on leaves/stems.*	176
	bacterial canker	*Wilting, lower leaves upwards. Brown-black edges/leaves. White, raised spots on fruits.*	180
	anthracnose	*Yellow/brown/purple spots on stems/leaves/fruits. Dark, depressed spots.*	180
	anthracnose	*Small, depressed spots on fruits; enlarging/rings/dark specks.*	181
	tomato stem rot	*Brown-black cankers near base of stems; black dots.*	184
	powdery mildew	*Grey-white powder on plants; young leaves distorted/shed.*	188
	tomato leaf mould	*Under glass: purple-brown mould under leaves, yellow blotches above.*	190
	fusarium wilt (tomatoes)	*Wilting; lower leaves yellow.*	191
	big bud, greening, virescence	*Unnaturally bushy growth; stems thickened.*	197
	damping off	*Seedlings collapse; blacken, wither.*	202
	late blight, tomato blight	*Yellow-brown patches on leaves; dry, curl. Black patches on stems; fruits brown, rot.*	203

'San Marzano' tomatoes

'Tigerella' tomatoes

'Red Peach' tomatoes

PLANT	PROBLEM	SYMPTOMS/DESCRIPTION	PAGE
Lycopersicon esculentum **tomato**	sclerotium stem rot, southern blight	*Leaves yellow; watery lesions at base of plants; white growth.*	212
	powdery scab, corky scab	*Brown blisters on tubers; brown spores.*	215
	verticillium wilt	*Wilting from lower leaves up.*	218
	bacterial spot	*Small, dark, watery spots on leaves; sunken streaks on stems; small, growing darkening spots on fruits.*	220
	beet curly top	*Leaves crinkled; veins swollen; yellowing.*	223
	cucumber mosaic virus	*Stunting, distortion, yellow mosaic pattern on leaves.*	224
	leaf roll	*Leaves curl; plants stunted, stiff upright.*	224
	pepino mosaic virus	*Leaves distorted, mosaic pattern; lower leaves darker, yellow spots; fruits marbled.*	226
	tomato mosaic virus, bronzing of tomatoes	*Leaves mottled/distorted/curled.*	226
	tobacco ring spot, bouquet disease, tomato ring spot, bud blight	*Stunting, distortion; small brown-yellow, raised rings/circles on leaves/fruits.*	226
	moist atmosphere	*Fungal diseases.*	232
	blossom end rot	*Circular brown-green-black patch opposite stalk on fruits.*	237
	greenback	*Hard green-yellow patches on fruits.*	240
	blotchy ripening	*Hard green-yellow patches on fruits.*	241
	chats	*Fruits small.*	241
	dry set	*Fruits fail to swell; dry, brown.*	241
	magnesium deficiency	*Leaves yellow, oldest first, later orange-red, drop.*	249
	potassium deficiency	*Leaves bluish, brown spots/tips; curl downwards.*	249

M

PLANT	PROBLEM	SYMPTOMS/DESCRIPTION	PAGE
Macadamia **macadamia**	macadamia leafminer	*Moth. Larvae cause white lines and blisters on leaves.*	112
	fruitspotting bug	*Green bug, red/black nymph. Sunken dark spots on leaves.*	115
	yellow peach moth	*Large pink caterpillars tunnel into plants/fruits. Die-back.*	125
	macadamia flower caterpillar	*Grey moth. Larvae feed on buds/flowers.*	126
	macadamia nutborer	*Pink larvae of moths feed on nuts.*	126
	macadamia felted coccid	*White-brown insect. Distorted/stunted growth, spotted leaves.*	133
	latania scale	*Grey scales; leaves drop.*	139
	macadamia cup moth	*Yellow-striped, oval larvae eat leaves.*	145
	redshouldered leaf beetle	*Yellow/red beetle eats leaves/flowers.*	147
	macadamia twig-girdler	*White moth. Brown-mottled larvae spin webs, eat bark/leaves, tunnel in nuts.*	169
Magnolia **magnolia**	hibiscus flower beetle	*Black beetle eats holes in petals.*	113
	pink wax scale	*Pink or grey scales; honeydew attracts sooty mould.*	122
	cottonycushion scale	*Brown scale. Honeydew, sooty mould.*	140
	white palm scale	*Scales under leaves. Yellow blotches.*	154
	coral spot	*Die-back; pink-red, cushion-like pustules.*	198
	frost damage	*Petals brown-edged; bark cracks.*	233
	iron deficiency, lime-induced chlorosis	*Young leaves yellow/scorched.*	248
Malus **crab apple**	woolly aphid, woolly apple aphid	*Brown aphid, white covering; soft galls.*	134
	mussel scale	*Brown scale. Die-back.*	141
	leopard moth	*White/black-spotted moth. Black-spotted larvae tunnel into wood.*	169

Tomatoes

Magnolia grandiflora

Magnolia sprengeri

'John Downie' crab apples

PLANT	PROBLEM	SYMPTOMS/DESCRIPTION	PAGE
Malus **crab apple**	apple scab	Brown blotches on leaves; rough, corky patches on fruits.	218
	apple mosaic	Green-yellow-cream mottling on leaves.	222
Malus domestica **apple**	fruitspotting bug	Green bug, red/black nymph; fruits spotted/shed.	115
	apple blossom weevil	Flowers fail to develop and fruit is not set.	115
	fruittree leafroller	Moth's green caterpillars eat plant parts, roll up in leaves.	116
	bryobia mite	Red, then brown-grey mites; white-mottled leaves.	119
	inland katydid	Grasshopper-like. Leaves skeletonized/holed; fruits gnawed.	120
	pear and cherry slugworm caterpillar pear and cherry slug	Sawfly. Dark green larvae eat leaves causing vein network.	120
	apple dimpling bug	Green bug causes indentations on fruits.	120
	plum curculio	Larvae tunnel into developing fruit. Fruits drop.	125
	green June beetle and fig beetle	Adults eat holes in leaves/fruits. Larvae eat roots.	126
	codling moth	White-pink caterpillars tunnel into fruits. White excreta.	127
	harlequin bug	Large black/red bug. Frass. Plants wilt, can die.	130
	apple leafhopper, canary fly	Yellow cicada-type. Grey-mottled leaves.	130
	rose leafhopper	Yellow insect, white nymphs, under leaves. Pale leaf mottling.	130
	potato leafhopper	Green insect, pale nymph. Leaves spotted/distorted/rolled.	131
	lightbrown apple moth	Green larvae roll/web leaves, eat leaves/fruits.	132
	mottled umber moth	Brown/yellow/striped larvae eat leaves.	132
	pearleaf blister mite	Discoloured blisters on leaves, spotted/distorted fruits.	133
	woolly aphid, woolly apple aphid	Brown aphid, white covering; soft galls.	134
	oriental fruit moth	White-pink caterpillars tunnel into shoots/fruits.	137
	budworms	Moth's caterpillars eat holes in leaves/flowers/fruits.	138
	apple sawfly, European apple sawfly	Maggots tunnel into fruits. Scarring.	140
	mussel scale	Brown scale. Die-back.	141
	fruit-tree root weevil	Adults eat young growth. Leaves folded. Larvae eat roots.	142
	periodical cicada	Slits in bark for eggs.	144
	tent caterpillars	Black, white striped/spotted caterpillars eat leaves, make webs.	144
	elephant weevil	Grey-black adult. Larvae tunnel in trunks/roots.	150
	vine weevil, black vine weevil	Black weevil. Grubs eat roots.	151
	fruit tree red spider mite, European red mite	Yellow-mottled leaves.	152
	oak leafminer	Fine lines/blisters on leaves.	155
	apple capsid	Green insect. Scabs/lumps on fruits, holes in leaves.	158
	apple sucker	Green-brown, aphid-like. Petals browned.	159
	San Jose scale	Well-camouflaged scale. Rough texture; fruits damaged.	160
	apple maggot	Black fly, eggs in holes in fruit. Maggots tunnel in fruit.	161
	buffalo treehopper	Triangular, green insect. Yellow eggs in slits in bark.	164
	apple curculio	Brown-red weevil. Larvae tunnel in fruits; scarred, dropped.	165
	painted apple moth	Black-tufted caterpillars chew leaves.	165
	spider mites	Fine webbing. Leaves speckled/yellow-brown.	166
	plague thrips	Tiny insect; colourless yellow nymph. Petals browned.	167
	wasps, hornet, yellow jackets	Black-yellow striped insects eat holes in fruit.	169
	powdery mildew	Grey-white powder on plants; young leaves distorted/shed. Red-skinned varieties: thin yellow lines on fruits.	188
	sooty blotch	Dark circular, cloudy enlarging patches on fruit skins.	192
	bitter rot	Small brown spots on fruit skins; spots enlarge in rings; rotting.	192

'Granny Smith' apples

'Worcester Pearmain' apples

'Washington Red' apples

'Bramley's seedling' cooking apples

PLANT	PROBLEM	SYMPTOMS/DESCRIPTION	PAGE
Malus domestica **apple**	fly speck	*Small, circular specks on fruit skins; taste unaffected.*	196
	brown rot	*Small brown spots on petals/stems/fruits. Brown mould. Sunken brown cankers on twigs. Fruits rot; rings of grey spores.*	196
	apple canker	*Sunken, elliptical patches on bark; shoots girdled. White spores, red fungus.*	198
	brown rot of stone fruit	*Flowers turn brown, die. Fungi can cause die-back. Brown spots on skin.*	211
	replant disease	*New plantings replacing a similar plant fail to make good growth and can die.*	216
	apple scab	*Brown blotches on leaves; rough, corky patches on fruits.*	218
	apple mosaic	*Green-yellow-cream mottling on leaves.*	222
	cracked fruits	*Cropping is impaired.*	234
	papery bark	*Bark thin, peels.*	235
	russeting	*Rough patches on fruit skins.*	239
	Cox's spot	*Small brown spots on leaves.*	244
	June drop	*Small fruits drop.*	244
	replant disorder	*New plantings replacing a similar plant fail to thrive.*	245
	bitter pit	*Sunken pits on fruit skins; brown areas inside.*	246
Mangifera indica **mango**	California red scale, red scale	*Orange-pink scale; die-back, leaves shed.*	116
	pink wax scale	*Pink or grey scales; honeydew attracts sooty mould.*	122
	redshouldered leaf beetle	*Yellow/red beetle eats leaves/flowers/fruits.*	147
	fruitpiercing moths	*Holes in fruits.*	151
	large mango tipborer	*Moth. Green/red-spotted larvae eat leaves, bore twigs.*	153
	anthracnose	*Black, enlarging spots on leaves/flowers/fruits.*	182
	bacterial black spot	*Greasy patches on leaves; blacken. Black, gum-filled cankers on stems; raised, oval black spots on fruits.*	220
Marrubium vulgare **horehound**	horehound bug	*Bug sucks sap; shoots wilt.*	114
Matthiola **stocks**	downy mildew	*White, mealy growth under leaves.*	199
	damping off	*Seedlings collapse; blacken, wither.*	202
	club root	*Stunting; leaves discoloured. Roots thickened/distorted; galls.*	204
	collar rot, rhizoctonia disease	*Reddish sunken areas at base of stems.*	210
	black rot	*Wilting; lower leaves yellow.*	219
	mosaic	*Leaves distorted/mottled.*	225
Medicago sativa **alfalfa**	potato leafhopper	*Green insect, pale nymph. Leaves spotted/distorted/rolled.*	131
	Mexican bean beetle	*Brown, spotted beetle, yellow larvae, eat underside of leaves.*	132
Melaleuca **paperbark**	paperbark sawfly	*Larvae eat leaves, burrow into bark.*	160
Melia azedarach **bead tree**	white cedar moth	*Brown, hairy caterpillars eat leaves.*	142
Mentha **mint**	leafhoppers	*Yellow adults, white nymphs. Pale dotted leaves.*	144
	mint rust	*Small orange pustules; distorted growth.*	209

'French Golden Delicious' apples

'Braeburn' apples

Mentha

PLANT	PROBLEM	SYMPTOMS/DESCRIPTION	PAGE
Morus alba **mulberry**	California red scale, red scale	*Orange-pink scale; die-back, leaves shed.*	116
	redshouldered leaf beetle	*Yellow/red beetle eats leaves/flowers/fruits.*	147
	mulberry leaf spot	*Small brown spots on leaves; enlarge, turn paler.*	200
	bacterial blight	*New leaves blacken. Small brown-black, angular spots on leaves, distortion. Cankers on shoots.*	206
Musa spp. **banana**	banana-spotting bug	*Green bug, red/black nymph; spots/patches on fruits.*	115
	banana rust thrips	*Grubs of black beetle cause swellings on roots.*	122
	banana weevil borer, banana root borer	*Black weevil. Larvae tunnel through corms. Rotting, wilting.*	125
	African black beetle	*Adults eat stems below ground; grubs eat roots.*	139
	fruitpiercing moths	*Holes in fruits.*	151
	fruit flies	*Eggs laid under fruit skin; larvae feed inside fruits. Cracks/spots.*	166
	strawberry spider mite	*Fine webs. Leaves yellowed/shed; fruits discoloured.*	166
	banana fruit caterpillar	*Moth. Khaki caterpillars chew fruit skins/flesh.*	168
	leaf speckle	*Yellow areas under leaves; dark brown spots.*	196
	banana leaf spot, Sigatoka disease	*Yellow streaks on leaves, then brown-greying oval spots; black streaks.*	197
Musa textilis **Manila hemp**	banana weevil borer, banana root borer	*Black weevil. Larvae tunnel through corms. Rotting, wilting.*	125
Muscari **grape hyacinth**	smut	*Flowers distorted; black spores.*	218

N

PLANT	PROBLEM	SYMPTOMS/DESCRIPTION	PAGE
Nandina **bamboo**	Indian white wax scale	*White scales produce honeydew; sooty mould appears.*	122
	white wax scale	*White scales produce honeydew.*	122
Narcissus **daffodil**	narcissus eelworm, onion eelworm, phlox eelworm	*Nematode. Plants distorted/discoloured.*	130
	lesser bulb fly	*Black fly; yellow larvae eat bulb tops.*	135
	large narcissus bulb fly	*Hoverfly. Maggots tunnel into bulbs.*	146
	bulb mite	*Globular, yellow white mite. Bulbs destroyed.*	161
	bulb scale mite	*Leaves curled/notched; stems stunted/distorted.*	164
	bulb and stem nematode	*Rough yellow swellings on leaves; late flowering; spongy brownish areas on bulbs.*	185
	basal rot	*Base of bulb browns, shrivels, hardens.*	191
	white mould	*Dark green-yellow-brown patches on leaves; white spores.*	210
	grey bulb rot	*Dry, grey rot from tip of bulb; black fungus in soil.*	211
	smoulder	*Grey spores on leaves; flattened black fungus on bulbs.*	211
	leaf scorch, tip burn	*Brown blotches on leaves/stalks/petals; rotting; dark red-brown spots on bulbs.*	215
Nerium **oleander**	black scale, brown olive scale	*Soft scales. Honeydew, sooty mould.*	161
	bacterial gall	*Swellings on young stems; split; rough cankers, woody galls. Leaves/flowers distorted.*	207

Morus alba

Muscari

Narcissus

PLANT	PROBLEM	SYMPTOMS/DESCRIPTION	PAGE
Nicotiana **tobacco plant**	glasshouse leafhopper	*Yellow adult, creamy nymph. White dots on leaves.*	138
O *Olea europaea* **olive**	olive lace bug black scale, brown olive scale	*Brown bug. Leaves yellow-mottled, browned.* *Soft scales. Honeydew, sooty mould.*	135 161
P *Paeonia* **peony**	swift moth caterpillars armillaria root rot, honey fungus peony wilt conifer rusts	*Large white caterpillars feed on roots.* *Leaves wither (don't drop); die-back.* *Shoot bases brown, wilt. Grey, velvety mould; brown patches.* *Yellow blisters on swollen stems; powdery orange spores.*	139 175 178 182
Pandorea **pandorea**	Australian privet hawk moth	*Green/lilac/white, spined caterpillars eat leaves.*	159
Papaver **poppy**	blackfly onion thrips spotted wilt pedicel necrosis	*Tiny flies on young growth; leaves curl.* *Yellow-grey insect. Yellow nymph. Leaves blotched/distorted.* *Brown spots on leaves; stems streaked brown.* *Flower stalks blacken; buds brown.*	116 167 227 240
Parthenocissus quinquefolia **Virginia creeper** *P. tricuspidata* **Boston ivy**	painted vine moth caterpillar oleander scale, ivy scale grapevine hawk moth grapevine moth	*Black/orange/cream caterpillars eat holes in leaves.* *White-brownish circular scales.* *Large green-black caterpillars chew leaves.* *Black/white/pink caterpillars eat under leaves.*	113 117 139 154

Passiflora
passion flower
passion fruit
granadilla
	banana-spotting bug
	California red scale, red scale
	Fuller's rose weevil
	soft scale, brown soft scale, soft brown scale
	glasshouse thrips, greenhouse thrips
	green vegetable bug
	black scale, brown olive scale
	passionvine hopper
	fruit flies
	brown spot
	
	phytophthora blight
	
	septoria spot
	woodiness of passionfruit
		Grey bug, red/black nymph; spots/patches on fruits.
		Orange-pink scale; die-back, leaves shed.
		Grey-brown weevils eat leaves; larvae eat roots.
		Yellow-brown scales under leaves. Honeydew, sooty mould.
		Yellow-brown insects. Leaves/petals spotted/discoloured.
		Green-black bug, many-coloured nymph. Growth distorted, discoloured.
		Soft scales. Honeydew, sooty mould.
		Moth-like adult, green nymph. Leaves/fruits shrivel/drop.
		Eggs laid under fruit skin; larvae feed inside fruits. Cracks/spots.
		Brown spots on all parts above ground; leaves shed;
		  green-brown spots on fruits.
		Translucent-brown patches on leaves, from base up. Die-back;
		  stem girdled. Watery spots on fruits.
		Brown spots on leaves/fruits.
		Fruits distorted; leaves yellow-mottled or pale.
			115
			116
			117
			124
			138
			148
			161
			162
			166
			173
			
			203
			
			213
			227

Pastinaca sativa **parsnip**	root aphid celery leaf miner vegetable weevil	*Grey-white aphid attacks near soil level; poor growth.* *Fly; maggots inside leaves. Discoloured patches, stunted growth.* *Brown beetle. Cream-green larvae. Base of plants and roots eaten.*	115 134 142

Nicotiana

Paeonia

Passiflora

PLANT	PROBLEM	SYMPTOMS/DESCRIPTION	PAGE
Pastinaca sativa **parsnip**	black swallowtail butterfly, western parsleyworm, parsleyworm	*Brown-black/white butterfly, green/black larvae eat leaves.*	152
	carrot fly, carrot rust fly	*Maggots tunnel in roots.*	159
	parsnip canker	*Cankers/horizontal cracks around roots; red-brown-black lesions.*	194
	common scab, potato scab	*Corky lesions on roots.*	215
	splitting of roots	*Roots split.*	237
Pelargonium **geranium**	pelargonium rust	*Small green spots above leaves, blisters below.*	209
	black stem rot	*Stems blacken from base up.*	209
	bacterial leaf spot	*Small, enlarging brown spots on leaves; yellowing. Brown-black rot on stems.*	220
	oedema, dropsy	*Pimple-like growths under leaves; later corky.*	234
	splitting of stems	*Stem splits/peels.*	238
Peperomia **peperomia**	oedema, dropsy	*Pimple-like growths under leaves; later corky.*	234
Persea spp. **avocado**	metallic flea beetles	*Irregular holes in young leaves, buds.*	114
	banana-spotting bug	*Green bug; red/black nymph; spots/patches on fruit.*	115
	fruitspotting bug	*Green bug; red/black nymph; fruits spotted/shed.*	115
	pink wax scale	*Pink or grey scales; honeydew attracts sooty mould.*	122
	latania scale	*Grey scales. Fruits pitted, leaves drop.*	139
	redshouldered leaf beetle	*Yellow/red beetle eats leaves/flowers/fruits.*	147
	fruit flies	*Eggs laid under fruit skin; larvae feed inside fruits. Cracks/spots.*	166
	stem-end rot	*Brown-black rot in fruits.*	185
	anthracnose	*Small, circular, light brown spots on fruits; enlarge, darken; rotting. Pink spores.*	192
Persoonia **geebung**	grevillea looper	*Green caterpillars eat leaves.*	149
Petroselinum crispum **parsley**	black swallowtail butterfly, western parsleyworm, parsleyworm	*Brown-black/white butterfly, green/black larvae eat leaves.*	152
	carrot fly, carrot rust fly	*Maggots tunnel in roots.*	159
	leaf blight, alternaria blight	*Brown spots on leaves.*	173
	carrot motley dwarf disease	*Leaves yellow/pink, twisted.*	223
Petunia **petunia**	tomato russet mite	*Leaves grey-brown; stems brown; leaves, flowers shed.*	113
	beet leafhopper	*Green-brown adult, green nymph, spread viruses.*	124
	African black beetle	*Adults eat stems below ground; grubs eat roots.*	139
	chrysanthemum stunt viroid	*Stunting, brittle stems. Yellow spots on leaves; distortion.*	223
	cucumber mosaic virus	*Stunting, distortion, yellow mosaic pattern on leaves.*	224
Phaseolus coccineus **runner bean** *P. lunatus* **lima bean**	garden webworm	*Brown moths' green-black caterpillars eat leaves, spin webs.*	112
	bean weevil	*White grubs eat holes in beans/seeds.*	112
	greenfly (dwarf, runner)	*Tiny green flies on shoot tips, under leaves.*	113
	bean leaf beetle	*Orange-yellow adults eat leaves, grubs eat roots/stems.*	122

Parsnips

Pelargonium

Petunia

PLANT	PROBLEM	SYMPTOMS/DESCRIPTION	PAGE
Phaseolus vulgaris	beet leafhopper	*Green-brown adult, green nymph, spread viruses.*	124
French bean	bean seed fly, onion maggot	*White maggots eat seedlings, young growth.*	128
P. coccineus	leafeating ladybirds	*Yellow-spotted beetle. Spiny larvae eat below leaves.*	131
runner bean	potato leafhopper	*Green insect, pale nymph. Leaves spotted/distorted/rolled.*	131
P. lunatus	blister beetles	*Various beetles eat leaves/pods.*	131
lima bean	Mexican bean beetle (lima, snap)	*Brown, spotted beetle; yellow larvae eat underside of leaves..*	132
	loopers and semi-loopers	*Holes are chewed in leaves. Flowers can be damaged.*	136
	field cricket	*Brown-black insect chews seedlings/leaves/flowers/pods.*	138
	whitefringed weevil	*Grey-black/white adult; larvae eat roots/pods.*	137
	budworms	*Moth's caterpillars eat holes in leaves/flowers/pods.*	138
	corn earworm	*Moth's larvae eat plants. Moth's caterpillars eat inside pods.*	138
	tomato fruitworm	*Moth's larvae eat plants.*	138
	leaf miners	*Larvae in leaves. Lines/blotches seen.*	142
	bean podborer	*Moth. Green-yellow, spotted caterpillars eat flowers/stems/seeds.*	145
	bean blossom thrips (dwarf French, climbing)	*Young leaves/beans puckered/distorted.*	146
	redshouldered leaf beetle	*Yellow/red beetle eats leaves/flowers/pods.*	147
	green vegetable bug	*Green-black bug, many-coloured nymph. Growth distorted, discoloured.*	148
	Rutherglen bug	*Brown bug. Wilting.*	149
	bean fly (French, climbing)	*Black fly, yellow eggs. Larvae eat inside stems; swelling, wilting.*	150
	European corn borer	*Moth. Grey-pink caterpillars chew leaves.*	150
	stink bugs, earth mites	*Green-brown-grey bugs, evil smell. Distorted growth/pods.*	153
	broad mite (French)	*Distortion, discoloration; buds shed.*	158
	garden symphylan	*White, many-legged soil-dweller eats roots.*	162
	passionvine hopper	*Moth-like adult, green nymph. Leaves shrivel/drop.*	162
	pea and bean weevil	*Brown beetle eats notches in leaves.*	163
	bean root aphid (French, runner)	*Brown aphid feeds on roots. White powder.*	163
	fall armyworm	*Moth. Green-brown-black/yellow-striped caterpillars eat leaves/cobs.*	163
	spider mites	*Fine webbing. Leaves speckled/yellow-brown.*	166
	glasshouse red spider mite, red spider mite, two-spotted mite	*Fine webbing. Mottled, pale leaves.*	166
	strawberry spider mite	*Fine webs. Leaves yellowed/shed.*	166
	onion thrips	*Yellow-grey insect. Yellow nymph. Leaves blotched/distorted.*	167
	grass blue butterfly	*Larvae, white then green-pink-brown/white-striped, eat leaves.*	169
	leaf blight, alternaria blight	*Brown spots on leaves.*	173
	foot and root rot, black root rot	*Stem bases brown-black; leaves discoloured; die-back.*	174
	ascochyta blight	*Dark spots on leaves/stems.*	176
	pea pod spot	*Sunken, dark patches on leaves/stems/pods.*	176
	anthracnose	*Yellow/brown/purple spots on stems/leaves.*	180
	anthracnose (beans)	*Black-red-brown patches on pods/stems. Leaf veins blacken. Under glass, spots can be white encrusted.*	181
	bulb and stem nematode	*New leaves distorted, raised, yellow section. Pale streaks on stems/ flowers; distortion.*	185
	powdery mildew	*Grey-white powder on plants; young leaves distorted/shed.*	188
	fusarium wilt (dwarf, runner)	*Wilting; leaves yellow. Brown sunken lesions at base of stem; pink fungus; red-brown streaks in cut stem at base.*	192
	angular leaf spot (French)	*Angular, rounded spots on leaves; dark sunken patches on pods.*	200
	halo blight (dwarf, French, runner)	*Irregular angular, pale-edged spots on leaves. Lesions on stems/pods.*	205

Purple French (green) beans

'Achievement' runner beans

'Painted Lady' runner beans

Dwarf French beans

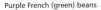

PLANT	PROBLEM	SYMPTOMS/DESCRIPTION	PAGE
Phaseolus coccineus **runner bean**	halo blight of beans (French, runner)	*Young plants yellow; angular spots on leaves; watery-greasy spots on pods/stems; white slime.*	206
P. lunatus **lima bean**	bacterial brown spot (French)	*Small, brown-red spots on leaves; dry out. Sunken brown spots on pods.*	207
P. vulgaris **French bean**	collar rot, rhizoctonia disease (French)	*Reddish sunken areas at base of stems.*	211
	sclerotium stem rot, southern blight	*Leaves yellow; watery lesions at base of plants; white growth.*	212
	bean rust	*Pale yellow spots above leaves; blisters below; blisters on pods.*	217
	verticillium wilt	*Wilting; leaves curl, yellow; die-back.*	218
	summer death of beans (French)	*Stunting, yellowing, sudden death.*	222
	bean mosaic, pea early browning virus	*Leaves yellow-mottled, brown; stems streaked yellow.*	222
	beet curly top	*Leaves crinkled; veins swollen; yellowing.*	223
	clover stunt virus, leaf roll, top yellows	*Plants small, upright, yellowish. Older leaves thickened.*	223
	failure to set fruit (runner)	*Plants flower but fruit not set.*	236
Philadelphus **mock orange**	blackfly	*Tiny flies on young growth; leaves curl.*	116
Phlomis **phlomis**	leafhoppers	*Yellow adults, white nymphs. Pale dotted leaves.*	144
Phlox **phlox**	phlox eelworm	*Nematode. Plants distorted/discoloured.*	130
	swift moth caterpillars	*Large white caterpillars feed on roots.*	139
	leafy gall	*Mass of abortive, distorted shoots at base.*	182
	splitting of stems	*Stems split.*	238
Photinia **photinia**	fireblight	*Leaves brown; wither. Shoots die back and cankers appear.*	186
Picea **spruce**	conifer red spider mites, spruce spider mite	*Green mite, red eggs. Webbing; leaves discoloured.*	149
	sirex wasp	*Blue female, blue/orange male. Larvae tunnel in wood.*	162
	stem canker	*Red fungus on dead wood; die-back.*	198
Pinus **pine**	woolly adelgid	*Some yellowing of foliage.*	113
	emperor gum moth (Monterey pine)	*Large green caterpillars chew leaves.*	150
	pine adelgid, woolly pine aphid	*Aphid. Woolly secretion; die-back.*	158
	sirex wasp	*Blue female, blue/orange male. Larvae tunnel in wood.*	162
	conifer rusts	*Yellow blisters on swollen stems; powdery orange spores.*	182
	shoot blight	*Needles yellow, then brown. Deformed growth.*	184
Pisum sativum **pea**	striped cucumber beetle	*Larvae eat roots, adults eat topgrowth.*	112
	bean weevil	*White grubs eat holes in pods/seeds.*	112
	garden webworm	*Brown moths' green-black caterpillars eat leaves, spin webs.*	112
	silver Y moth	*Green/white caterpillars eat flowers/leaves.*	118
	bean leaf beetle	*Orange-yellow adults eat leaves, grubs eat roots/stems.*	122
	pea moth	*Cream-white caterpillars eat peas inside pods.*	127
	blister beetles	*Various beetles eat leaves/pods.*	131
	field cricket	*Brown-black insect chews seedlings/leaves/flowers/pods.*	138
	budworms	*Moth's caterpillars eat holes in leaves/flowers/pods.*	138

Peas

Phlox

Picea

Pinus

PLANT	PROBLEM	SYMPTOMS/DESCRIPTION	PAGE
Pisum sativum	corn earworm, tomato fruitworm	*Moth's larvae eat plants.*	138
pea	pea thrips	*Black adult, yellow nymph. Pods discoloured/distorted.*	141
	green vegetable bug	*Green-black bug, many coloured nymph. Growth distorted, discoloured.*	148
	stink bugs, earth mites	*Green-brown-grey bugs, evil smell. Distorted growth.*	153
	pea and bean weevil	*Brown beetle eats notches in leaves.*	163
	beet armyworms	*Moth. Green/yellow stripy caterpillars spin webs, eat leaves/stems/roots.*	163
	grass blue butterfly	*Larvae, white then green-pink-brown/white-striped, eat leaves.*	169
	foot and root rot, black root rot	*Stem bases brown-black; leaves discoloured; die-back.*	174
	pea pod spot	*Sunken, dark patches on leaves/stems/pods.*	176
	anthracnose	*Yellow-brown-purplish spots on leaves/stems/pods darkening. Pinkish fungus.*	180
	bulb and stem nematode	*New leaves distorted, raised, yellow section. Pale streaks on stems/ flowers; distortion.*	185
	fusarium wilt	*Plants wilt. Lower leaves turn yellow, plants can die.*	192
	downy mildew	*Leaves yellow above, then brown; grey furry growth below. Cream patches on pods.*	199
	damping off	*Seedlings collapse; blacken, wither.*	202
	bacterial blight	*Watery, darkening spots at stem base. Yellow lesions on leaflets; brown, papery. Dark green-brown spots on pods.*	207
	sclerotium stem rot, southern blight	*Leaves yellow; watery lesions at base of plants; white growth.*	212
	bean mosaic, pea early browning virus	*Leaves yellow-mottled, brown; stems streaked yellow.*	222
	clover stunt virus, leaf roll, top yellows	*Plants small, upright, yellowish. Older leaves thickened.*	223
	manganese deficiency	*Leaves yellow/drop, oldest first.*	249
	marsh spot	*Dark red spot/cavity in centre of peas; yellow between leaf veins.*	247
Pittosporum	pink wax scale	*Pink or grey scales; honeydew attracts sooty mould.*	122
pittosporum	cottonycushion scale	*Brown scale. Honeydew, sooty mould.*	140
Platanus	anthracnose	*Leaves and shoots brown, buds may not open; leaves shed prematurely.*	193
plane			
Platycerium	staghorn fern beetle	*Black/red beetle. Brown-marked fronds.*	137
staghorn fern			
Plumeria	hemispherical scale	*Brown scales. Honeydew, sooty mould.*	161
frangipani			
Polygonatum x *hybridum*	Solomon's seal sawfly	*Black sawfly. Larvae eat leaves.*	156
Solomon's seal			
Polyscias	leaf blight	*Dark brown-black patches on leaves; distortion.*	173
polyscias			
Populus	bacterial canker of poplars	*Large cankers; die-back; creamy slime from cracks.*	175
poplar	silver leaf	*Leaves silver-brown; die-back. Mauve-white-brown brackets on dead wood.*	179
	poplar rust	*Yellow flecks on leaves; browned, shed.*	195

Platanus

Plumeria rubra

Plumeria alba

Polygonatum x hybridum

PLANT	PROBLEM	SYMPTOMS/DESCRIPTION	PAGE
Populus **poplar**	anthracnose yellow leaf blister	*Small brown spots on leaves; distorted, shed. Small dark cankers on shoots.* *Yellow blisters under leaves.*	194 216
Portulaca **purslane**	beet webworm	*Moth. Cream-green caterpillars eat leaves.*	140
Potentilla **potentilla**	red core, red stele	*Wilting, stunting. Leaves discoloured.*	203
Primula **primula**	glasshouse leafhopper foot and root rot, black root rot brown core (primulas) fasciation replant disorder	*Yellow adult, creamy nymph. White dots on leaves.* *Stem bases brown-black; leaves discoloured; die-back.* *Roots die back. Wilting.* *Growth flattened.* *New plantings replacing a similar plant fail to thrive.*	138 174 204 238 245
Prunus spp. **ornamental cherry**	pear and cherry slugworm caterpillar, 　pear and cherry slug blossom wilt bacterial canker brown rot of stone fruit leaf curl, peach leaf curl fasciation gumming	*Sawfly. Dark green larvae eat leaves causing vein network.* *Flowers wither, not shed. Leaves shrivel; die-back.* *Flat, elongated lesions on branches; sticky gum. Next year, bud* 　*distorted; leaves spotted/holes.* *Flowers turn brown, die. Fungi can cause die-back.* 　*Brown spots on fruit skin.* *Leaves pucker, thicken, curl; red blisters; pale fungal spores.* *Growth flattened.* *Beads of resin exuded from stems/fruits.*	120 196 206 211 215 238 248
Prunus armeniaca **apricot**	fruittree leafroller cup moths frosted scale emperor gum moth elephant weevil San Jose scale peachtree borers freckle brown rot bacterial canker shot hole leaf curl, peach leaf curl plum rust, peach rust plum pox, sharka	*Moth's green caterpillars eat plant parts, roll up in leaves.* *Cup-shaped cocoons. Spiny larvae eat leaves.* *Brown, white-coated scale. Honeydew, sooty mould.* *Large green caterpillars chew leaves.* *Grey-black adult. Larvae tunnel in trunks/roots.* *Well-camouflaged scale. Rough texture; fruits damaged* *Yellow-orange banded moth. Larvae bore base of trees/roots.* *Cream-pale green-black spots on fruits; cracking. Spots on leaves;* 　*black lesions on twigs.* *Small brown spots on petals/stems/fruits. Brown mould. Sunken* 　*brown cankers on twigs. Fruits rot; rings of grey spores.* *Die-back, brown spots on leaves; dark, sunken spots on fruits.* *Small brown spots/holes on leaves; scabs on fruits, gum; fuits crack;* 　*spots/gum on twigs.* *Leaves puckered/curled; red blisters, pale spores; leaves turn white.* *Yellow spores under leaves.* *Diffuse, pale rings/lines/blotches on leaves; rings/blotches on fruits.*	116 130 134 150 150 160 165 192 196 207 215 215 216 226
Prunus avium **cherry**	fruittree leafroller Fuller's rose weevil	*Moth's green caterpillars eat plant parts, roll up in leaves.* *Grey-brown weevils eat leaves; larvae eat roots.*	116 117

Potentilla

Primula

Prunus sargentii

Apricots

PLANT	PROBLEM	SYMPTOMS/DESCRIPTION	PAGE
Prunus avium **cherry**	pear and cherry slugworm caterpillar pear and cherry slug	*Sawfly. Dark green larvae eat leaves causing vein network.*	120
	plum curculio	*Larvae tunnel into developing fruit. Fruits drop.*	125
	mottled umber moth	*Brown/yellow/striped larvae eat leaves.*	132
	cherry aphid	*Brown-black aphid. New growth yellows/curls. Honeydew, sooty mould.*	147
	cherry fruit flies	*Black flies. Eggs in slits in fruit, maggots eat inside fruits.* *Distortion/early reddening.*	160
	apple maggot	*Black fly, eggs in holes in fruit. Maggots tunnel in fruit.*	161
	buffalo treehopper	*Triangular, green insect. Yellow eggs in slits in bark.*	164
	peachtree borers	*Yellow-orange banded moth. Larvae bore base of trees/roots.*	165
	black knot	*Leaves brown, not shed; shoots/flowers wither. Cankers in autumn,* *exudation in spring. May be red-brown under bark. Roots killed.*	183
	brown rot	*Small brown spots on petals/stems/fruits. Brown mould. Sunken* *brown cankers on twigs. Fruits rot; rings of grey spores.*	196
	bacterial canker	*Flat, elongated lesions on branches; sticky gum. Next year, buds* *distorted; leaves spotted/holes.*	206
	bacterial canker	*Die-back, brown spots on leaves; dark, sunken spots on fruits.*	207
	shot hole	*Small brown spots/holes on leaves; fuits crack; spots/gum on twigs.*	215
	replant disease	*New plantings, replacing a similar plant, fail to thrive.*	216
	tan bark	*Small eruptions on shoots; tan powder; outer bark peels.*	234
	replant disorder	*New plantings replacing a similar plant fail to thrive.*	245
	gumming	*Beads of resin exuded from stems/fruits.*	248
Prunus domestica **plum**	bryobia mite	*Red, then brown-grey mites; white-mottled leaves.*	119
	pear and cherry slugworm caterpillar pear and cherry slug	*Sawfly. Dark green larvae eat leaves causing vein network.*	120
	plum curculio	*Larvae tunnel into developing fruit. Fruits drop.*	125
	apple leafhopper, canary fly	*Yellow cicada-type. Grey-mottled leaves.*	130
	mottled umber moth	*Brown/yellow/striped larvae eat leaves.*	132
	gall mites, rust mites	*Galls on leaves/stems.*	133
	frosted scale	*Brown, white-coated scale. Honeydew, sooty mould.*	134
	plum sawfly	*Larvae tunnel into fruits. Black excreta, fruits drop.*	140
	leafhoppers	*Yellow adults, white nymphs. Pale dotted leaves.*	144
	redshouldered leaf beetle	*Yellow/red beetle eats leaves/flowers/fruits.*	147
	fruit tree red spider mite, European red mite	*Yellow-mottled leaves.*	152
	San Jose scale	*Well-camouflaged scale. Rough texture; fruits damaged.*	160
	cherry fruit flies	*Black flies. Eggs in slits in fruit, maggots eat inside fruits.* *Distortion/early reddening.*	160
	apple maggot	*Black fly, eggs in holes in fruit. Maggots tunnel in fruit.*	161
	peachtree borers	*Yellow-orange banded moth. Larvae bore base of trees/roots.*	165
	plague thrips	*Tiny insect; colourless yellow nymph. Petals browned.*	167
	wasps, hornet, yellow jackets	*Black-yellow striped insects eat holes in fruit.*	169
	silver leaf	*Leaves silver-brown; die-back. Mauve-white-brown* *brackets on dead wood.*	179
	black knot	*Leaves brown, not shed; shoots/flowers wither. Cankers in autumn,* *exudation in spring. May be red-brown under bark. Roots killed.*	183
	bacterial canker (stone fruits)	*Die-back, brown spots on leaves; dark, sunken spots on fruits.*	207

Cherry

Prunus avium

P. avium

PLANT	PROBLEM	SYMPTOMS/DESCRIPTION	PAGE
Prunus domestica **plum**	shot hole	*Small brown spots-holes on leaves; fruits crack; spots/gum on twigs.*	215
	plum rust, peach rust	*Yellow spores under leaves.*	216
	plum pox, sharka	*Diffuse, pale rings/lines/blotches on leaves; rings/blotches on fruits.*	226
	gumming	*Beads of resin exuded from stems/fruits.*	248
Prunus domestica italica **greengage**	shot hole	*Small brown spots-holes on leaves; fruits crack; spots/gum on twigs.*	215
	plum pox, sharka	*Diffuse, pale rings/lines/blotches on leaves; rings/blotches on fruits.*	226
Prunus dulcis **almond**	bryobia mite	*Red, then brown-grey mites; white-mottled leaves.*	119
	oriental fruit moth	*White-pink caterpillars tunnel into shoots.*	137
	San Jose scale	*Well-camouflaged scale. Rough texture.*	160
	brown rot	*Small brown spots on petals/stems. Brown mould. Sunken brown cankers on twigs.*	196
	leaf curl, peach leaf curl	*Leaves pucker/thicken/curl; red blisters, later pale fungal spores. Leaves later turn white and can be shed.*	215
	plum pox, sharka	*Diffuse, pale rings/lines/blotches on leaves.*	226
Prunus persica **peach**	fruitspotting bug	*Green bug, red/black nymph; fruits spotted/shed.*	115
	Fuller's rose weevil	*Grey-brown weevils eat leaves; larvae eat roots.*	117
	inland katydid	*Grasshopper-like. Leaves skeletonized/holed; fruits gnawed.*	120
	soft scale, brown soft scale, soft brown scale	*Yellow-brown scales under leaves. Honeydew, sooty mould.*	124
	yellow peach moth	*Large pink caterpillars tunnel into plants/fruits. Die-back.*	125
	plum curculio	*Larvae tunnel into developing fruit. Fruits drop.*	125
	green June beetle and fig beetle	*Adults eat holes in leaves/fruits. Larvae eat roots.*	126
	frosted scale	*Brown, white-coated scale. Honeydew, sooty mould.*	134
	oriental fruit moth	*White-pink caterpillars tunnel into shoots/fruits.*	137
	periodical cicada	*Slits in bark for eggs.*	144
	redshouldered leaf beetle	*Yellow/red beetle eats leaves/flowers/fruits.*	147
	Rutherglen bug	*Brown bug. Wilting; fruits pitted.*	149
	elephant weevil	*Grey-black adult. Larvae tunnel in trunks/roots.*	150
	San Jose scale	*Well-camouflaged scale. Rough texture; fruits damaged.*	160
	passionvine hopper	*Moth-like adult, green nymph. Leaves/fruits shrivel/drop.*	162
	buffalo treehopper	*Triangular, green insect. Yellow eggs in slits in bark.*	164
	peachtree borers	*Yellow-orange banded moth. Larvae bore base of trees/roots.*	165
	powdery mildew	*Grey-white powder on plants; young leaves distorted/shed.*	188
	freckle	*Cream-pale green-black spots on fruits; cracking. Spots on leaves; black lesions on twigs.*	192
	sooty blotch	*Dark circular, cloudy enlarging patches on fruit skins.*	192
	fly speck	*Small, circular specks on fruit skins; taste unaffected.*	196
	bacterial canker	*Die-back, brown spots on leaves; dark, sunken spots on fruits.*	207
	leaf curl, peach leaf curl	*Leaves pucker, thicken, curl; red blisters; pale fungal spores.*	215
	shot hole	*Small brown spots-holes on leaves; fruits crack; spots/gum on twigs.*	215
	peach rust	*Yellow spores under leaves.*	216
	plum pox, sharka	*Diffuse, pale rings/lines/blotches on leaves; rings/blotches on fruits; new leaves distorted.*	226
	split stone	*Deep cleft in fruits; stone (US pit) split.*	237

Damson plums

Plums

Peaches

PLANT	PROBLEM	SYMPTOMS/DESCRIPTION	PAGE
Prunus persica **peach**	gumming iron deficiency, lime-induced chlorosis	*Beads of resin exuded from stems/fruits.* *Young leaves yellow/scorched.*	248 248
Prunus persica nectarina **nectarine**	fruitspotting bug frosted scale oriental fruit moth peachtree borers freckle bacterial canker shot hole leaf curl, peach leaf curl peach rust plum pox, sharka	*Green bug, red/black nymph; fruits spotted/shed.* *Brown, white-coated scale. Honeydew, sooty mould.* *White-pink caterpillars tunnel into shoots/fruits.* *Yellow-orange banded moth. Larvae bore base of trees/roots.* *Cream-pale green-black spots on fruits; cracking. Spots on leaves;* *black lesions on twigs.* *Die-back, brown spots on leaves; dark, sunken spots on fruits.* *Small brown spots/holes on leaves; fruits crack; spots/gum on twigs.* *Leaves pucker, thicken, curl; red blisters; pale fungal spores.* *Yellow spores under leaves.* *Diffuse, pale rings/lines/blotches on leaves; rings/blotches on fruits.*	115 134 137 165 192 207 215 215 216 226
Prunus triloba **flowering almond**	bacterial canker	*Flat, elongated lesions appear on branches, exuding a sticky gum.*	206
Pseudotsuga **Douglas fir**	woolly adelgid phomopsis disease	*Some yellowing of foliage.* *Die-back. Cankers, small black fungi.*	113 201
Psidium **guava**	fruitspotting bug yellow peach moth cup moths fruitpiercing moths fruit flies	*Green bug, red/black nymph; fruits spotted/shed.* *Large pink caterpillars tunnel into plants/fruits. Die-back.* *Cup-shaped cocoons. Spiny larvae eat leaves.* *Holes in fruit.* *Eggs laid under fruit skin; larvae feed inside fruits. Cracks/spots.*	115 125 130 151 166
Pyracantha **firethorn**	Indian white wax scale white wax scale woolly aphid, woolly apple aphid leaf miners woolly vine scale San Jose scale fireblight scab	*White scales produce honeydew; sooty mould appears.* *White scales produce honeydew.* *Brown aphid, white covering; soft galls.* *Larvae in leaves. Lines/blotches seen.* *Large, oval, brown scales.* *Well-camouflaged scale. Rough texture; fruits damaged.* *Leaves brown; wither. Shoots die back and cankers appear.* *Green-brown patches on leaves; brown-black scabs on fruits.*	122 122 134 142 160 160 186 214
Pyrus communis **pear**	fruittree leafroller bryobia mite pear psylla inland katydid pear and cherry slugworm caterpillar pear and cherry slug soft scale, brown soft scale, soft brown scale plum curculio pear midge green June beetle and fig beetle codling moth	*Moth's green caterpillars eat plant parts, roll up in leaves.* *Red, then brown-grey mites; white-mottled leaves.* *Brown adult, yellow then green nymph. Spotted leaves, scarred fruit.* *Grasshopper-like. Leaves skeletonized/holed; fruits gnawed.* *Sawfly. Dark green larvae eat leaves causing vein network.* *Yellow-brown scales under leaves. Honeydew, sooty mould.* *Larvae tunnel into developing fruit. Fruits drop.* *Orange-white larvae in fruitlets cause swelling/blackening.* *Adults eat holes in leaves/fruits. Larvae eat roots.* *White-pink caterpillars tunnel into fruits. White excreta.*	116 119 120 120 120 124 125 125 126 127

Guava

Pseudotsuga

Pyracantha

Pears

PLANT	PROBLEM	SYMPTOMS/DESCRIPTION	PAGE
Pyrus communis **pear**	mottled umber moth	*Brown/yellow/striped larvae eat leaves.*	132
	gall mites, rust mites	*Galls on leaves/stems.*	133
	pearleaf blister mite	*Discoloured blisters on leaves, spotted/distorted fruits.*	133
	woolly aphid, woolly apple aphid	*Brown aphid, white covering; soft galls.*	134
	oriental fruit moth	*White-pink caterpillars tunnel into shoots/fruits.*	137
	budworms	*Moth's caterpillars eat holes in leaves/flowers/fruits.*	138
	fruit-tree root weevil	*Adults eat young growth. Leaves folded. Larvae eat roots.*	142
	periodical cicada	*Slits in bark for eggs.*	144
	tent caterpillars	*Black, white striped/spotted caterpillars eat leaves, make webs.*	144
	fruit tree red spider mite, European red mite	*Yellow-mottled leaves.*	152
	pearleaf blister mite	*Pink-red pustules on unfurled leaves. Yellow/red/green blisters on both leaf surfaces, turn brown, then black. Leaf dies.*	157
	pear sucker	*Green-brown insect. Petals browned. Honeydew, sooty mould.*	160
	San Jose scale	*Well-camouflaged scale. Rough texture; fruits damaged.*	160
	cherry fruit flies	*Black flies. Eggs in slits in fruit, maggots eat inside fruits. Distortion.*	160
	buffalo treehopper	*Triangular, green insect. Yellow eggs in slits in bark.*	164
	apple curculio	*Brown-red weevil. Larvae tunnel in fruits; scarred, dropped.*	165
	plague thrips	*Tiny insect; colourless yellow nymph. Petals browned.*	167
	wasps, hornet, yellow jackets	*Black-yellow striped insects eat holes in fruit.*	169
	leopard moth	*White/black-spotted moth. Black-spotted larvae tunnel into wood.*	169
	quince leaf blight, fleck	*Small, irregular spots on leaves, red then black.*	184
	powdery mildew	*Grey-white powder on plants; young leaves distorted/shed.*	188
	sooty blotch	*Dark circular, cloudy enlarging patches on fruit skins.*	192
	bitter rot	*Small brown spots on fruit skins, spots enlarge in rings, rotting.*	192
	brown rots	*Small brown spots on petals/stems/fruits. Brown mould. Sunken, brown cankers on twigs. Fruits rot, rings of grey spores.*	196
	flyspeck	*Small, circular, cloudy enlarging patches on fruit skins.*	196
	apple canker	*Sunken, elliptical patches on bark; shoots girdled. White spores, red fungus.*	198
	brown rot of stone fruit	*Flowers brown, die. Fungi can cause die-back. Brown spots on fruit skin.*	211
	apple scab	*Brown blotches on leaves; rough, corky patches on fruits.*	218
	stony pit	*Bark cracked; fruits distorted/hard.*	226
	cracked fruits	*Cropping is impaired.*	234
	June drop	*Small fruits drop.*	244
	boron deficiency	*Fruits distorted, brown patches within; bark rough; leaves distorted; die-back.*	246
Q *Quercus* **oak**	gall wasps	*Galls on all parts of tree. Spots on leaves.*	127
	mottled umber moth	*Brown/yellow/striped larvae eat leaves.*	132
	periodical cicada	*Slits in bark for eggs.*	144
	angle shades moth	*Green-brown caterpillars eat flowers/leaves.*	154
	oak leafminer	*Fine lines/blisters on leaves.*	155
	sudden oak death	*Dark red-black sap from lesions on trunk.*	204

Pears

Pear blossom

Quercus

Quercus

PLANT	PROBLEM	SYMPTOMS/DESCRIPTION	PAGE
R			
Raphanus sativus **radish**	cabbage root fly and maggots, cabbage maggot	*Green fly. Maggots tunnel into roots and stems.*	128
	vegetable weevil	*Brown beetle. Cream-green larvae. Base of plants and roots eaten.*	142
	calico back bug	*Red/black beetle. White/yellow blotched leaves; wilting.*	147
	flea beetles	*Dry areas on leaves; seedlings killed.*	156
	small cabbage white butterfly, cabbage white butterfly imported cabbageworm	*Green/yellow caterpillars eat leaves.*	157
	white blister, white rust	*White blisters/rings on leaves. Stunting/distortion.*	172
	black root	*Black patches on roots; splitting.*	174
	downy mildew	*White, mealy-furry growths under leaves; pale green-yellow-brown above.*	178
	common scab, potato scab	*Corky lesions on roots.*	215
Rhaphiolepis x *delacourii* *R. indica* **Indian hawthorn**	Indian hawthorn leaf spot	*Grey, brown-edged spots on leaves; yellow-red, dropped.*	186
Rheum raphonticum **rhubarb**	harlequin bug	*Large black/red bug. Frass. Plants wilt, can die.*	130
	potato leafhopper	*Green insect, pale nymph. Leaves spotted/distorted/rolled.*	131
	grapevine hawk moth	*Large green-black caterpillars chew leaves.*	139
	passionvine hopper	*Moth-like adult, green nymph. Leaves shrivel/drop.*	162
	crown gall	*Large galls on tree roots; small, soft galls on shrubs.*	172
	leaf spot	*Small, round, brown spots on leaves/stalks. Spots enlarge.*	176
	crown rot	*Buds rot; soft brown rot in crown.*	188
	downy mildew	*Irregular, spreading, brown patches above leaves; furry growth below.*	199
	rhubarb leaf spot	*Irregular brown spots on leaves fall away to leave holes.*	210
	sclerotium stem rot, southern blight	*Leaves yellow; watery lesions at base of plants; white growth.*	212
Rhododendron **(azalea varieties)** **azalea**	azalea leafminer	*Moth's caterpillars cause white streaks, brown patches, curled/webbed leaf tips.*	120
	cyclamen mite	*Mite inside buds, under leaves. Discoloration/distortion.*	157
	azalea gall, leaf gall	*Young leaves/buds pale, (redden), swell. Small galls; spores turn white/waxy, then brown, then shrivel.*	189
Rhododendron **rhododendron**	rhododendron whitefly	*Tiny flies under leaves; green nymphs. Honeydew, sooty mould.*	129
	rhododendron leafhoppers	*Turquoise/red adult, green nymph.*	136
	azalea whitefly	*White adult, green nymph. Honeydew, sooty mould.*	152
	azalea lace bug	*Black beetle. Nymphs feed under leaves; brown excreta.*	164
	rhododendron lace bug	*Brown bug feeds under leaves. Yellow/brown mottling.*	164
	silver leaf	*Leaves silver-brown; die-back. Mauve-white-brown brackets on wood.*	179
	azalea gall, leaf gall	*Young leaves/buds pale, (redden), swell. Small galls; spores turn white/waxy, then brown, then shrivel.*	189
	petal blight	*White-brown spots on petals; slimy, then dry; not shed.*	198
	sudden oak death	*Shoots discolour; leaves spotted; die-back.*	204
	green algae	*Thick green deposit on leaves.*	205
	rhododendron bud blast	*Flower buds brown-black-silver; black bristly spores.*	209

Rhaphiolepis indica

Rhubarb

Rhododendron

PLANT	PROBLEM	SYMPTOMS/DESCRIPTION	PAGE
Rhododendron	frost damage	*Petals brown-edged; bark cracks.*	233
rhododendron	iron deficiency, lime-induced chlorosis	*Young leaves yellow/scorched.*	248
Ribes nigrum	magpie moth caterpillar	*White/black/yellow caterpillars eat leaves.*	112
blackcurrants	big bud mite, currant bud mite	*Rounded, swollen buds in winter.*	121
R. rubrum	currant blister aphid	*Yellow aphid causes blisters, red/yellow leaves.*	126
red currants	gooseberry sawfly caterpillar	*Green/spotted caterpillars eat leaves.*	148
R. sativum	woolly vine scale	*Large, oval, brown scales.*	160
white currants	currant clearwing moth, currant borer moth	*Larvae feed inside stems. Small, yellow leaves; pupal cases appear.*	165
	leaf nematode (blackcurrants)	*Yellow-brown patches on leaves.*	175
	silver leaf	*Leaves silver-brown; die-back. Mauve-white-brown brackets on wood.*	179
	conifer rusts (blackcurrant bushes)	*Yellow blisters on swollen stems; powdery orange spores.*	182
	coral spot	*Die-back; pink-red, cushion-like pustules.*	198
	blackcurrant leaf spot	*Angular, grey, purple-edged spots on leaves.*	213
	American gooseberry mildew (blackcurrants)	*White, powdery patches on young growth/fruits; browning, distortion.*	214
	potassium deficiency	*Leaves bluish, brown spots/tips; curl downwards.*	249
Ribes uva-crispa	magpie moth caterpillar	*White/black/yellow caterpillars eat leaves.*	112
gooseberry	gooseberry sawfly caterpillar	*Green/spotted caterpillars eat leaves.*	148
	woolly vine scale	*Large, oval, brown scales.*	160
	currant clearwing moth, currant borer moth	*Larvae feed inside stems. Small, yellow leaves; pupal cases appear.*	165
	American gooseberry mildew	*White, powdery patches on young growth/fruits; browning, distortion.*	214
	scald (gooseberries)	*Depressed white patches on fruits.*	242
Rosa	greenfly	*Tiny green flies on shoot tips, under leaves.*	113
rose	California red scale, red scale	*Orange-pink scale; die-back, leaves shed.*	116
	scurfy scale, rose scale	*Grey-white scale on stems.*	117
	leaf-rolling rose sawfly	*Rolled leaves. Green caterpillars emerge, eat leaves.*	118
	rose leafhopper	*Yellow insect, white nymphs, under leaves. Pale leaf mottling.*	130
	rose slugworm larva	*Green caterpillars eat underside of leaves.*	131
	budworm	*Moth's caterpillars eat holes in leaves/flowers.*	138
	cottony cushion scale	*Brown scale. Honeydew, sooty mould.*	140
	capsid bugs	*Green insects eat young leaves. Growth distorted.*	143
	leaf-cutting bee	*Round holes in leaves.*	146
	redshouldered leaf beetle	*Yellow/red beetle eats leaves/flowers.*	147
	fruit tree red spider mite, European red mite	*Yellow-mottled leaves.*	152
	glasshouse red spider mite, red spider mite, two-spotted mite	*Fine webbing. Mottled, pale leaves.*	166
	rose thrips	*Brown-streaked petals, distorted flowers.*	167
	crown gall	*Small, soft galls.*	172
	canker	*Brown patches on shoots; die-back. Cankers near ground swelling, cracking, white spores, red fungus.*	180
	rose canker	*Die-back from pruning cuts. Pale yellow-red spots on stems/cracking.*	182
	black spot	*Round, brown-black spots on leaves; yellowing.*	184
	powdery mildew	*Grey-white powder on plants; young leaves distorted/shed.*	188
	root knot nematodes	*Galls/scabby lesions/swellings on roots. Stunting, wilting.*	196

Gooseberries

White currants

Rosa

PLANT	PROBLEM	SYMPTOMS/DESCRIPTION	PAGE
Rosa **rose**	downy mildew	*Purple-red-dark brown spots on leaves; furry growth below.* *Stems split; flowers browned, distorted.*	199
	rust	*Orange patches on stems. Yellow spots above leaves; orange pustules* *below, turning brown-black.*	201
	anthracnose	*Small, enlarging black spots on leaves.*	214
	mosaic	*Yellow blotches/lines on leaves.*	225
	rose wilt	*Young leaves curled, older leaves droop/yellow; die-back.* *Purplish blotches on stems.*	226
	capping	*Flower buds fail to open fully.*	235
	proliferation	*Stems grow through open flowers; further flowers/buds.*	239
	pedicel necrosis	*Flower stalks blacken; buds brown.*	240
	dumpy bud	*Buds fail to open, or flowers flattened.*	241
	hormone weedkiller damage	*Check in growth.*	243
	replant disorder	*New plantings replacing a similar plant fail to thrive.*	245
	potassium deficiency	*Leaves bluish, brown spots/tips; curl downwards.*	249
	magnesium deficiency	*Leaves yellow, oldest first, later orange-red, drop.*	249
Rubus fruticosus **blackberry, bramble** *R. idaeus* **raspberry** *R. loganobaccus* **loganberry**	Fuller's rose weevil (blackberries)	*Grey-brown weevils eat leaves; larvae eat roots.*	117
	raspberry beetles	*Brown adult; pale brown larvae damage fruit.*	119
	leafhoppers	*Yellow adults, white nymphs. Pale dotted leaves.*	144
	strawberry root weevils (raspberries)	*Brown-black adults eat leaves/stalks; larvae eat roots.*	151
	fruit tree red spider mite, European red mite (raspberries)	*Yellow-mottled leaves.*	152
	bramble sawfly (loganberries, blackberries)	*Larvae eat leaves.*	154
	leaf and bud mites (raspberries, blackberries)	*Yellow blotches on leaves.*	155
	raspberry sawfly (raspberries, blackberries)	*Black adult; yellow/brown/white-striped larvae eat leaves.*	159
	currant clearwing moth, currant borer moth	*Larvae feed inside stems. Small, yellow leaves; pupal cases appear.*	165
	glasshouse red spider mite, red spider mite, two-spotted mite	*Fine webbing. Mottled, pale leaves.*	166
	plague thrips	*Tiny insect; colourless yellow nymph. Petals browned.*	167
	crown gall (blackberries, brambles)	*Small, soft galls.*	172
	grey mould	*Pale/silvery stems, velvety grey growths; grey-brown fluff on fruits/* *stems/leaves.*	177
	anthracnose	*Yellow-brown-purplish spots on leaves/stems/fruit; darkening.* *Pinkish fungus.*	180
	spur blight (raspberries, loganberries)	*Blotches on canes, purple-brown; then silver; tiny black growths.*	183
	cane spot, anthracnose	*On canes, small purple spots, then oval, purple-edged; pits/cankers;* *bark killed; spots on leaves/fruits.*	186
	cane blight	*Dark patches at base of canes; brittle; leaves wither.*	194
	raspberry rust	*Orange pustules above leaves; later, orange patches below.*	201
	iron deficiency, lime-induced chlorosis	*Young leaves yellow/scorched.*	248

S

Saccharum officinarum **sugar cane**	banana weevil borer, banana root borer	*Black weevil. Larvae tunnel through roots. Rotting, wilting.*	125

Rosa   Blackberries   Raspberries

PLANT	PROBLEM	SYMPTOMS/DESCRIPTION	PAGE
Saintpaulia **African violet**	glasshouse thrips, greenhouse thrips	*Yellow-brown insects. Leaves/petals spotted/discoloured.*	138
	tarsenomid mite, Michaelmas daisy mite, strawberry mite	*Mite inside buds. Scarring/distortion.*	156
	cyclamen mite	*Mite inside buds, under leaves. Discoloration/distortion.*	157
	leaf nematodes	*Yellow-brown patches on leaves.*	175
	ring pattern	*Large yellow rings on leaves.*	242
Salix **willow**	California red scale, red scale	*Orange-pink scale; die-back, leaves shed.*	116
	willow scale	*Vigour is reduced; dieback can occur.*	123
	katydids	*Grasshopper-like. Leaves eaten.*	146
	San Jose scale	*Well-camouflaged scale, rough texture.*	160
	silver leaf	*Leaves silver-brown; die-back. Mauve-white-brown brackets on dead wood.*	179
	anthracnose	*Small brown spots on leaves; distorted, shed. Small dark cankers on shoots.*	194
Salvia **salvia**	leafhoppers	*Yellow adults, white nymphs. Pale dotted leaves.*	144
Schefflera arboricola *S. actinophylla* **Queensland umbrella tree**	soft scale, brown soft scale, soft brown scale	*Yellow-brown scales under leaves. Honeydew, sooty mould.*	124
	leaf blight	*Pale spots on leaves; distortion.*	173
Schinus molle **Californian pepper-tree**	emperor gum moth	*Large green caterpillars chew leaves.*	150
Scorzonera hispanica **scorzonera**	white blister, white rust	*White blisters/rings on leaves. Stunting/distortion.*	172
Sedum **sedum**	waterlogging	*Leaves discoloured/die-back.*	232
	crown rot	*Crowns soft, slimy.*	234
Senecio **cineraria**	cineraria leafminer	*Small black fly. Larvae inside leaves cause silver lines, wilting.*	123
	chrysanthemum leaf miner grub	*Fly. Maggots inside leaves; discoloration.*	156
	English marigold rust	*Pale green-yellow spots on leaves/stems; small "cups" on leaves.*	208
Solanaceae	Colorado beetle, Colorado potato beetle	*Orange/black adults and larvae eat leaves.*	141
	potato moth, potato tuberworm	*Larvae mine leaves/stems/tubers/fruits.*	155
	flea beetles	*Dry areas on leaves; seedlings killed.*	156
	target spot	*Brown-black spots/rings on leaves.*	174
	ascochyta blight	*Dark spots on leaves/stems.*	176
	late blight, tomato blight	*Yellow-brown patches on leaves; leaves/stems blacken, rot. White threads, under leaves. Red-brown rot inside tubers.*	203
	powdery scab, corky scab	*Brown blisters on tubers; brown spores.*	215
	potato mosaic	*Leaves mottled/spotted yellow-green; crinkled; black veins.*	222
	leaf roll	*Leaves curl; plants stunted, stiff upright. Brown-black netting inside tubers.*	224

Salix

Salvia

Sedum

PLANT	PROBLEM	SYMPTOMS/DESCRIPTION	PAGE
Solanaceae	pepino mosaic virus	*Leaves distorted, mosaic pattern; lower leaves darker, yellow spots; fruits marbled.*	226
	tobacco ring spot, bouquet disease, tomato ring spot, bud blight	*Stunting, distortion; small brown-yellow, raised rings/circles on leaves/fruits.*	226
Solanum melongena **aubergine (eggplant)**	tomato russet mite	*Leaves grey-brown; stems brown; leaves, flowers shed.*	113
	flea beetle, leaf beetle, striped flea beetle	*Adults eat holes in leaves; larvae eat roots.*	123
	beet leafhopper	*Green-brown adult, green nymph, spread viruses.*	124
	potato leafhopper	*Green insect, pale nymph. Leaves spotted/distorted/rolled.*	131
	Colorado beetle, Colorado potato beetle	*Orange/black adults and larvae eat leaves.*	141
	tomato hornworm	*Large moth. Green/black-horned caterpillars eat leaves/fruits.*	145
	broad mite	*Distortion, discoloration; buds shed.*	158
	fruit flies	*Eggs laid under fruit skin; larvae feed inside fruits. Cracks/spots.*	166
	spider mites	*Fine webbing. Leaves speckled/yellow-brown.*	166
	target spot	*Brown-black spots/rings on leaves.*	174
	verticillium wilt	*Wilting; leaves curl, yellow; die-back.*	218
Solanum tuberosum **potato**	tomato russet mite	*Leaves grey-brown; stems brown; leaves shed.*	113
	wireworm	*Adults chew leaves; larvae tunnel in tuberous roots.*	114
	metallic flea beetle	*Irregular holes in young leaves, buds.*	114
	spotted cucumber beetle, Southern corn rootworms	*Yellow/black beetle chews leaves. Long, thin larvae eat roots/crowns.*	128
	potato leafhopper	*Green insect, pale nymph. Leaves spotted/distorted/rolled.*	131
	leafeating ladybird	*Yellow-spotted beetle. Spiny larvae eat below leaves.*	131
	blister beetles	*Various beetles eat leaves.*	131
	snails and slugs	*Holes eaten in tubers.*	135
	loopers and semi-looper	*Holes are chewed in leaves.*	136
	potato cyst eelworm	*Cysts on roots. Leaves yellowed from base up.*	136
	whitefringed weevil	*Grey-black/white adult; larvae eat roots/tubers.*	137
	corn earworm, tomato fruitworm	*Moth's larvae eat plants.*	138
	Colorado beetle, Colorado potato beetle	*Orange/black adults and larvae eat leaves.*	141
	lily beetle, lily leaf beetle	*Red adults and larvae eat leaves.*	142
	leaf miners	*Larvae in leaves. Lines/blotches seen.*	142
	tomato hornworm	*Large moth. Green/black-horned caterpillars eat leaves.*	145
	green vegetable bug	*Green-black bug, many-coloured nymph. Growth distorted/discoloured.*	148
	Rutherglen bug	*Brown bug. Wilting.*	149
	European corn borer	*Moth. Grey-pink caterpillars chew leaves.*	150
	potato moth, potato tuberworm	*Larvae mine leaves/stems/tubers.*	155
	June beetle, May beetle	*Adults eat leaves, grubs eat roots.*	156
	flea beetles	*Dry areas on leaves; seedlings killed.*	156
	bulb mite	*Globular, yellow-white mite. Bulbs destroyed.*	161
	beet armyworm	*Moth. Green/yellow stripy caterpillars spin webs, eat leaves/stems/roots.*	163
	fall armyworm	*Moth. Green-brown-black/yellow-striped caterpillars eat leaves.*	163
	false wireworm	*Beetles. Shiny brown-yellow larvae eat underground/ ground-level plant parts.*	166
	onion thrips	*Yellow-grey insect. Yellow nymph. Leaves blotched/distorted.*	167
	target spot	*Brown-black spots/rings on leaves; tubers pitted.*	174

Aubergine (eggplant)

Potatoes

'Alisa' potatoes

'Ambo' potatoes

PLANT	PROBLEM	SYMPTOMS/DESCRIPTION	PAGE
Solanum tuberosum **potato**	bacterial ring rot of potato	*Wilting, late in season. Cut stems exude cream liquid. Tubers rot.*	180
	bacterial soft rot	*Small, watery spots on leaves/roots/stored crops. Spots enlarge, slimy; tissue softens, liquefies.*	187
	bacterial soft rot, blackleg	*Black lesions at base of stem; lower leaves yellow-brown, drop. Stems collapse; dark slime. Erect growth.*	187
	violet root rot	*Violet, web-like strands on roots; roots die.*	193
	root knot nematodes	*Galls/scabby lesions/swellings on roots/tubers. Stunting, wilting.*	196
	big bud, greening, virescence	*Unnaturally bushy growth.*	197
	purple top wilt	*Young leaves curled; stems collapse.*	197
	gangrene	*Round, brown depressions on stored tubers; enlarged; rotting, hollowing.*	200
	late blight, tomato blight	*Yellow-brown patches on leaves; leaves/stems blacken, rot. White threads under leaves. Red-brown rot inside tubers.*	203
	rhizoctonia scab	*Shoots rot; red-yellow areas on leaves; distortion. Tubers cracked/distorted; black lumps.*	210
	sclerotium stem rot, southern blight	*Leaves yellow; watery lesions at base of plants; white growth.*	212
	powdery scab, corky scab	*Brown blisters on tubers; brown spores.*	215
	common scab, potato scab	*Corky lesions on roots.*	215
	verticillium wilt	*Wilting; leaves curl, yellow; die-back.*	218
	potato mosaic	*Leaves mottled/spotted yellow-green; crinkled; black veins.*	222
	leaf roll	*Leaves curl; plant stunted, stiff upright. Brown-black netting inside tubers.*	224
	tobacco ring spot, bouquet disease, tomato ring spot, bud blight	*Stunting, distortion; small brown-yellow, raised rings/circles on leaves.*	226
	spraing, tobacco rattle virus, potato mop-top virus	*Red-brown lesions inside tubers.*	227
	cracks	*Cracks in tubers; holes inside.*	234
	blackening	*Flesh blackens, often after cooking.*	248
	potassium deficiency	*Leaves bluish, brown spots/tips; curl downwards.*	249
Sorbus **rowan/mountain ash**	pearleaf blister mite	*Discoloured blisters on leaves, spotted/distorted fruits.*	133
	leopard moth	*White/black-spotted moth. Black-spotted larvae tunnel into wood.*	169
	conifer rusts	*Horn-like gelatinous masses of orange spores on swollen shoots.*	182
	fireblight	*Leaves brown; wither. Shoots die back and cankers appear.*	186
Sorghum **sorghum**	southwestern corn borer	*Large moth. White/spotted caterpillars eat leaves, bore into stalks.*	129
	corn leaf blight (southern)	*Small, pale spots; long, narrow, brown-edged lesions; black spores.*	176
	corn leaf blight (northern)	*Long, grey-green lesions on leaves, from base up. Lesions turn tan; drying. Dark green-black spores.*	189
Spinacia oleracea **spinach**	root aphid	*Grey-white aphid attacks near soil level; poor growth.*	115
	beet leafhopper	*Green-brown adult, green nymph, spread viruses.*	124
	celery leaf miner	*Fly; maggots inside leaves. Discoloured patches, stunted growth.*	134
	leaf miners	*Larvae in leaves. Lines/blotches seen.*	142
	vegetable weevil	*Brown beetle. Cream-green larvae. Base of plants and roots eaten.*	142
	green vegetable bug	*Green-black bug, many-coloured nymph. Growth distorted/discoloured.*	148
	fall armyworm	*Moth. Green-brown-black/yellow-striped caterpillars eat leaves.*	163
	cabbage looper	*Moth. Green pale-striped caterpillars eat leaves.*	168
	cucumber mosaic virus	*Stunting, distortion; yellow mosaic pattern on leaves.*	224

'Arran Victory' potatoes

'Centennial Russet' potatoes

Sorbus

Spinach

PLANT	PROBLEM	SYMPTOMS/DESCRIPTION	PAGE
Spinacia oleracea **spinach**	tobacco ring spot, bouquet disease, tomato ring spot, bud blight	*Stunting, distortion; small brown-yellow, raised rings/circles on leaves.*	226
Streptocarpus **Cape primrose**	glasshouse thrips, greenhouse thrips	*Yellow-brown insects. Leaves/petals spotted/discoloured.*	138
Syringa **lilac**	privet thrips	*Thin, black or yellow insect. Leaves turn dull/brown.*	128
	leaf-cutting bees	*Round holes in leaves.*	146
	Australian privet hawk moth	*Green/lilac/white, spined caterpillars eat leaves.*	159
	leopard moth	*White/black-spotted moth. Black-spotted larvae tunnel into wood.*	169
	lilac blight, bacterial leaf spot	*Angular, brown watery spots on leaves/stems. Shoots blacken.*	207

T

PLANT	PROBLEM	SYMPTOMS/DESCRIPTION	PAGE
Tanacetum coccineum **pyrethrum**	pedicel necrosis	*Flower stalks blacken; buds brown.*	240
Telopea **waratah**	macadamia cup moth	*Yellow-striped, oval larvae eat leaves.*	145
Thuja **arborvitae**	conifer red spider mites, spruce spider mite	*Green mite; red eggs. Webbing; leaves discoloured.*	149
Thuja plicata **western red cedar**	thuja blight	*Needles brown; brown-black fungus. Needles drop.*	183
Tigridia **tiger flower**	gladiolus thrips	*Brown-black insect, yellow nymph. Leaves mottled, flowers flecked; stored corms attacked.*	167
Tilia **lime**	gall mites, rust mites	*Galls on leaves/stems.*	133
	nail gall mite	*Red galls on leaves.*	134
Tragopogon porrifolius **salsify**	white blister, white rust	*White blisters/rings on leaves. Stunting/distortion.*	172
Tristania conferta **brush box**	*see Lophostemon confertus*		123 186
Trollius **globeflower**	smut	*Blisters on leaves/stems; black spores.*	218
Tropaeolum **nasturtium**	blackfly	*Tiny flies on young growth; leaves curl.*	116
	cineraria leafminer	*Small black fly. Larvae inside leaves cause silver lines, wilting.*	123
	cabbage white butterfly, large white butterfly	*Yellow/black caterpillars eat leaves.*	157
	small cabbage white butterfly, cabbage white butterfly, imported cabbageworm	*Green/yellow caterpillars eat leaves.*	157

Spinach

Tilia

Tilia

PLANT	PROBLEM	SYMPTOMS/DESCRIPTION	PAGE
Tulipa **tulip**	snails and slugs	*Bulbs eaten.*	135
	bulb mite	*Globular, yellow-white mite. Bulbs destroyed.*	161
	tulip fire	*Leaf tips "scorched", grey mould. Brown spots on leaves/flowers. Black* *fungus on bulbs/rotting.*	178
	bulb and stem nematode	*White-purplish marks at top of stem before flowering. Grey/shiny* *brown patches on bulbs.*	185
	blue mould, soft rot	*Red-brown sunken patches on stored bulbs; blue mould, rotting.*	198
	grey bulb rot	*Dry, grey rot from tip of bulb; black fungus in soil.*	211
	tulip breaking virus	*Flowers streaked; leaves yellow-streaked, tattered.*	227
	chalkiness and hardness of bulbs	*Dormant bulbs in storage harden.*	243

U

Ulmus **elm**	Dutch elm disease	*Rapid death.*	178

V

Vaccinium corymbosum var. *ashei* **blueberry**	plum curculio	*Larvae tunnel into developing fruits. Fruits drop.*	125
	vine weevil, black vine weevil	*Black weevil. Grubs eat roots.*	151
	apple maggot	*Black fly, eggs in holes in fruit. Maggots tunnel in fruit.*	161
	azalea gall, leaf gall	*Young leaves/buds pale, (redden), swell. Small galls; spores turn* *white/waxy, then brown, then shrivel.*	189
	tobacco ring spot	*Stunting, distortion; brown-yellow, raised rings/circles on leaves/fruits.*	226
Viburnum **viburnum**	blackfly	*Tiny flies on young growth, leaves curl.*	116
	oleander scale, ivy scale	*White-brownish circular scales.*	117
	white palm scale	*Scales under leaves. Yellow blotches.*	154
	crown gall	*Small, soft galls.*	172
	sudden oak death	*Wilting from base up. Die-back.*	204
	papery bark	*Bark thin, peels.*	235
Vicia faba **broad (fava) bean**	bean weevil	*Pear-shaped olive-brown insect lays eggs. Small white grubs.*	112
	garden webworm	*Moth. Larvae spin webs and chew holes in leaves.*	112
	blackfly	*Tiny flies on young growth; leaves curl.*	116
	bean leaf beetle	*Orange-yellow adults eat leaves, grubs eat roots/stems.*	122
	bean root aphid	*Brown aphid feeds on roots. White powder.*	163
	chocolate spot	*Chocolate brown spots/streaks/patches on leaves/stems. Blackening.*	178
	clover stunt virus, leaf roll, top yellows	*Plants small, upright, yellowish. Older leaves thickened.*	223
	broad bean wilt	*Tips blacken; base/roots black, rotted. Leaves mottled/curled.*	223
Vignis sinensis **cow pea**	Mexican bean beetle	*Brown, spotted beetle, yellow larvae eat underside of leaves.*	132
Viola **pansy, violet, viola**	violet leaf midge	*Orange-white maggots feed on leaves, which curl/thicken. Plants can die.*	127
	harlequin bug	*Large black/red bug. Frass. Plants wilt, can die.*	130
	leaf spot	*Brown spots on leaves.*	179

Tulipa

Viburnum

Broad beans

PLANT	PROBLEM	SYMPTOMS/DESCRIPTION	PAGE
Viola	pansy rust	*Stems swollen; pustules of spores, yellow-orange then brown.*	209
pansy, violet, viola	pansy sickness	*Yellowing, wilting.*	210
	violet scab	*Tiny watery spots on stems/leaves grey patches; scabby.*	214
	smut	*Leaves/stems develop blisters; powdery black spores.*	217
Vitis	painted vine moth caterpillar	*Black/orange/cream caterpillars eat holes in leaves.*	113
grape, vine	metallic flea beetle	*Irregular holes in young leaves, buds.*	114
	oleander scale, ivy scale	*White-brownish circular scales.*	117
	bunch mite	*Leaves brown/rough. Grapes shrivel/crack/drop.*	119
	inland katydid	*Grasshopper-like. Leaves skeletonized/holed; fruits gnawed.*	120
	grapeleaf rust mite	*Red-brown areas on leaves; may drop.*	120
	soft scale, brown soft scale, soft brown scale	*Yellow-brown scales under leaves. Honeydew, sooty mould.*	124
	grapeleaf blister mite	*Cream/brown patches under leaves, blisters above.*	125
	grape phylloxera	*Growth is weakened; fruiting is impaired.*	127
	harlequin bug	*Large black/red bug. Frass. Plants wilt, can die.*	130
	lightbrown apple moth	*Green larvae roll/web leaves, eat leaves/fruits.*	132
	grapeleaf skeletonizers	*Moth. Cream-yellow/purple-black stripy larvae eat under leaves.*	137
	glasshouse thrips, greenhouse thrips	*Yellow-brown insects. Leaves/petals spotted/discoloured.*	138
	African black beetle	*Adults eat stems below ground; grubs eat roots.*	139
	grapevine hawk moth	*Large green-black caterpillars chew leaves.*	139
	periodical cicada	*Slits in bark for eggs.*	144
	crusader bug	*Brown bug, yellow cross. Yellos dots on nymph. Plants wilt.*	146
	redshouldered leaf beetle	*Yellow/red beetle eats leaves/flowers/fruits.*	147
	Rutherglen bug	*Brown bug. Wilting; fruits pitted.*	149
	elephant weevil	*Grey-black adult. Larvae tunnel in trunks/roots.*	150
	vine weevil, black vine weevil	*Black weevil. Grubs eat roots.*	151
	fruit tree red spider mite, European red mite	*Yellow-mottled leaves.*	152
	grapevine moth	*Black/white/pink caterpillars eat under leaves.*	154
	passionvine hopper	*Moth-like adult, green nymph. Leaves/fruit shrivel/drop.*	162
	fruit flies	*Eggs laid under fruit skin; larvae feed inside fruits. Cracks/spots.*	166
	plague thrips	*Tiny insect; colourless-yellow nymph. Petals browned.*	167
	wasps, hornet, yellow jackets	*Black-yellow striped insects eat holes in fruit.*	169
	crown gall	*Small, soft galls.*	172
	armillaria root rot, honey fungus	*Fan-shaped honey-coloured fungus on roots/at base; white mycelium under bark. Leaves wither (don't drop); die-back.*	175
	black rot	*Brown-black spots on stems; flowers/fruits drop. Grey-black spots, then holes, on leaves; spots on fruits.*	185
	powdery mildew	*Grey-white powder on plants; young leaves distorted/shed.*	188
	downy mildew	*Light green blotches above leaves, downy below; drying leaves curl, drop; fruits shrivel/brown.*	205
	moist atmosphere	*Fungal diseases.*	232
	shanking	*Fruit stalks shrivel; fruits fail to develop.*	236
	scald in the greenhouse	*Discoloured sunken patches on fruits.*	242
	hormone weedkiller damage	*Check in growth.*	243

Vitis vinifera

White grapes

Black grapes

Vitis vinifera

PLANT	PROBLEM	SYMPTOMS/DESCRIPTION	PAGE
W			
Wisteria	leaf-cutting bees	*Round holes in leaves.*	146
wisteria	iron deficiency, lime-induced chlorosis	*Young leaves yellow/scorched.*	248
Z			
Zantedeschia	arum corm rot	*Plants wither, collapse. Brown patches on corms; roots rot.*	188
arum lily			
Zea mays	striped cucumber beetle	*Larvae eat roots, adults eat topgrowth.*	112
sweet corn (corn)	wireworm	*Adults chew leaves; larvae eat roots.*	114
	flea beetles, leaf beetle, striped flea beetle	*Adults eat holes in leaves; larvae eat roots.*	123
	yellow peach moth	*Large pink caterpillars tunnel into plants. Die-back.*	125
	green June beetle and fig beetle	*Adults eat holes in leaves. Larvae eat roots.*	126
	corn rootworms (northern and western)	*Yellow-green beetles eat cobs; grubs tunnel into roots.*	128
	spotted cucumber beetle, Southern corn rootworm	*Yellow/black beetle chews leaves. Long, thin larvae eat roots/crowns.*	128
	southwestern corn borer	*Large moth. White/spotted caterpillars eat leaves, bore into stalks/husks.*	129
	budworms	*Moth's caterpillars eat holes in leaves/flowers.*	138
	corn earworm	*Moth's caterpillars eat inside husks.*	138
	corn earworm, tomato fruitworm	*Moth's larvae eat plants.*	138
	African black beetle	*Adults eat stems below ground; grubs eat roots.*	139
	grasshoppers, locusts	*Stems/leaves eaten.*	143
	redshouldered leaf beetle	*Yellow/red beetle eats leaves/flowers.*	147
	frit fly (seedlings up to five-leaf stage)	*Tiny black fly. Maggots feed inside shoots.*	150
	European corn borer	*Moth. Grey-pink caterpillars chew leaves, enter husks/stalks.*	150
	stink bugs, earth mites	*Green-brown-grey bugs; evil smell. Distorted growth.*	153
	fall armyworm	*Moth. Green-brown-black/yellow-striped caterpillars eat leaves/cobs.*	163
	corn leaf blight (southern)	*Small, pale spots; long, narrow, brown-edged lesions; black spores.*	176
	leaf blight	*Thin, grey-green patches on leaves.*	185
	corn leaf blight (northern)	*Long, grey-green lesions on leaves, from base up. Lesions turn tan; drying. Dark green-black spores.*	189
	smut (sweet corn)	*White galls; black spores.*	218
Zinnia	beet leafhopper	*Green-brown adult, green nymph, spread viruses.*	124
zinnia	seedling blight	*Red-brown/grey centred spots on leaves; brown cankers on stems.*	174
	big bud, greening, virescence	*Unnaturally bushy growth.*	197
	damping off	*Seedlings collapse; blacken, wither.*	202
	angular leaf spot	*Angular-circular red-brown spots on leaves; new growth killed.*	220
	spotted wilt	*Brown spots on leaves; stems streaked brown.*	227

Wisteria sinensis   Zantedeschia

Sweet corn

Zinnia

Plant list by general plant group

The following list contains pests, diseases and physiological problems that can affect any or most plants if the conditions in the garden are favourable. It also includes problems that are specific to certain groups of plants, such as citrus fruits or legumes.

PLANT GROUP	PROBLEM	SYMPTOMS/DESCRIPTION	PAGE
GENERAL: A WIDE RANGE OF PLANTS ARE SUSCEPTIBLE TO THE FOLLOWING	striped cucumber beetle	*Larvae eat roots, adults eat topgrowth.*	112
	greenfly	*Tiny green flies on shoot tips, under leaves.*	113
	bogong moth caterpillar (leafy plants)	*Caterpillars eat leaves.*	114
	whitefly	*Tiny white insects; yellow mottled leaves.*	114
	metallic flea beetles	*Irregular holes in young leaves, buds.*	114
	eelworm	*Tiny soil-dwellers eat roots, other parts.*	116
	New Zealand flatworm	*Large leech-like worm; round black eggs.*	117
	green looper	*Moth's large caterpillars eat leaves. Brown droppings.*	123
	soft scales	*Honeydew excreted by scales attracts sooty mould.*	124
	lightbrown apple moth	*Green larvae roll/web leaves, eat leaves/fruits.*	132
	frosted scale	*Brown, white-coated scale. Honeydew, sooty mould.*	134
	Australian flatworm	*Brown, leech-like worm eats earthworms. Black eggs.*	136
	ants	*Nests can cause drought to plants.*	135
	slugs and snails	*All soft parts eaten. Plants can be defoliated.*	135
	whitefringed weevil	*Grey-black/white adult; larvae eat roots/tubers.*	137
	swift moth caterpillars	*Large white caterpillars feed on roots.*	139
	tarnished plant bug	*Yellow-brown adult, yellow/spotted nymph. Buds/leaves blackened, fruits puckered.*	143
	praying mantids	*Large green-brown insect, light brown egg cases (on stems).*	145
	fruit-tree borer	*White moth. Larvae tunnel into wood.*	145
	calico back bug	*Red/black beetle. White/yellow blotched leaves; wilting.*	147
	green vegetable bug	*Green-black bug, many-coloured nymph. Growth distorted/discoloured.*	148
	elephant weevil	*Grey-black adult. Larvae tunnel in trunks/roots.*	150
	European corn borer	*Moth. Grey-pink caterpillars chew leaves, enter husks/stalks.*	150
	strawberry root weevils	*Brown-black adults eat leaves/stalks; larvae eat roots/crowns.*	151
	June beetle, May beetle	*Adults eat leaves, grubs eat roots.*	156
	broad mite	*Distortion, discoloration; buds shed.*	158
	cabbage moth	*Green caterpillars tunnel through leaves; small holes.*	158
	Japanese beetle	*Blue-black adults eat leaves/flowers; larvae eat roots.*	158
	San Jose scale	*Well-camouflaged scale. Rough texture; fruits damaged.*	160
	garden symphylan	*White, many-legged soil-dweller eats roots.*	162
	woollybear caterpillar	*Moth. Hairy caterpillars eat leaves.*	163
	cluster caterpillar	*White moth. Green-brown/black triangle-marked caterpillars eat plants.*	163

Ornamentals commonly suffer attack from garden pests and diseases.

The herb garden is less appealing to insect pests.

PLANT GROUP	PROBLEM	SYMPTOMS/DESCRIPTION	PAGE
	cabbage looper	*Moth. Green pale-striped caterpillars eat leaves.*	168
	crown gall	*Large galls on tree roots; small, soft galls on shrubs.*	172
	leaf spot	*Brown/black spots on leaves/flowers.*	172
	leaf blight, alternaria blight	*Brown spots on leaves.*	173
	foot and root rot, black root rot	*Stem bases brown-black; leaves discoloured; die-back.*	174
	leaf nematodes	*Leaves show yellow patches turning brown. Damage can be extensive.*	175
	ascochyta blight	*Dark spots on leaves/stems.*	176
	grey mould	*Grey-brown, velvety fungal growth; wilting.*	177
	fusarium wilt	*Leaves wilt, oldest first. Yellow-brown patches. Brown-black lesions on lower stems/roots.*	190
	rusts	*Red-brown-yellow patches on leaves/flowers/fruits. Galls, swellings.*	195
	phytophthora root rot	*Roots rot, smallest first. Leaves yellow; die-back.*	201
	collar rot, rhizoctonia disease	*Sunken patches at base of stems.*	210
	sclerotinia disease, sclerotinia rot, sclerotinia wilt, white mould	*Stems rot; fluffy white growth inside; hard black fungi; flowers/buds rot.*	212
	sooty moulds	*Soot-like fungus on plants.*	221
	arabis mosaic virus	*Mosaic-like marks on leaves; distortion.*	222
	beet curly top	*Leaves crinkled; veins swollen; yellowing.*	223
	spotted wilt	*Brown spots on leaves; stems streaked brown.*	227
	severe weather injuries	*Parts ripped off; leaves torn.*	230
	drought	*Plants wilt, die.*	231
	chronic lack of water	*Leaves yellow-brown, drop.*	231
	acute water deficiency (sudden)	*Wilting.*	231
	lack of water at critical times	*Fruits crack/split; vegetable crops fail, new plants die.*	231
	sporadic water supply	*Uneven growth; poor flowering/fruiting.*	231
	waterlogging	*Leaves discoloured/die-back; bark peels.*	232
	cold	*Stems wither, die-back. Leaves discolour, drop.*	233
	frost damage	*Petals brown-edged; bark cracks.*	233
	faulty root action	*Leaves discoloured/blackened; die-back.*	235
	die-back	*Tips blacken/wither; leaves drop.*	236
	bud drop/aborted flowers	*Flower buds shrivel/drop.*	240
	poor light	*Growth long, thin, pale.*	242
	hormone weedkiller damage	*Check in growth.*	243
	chemical injuries	*Growth stunted; leaves misshapen/discoloured.*	243
	injuries by gardeners	*A range of physical damage.*	243
	leaf blotches	*Irregular yellow-brown-black patches on leaves.*	244
	poor flowering	*Few, or no, flowers.*	245
	manganese deficiency	*Leaves yellow/drop, oldest first.*	247
	malnutrition	*Failure to thrive.*	247
	nitrogen deficiency	*Growth stunted, spindly; leaves yellow.*	247
	phosphorus deficiency	*Leaves bluish-purplish-bronze; purple-brown spots; fruits soft.*	247

In the summer garden insect pests proliferate.

Vegetables are host to many specific garden problems.

PLANT GROUP	PROBLEM	SYMPTOMS/DESCRIPTION	PAGE
	excess nitrogen	*Excess of soft growth; poor flowering/fruiting.*	248
	magnesium deficiency	*Leaves yellow, oldest first, later orange-red, drop.*	249
	potassium deficiency	*Leaves bluish, brown spots/tips; curl downwards.*	249
FRUIT	fruitspotting bug	*Green bug, red/black nymph; fruits spotted/shed.*	115
Citrus	banana-spotting bug	*Green bug, red/black nymph; spots/patches on fruit.*	115
citrus fruit	California red scale, red scale	*Orange-pink scale; die-back, leaves shed.*	116
	Fuller's rose weevil	*Grey-brown weevils eat leaves; larvae eat roots.*	117
	spined citrus bug	*Green, horned adult, yellow/black nymph; browned fruits.*	118
	large auger beetle	*White larvae tunnel through wood.*	118
	citrus gall wasp	*Galls appear; plants weakened.*	119
	bunch mite	*Leaves brown/rough.*	119
	citrus katydid	*Grasshopper-like. Nymphs eat holes in leaves/fruits.*	120
	pink wax scale	*Pink or grey scales; honeydew attracts sooty mould.*	122
	banana rust thrips	*Grubs of black beetle cause swellings on roots.*	122
	soft scale, brown soft scale, soft brown scale	*Yellow-brown scales under leaves. Honeydew, sooty mould.*	124
	hard scales, armoured scales	*Yellow-blotches leaves may be shed. Die-back.*	129
	small citrus butterfly, dingy swallowtail	*Black/gre/white butterfly. Large caterpillars eat leaves..*	131
	potato leafhopper	*Green insect, pale nymph. Leaves spotted/distorted/rolled.*	131
	lightbrown apple moth	*Green larvae roll/web leaves, eat leaves.*	132
	citrus bud mite	*Blackened buds/fruits, distorted leaves/flowers/fruits.*	134
	fruit-tree root weevil	*Adults eat young growth. Leaves folded. Larvae eat roots.*	142
	katydids	*Grasshopper-like. Leaves eaten*	143
	crusader bug	*Brown bug, yellow cross. Yellow dots on nymph. Plants wilt.*	146
	redshouldered leaf beetle	*Yellow/red beetle eats leaves/flowers/fruits.r*	147
	bronze orange bug	*Brown-black bug; evil smell. Flowers/fruits shed; shoots wilt.*	147
	elephant weevil	*Grey-black adult. Larvae tunnel in trunks/roots.*	150
	fruitpiercing moths	*Holes in fruit.*	151
	citrus leafminer	*White/yellow moth. Larvae inside leaves; white lines, distortion.*	155
	broad mite	*Distortion, discoloration; buds shed.*	158
	large citrus butterfly	*Black/yellow/red male, brown/orange/blue female. Larvae like bird droppings, then fat, green/brown/white banded. Leaves eaten.*	159
	black scale, brown olive scale	*Soft scales. Honeydew, sooty mould.*	161
	passionvine hopper	*Moth-like adult, green nymph. Leaves/fruits shrivel/drop.*	162
	fruit flies	*Eggs laid under fruit skin; larvae feed inside fruits. Cracks/spots.*	166
	spider mites	*Fine webbing. Leaves speckled/yellow-brown.*	166
	plague thrips	*Tiny insect; colourless; yellow nymph. Petals browned.*	167
	white louse scale	*White male, brown female scale. Leaves yellow; die-back.*	168
	sooty blotch	*Dark circular, cloudy enlarging patches on fruit skins.*	192
	fly speck	*Small, circular specks on fruit skins; taste unaffected.*	196

Careful vigilance will ensure fruit crops are productive.

Citrus fruit suffer different problems to orchard fruits.

PLANT GROUP	PROBLEM	SYMPTOMS/DESCRIPTION	PAGE
	brown rots	*Brown rot on fruits. Leaves shed, die-back.*	201
	collar rot	*Gum from bark at base; bark dies, splits.*	202
	citrus scab	*Brown-pink-grey scabs on leaves; fruits shed or enlarged/distorted.*	213
pome fruits	lightbrown apple moth	*Green larvae roll/web leaves, eat leaves/fruits.*	132
	fruit flies	*Eggs laid under fruit skin; larvae feed inside fruits. Cracks/spots.*	166
stone fruits (those with pits)	driedfruit beetles	*Fruit rots.*	121
	budworms	*Moth's caterpillars eat holes in leaves/flowers/fruits.*	138
	Rutherglen bug	*Brown bug. Wilting; fruits pitted.*	149
	oak leafminer	*Fine lines/blisters on leaves.*	155
	fruit flies	*Eggs laid under fruit skin; larvae feed inside fruits. Cracks/spots.*	166
	freckle	*Cream-pale green-black spots on fruits; cracking. Spots on leaves; black lesions on twigs.*	192
	bacterial canker	*Die-back, brown spots on leaves; dark, sunken spots on fruits.*	207
	brown rot of stone fruit	*Flowers brown; die-back; brown spot on fruits, rotting.*	211
	plum rust, peach rust	*Yellow spores under leaves.*	216
fruiting plants	tarnished plant bug	*Yellow-brown adult, yellow/spotted nymph. Buds/leaves blackened, fruits puckered.*	143
	Japanese beetle	*Blue-black adults eat leaves/flowers; larvae eat roots.*	158
	anthracnose	*Small depressed spots on fruits; fruits can rot.*	181
	lack of pollination	*No fruit.*	241
	potassium deficiency	*Leaves bluish, brown spots/tips; curl downwards.*	249
fruiting trees	March moth	*Caterpillars eat small holes in leaves.*	114
	large auger beetle	*White larvae tunnel through wood.*	118
	codling moth	*White-pink caterpillars tunnel into fruits. White excreta.*	127
	apple leafhopper, canary fly	*Yellow cicada-type. Grey-mottled leaves.*	130
	fall webworm	*Moth. White/spotted caterpillars eat leaves, make webs.*	140
	cottonycushion scale	*Brown scale. Honeydew, sooty mould.*	140
	fruit-tree root weevil	*Adults eat young growth. Leaves folded. Larvae eat roots.*	142
	tent caterpillars	*Black, white striped/spotted caterpillars eat leaves, make webs.*	144
	fruit-tree borer	*White moth. Larvae tunnel into wood.*	145
	calico back bug	*Red/black beetle. White/yellow blotched leaves; wilting.*	147
	winter moth	*Green/striped caterpillars eat young leaves/flowers/fruits, spin silk.*	150
	strawberry root weevil	*Brown-black adults eat leaves; larvae eat roots.*	151
	wingless grasshopper	*Brown grasshopper eats plants/fruits.*	154
	wasps, hornet, yellow jacket	*Black-yellow striped insects eat holes in fruits.*	169
	leopard moth	*White/black-spotted moth. Black-spotted larvae tunnel into wood.*	169

Favourable growing conditions will produce strong trees and shrubs.

Careful pruning will ensure these fruit trees remain productive.

PLANT GROUP	PROBLEM	SYMPTOMS/DESCRIPTION	PAGE
	silver leaf	*Leaves silver-brown; die-back. Mauve-white-brown brackets on dead wood.*	179
	blossom wilt	*Flowers wither, not shed. Leaves shrivel; die-back.*	196
	lack of water at critical times	*Fruits crack.*	231
	frost damage	*Petals brown-edged; bark cracks; fruits distorted.*	233
	false silver leaf	*Leaves silvery.*	236
	fruit drop	*Fruits drop prematurely.*	241
	glassiness or water core	*Flesh of fruits waterlogged.*	244
fruiting vines	brown scale	*Honeydew, sooty mould.*	152
	grapevine scale	*Brown scale. Honeydew, sooty mould.*	152
	grapevine moth	*Black/white/pink caterpillars eat under leaves.*	154
	woolly vine scale	*Large, oval, brown scales.*	160
	lack of water at critical times	*Fruits crack.*	231
soft fruit	fruittree leafroller	*Moth's green caterpillars eat plant parts, roll up in leaves.*	116
	green June beetle and fig beetle	*Adults eat holes in leaves/fruits. Larvae eat roots.*	126
	millipedes	*Holes eaten in fruits; roots can be eaten.*	130
	gall mites, rust mite	*Galls on leaves/stems.*	133
	gypsy moth	*Grey/spotted, hairy caterpillars eat leaves.*	144
	strawberry root weevil	*Brown-black adults eat leaves/stalks; larvae eat roots/crowns.*	151
	stink bug, earth mite	*Green-brown-grey bugs; evil smell. Distorted growth/fruits.*	153
vegetables	garden webworm	*Brown moth's green-black caterpillars eat leaves, spin webs.*	112
	green looper	*Moth's large caterpillars eat leaves. Brown droppings.*	123
	blister beetles	*Various beetles eat leaves/fruits.*	131
	African black beetle	*Adults eat stems below ground; grubs eat roots.*	139
	leaf miners	*Larvae in leaves. Lines/blotches seen.*	142
	tarnished plant bug	*Yellow-brown adult, yellow/spotted nymph. Buds/leaves blackened, fruits puckered.*	143
	wingless grasshopper	*Brown grasshopper eats plants/fruits.*	154
	Japanese beetle	*Blue-black adults eat leaves/flowers; larvae eat roots.*	158
	garden symphylan	*White, many-legged soil-dweller eats roots.*	162
	cluster caterpillar	*White moth. Green-brown/black triangle-marked caterpillars eat plants.*	163
	collar rot, rhizoctonia disease	*Reddish sunken areas at base of stems.*	210
	wirestem fungus	*Stems hard, brown, shrunken at base.*	216
	verticillium wilt	*Wilting; leaves curl, yellow; die-back.*	218
	spotted wilt	*Brown spots on leaves; stems streaked brown.*	227
	lack of water at critical times	*Vegetables crack.*	231
	splitting of roots	*Roots split.*	237
	bolting	*Crops run to seed prematurely.*	240

Rotating crops over the years ensures the soil remains as healthy as possible.

Net soft fruit to protect it from flying insect pests and birds.

PLANT GROUP	PROBLEM	SYMPTOMS/DESCRIPTION	PAGE
	phosphorus deficiency	*Leaves bluish-purplish-bronze; purple-brown spots; fruits soft.*	247
crucifers	cabbage moth	*Green caterpillars tunnel through leaves; small holes.*	144
	onion thrips	*Yellow-grey insect. Yellow nymph. Leaves blotched/distorted.*	167
	cabbage looper	*Moth. Green pale-striped caterpillars eat leaves.*	168
	black leg	*Wilting, red-edged leaves, stems/roots crack. Seedlings have brown-black sunken area at base.*	194
	downy mildew (crucifers)	*White, mealy growth on the undersides of leaves. Growth is checked.*	199
	beet curly top	*Leaves crinkled; veins swollen; yellowing.*	223
	mosaic	*Yellow rings on young leaves; green mottling; black rings.*	225
cucurbits	greenfly	*Tiny green flies on shoot tips, under leaves.*	113
	pumpkin beetle	*Orange/black adult eats leaves, flowers.*	118
	spotted cucumber beetle, Southern corn rootworm	*Yellow/black beetle chews leaves/fruits. Long, thin larvae eat roots/crowns.*	128
	pickleworm	*Brown moth. Yellow/spotted, then green or pink larvae eat buds/fruits/stems.*	129
	leafeating ladybird	*Yellow, spotted beetle. Spiny larvae eat below leaves.*	131
	squash vine borer	*Moth. Larvae chew bases of stems.*	146
	fruit fly	*Eggs laid under fruit skin; larvae feed inside fruits. Cracks/spots.*	166
	spider mite	*Fine webbing. Leaves speckled/yellow-brown.*	166
	leaf blight, alternaria blight	*Brown spots on leaves/fruits; leaves curl.*	173
	gummy stem blight	*Watery areas/sunken cankers on stems; black spots on leaves/fruits.*	183
	bacterial wilt	*Large, dull, irregular patches on leaves; die-back. White "milk" from cut stems.*	188
	powdery mildew	*White spots below leaves. Grey-white powder on plants; young leaves distorted/shed.*	188
	fusarium wilt	*Wilting; damping off.*	190
	angular leaf spot	*Water-soaked spots on leaves turn yellow then brown. Fruits shed.*	206
	sclerotinia disease, sclerotinia rot, sclerotinia wilt, white mould	*Stems rot; fluffy white growth inside; hard black fungi; flowers/buds rot.*	212
	verticillium wilt	*Wilting; leaves curl; yellow; die-back.*	218
	cucumber mosaic virus	*Stunting, distortion, yellow mosaic pattern on leaves.*	224
	tobacco ring spot, bouquet disease, tomato ring spot, bud blight	*Stunting, distortion; small brown-yellow, raised rings/circles on leaves/fruits.*	226
	watermelon mosaic virus	*Leaves mottled/distorted. Hollows/raised marbling on fruits.*	227
legumes	spittlebug	*Green nymphs hide in white froth on plants.*	121
	bean podborer	*Moth. Green-yellow, spotted caterpillars eat flowers/stems/seeds.*	145
	pea pod spot	*Sunken, dark patches on leaves/stems/pods.*	176
	ascochyta blight	*Dark spots on leaves/stems.*	176

Cruciferous vegetables are particularly attractive to caterpillars.

Peas, beans and other legumes suffer from many of the same garden pests.

PLANT GROUP	PROBLEM	SYMPTOMS/DESCRIPTION	PAGE
	anthracnose ·	*Black-red-brown patches on pods/stems. Leaf veins blacken. Under glass, spots can be white-encrusted.*	181
	halo blight of beans	*Young plants yellow; angular spots on leaves; watery-greasy spots on pods/stems; white slime.*	206
	sclerotium stem rot, southern blight	*Leaves yellow; watery lesions at base of plants; white growth.*	212
	bean rust	*Pale yellow spots above leaves, blisters below; blisters on pods.*	217
	verticillium wilt	*Wilting; leaves curl, yellow; die-back.*	218
	bean mosaic, pea early browning virus	*Leaves yellow-mottled, brown; stems streaked yellow.*	222
	beet curly top	*Leaves crinkled; veins swollen; yellowing.*	223
	clover stunt virus, leaf roll, top yellows	*Plants small, upright, yellowish. Older leaves thickened.*	223
	potassium deficiency	*Leaves bluish, brown spots/tips; curl downwards.*	249
WOODY PLANTS **shrubs**	greenfly	*Tiny green insects suck sap.*	113
	bogong moth caterpillar	*Caterpillars eat leaves*	114
	longicorns, long horn beetles	*Beetle's larvae tunnel uner bark; cracks appear.*	121
	gall mites, rust mites	*Galls on leaves/stems.*	133
	frosted scale	*Brown, white-coated scale. Honeydew, sooty mould.*	134
	garden soldier fly, garden maggot	*Slender black fly.*	135
	whitefringed weevil	*Grey-black/white adult; larvae eat roots/tubers.*	137
	fall webworm	*Moth. White/spotted caterpillars eat leaves, make webs.*	140
	leaf miners	*Larvae in leaves. Lines/blotches seen.*	142
	gypsy moth	*Grey/spotted, hairy caterpillars eat leaves.*	144
	periodical cicada	*Slits in bark for eggs.*	144
	brown scale	*Honeydew, sooty mould.*	152
	white palm scale	*Scales under leaves. Yellow blotches.*	154
	angle shades moth	*Green-brown caterpillars eat flowers/leaves.*	154
	leopard moth	*White/black-spotted moth. Black-spotted larvae tunnel into wood.*	169
	foot and root rot, black root rot	*Leaves discoloured; die-back.*	174
	armillaria root rot, honey fungus	*Plants collapse and die.*	175
	grey mould	*Die-back; cracks, grey pustules, black threads.*	177
	bracket fungi, wood rots	*Bracket-shaped growths on trunks/branches.*	190
	witches' brooms	*Broom-like mass of erect shoots.*	195
	phytophthora root rot	*Roots rot, smallest first. Leaves yellow; die-back.*	201
	green algae	*Thick green deposit on leaves.*	205
	lichens and mosses	*Moss: cushion-like tufty growth. Lichen: thin, flat crust.*	221
	slime fluxes, wetwood	*Orange-pink-white fluid exuded from stems.*	221
	severe weather injuries	*Parts ripped off; leaves torn.*	230
	wind damage	*Plants flattened; dead patches on evergreens.*	230
	cold	*Stems wither, die-back. Leaves discolour, drop.*	233
	faulty root action	*Leaves discoloured/blackened; die-back.*	235
	discoloured leaves	*Leaves discoloured.*	237

Many tall, woody plants suffer the effects of wind damage.

Companion planting is a traditional method of keeping pests at bay.

PLANT GROUP	PROBLEM	SYMPTOMS/DESCRIPTION	PAGE
	fasciation	*Growth flattened.*	238
trees *see also fruiting trees*	jewel beetles	*White larvae tunnel under bark.*	119
	longicorns, long horn beetles	*Beetle's larvae tunnel under bark; cracks appear.*	121
	gall mites, rust mites	*Galls on leaves/stems.*	133
	termites	*White-cream insects chew wood.*	141
	periodical cicada (deciduous)	*Slits in bark for eggs.*	144
	gypsy moth	*Grey/spotted, hairy caterpillars eat leaves.*	144
	angle shades moth	*Green-brown caterpillars eat flowers/leaves.*	154
	leafblister sawflies	*Larvae inside leaves. Blisters/lumps.*	154
	black field cricket	*Leaves/shoots/fruits chewed.*	165
	armillaria root rot, honey fungus	*Fan-shaped honey-coloured fungus on roots/at base; white mycelium under bark. Leaves wither (don't drop); die-back.*	175
	bracket fungi, wood rots	*Bracket-shaped growths on trunks/branches.*	190
	witches' brooms	*Broom-like mass of erect shoots.*	195
	phytophthora root rot	*Roots rot, smallest first. Leaves yellow; die-back.*	201
	green algae	*Thick green deposit on leaves.*	205
	verticillium wilt	*Wilting; leaves curl, yellow; die-back.*	218
	slime fluxes, wetwood	*Orange-pink-white fluid exuded from stems.*	221
	severe weather injuries	*Parts ripped off; leaves torn.*	230
conifers	cypress bark weevil	*Young growth eaten; tips die; larvae under bark weaken/kill tree.*	113
	gypsy moth	*Grey/spotted, hairy caterpillars eat leaves.*	144
	cypress bark beetle	*Brown-black adult. Larvae tunnel in wood.*	154
	armillaria root rot, honey fungus	*Fan-shaped honey-coloured fungus on roots/at base; white mycelium under bark. Leaves wither (don't drop); die-back.*	175
	fomes root and butt rot	*Die-back; heartwood rots; roots die. Red-brown/white fungus at base.*	193
	severe weather injuries	*Parts ripped off; leaves torn.*	230
GREENHOUSE, HOUSEPLANTS, EXOTICS	whitefly	*Tiny white insects; yellow mottled leaves.*	114
	fern eelworm, chrysanthemum eelworm	*Tiny creatures inside leaves cause browning.*	116
	silver Y moth	*Green/white caterpillars eat flowers/leaves.*	118
	mottled arum aphid	*Yellow-green aphid. Leaves puckered, poor growth.*	117
	carnation tortrix caterpillar	*Moth's green caterpillars fold and eat leaves.*	119
	green looper	*Moth's large caterpillars eat leaves. Brown droppings.*	123
	loopers and semi-loopers	*Holes are chewed in leaves. Flowers can be damaged.*	136
	glasshouse leafhopper	*Yellow adult, creamy nymph. White dots on leaves.*	138
	scales	*Scales suck sap. Honeydew; sooty mould.*	139
	peach-potato aphid, green peach aphid, spinach aphid	*Greenfly. Leaves puckered. Honeydew, sooty mould.*	148
	angle shades moth	*Green-brown caterpillars eat flowers/leaves.*	154

Conifers are host to certain specific insect pests.

Some species of tree have been almost eradicated by some diseases.

PLANT GROUP	PROBLEM	SYMPTOMS/DESCRIPTION	PAGE
	broad mite	*Distortion, discoloration; buds shed.*	158
	mealybugs	*Growth wilts; distorted. Honeydew; sooty mould.*	159
	black scale, brown olive scale	*Soft scales. Honeydew, sooty mould.*	161
	hemispherical scale	*Brown scales. Honeydew, sooty mould.*	161
	spider mites	*Fine webbing. Leaves speckled/yellow-brown.*	166
	glasshouse red spider mite, red spider mite, two-spotted mite	*Fine webbing. Mottled, pale leaves.*	166
	thrips	*Black insect; yellow nymph. Leaves/flowers discoloured.*	167
	glasshouse whitefly	*Scale-like, green nymphs feed under leaves. Honeydew, sooty mould.*	168
	powdery mildew	*Grey-white powder on plants; young leaves distorted/shed.*	188
	root knot nematodes	*Galls/scabby lesions/swellings on roots/tubers. Stunting, wilting.*	196
	damping off	*Seedlings collapse; blacken, wither.*	202
	dry atmosphere	*Growth slows; browning.*	232
	bud drop/aborted flowers	*Flower buds shrivel/drop.*	240
	tip scorch	*Leaf tips brown.*	241
	poor light	*Growth long, thin, pale.*	242
	sun scorch under glass	*Pale brown areas on leaves.*	242
	exudation	*Small round droplets on leaves/stems.*	244
orchids	oleander scale, ivy scale	*White-brownish circular scales.*	117
	orchid scale	*Scales at base of plant; yellowing leaves.*	129
	orchid beetle, dendrobium beetle	*Orange/black spotted beetle eats buds/flowers/leaves.*	164
	black pseudobulb rot	*Pseudobulb turns brown-black; leaves yellow.*	209
	cymbidium virus	*Leaves mottled; black spots.*	224
palms	orange palmdart	*Orange/brown moth's green caterpillars wrapped in/feeding on leaves.*	121
	orchid scale	*Scales at base of plant; yellowing leaves.*	129
	white palm scale	*Scales under leaves. Yellow blotches.*	154
	mealybugs	*Growth wilts; distorted. Honeydew; sooty mould.*	159
succulents	mealybugs	*Growth wilts; distorted. Honeydew; sooty mould.*	159
	waterlogging	*Roots rot; topgrowth wilts or rots.*	232
	crown rot	*Crowns soft, slimy.*	234
BULBS, RHIZOMES, CORMS, TUBERS	swift moth caterpillars	*Large white caterpillars feed on roots.*	139
	frost damage to stored corms	*Stored corms soften.*	239
bulbous plants	blindness of bulbs	*Leaves grow, but no flowers.*	237
	crinkling of leaves	*Leaves crinkled.*	238
	chalkiness and hardness of bulbs	*Dormant bulbs in storage harden.*	243

For healthy plants, store bulbs, corms, rhizomes and tubers in a cool place.

Cacti and succulents prefer the conditions of their natural environment.

PLANT GROUP	PROBLEM	SYMPTOMS/DESCRIPTION	PAGE
YOUNG PLANTS seeds and seedlings	bean weevil	*White grubs eat holes in beans/seeds.*	112
	springtails	*Seeds/seedlings chewed.*	124
	millipedes	*Roots can be eaten.*	130
	slugs and snails	*Plants can be destroyed.*	135
	woodlice	*Seedlings are eaten.*	149
	strawberry root weevils	*Brown-black adults eat leaves/stalks; larvae eat roots/crowns.*	151
	fungus gnats	*Hovering flies. Larvae eat roots. Slimy trail on soil.*	162
	black field cricket	*Leaves/shoots/fruits chewed.*	165
	damping off	*Seedlings collapse after germinating.*	202
	collar rot, rhizoctonia disease	*Sunken patches at base of stems.*	210
	wirestem fungus	*Stems shrink; roots blacken.*	216
	moist atmosphere	*Fungal diseases.*	232
	cold	*Stems wither, die-back. Leaves discolour, drop.*	233
	poor light	*Growth long, thin, pale.*	242
cuttings	fungus gnats	*Hovering flies. Larvae eat roots. Slimy trail on soil.*	162
	moist atmosphere	*Fungal diseases.*	232
	low temperatures	*Leaves discoloured/distorted; poor growth.*	232
evergreens	low temperatures	*Leaves discoloured/distorted; poor growth.*	232
	frost damage	*Petals brown-edged; bark cracks.*	233
ferns	fern eelworm, chrysanthemum eelworm	*Tiny creatures inside leaves cause browning.*	116
	oleander scale, ivy scale	*White-brownish circular scales.*	117
	soft scale, brown soft scale, soft brown scale	*Yellow-brown scales under leaves. Honeydew, sooty mould.*	124
	mealybugs	*Growth wilts; distorted. Honeydew; sooty mould.*	159
	hemispherical scale	*Brown scales. Honeydew, sooty mould.*	161
grains	corn rootworms (northern and western)	*Yellow-green beetles eat cobs; grubs tunnel into roots.*	128
grasses	spittlebugs, froghoppers	*Green nymphs hide in white froth on plants.*	121
	corn rootworms (northern and western)	*Yellow-green beetles eat cobs; grubs tunnel into roots.*	128
	southwestern corn borer	*Large moth. White/spotted caterpillars eat leaves, bore into stalks/husks.*	129
	June beetle, May beetle	*Adults eat leaves, grubs eat roots.*	156
	false wireworms	*Beetles. Shiny brown-yellow larvae eat underground/ground-level plant parts.*	166
	corn leaf blight (southern)	*Small, pale spots; long, narrow, brown-edged lesions; black spores.*	176
	corn leaf blight (northern)	*Long, grey-green lesions on leaves, from base up. Lesions turn tan; drying. Dark green-black spores.*	189

Ornamental grasses are attractive to some insect pests.

Young bedding plants in pots require careful attention and vigilance.

Insects and Other Invertebrates

The following directory lists invertebrate plant pests in Latin name alphabetical order; the parts of the world where they are likely to occur; and the plants commonly attacked by them. Descriptions of the adult pest (and its younger stages and eggs, where relevant), details of its feeding habits, and the damage it creates should help establish the cause of the problem you have encountered. Advice is given on dealing with the immediate problem and preventing further damage by the pest.

Left: A praying mantid.

Insect and other invertebrate pests

The entries that follow are in Latin name alphabetical order. To locate a problem by common name entry, use the index.

MAGPIE MOTH CATERPILLAR (gooseberries, white currants, red currants)
Abraxas grossulariata
Range: Europe to Japan.
Description: The adult is a moth, to 2.5cm (1in) across with orange and black markings. Caterpillars are white, marked with black, with yellow stripes down their sides.
Damage: Leaves are eaten.
Plants affected: Gooseberries, white currants and red currants.
Prevention and control: *Chemical:* Spray with permethrin or fenitrothion. *Non-chemical/organic:* Spray with derris.

STRIPED CUCUMBER BEETLE
Acalymma vittatum
Range: North America, except the far west.
Description: The adult is a yellow to orange beetle, 7mm (¼in) long, striped black and with a black head. It lays its eggs in the soil at the base of plants. Larvae are white, up to 2cm (⅘in) long, with a brown head and tail. There are one or two generations per year, depending on climate.
Damage: Larvae feed on plant roots, leading to stunted growth or even death in seedlings.

Below: Magpie moth caterpillars eat the leaves of fruit bushes and are active in spring.

Adults chew leaves and flowers and can transmit viruses.
Plants affected: Cucumbers, melons and squashes; also peas and sweet corn. The flowers of ornamental plants are eaten.
Prevention and control: *Chemical:* Spray with permethrin, pirimiphos-methyl or fenitrothion. *Non-chemical/organic:* Spray with kaolin or canola oil. Rotate crops. Grow on seedlings under floating mulches or cloches. Larvae can be controlled with the parasitic nematode *Heterorhabditis bacteriophora.*

BEAN WEEVIL
Acanthoscelides obtectus
Range: Cosmopolitan.
Description: The adult is a pear-shaped, olive brown insect, 3mm (⅛in) long, that lays its eggs in holes chewed from pods or in other cracks. The larvae are small, hairy, white grubs that tunnel into the seeds. There can be up to seven generations per year.
Damage: Holes are eaten in beans and seeds of other plants.
Plants affected: Beans, lentils, peas and other seeds (including stored crops).
Prevention and control: *Non-chemical/organic:* Destroy plants after cropping to reduce the weevil population. Seeds for

Below: This broom shrub has suffered as a result of broom gall mites.

storing should be thoroughly dried then frozen for 48 hours; alternatively, heat them to 57°C (135°F) for half an hour.

BROOM GALL MITE
Aceria genistae
Range: Europe.
Description: The pest is microscopic, living within plant tissue. Infested plants form soft green galls in spring, towards the centre of the bush initially, later spreading to outer branches. By late summer, the galls harden and turn brown.
Damage: Growth is impaired.
Plants affected: Broom (*Cytisus*).
Prevention and control: *Chemical:* None available. *Non-chemical/organic:* Remove galls as they form in spring and burn them. Badly affected plants should be dug up and burnt.

GARDEN WEBWORM
Achyra rantalis
Range: Throughout North America.
Description: The adult is a brownish-yellow moth, about 2cm (⅘in) across, with grey, gold and brown markings, that lays its eggs in clusters on leaves. The caterpillars, up to 2cm (⅘in) long, vary from light green to almost black. There are two to five generations per year. Larvae spin webs between leaves and chew holes in leaves. They are often found on weeds.
Damage: Leaves are eaten. In severe cases, webbing covers plants, which are then completely defoliated.
Plants affected: Beans, peas and some other vegetables; also strawberries.
Prevention and control: *Non-chemical/organic:* Keep the kitchen garden free of weeds. Pick off larvae and their webs by hand.

Above: Macadamia leafminers have severely damaged some sections of these leaves.

After cropping, dig over the soil to expose the pupae to predatory birds.

MACADAMIA LEAFMINER
Acrocercops chionosema
Range: Tropical and subtropical areas.
Description: The adult is a small, white moth that lays its eggs on the surface of leaves. Emerging larvae burrow directly into the leaf.
Damage: White lines appear on leaves – the first sign of pest activity. Whitish, papery blisters develop, sometimes covering the leaf surface completely. On badly affected plants, growth slows down appreciably.
Plants affected: Macadamias.
Prevention and control: *Non-chemical/organic:* Prune out affected growth as soon as white lines are noticed.

WATTLE LEAFMINER
Acrocercops plebeia
Range: Australia (native; not verified in central regions).
Description: The adult is a small, white, generally inconspicuous moth; its larvae are active within the body of the plant.
Damage: Larvae tunnel through leaves, producing pinkish blisters in which they pupate.

Above: Greenfly infestations appear quickly, but are easily controlled.

The leaf surface turns brown and flakes off.
Plants affected: Species of wattle (*Acacia*) with flattened leaf stalks.
Prevention and control: *Chemical:* Spray with fenthion. *Non-chemical/organic:* Prune out and destroy blistered growth to prevent spread of the pest.

GREENFLY
Acyrthosiphon pisum and other species
Range: Europe.
Description: The pest that is commonly known as greenfly is a tiny green insect about 3mm (⅛in) in length. Greenfly are active on shoot tips from spring into summer, sucking sap and spreading viral diseases. In cases of severe infestation, the plants may be rendered completely unproductive.
Damage: Leaves are curled and distorted, growth is slowed and yields of fruit and vegetables are reduced.
Plants affected: A wide range of plants, including dwarf and runner beans, cucumbers and other cucurbits, and many ornamentals, especially roses (*Rosa*).
Prevention and control: *Chemical:* Spray with bifenthrin, pirimicarb, dimethoate, hepten-ophos or permethrin. *Non-chemical/organic:* Spray with pyrethrum or an insecticidal soap.

TOMATO RUSSET MITE
Aculops lycopersici
Range: Cosmopolitan.
Description: This microscopic mite is usually observable only when present in large numbers. Yellowish areas can sometimes be seen under leaves and on stems and fruits.
Damage: Lower leaves turn grey, then brown, and dry out. Stems can turn brown and develop cracks. In severe infestations, flowers and fruits can be shed. If only leaves are dropped, new fruits may get scorch.
Plants affected: Aubergines (eggplants), peppers, potatoes, tomatoes; petunias (*Petunia*).
Prevention and control: *Chemical:* Spray with dimethoate or maldison as soon as damage is noticed. *Non-chemical/organic:* Use a product based on flowers of sulphur.

WOOLLY ADELGIDS (fir, larch, Douglas fir)
Adelges spp.
Range: Europe.
Description: Sap-feeding insects that attack leaves and stems of certain conifers. They have a waxy coating that camouflages them.
Damage: Negligible; some yellowing of the foliage can occur, but plants continue to grow normally.
Plants affected: Firs (*Abies*), larches (*Larix*), pines (*Pinus*)

and Douglas firs (*Pseudotsuga*).
Prevention and control: *Chemical:* Spray with malathion in late winter to early spring, if necessary.

CYPRESS BARK WEEVIL
Aesiotes leucurus
Range: Australia (mainly eastern).
Description: The adult is a dark grey to dark brown insect, about 2cm (⅘in) long, active in spring and summer, that feeds on the young growth of conifers. The white larvae, about 2cm (⅘in) long, feed beneath the bark. On reaching adulthood, they emerge through holes chewed in the bark.
Damage: Young growth is eaten. Shoot tips die. Larvae that chew right around some branches, or even the trunk, can cause the death of the tree.
Plants affected: Cypress (*Cupressus*), false cypress (*Chamaecyparis*) and some other conifers. They are particularly vulnerable to infestation during times of drought.
Prevention and control: *Non-chemical/organic:* Cut back dead growth and water the tree to keep it growing strongly.

HIBISCUS FLOWER BEETLE
Aethina concolor, syn. *Olliffura concolor*
Range: Australia.
Description: A black beetle about 3mm (⅛in) in length,

which is often found in large numbers on the flowers of hibiscus. It feeds mainly on the pollen.
Damage: Holes are chewed in petals. Buds dropped by the plant, however, are more likely to be the result of a physiological problem – for instance, a sudden cold spell after a warm spring or excessive dryness at the roots.
Plants affected: Hibiscus (*Hibiscus*) and magnolias (*Magnolia*).
Prevention and control: *Chemical:* Spray with carbaryl or diazinon, if necessary. *Non-chemical/organic:* Remove any damaged or dropped flowers and buds.

PAINTED VINE MOTH CATERPILLAR
Agarista agricola
Range: North-eastern Australia.
Description: The adult is a predominantly black moth about 6.5cm (2¼in) across. Larvae are striped black, orange and cream.
Damage: Larvae eat holes in leaves.
Plants affected: Cissus (*Cissus*), grapes and *Parthenocissus*.
Prevention and control: *Chemical:* Spray with carbaryl. *Non-chemical/organic:* Pick off the caterpillars by hand.

Below: The presence of woolly adelgids is clearly visible on these pine needles.

HOREHOUND BUG
Agonoscelis rutila

Range: Eastern Australia
(native).
Description: This sap-sucking,
shield bug, 12mm (½in) long,
is orange with black markings
on the top and underside of the
body. It has five nymphal stages
and tends to swarm.
Damage: Shoots wilt.
Plants affected: Horehounds
(*Marrubium vulgare*), occasionally
other plants.
Prevention and control:
Chemical: Spray swarms with
dimethoate or maldison.

WIREWORMS
Agriotes spp., *Limonius spp.*

Range: Europe to Asia; North
America.
Description: Wireworms are the
larvae of click beetles. Adults,
which lay their eggs in the soil,
are brown or black and
8.5mm–2cm (⅓–⅜in) long.
Larvae are orange-brown and to
2.5cm (1in) long. They feed
underground. Depending on the
climate, there can be up to three
or more generations per year.
Damage: Larvae tunnel in
tuberous roots. Seedlings can be
killed outright if the wireworms
eat through the underground
tissue. Adults chew holes in
plant leaves. They are also
vectors of cucumber mosaic
virus and other diseases.
Plants affected: Potatoes,
carrots, cucumbers, peanuts and
sweet corn.
Prevention and control:
Chemical: Dust seedlings with
lindane or pirimiphos-methyl.
Non-chemical/organic: Use canola

Below: A wireworm.

Above: The bogong moth begins
life as a cream caterpillar. In later
stages its skin becomes pale green
with line markings. It has a black
head. In its final stages it turns
brown in colour, often with an
orange tint.

oil or kaolin to protect against
adults. *Potatoes:* Lift tubers for
storage as early as possible.
Cucumbers: Sow varieties known
to be virus-resistant.

BOGONG MOTH
CATERPILLAR
Agrotis infusa

Range: North Australia.
Description: The adult is a
moth that lays its eggs in late
summer. Larvae feed on fresh
new growth produced in
autumn, winter and early spring.
Damage: Leaves are eaten.
Plants affected: A wide range of
leafy plants.
Prevention and control:
Chemical: Spray or dust with
carbaryl. *Non-chemical/organic:*
Pick off larvae by hand and
dispose of them.

CABBAGE
WHITEFLY
Aleyrodes proletella

Range: Europe.
Description: The adult is a tiny,
white, moth-like insect. Larvae
are flat, oval and scale-like. Both
suck sap from the underside of
leaves. Usually only the outer
leaves are attacked, so low
infestations can be tolerated.
Damage: Outer leaves are
covered with a black mould that
clings to the pests' excreta.
Plants affected: Cabbages and
other brassicas.
Prevention and control:
Chemical: Spray with permethrin,

Above: The outer leaf of this
cabbage is covered in cabbage
whitefly larvae.

bifenthrin or pirimiphos-
methyl. Repeated applications
of these chemicals may be
necessary.

WHITEFLY
Aleyrodidae

Range: Cosmopolitan.
Description: Whiteflies are
white, moth-like insects, to
3mm (⅛in) across. Eggs are
laid on the undersides of leaves.
Whiteflies suck sap and excrete
honeydew. When disturbed,
they fly quickly from the plant,
but return.
Damage: Yellow mottling
appears on the upper leaf
surfaces. Honeydew attracts
sooty mould.
Plants affected: A wide range,
including plants grown under
glass.
Prevention and control:
Some strains have developed
resistance to chemical
insecticides. *Chemical:* Spray
with dimethoate, permethrin,
bifenthrin or pirimiphos-methyl.
Non-chemical/organic: The parasitic
wasp *Encarsia formosa* can be used
to control whiteflies.

Below: Whiteflies, though
miniscule, are easily visible on
leaves because of their colour.

MARCH MOTH
(fruit trees)
Alsophila aescularia

Range: Europe.
Description: The adult male is
a grey to brownish moth, to
2cm (⅚in) across; females are
wingless, and crawl up fruit tree
trunks to lay their eggs among
the branches. Caterpillars, active
in late spring to early summer,
feed on new leaves, flowers and
developing fruits. They bind
leaves together with silky
threads.
Damage: Small holes are eaten
in leaves (most noticeable
when leaves are fully open).
Blossom can be eaten and fruits
are misshapen.
Plants affected: Fruit trees.
Prevention and control:
Chemical: Spray with permethrin,
bifenthrin, pirimiphos-methyl
or fenitrothion when new
growth emerges in spring. *Non-
chemical/organic:* Prevent egg-
laying by binding tree trunks
with grease bands over winter to
trap the females.

METALLIC FLEA
BEETLES
Altica spp.

Range: Cosmopolitan.
Description: The adult beetles
are about 3mm (⅛in) long and
have shiny, metallic-looking
bodies. They move by jumping.
Larvae, which do little harm,
emerge in the stems of plants.
Damage: Irregularly shaped
holes are eaten by the beetles
in shoot tips and the upper
surfaces of young leaves; buds

Below: A plum leaf provides food
for a March moth caterpillar, active
in late spring.

Above: A large metallic flea beetle has eaten the holes in the petals of this shrubby potentilla.

Above: This squash bug has clearly defined characteristics.

are also damaged by the beetles. Heavy attacks can kill seedlings and young plants.
Plants affected: A wide range of ornamentals and crops, including avocados, dahlias (*Dahlia*), grapes (including fruiting varieties), hibiscus (*Hibiscus*), potatoes and sweet potatoes; weeds can also be infested.
Prevention and control: *Chemical:* Spray with carbaryl.

BANANA-SPOTTING BUG
Amblypelta lutescens
Range: Australia (mainly bushland areas of Queensland).
Description: The adult is a green bug, about 1.5cm (⅝in) long. Nymphs are light red with black spots on the abdomen.
Damage: Young shoots and fruits are attacked. *Avocados:* Watersoaked areas appear on fruits, which exude sap. These dry out. The flesh beneath the spots is discoloured. *Bananas:* Skins of fruits show dark, sunken patches.
Plants affected: A range of fruiting plants, including avocados, bananas, citrus, lychees and passion fruit.
Prevention and control: Early detection is desirable; non-chemical methods of control are preferable. *Chemical:* Spray bugs with trichlorfon. *Non-chemical/organic:* Spray with a soap spray. Check plants regularly at the flowering stage

and as the fruits are forming. Treat infestations as soon as they are spotted.

FRUITSPOTTING BUG
Amblypelta nitida
Range: South-eastern Australia.
Description: The adult is a green bug about 1.5cm (⅝in) in length. Nymphs are reddish-black with two black spots on the abdomen. Both adults and nymphs suck sap. Fertility rises during warm weather, when numbers can rapidly increase. Fruitspotting bugs often occur together with the *banana-spotting bug*.
Damage: *Avocados:* Watersoaked areas appear on fruits, which exude sap. The flesh beneath the spots is discoloured. *Macadamias:* Green nuts have slightly sunken, dark spots and are shed by the plant. Kernels can be deformed. *Papayas:* Fruits are shed. *Peaches:* Fruits exude a sticky gum and can be shed.
Plants affected: Many fruiting plants including apples, avocados, citrus, macadamias, nectarines, guavas, peaches and persimmons.
Prevention and control: Early detection is desirable; non-chemical methods of control are preferable. *Chemical:* Spray with trichlorfon. *Non-chemical/organic:* Spray with a soap spray. Check plants regularly at the flowering stage and as the fruits are forming.

SQUASH BUG
Anasa tristis
Range: Throughout North America.
Description: Adults are dark brown to black bugs, about 1.5cm (⅝in) long, that lay their eggs in groups on leaves. The nymphs are pale grey to green. Both suck sap.
Damage: Leaves wilt, blacken, then dry out and die. Small plants can be killed outright.
Plants affected: Cucumbers, melons, pumpkins and squashes.
Prevention and control: *Chemical:* Chemical control is unlikely to be successful. *Non-chemical/organic:* Cover seedlings with floating cloches. Pick off pests and eggs.

CHRISTMAS BEETLES (eucalyptus)
Anoplognathus spp.
Range: Australia.
Description: The adults are shiny beetles, brown with a green tinge. They are active from November to January. The larvae are white grubs that live in the soil, feeding on the roots of grasses and other small plants.
Damage: Characteristic "saw-tooth" holes are eaten in leaves.
Plants affected: Eucalyptus (*Eucalyptus*) (particularly specimens over 3m/10ft tall).
Prevention and control: Seriously infested trees are best grubbed up and destroyed.

ROOT APHID (parsnips, spinach)
Anuraphis subterranea
Range: Europe.
Description: A greyish-white aphid that feeds on parsnips. It is most common during late summer.
Damage: The shoulders of roots and the base of the leaves are attacked around soil level. Plants grow slowly and tend to wilt in warm weather. Roots may be coated with a white powder.
Plants affected: Parsnips, annual spinach.
Prevention and control: *Chemical:* Drench the soil with dimethoate, heptenophos with permethrin, pirimicarb or pirimiphos-methyl. *Non-chemical/organic:* Practise crop rotation.

APPLE BLOSSOM WEEVIL
Anthonomus pomorum
Range: Europe. The pest is now less common than formerly.
Description: The adult is a small brown beetle that lays its eggs in unopened flower buds. The larvae are small white grubs, which eat the flowers from the inside.
Damage: Flowers fail to develop and fruit is not set.
Plants affected: Apples.
Prevention and control: *Chemical:* Spray with fenitrothion, pirimiphos-methyl or bifenthrin as the buds are about to burst.

Below: Adult Christmas beetles bite holes in leaves.

Above: A citrus fruit covered in California red scale.

CALIFORNIA RED SCALE, Red Scale

Aonidiella aurantii

Range: Australia, North America and Europe (where citrus are grown).
Description: This hard scale insect is orange to orange-pink; the adult red scale is about 1.5mm (¹⁄₁₆ in) across. It generally appears only on those parts of plants that receive the highest light levels.
Damage: *Citrus*: Branches dry out, leaves turn yellow and are shed. Fruits are encrusted.
Plants affected: Citrus; also wattles (*Acacia*), ivies (*Hedera*), hollies (*Ilex*), mangoes, mulberries, passion fruit, roses (*Rosa*) and willow (*Salix*).
Prevention and control: *Chemical:* Spray with malathion. *Non-chemical/organic:* Canola oil.

EELWORMS

Aphelenchoides spp., other species

Range: Cosmopolitan.
Description: Eelworms, or nematodes, are microscopic, worm-like creatures that live in the soil. Many cause little harm to plants, and can be beneficial, since they feed on fungi, bacteria and other micro-organisms. Some feed within host plants and can be carriers of viral diseases. Most are host specific.
Damage: Roots and other plant parts are eaten.
Plants affected: A large range of garden plants.
Prevention and control: *Non-chemical/organic:* Do not replant areas of the garden affected by eelworms with the same plant. Practise crop rotation in the vegetable garden.

FERN EELWORM, Chrysanthemum Eelworm

Aphelenchoides fragariae, A. ritzemabosi

Range: Temperate and tropical regions.
Description: Microscopic worm-like creatures that feed inside the leaves of certain plants grown under glass.
Damage: Brown areas appear on the surfaces of leaves where the eelworms are active. With severe infestation, entire leaves turn brown and then black. The foliage dries up from the base of the plant upwards.
Plants affected: A range of plants cultivated under glass, especially ferns and chrysanthemums.
Prevention and control: *Non-chemical/organic:* Dig up and destroy affected plants.

Below: This leaf has been damaged by chrysanthemum eelworm.

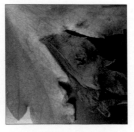

Chrysanthemums, however, can be saved to provide propagation material. Dig up the dormant stools, shake away any soil and plunge them into a bath of hot water held at 46°C/115°F for five minutes. Any more heat will damage the plant. Take cuttings from the new shoots in late winter/spring.

BLACKFLY

Aphis fabae

Range: Europe.
Description: The adult is a black (sometimes green) insect, to 2mm (¹⁄₁₂in) long, that lays its eggs on spindles (*Euonymus*) or other shrubs. Blackfly suck sap from a range of garden plants, sometimes in dense colonies, during spring and summer. A number of other aphid species have the common name blackfly.
Damage: Leaves curl at the shoot tips. Affected plants are weakened. *Beans:* Pods fail to develop.
Plants affected: A wide range, including broad (fava) beans and globe artichokes; dahlias (*Dahlia*), poppies (*Papaver*), nasturtiums (*Tropaeolum*), viburnum (*Viburnum*) and mock orange (*Philadelphus*).
Prevention and control: *Chemical:* Spray with hepteophos with permethrin, dimethoate, pirimicarb, bifenthrin, pirimiphos-methyl or malathion. *Non-chemical/organic:* Substitute pyrethrum, derris or an insecticidal soap.

Below: Blackflies usually appear in large groups on stems and the undersides of leaves.

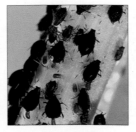

FRUITTREE LEAFROLLERS

Archips argyrospila, other species

Range: North America.
Description: The adult is a brown moth, about 2.5cm (1in) across, with gold-mottled wings, that lays its eggs on bark. The caterpillars, up to 2cm (⁴⁄₅in) long, are green with dark brown or black heads. There is one generation per year. Larvae emerge in spring to feed on leaves, buds, flowers and developing fruit, then roll leaves around themselves to pupate.
Damage: Leaf damage is minor. Fruit can be deeply scarred.
Plants affected: Apples, apricots, cherries, pears, soft fruits and some others.
Prevention and control: *Chemical:* Spray with pirimiphos-methyl or permethrin. *Non-chemical/organic:* Pick off rolled-up leaves. Spray with canola oil or kaolin before petal fall or use *Bacillus thuringinensis* var. *kurstaki*.

ACER PIMPLE GALL MITE, Acer Gall Mite

Artacris macrorhynchus, Eriophyes eriobus

Range: Europe.
Description: These tiny gall mites live within the plant tissue of maples.

Below: The inside of this maple leaf has become infested with acer pimple gall mites.

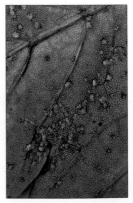

Below: The brown patches on this leaf indicate eelworm attack.

Damage: Reddish, raised pimples appear on the surfaces of leaves. Heavily infested leaves show some distortion.
Plants affected: Maples (*Acer*).
Prevention and control: *Chemical:* There is no form of chemical control. While unsightly, the pest does little damage. *Non-chemical/organic:* If necessary on small plants, remove all the affected leaves.

NEW ZEALAND FLATWORM
Artioposthia triangulata
Range: Australasia; introduced into Europe.
Description: A leech-like creature, 10–15cm (4–6in) long. Its purplish brown body is paler at the flattened edges. It is mainly nocturnal, spending the daylight hours curled up under stones. Flatworms are often unwittingly introduced into gardens in the roots of bought container-grown plants. They prey on earthworms and are a very serious pest.
Damage: Flatworms do not damage plants directly, but the reduction of earthworm populations results in poor drainage and aeration of the soil. Plant growth suffers.
Plants affected: Potentially all garden plants.

Below: The rust-coloured speckles of oleander scale can spoil the appearance of leaves.

Prevention and control: None possible. Soak newly purchased container-grown plants in water to encourage any flatworms to emerge. Wash the roots carefully before planting out (eggs are blackcurrant-like). Contact your local agriculture office.

OLEANDER SCALE, Ivy Scale
Aspidiotus nerii
Range: Australia and New Zealand.
Description: A roughly circular scale insect up to about 2mm (⅒in) across and white to brownish in colour. Oleander scales appear on bark, leaves and fruits.
Damage: Plants are disfigured.
Plants affected: A wide range, including wattles (*Acacia*), buddleias (*Buddleja*), camellias (*Camellia*), daphnes (*Daphne*), ferns, ivies (*Hedera*), hollies (*Ilex*), orchids, Boston ivy (*Parthenocissus tricuspidata*), viburnums (*Viburnum*); also grapes.
Prevention and control: *Non-chemical/organic:* Spray with white oil.

FULLER'S ROSE WEEVIL
Asynonychus cervinus
Range: Australia.
Description: The adult is a grey-brown weevil about 7mm (³⁄₁₀in) long, active in summer and autumn. It lays its eggs beneath loose bark or in curled leaves on the ground, and feeds on leaves. Larvae, 6mm (¼in)

Above: Fuller's rose weevil is a beetle-like insect that does no long-term damage.

long and grey-white, live underground, where they feed on plant roots but cause little long-term harm.
Damage: Roots are damaged. Large plants survive, but small tomato plants can suffer.
Plants affected: A wide range, including blackberries, cherries, citrus, passion fruit and peaches; susceptible ornamentals include camellias (*Camellia*), dahlias (*Dahlia*) and gardenias (*Gardenia*). Weeds such as fat hen can harbour the pest.
Prevention and control: *Chemical:* Spray with carbaryl as soon as young adults are seen.

SCURFY SCALE, Rose Scale
Aulacaspis rosae
Range: Cosmopolitan.
Description: The adult is a greyish-white, circular scale about 3mm (⅛in across). They encrust stems.

Below: The stem of this rose is covered in scurfy scale, which will hinder its growth.

Damage: Growth is impaired.
Plants affected: Roses (*Rosa*).
Prevention and control: *Chemical:* Spray with malathion in early autumn.

MOTTLED ARUM APHID
Aulacorthum circumflexum
Range: Europe.
Description: This aphid is a type of greenfly that sucks sap from plants. The adult is yellow-green and excretes honeydew. The skins that are shed by the insect as it grows stick to this honeydew and may easily be mistaken for *whitefly* infestation. The mottled arum aphid sometimes also occurs on plants in association with the *peach-potato aphid* (*Myzus persicae*).
Damage: Leaves are puckered and plants grow more slowly than usual. Leaves and fruits become shiny and sticky with honeydew, then blacken with *sooty mould* in humid conditions under glass.
Plants affected: A range of plants grown under glass.
Prevention and control: *Chemical:* Spray with pirimicarb, pirimiphos-methyl, permethrin or heptenophos. *Non-chemical/organic:* Spray with pyrethrum.

Below: Both female mottled arum aphids and nymphs are sucking sap from this hothouse ornamental.

PUMPKIN BEETLE (cucurbits)

Aulacophora hilaris

Range: Central to eastern Australia.
Description: The adult, about 6mm (¼in) long, is a yellow-orange beetle with four black spots. Pumpkin beetles prefer warm, dry conditions and are most numerous from late spring to early autumn. Larvae are active either below ground or at soil level but do little harm.
Damage: Adults chew leaves and flowers. Young plants can be completely decimated, but light infestations on more developed plants can be tolerated.
Plants affected: Cucurbits; other plants occasionally suffer.
Prevention and control: *Chemical:* Dust young plants with maldison dust; spray older ones with carbaryl. *Non-chemical/organic:* Dust with derris.

SILVER Y-MOTH

Autographa gamma

Range: Europe.
Description: The adult moth is grey- to violet-brown, to 2cm (⅘in) across. The caterpillars, to 2.5cm (1in) long, yellowish- to bluish-green, lined and ringed white, are active at night.
Damage: Caterpillars eat flowers and leaves.
Plants affected: Ornamentals under glass; occasionally also peas and cabbages.
Prevention and control: *Chemical:* Spray with pirimiphos-methyl or permethrin.

Below: The caterpillar of the silver Y-moth is seen here feeding on a buddleia leaf.

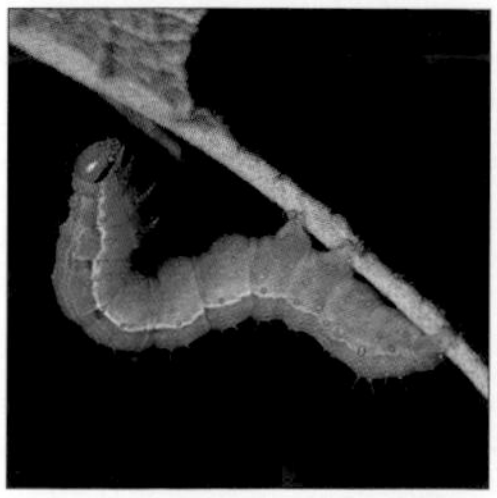

Non-chemical/organic: Hunt for caterpillars at night and pick them off by hand.

SPINED CITRUS BUG

Biprorulus bibax

Range: Eastern Australia.
Description: The adult is a green bug, 2cm (⅘in) long, with a pronounced horn to each side of the head. Nymphs are yellow and black or orange and black, gradually turning green. Both stages attack fruit.
Damage: Sap is sucked from fruits, creating dry patches. Gumming and browning can occur inside fruits, and fruits can be shed.
Plants affected: Citrus and related fruits, particularly mandarins, also lemons, limes.
Prevention and control: *Chemical:* Spray with maldison or dimethoate. *Non-chemical/organic:* Set pheromone traps; pick off.

LEAF-ROLLING ROSE SAWFLY

Blennocampa pusilla

Range: Europe.
Description: The adult is a black sawfly that lays its eggs on rose leaves in late spring. Female secretions cause the leaves to roll around the eggs, which hatch into small, pale green caterpillars. There is usually only one generation per year.
Damage: Leaves are rolled. The developing caterpillars feed on the leaves.

Below: The "Y" marking can be seen on this moth, despite its brownish colouring.

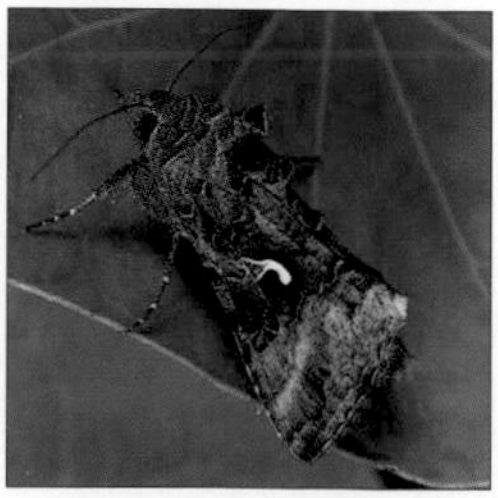

Above: These rose leaves are rolled around rose sawfly eggs.

Plants affected: Roses (*Rosa*).
Prevention and control: *Chemical:* Spray with pirimiphos-methyl from mid-spring. *Non-chemical/organic:* Pick off individual caterpillars or rolled leaves by hand.

LARGE AUGER BEETLE

Bostrychopsis jesuita

Range: Australia.
Description: The adult is a black beetle about 1–2cm (⅖–⅘in) long. The larvae are creamy white. They tunnel through sapwood, emerging through the bark on adulthood. Trees that are already dead or dying are prone to infestation.
Damage: Death and decay of already dying trees is accelerated.
Plants affected: A wide range, including citrus and other fruit trees, wattles (*Acacia*) and eucalyptus (*Eucalyptus*).
Prevention and control: None

Below: Caraway, coriander, dill, mint, fennel, potentillas and statice (*Limonium*) attract braconid wasps.

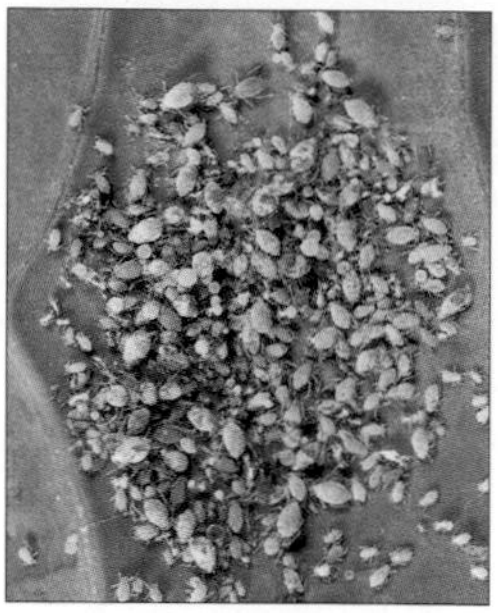

Above: Mealy cabbage aphids suck sap from an oilseed rape leaf.

necessary. Replace affected trees with healthy stock appropriate to the local conditions.

BRACONID WASPS

Braconidae

Range: Cosmopolitan.
Description: Adults are black or brown or reddish insects, to 1.25cm (½in) long depending on the species. Braconid wasps are beneficial insects; eggs are laid into the bodies of host insects. Larvae are small, white grubs that feed on the host insect from inside its body. They emerge to spin their cocoons either on the insect's body or nearby. There can be several generations per year. For details of wasps that cause damage to plants, see under *Vespula* spp.
Damage: The activities of braconid wasps cause no direct damage to plants.
Prevention and control: Not necessary.

MEALY CABBAGE APHID

Brevicoryne brassicae

Range: Europe; North America.
Description: The adult is a bluish-grey aphid, covered in a waxy powder, that sucks sap from the underside of leaves. Large colonies build up from late spring to autumn. Eggs are laid towards the end of the season and hatch the following spring. Young plants can be severely damaged.

Damage: Foliage turns yellow and growth is stunted. Plants can be rendered inedible.
Plants affected: Mainly cabbages; also Brussels sprouts, cauliflowers and swedes (rutabagas).
Prevention and control: Check regularly for infestations from spring onwards. *Chemical:* Spray with dimethoate, heptenophos or pirimicarb. To limit the spread of the aphid, dip transplants in insecticide before replanting them. *Non-chemical/organic:* Dig up affected plants after cropping and burn them to destroy any eggs.

BUNCH MITE
(grapes, citrus)
Brevipalpus californicus
Range: Eastern Australia; parts of North America.
Description: This microscopic mite feeds on leaves close to bunches of grapes or on the fruits themselves, sometimes impeding the flow of water to the truss. It overwinters in the cracks in bark.
Damage: Leaves turn brown and develop a rough appearance. Grapes shrivel and/or drop. Skins of fruits can thicken and crack.
Plants affected: Grapes; woolly-leaved varieties are especially vulnerable. Also citrus.
Prevention and control: *Chemical:* Treat with dicofol. *Non-chemical/organic:* Spray with sulphur. Spray plants affected the previous year with lime sulphur as the buds burst.

CITRUS GALL WASP
Bruchophagus fellis
Range: Eastern Australia.
Description: The adult is a tiny black wasp that lays its eggs on the soft growth of citrus. The activity of the larvae causes galls to form that reach full size by autumn. Later generations reinfest the same tree. In some areas, control is a legal requirement.
Damage: Plants are weakened

Above: The citrus gall wasp has damaged this tree.

and become unproductive.
Plants affected: Citrus, especially rough lemons and grapefruits.
Prevention and control: *Non-chemical/ organic:* Cut the galls from affected plants and burn.

BRYOBIA MITE
Bryobia rubrioculus
Range: Australia; also parts of North America.
Description: The adult is a purplish-brown to greenish-grey mite, about 1mm (¹⁄₂₅in) long, that lays its eggs on tree bark or among branches and twigs. Young mites, initially bright red, emerge in spring, feeding on new leaves, usually at night.
Damage: Leaves are mottled white, eventually turning pale all over. Plant vigour is affected; fruits are smaller and less numerous.
Plants affected: Many fruiting trees, including almonds, apples, pears and plums; also hawthorns (*Crataegus*).
Prevention and control: *Chemical:* Spray with difocol as soon as leaf damage is seen. *Non-chemical/organic:* Spray with sulphur at the first sign of damage. Overwintering eggs can be killed by spraying bark with white oil in spring.

JEWEL BEETLES
Buprestidae
Range: Tropical regions.
Description: This family of beetles comprises hundreds of species that vary in size and colour. Adults are active at night, chewing leaves and flowers, but the real damage is

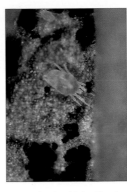
Above: A female adult bryobia mite.

done by the larvae, which are white and look like tiny cobras. They tunnel through wood beneath tree bark, favouring trees that have already been damaged or are growing poorly. These pests can often be detected only by removing sections of bark and examining the live tissue.
Damage: Holes are tunnelled through wood.
Plants affected: A variety of trees; some species are associated with particular trees.
Prevention and control: None possible. Severely affected trees are best removed.

RASPBERRY BEETLE
Byturus tomentosus
Range: Central Europe to the British Isles.
Description: The adult is a small brown beetle that lays its eggs on the flowers of some cane fruits in early to midsummer. The larvae, which are pale brown and up to 8mm

(¹⁄₁₆in) long, feed on the developing fruits.
Damage: Fruits dry up.
Plants affected: Blackberries, loganberries and raspberries.
Prevention and control: *Chemical:* Spray with fenitrothion. *Non-chemical/organic:* Spray with derris as follows: on blackberries when the first flowers open, on loganberries when 80 per cent of petals have fallen and on raspberries when the first pink fruits are seen. Avoid spraying all plants at the peak of flowering, when pollinating insects are active.

CARNATION
TORTRIX
CATERPILLAR
Cacoecimorpha pronubana
Range: Europe.
Description: The adult is a small brown moth. Caterpillars are up to 2cm (⅝in) in length and are pale green with a brown head. Several generations can be produced in one year, and caterpillars can be found all year round.
Damage: Young larvae make folds in the edges of leaves or bind leaves together, feeding on inner surfaces. Larger larvae eat holes in leaves.
Plants affected: Carnations (*Dianthus*) and other ornamentals under glass.
Prevention and control: *Chemical:* Spray with pirimiphos-methyl or permethrin. *Non-chemical/organic:* Look for evidence of young larva activity and either pick off affected leaves or squash the culprit flat.

Below: A raspberry beetle larva in a damaged fruit.

Below: A carnation tortrix caterpillar feeding on a leaf.

PEAR PSYLLA (pears and quinces)
Cacopsylla pyricola

Range: Eastern North America and Pacific North-West (similar species occur elsewhere in North America).

Description: The adult is a greenish- or reddish-brown insect, about 3mm (⅛in) long, marked with red or green, that lays its eggs on bark and around buds. The nymphs are initially yellow, later turning green. Both adults and nymphs suck the sap from stems and leaves and feed on fruit. There are three to five generations per year. Earwigs are among their predators.

Damage: Leaves develop brown spots and can be shed. Buds may fail to develop. Fruits are scarred. Honeydew excreted by the pest attracts *sooty mould*.

Plants affected: Pears and quinces.

Prevention and control: *Chemical:* Spray with dimethoate, pirimiphos-methyl or fenitrothion. *Non-chemical/organic:* Prune out water shoots, which can harbour the pest. At the time of bud break, spray with kaolin.

INLAND KATYDID
Caedicia simplex

Range: South-eastern Australia.

Description: The adult is a grasshopper-like insect, about 5cm (2in) long, that lays its eggs in the soil around plants. The nymphs are active in early spring, starting to feed around the base of plants, later climbing higher. The adults

Below: Control of the inland katydid is best undertaken at night.

feed mainly at night.

Damage: Leaves low down on the plant are skeletonized. Holes are chewed in leaves further up the plant. Adults gnaw at fruits.

Plants affected: Mainly peaches; also apples, grapes and pears.

Prevention and control: *Chemical:* Spray with carbaryl or fenthion. Repeated applications may be necessary.

CITRUS KATYDID
Caedicia strenua

Range: South-eastern Australia.

Description: The adult is a green, grasshopper-like insect, about 4.5cm (1¼in) long. Nymphs feed on young leaves first, then move on to older leaves and developing fruits.

Damage: Holes are chewed in leaves. Patches are removed from the surface of small fruits. These appear white initially, turning grey as the fruit grows. Fungi sometimes take hold in damaged fruits.

Plants affected: Citrus (lemons only rarely).

Prevention and control: *Chemical:* Spray with carbaryl or fenthion.

GRAPELEAF RUST MITE
Calepitrimerus vitis

Range: Australia

Description: This mite is microscopic. Colonies build up

Below: Detection of the grapeleaf rust mite is possible with a magnifying glass.

on the surfaces of leaves, giving a reddish-brown appearance. Fruiting capacity does not seem to be affected.

Damage: Leaves discolour and can be shed prematurely.

Plants affected: Grapevines.

Prevention and control: *Non-chemical/organic:* Spray with lime sulphur as the buds begin to swell in spring, aiming to wet the whole plant.

PEAR AND CHERRY SLUGWORM CATERPILLAR, Pear and Cherry Slug
Caliroa cerasi

Range: Europe, North America and Australia.

Description: The adult is a shiny black sawfly, to 8mm (⅛in) long. The slimy, dark green larvae, to 1cm (⅜in) long, feed mostly on the upper surfaces of leaves, leaving a network of veins. Damaged areas dry out.

Damage: Leaves have a white or brown appearance. Light infestations cause little damage.

Plants affected: Apples, pears, quinces, cherries and plums; also hawthorns (*Crataegus*).

Prevention and control: *Chemical:* Spray with permethrin, fenitrothion, pirimiphos-methyl or carbaryl. *Non-chemical/organic:* Substitute pyrethrum or derris, or hose the pests from the leaves with water.

Below: There are two or more generations of pear and cherry slugworm per year.

Above: These brown blisters are caused by the mining activities of the azalea leafminer.

AZALEA LEAF-MINER
Caloptilia azaleella

Range: Cosmopolitan.

Description: The adult is a moth, about 1cm (⅜in) across, that lays its eggs near the mid-rib of leaves. Caterpillars feed within the leaf.

Damage: Mining by the larvae results in white streaks visible on the underside of leaves. These develop as brown patches or blisters. Caterpillars eventually curl leaf tips and web them in place.

Plants affected: Azaleas (*Rhododendron*).

Prevention and control: *Chemical:* Spray with dimethoate or a systemic insecticide.

APPLE DIMPLING BUG
Campylomma liebknechti

Range: Australia (native).

Description: This is a pale green bug, about 2mm (¹⁄₁₀in) long, that sucks sap from blossom and developing fruits. The damage is similar in appearance to *boron deficiency*. The level of damage varies each year, depending on climate. To a certain extent the pest can be tolerated, since it attacks aphids.

Damage: Indentations appear on the surface of fruits.

Plants affected: Apples, particularly 'Granny Smith' and 'Delicious'.

Prevention and control: *Chemical:* Spray heavy infestations with omethoate. *Non-chemical/organic:* Shake the tree to dislodge the pests and trap them on sticky yellow traps hung from the branches.

BROWN BASKET LERP (eucalyptus)
Cardiaspina fiscella
Range: North-eastern Australia. Description: This is a sap-sucking insect that feeds within the leaves of trees.
Damage: Upper surfaces of leaves develop red or yellow blotches. Leaves eventually turn brown. In severe cases, trees are killed.
Plants affected: Eucalyptus (*Eucalyptus*), especially *E. robusta*.
Prevention and control: *Chemical:* Where practical, spray trees with maldison.

DRIED FRUIT BEETLES
Carpophilus spp.
Range: Widely distributed. Description: The adults are dark brown beetles, about 3mm (⅛in) long, laying their eggs in over-ripe or rotting fruit on plants or on the ground. They also carry *brown rot*.
Damage: Fruits rot.
Plants affected: Many fruits, including stone fruits (those with pits) and tomatoes.
Prevention and control: *Chemical:* Spray with maldison at regular intervals when the beetles are active. *Non-chemical/organic:* Remove shed fruit from the ground to eliminate larvae and restrict the spread of disease.

TEA TREE WEB MOTH
Catamola thyrisalis
Range: Australia.
Description: The adult is a moth that lays its eggs on and around trees. The larvae shelter by day in a mass of silk webbing, emerging at night to feed.

Damage: Webs spun by the larvae are unsightly.
Plants affected: Tea trees (*Leptospermum*).
Prevention and control: *Chemical:* Spray with carbaryl. *Non-chemical/organic:* Remove the webs by hand.

BIG BUD MITE, Currant Bud Mite (blackcurrants)
Cecidophyopsis ribis
Range: Europe, Australia and New Zealand.
Description: This tiny mite lives inside blackcurrant buds. Affected buds (most obvious in winter) are enlarged, swollen and rounded. The mites are also the carriers of reversion disease.
Damage: Affected buds fail to open, or produce distorted growth as the mites emerge in spring in search of fresh buds.
Plants affected: Blackcurrants.
Prevention and control: *Chemical:* Spray with carbendazim as the flowers open. Repeated applications may be necessary. *Non-chemical/organic:* Pick off and burn enlarged buds in winter. Complete control is difficult, however, and severely affected bushes should be dug up and burnt. Some varieties of blackcurrant have a resistance to the mite.

Below: This blackcurrant shoot has the typical swollen buds of a big bug mite infection.

Above: The adult longicorn is a uniform brown colour.

ORANGE PALMDART (palms)
Cephrenes augiades sperthias
Range: Coastal regions of Australia.
Description: The adult is an orange and brown moth (or skipper). The caterpillars are pale bluish-green with a distinct head. They wrap sections of leaves around themselves, in which they feed.
Damage: Leaves are tattered.
Plants affected: Palms, especially *Archontophoenix cunninghamiana* and *Livistona australis*.
Prevention and control: *Chemical:* Spray with carbaryl. *Non-chemical/organic:* Unfold affected leaves and dispose of the larvae.

LONGICORNS, Long Horn Beetles
Cerambycidae
Range: Mainly tropical regions. Description: The adult beetles lay their eggs in the cracks in bark of woody plants. The fleshy and cream-coloured larvae tunnel through the wood

Above: This red-and-black spittlebug is an example of the species *Cercopis vulnerata*.

beneath the bark. Cracks in the bark, which are more noticeable on smooth-barked trees, indicate their activity. There are many species of these beetles, all of which cause considerable damage, though they usually attack only trees that have already been weakened, either through old age or as a result of disease.
Damage: Plants lose their vigour and can die if the infestation is severe.
Plants affected: A range of trees and shrubs and some climbers.
Prevention and control: *Non-chemical/organic:* Prune off affected branches where practical and keep the tree growing strongly.

SPITTLEBUGS, Froghoppers
Cercopidae
Range: Cosmopolitan.
Description: The adults ("froghoppers") are usually brown or green, and 3–6mm (⅛–¼in) long. The nymphs are pale green and wingless. Both adults and nymphs suck sap from plants.
Damage: Damage from sap-sucking is minimal, but the froth (known as "cuckoo spit") secreted by the nymphs is unsightly.
Plants affected: A wide range, including legumes, strawberries, grasses and many weeds.
Prevention and control: Unnecessary. Cuckoo spit can be hosed off the stems with a jet of water.

Below: Spittlebug damage or "cuckoo spit" does no damage to plants but is unsightly.

Above: Honeydew from wax scale insects has encouraged sooty mould on this leaf.

INDIAN WHITE WAX SCALE

Ceroplastes ceriferus
Range: Cosmopolitan.
Description: This scale has a white waxy covering. It is similar to the white wax scale, *Ceroplastes destructor*, though slightly smaller.
Damage: A build-up of honeydew results in a loss of vigour. Disease can take hold.
Plants affected: A range of ornamentals, including Michaelmas daisies (*Aster*), sacred bamboos (*Nandina*), barberries (*Berberis*), chrysanthemums (*Chrysanthemum*) and firethorns (*Pyracantha*).
Prevention and control:
Chemical: Spray with malathion. *Non-chemical/organic:* Spray with white oil when the crawlers are active in summer. Remove mature scales with a stiff brush.

WHITE WAX SCALE

Ceroplastes destructor
Range: Australia and New Zealand.
Description: This scale, which can reach a length of 1cm (⅜in), has a waxy, whitish covering and is found on the twigs of certain plants. The crawlers initially feed on leaves, moving to the twigs to produce their covering as they reach the adult stage. The white wax scale causes little harm in itself, but its honeydew attracts ants and encourages *sooty mould*, besides disfiguring the plant.

Damage: A build-up of honeydew results in a loss of vigour. Disease can take hold.
Plants affected: A range of ornamentals, including Michaelmas daisies (*Aster*), barberries (*Berberis*), chrysanthemums (*Chrysanthemum*), bay laurels (*Laurus nobilis*), bamboo (*Nandina*) and firethorns (*Pyracantha*).
Prevention and control:
Chemical: Spray with malathion. *Non-chemical/organic:* Spray with white oil when the crawlers are active in summer. Remove mature scales with a stiff brush.

PINK WAX SCALE

Ceroplastes rubens
Range: Tropical and subtropical areas; also found in warm areas of Europe.
Description: The adult, up to 3mm (⅛in) long, is covered with hard, pink or greyish wax. Scales appear on the midribs of leaves and on twigs, producing quantities of honeydew. They are a problem in wet summers.
Damage: Plants lose vigour in severe cases. The honeydew attracts *sooty mould*.

Below: Pink wax scale is highly visible on the insides of leaves.

Plants affected: Avocados, citrus, custard apples, figs, mangoes; also holly (*Ilex*), magnolias (*Magnolia*), pittosporums (*Pittosporum*), ivies (*Hedera*), and some others.
Prevention and control:
Chemical: Spray with carbaryl before the scales are 1mm (½in) long (older scales are difficult to kill). *Non-chemical/organic:* Remove scales by hand.

BEAN LEAF BEETLE (soya and other beans and peas)

Cerotoma trifurcata
Range: Eastern North America (into Canada), Texas, Kansas and New Mexico.
Description: The adult is a reddish-orange to yellow beetle, 6.5mm (¼in) long, that lays orange, oval eggs on the undersides of leaves. The larvae are thin white grubs with brown heads. There are two or three generations per year. They are particularly common in areas where soya crops are grown.
Damage: Larvae tunnel through plant roots and sometimes stems. Adults feed on leaves and help in the spread of viruses.
Plants affected: Soya and other beans and peas.
Prevention and control:
Chemical: Spray with permethrin, pirimiphos-methyl or femitrothion. *Non-chemical/organic:* Spray with canola oil or pyrethrum. Pick off adults where they are found. In areas where infestations are likely, delay sowing until late spring (to miss the beetle's first generation).

TURNIP GALL WEEVIL (brassicas)

Ceutorhynchus pleurostigma
Range: Europe.
Description: The adult is a black beetle. The larvae are small white grubs that cause swelling of the roots (galls) in which they live initially, emerging to pupate in the soil. The damage is easily mistaken

for *club root*. There is usually only one generation per year. (The beetle can also lay its eggs on leafy brassicas such as cabbages and broccoli, but does not cause them serious harm.)
Damage: Damage to established plants is not serious, but young plants' growth can be checked.
Plants affected: Brassicas, including swedes (rutabagas) and turnips.
Prevention and control:
Chemical: To protect seedlings, dust the seed drill with lindane or pirimiphos-methyl.

BANANA RUST THRIPS (banana and giant taro)

Chaetanaphothrips signipennis
Range: Tropical areas.
Description: The adult is a yellow insect, about 1.5mm (¹⁄₁₆in) long. They feed on leaves and fruits, though damage may not be serious if a fruit is already well developed by the time the infestation begins. Populations are highest in summer.
Damage: Reddish areas appear on leaves. Fruit skins are roughened and become dull grey, later turning red or reddish-brown and cracking.
Plants affected: Bananas; also citrus and the giant taro (*Alocasia macrorrhiza*).
Prevention and control:
Chemical: Spray all parts thoroughly with maldison at intervals, also wetting the soil around the plants.

Below: Leaf blotches show damage caused by banana rust thrips.

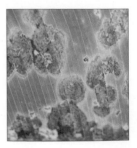

STRAWBERRY APHID
Chaetosiphon fragaefolii
Range: Widely distributed in areas where strawberries are grown.
Description: This aphid grows to 1.5mm (⅟₁₆in) and is pale green-yellow with translucent legs. It sucks sap from leaves and can also spread viruses.
Damage: Plant growth is affected if the infestation is severe.
Plants affected: Strawberries.
Prevention and control: *Chemical:* Spray with an insecticide just before flowers open in spring. Repeat once the crop is harvested.

WHITESTEMMED GUM MOTH (eucalyptus and brush box)
Chelepteryx collesi
Range: South-eastern Australia.
Description: The adult is a greyish-brown moth, about 15cm (6in) across. The larvae, which grow to 11cm (4½in), are covered in spines or hairs that can cause irritation if they are handled. They are active by night from winter to midsummer. Despite the large size of the larvae, they do little harm.
Damage: Tree bark is damaged.
Plants affected: Scribbly gum (*Eucalyptus haemastoma*) and brush box (*Tristania conferta*).
Prevention and control: *Chemical:* Spray with maldison, if necessary.

Below: Whitestemmed gum moth caterpillars have bands of colour and can grow very long.

Above: Centipedes are beneficial creatures in the garden.

CENTIPEDES
Chilopoda
Range: Cosmopolitan.
Description: Centipedes are many-legged creatures, to 7.5cm (3in) long, depending on the species. They overwinter in the soil. There is one generation per year. Centipedes are beneficial creatures that prey on slugs, pupae and other soil-dwelling invertebrates. They are not to be confused with millipedes (Diplopoda), which can cause damage. (Centipedes have one pair of legs per body segment, while millipedes have two pairs of very short legs per segment.)
Damage: Minimal, though centipedes occasionally prey on earthworms.
Plants affected: None.
Prevention and control: Not necessary.

WILLOW SCALE (willows)
Chionaspis salicis
Range: Europe.
Description: A pear-shaped scale about 2mm (⅟₁₆in) long

Below: Whitestemmed gum moths are so large that they may be mistaken for bats.

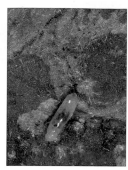

Above: A dissected chrysanthemum leaf shows a leafminer in its mine.

that attacks willows. Dense colonies can form on older branches.
Damage: Vigour is reduced. Die-back occurs in severe cases.
Plants affected: Willows (*Salix*).
Prevention and control: *Chemical:* Spray with malathion at intervals during the period when the eggs are hatching.

CINERARIA LEAFMINER
Chromatomyia syngenesiae
Range: Europe, North America, Australia.
Description: The adult is a black fly, about 2mm (⅟₁₆in) long, that lays its eggs on the underside of leaves. The larvae mine the leaves, producing silvery grey lines on the surface. A mild infestation of this leafminer may not inhibit normal flowering. It is also often found on weeds.
Damage: Plants wilt and in severe cases die.
Plants affected: Weeds, chrysanthemums (*Chrysanthemum*), cinerarias (*Senecio*), and nasturtiums (*Tropaeolum*); lettuces.
Prevention and control: *Chemical:* Spray with a systemic insecticide such as dimethoate. Repeated applications may be necessary. *Non-chemical/organic:* Remove affected leaves when noticed. Keep areas where vulnerable plants are grown weed-free.

GREEN LOOPERS
Chrysodeixis spp.
Range: Widely distributed.
Description: The adults are brown moths, about 3–4cm (1¼–1½in) across. The caterpillars, which grow to 4cm (1½in), are green and inconspicuous among plant foliage; they are active by night. Their activity is sometimes betrayed by dry brown droppings on leaves or around the base of plants.
Damage: Leaves are eaten.
Plants affected: A range of vegetables, annuals and soft-stemmed perennials, including plants under glass.
Prevention and control: *Chemical:* Spray with carbaryl. *Non-chemical/organic:* Pick off the larvae by hand.

FLEA BEETLES, Leaf Beetles, Striped Flea Beetles
Chrysomelidae
Range: Cosmopolitan.
Description: Adults vary in size and colour depending on species; most are shiny brown or black and 2mm (⅟₁₆in) long, sometimes longer. Females lay eggs at the base of plants and the emerging larvae feed on plant roots. Flea beetles can be vectors of some plant diseases. They are active from mid-spring to late summer.
Damage: The larvae eat plant roots (including tubers). Adults chew rounded holes in leaves and affected leaves can turn brown. Affected seedlings can

Below: Flea beetles can produce four generations a year, depending on the species.

Above: This adult turnip flea beetle is feeding on an oilseed rape plant.

be killed outright, though older plants generally recover.
Plants affected: Brassicas; sweet corn, aubergines (eggplants) and sweet potatoes; fuchsias (*Fuchsia*). Weeds can harbour the pests.
Prevention and control: *Chemical*: Treat with derris or bifenthrin, lindane or pirimiphos-methyl. *Non-chemical/organic*: Substitute pyrethrum. Protect seedlings with a floating mulch. Keep a weed-free vegetable garden.

BEET LEAFHOPPER
Circulifer tenellus
Range: North America, Europe, Asia.
Description: The adult is a pale green to brown insect, to 3mm (⅛in) long, capable of rapid hopping and flying. Nymphs are pale green and lack wings. Both adults and nymphs are vectors of a number of plant diseases, including beet curly top (Western yellow blight). There are one to three generations per year.
Damage: Adults and nymphs suck sap from plants. This generally causes little damage in

Below: A shiny, black cabbage stem flea beetle.

itself, but can result in harmful viral infections.
Plants affected: Beans, beets, carrots, aubergines (eggplants), spinach and tomatoes; also delphiniums (*Delphinium*), carnations (*Dianthus*), petunias (*Petunia*) and zinnias (*Zinnia*); and weeds.
Prevention and control: *Chemical*: Spray with dimethoate, malathion, permethrin or pirimiphos-methyl. *Non-chemical/organic*: Protect vulnerable crops with a floating mulch when the pests are active. Clear the garden of weeds that can harbour the pest.

SOFT SCALES
Coccidae
Range: Cosmopolitan.
Description: Soft scales are sap-sucking insects, which have a tough outer skin, or cover themselves with wax. Many species have no males. Females lay eggs that hatch into crawlers, which wander about until they find a suitable resting place. Their feeding activities cause little direct harm, but the honeydew they excrete is damaging.
Damage: Honeydew excreted by the scales attracts *sooty mould*.
Plants affected: A wide range; some species have specific hosts.
Prevention and control: *Chemical*: Spray with dimethoate or insecticidal soap. *Non-chemical/organic*: Brush off scales by hand. Control ants, which deter the scales' natural predators.

Below: White soft scale insects on some new laurel growth.

Above: Scale insects have excreted honeydew on to this leaf.

COCCID GALLS (eucalyptus)
Coccoidea
Range: Widely distributed.
Description: A number of sap-sucking insects can cause galls to appear on eucalyptus. The size and shape of the galls vary according to the species of pest and its sex.
Damage: Unsightly galls appear on the stems and leaves of eucalyptus.
Plants affected: Eucalyptus (*Eucalyptus*), especially young plants.
Prevention and control: *Non-chemical/organic*: Prune affected growth if necessary; feed and water the plant well.

SOFT SCALE, Brown Soft Scale, Soft Brown Scale
Coccus hesperidum
Range: Europe, North America, Australia and New Zealand.
Description: This scale is a sap-sucking insect that is capable of breeding throughout the year in favourable conditions. Scales are yellow-brown and roughly oval, to 4mm (⅛in) long, and are usually found on the undersides

Below: This coffee leaf has been heavily infested with soft scales.

Above: These overturned leaves are infested with young scale insects.

of leaves. The honeydew they excrete drips down and forms sticky areas on the upper sides of leaves lower down the plant. Infestations are worse in hot, dry climates.
Damage: Honeydew attracts *sooty mould*.
Plants affected: Many plants commonly grown under glass, including citrus, grapes, figs, passion fruit, peaches and pears; also ornamental plants such as ferns, ivies (*Hedera*), *Ficus* and *Schefflera*.
Prevention and control: *Chemical*: Spray with malathion. *Non-chemical/organic*: The parasitic wasp *Metaphycus helvolus* provides some control. *Ferns*: Cut back affected growth. Heavily infested specimens are best discarded.

SPRINGTAILS
Collembola
Range: Cosmopolitan.
Description: Springtails are small, white insects that feed on moist, decaying organic matter. The most commonly seen species are less than 2mm (½in) long. They are found in compost heaps, and sometimes

Below: A large colony of brown scale insects lives on this grapevine.

Above: This adult springtail is visible beneath the lens of a microscope.

among the roots of pot plants. They feed on already damaged plant material, such as strawberry fruits.
Damage: Most springtails do little damage, but the lucerne fly (*Sminthurus viridis*) feeds off the leaf surfaces of some vegetables.
Plants affected: Seeds and seedlings are occasionally chewed, where springtails are present in sufficient quantities.
Prevention and control: Not usually necessary. *Chemical*: Spray with dimethoate or maldison. *Non-chemical/organic*: Fork over the soil where the springtails are found to be active to dry it out.

GRAPELEAF BLISTER MITE
Colomerus vitis
Range: Australia, New Zealand and parts of Europe and North America where grapes are grown.
Description: This microscopic

Below: Grapeleaf blister mites on a vine leaf.

mite attacks the new leaves of grapevines in spring, feeding on the undersides. Damage is unsightly rather than serious, since cropping is not affected. Attacks are most likely during wet springs.
Damage: Cream, then brown, felted patches appear on the underside of leaves. These cause the upper surface to bubble up.
Plants affected: Grapevines. Some varieties show resistance to the pest.
Prevention and control: *Chemical*: Treat with dicofol. *Non-chemical/organic*: Spray the vine with lime sulphur just before the leaves unfurl.

YELLOW PEACH MOTH
Conogethes punctiferalis
Range: Tropical areas.
Description: The adult is a yellow or orange moth, about 2.5cm (1in) across, with black spots. The larvae are pinkish caterpillars that can grow to 3.5cm (1½in). They tunnel into plants and fruits, their presence often betrayed by their droppings ("frass").
Damage: Shoot tips of plants are damaged, weakening the plant or causing die-back. Holes are bored in macadamia nuts. Gumming can occur on the surface of fruits such as peaches.
Plants affected: A range of edible plants, including guavas, macadamias, papayas, peaches and sweet corn.

Prevention and control: *Chemical*: Spray with carbaryl. Repeated applications may be necessary. *Non-chemical/organic*: Remove all affected fruits from the plant and destroy them.

PLUM CURCULIO
Conotrachelus nenuphar
Range: Eastern North America.
Description: The adult is a dark brownish insect, 5mm (⅕in) long, with warty wing covers. It lays its eggs on fruit trees at flowering time. The larvae tunnel into the developing fruit. There are one or two generations per year, depending on the climate.
Damage: Fruits are spoilt and drop early. Scars made by adults are open to disease.
Plants affected: Plums; also apples, blueberries, cherries, peaches, pears and quinces.
Prevention and control: *Chemical*: Spray with fenitrothion, pirimiphos-methyl or bifenthrin. *Non-chemical/organic*: Spray with kaolin at petal fall. Collect and destroy shed fruits.

PEAR MIDGE
Contarinia pyrivora
Range: Europe. The pest seems to favour particular localities.
Description: The adult is a small fly or midge that lays its eggs in unopened flower buds. Larvae, which feed in the developing fruits, are orange-white and may be up to 3mm (⅛in) long.

Below: An early invasion by pear midge larvae has caused these fruitlets to swell.

Damage: Affected fruitlets show accelerated growth before turning black and falling. In severe cases, nearly the whole crop may be lost.
Plants affected: Pears.
Prevention and control: *Chemical*: Spray with pirimiphos-methyl or fenitrothion when the flower buds start to show colour. *Non-chemical/organic*: Pick and dispose of affected fruitlets to prevent the pest pupating.

BANANA WEEVIL BORER, Banana Root Borer
Cosmopolites sordidus
Range: Tropical areas.
Description: The adult is a black weevil, 1.2cm (½in) long, active at night; it lays its eggs on the base of pseudo-stems or among old leaves. The larvae, which grow up to 1.2cm (½in) long, are creamy white and have a brown head. They tunnel through corms and pseudo-stems. Control of this pest is a legal requirement.
Damage: Parts of the plant rot and new leaves wilt. Plants may break. Fruiting is impaired.
Plants affected: Bananas and other *Musa*, some agricultural crops such as Manila hemp, sugar cane.
Prevention and control: Consult the local agriculture office in the first instance.

MOTH BORERS

Cossidae* and *Oecophoridae

Range: Widely distributed.

Description: Adults are grey or brown moths and very large, up to 25cm (10in) across. Females lay eggs on bark, usually where some damage has occurred. Larvae tunnel into the wood (sometimes feeding there for several years). Moths of the Oecophoridae family are also referred to as "moth borers".

Damage: Infested branches are weakened and are vulnerable to storm damage. Small trees can be blown over. Where several larvae are present, trees can be ringbarked.

Plants affected: Eucalyptus (*Eucalyptus*), wattles (*Acacia*) and smooth-barked apples (*Angophora costata*).

Prevention and control: *Non-chemical/organic*: Feed and water to maintain the vigour of affected trees. Dig up and destroy badly affected trees.

GREEN JUNE BEETLE and Fig Beetle

Cotinis nitida* and *C. texana

Range: South-eastern USA (*Cotinis nitida*); south-western USA (*C. texana*).

Description: The adults are copper green beetles, up to 2.5cm (1in) long, that lay eggs in soil high in decaying organic matter. The larvae, about 5cm (2in) long, are cream and eat organic matter underground.

Damage: Adults eat holes in leaves and fruits. Larvae eat plant roots, though the damage is rarely serious. In large numbers, they can cause damage by tunnelling in seed beds.

Plants affected: A wide range of fruit, including apples, figs, soft fruit, melons, peaches and pears; susceptible vegetable crops include sweet corn.

Prevention and control: *Non-chemical/organic:* Pick off adults by hand. Avoid creating deep piles of organic matter near vulnerable crops.

Below: The green June beetle is a shield beetle.

SPOTTED ASPARAGUS BEETLE

Crioceris asparagi, C. duodecimpunctata

Range: Europe; introduced into North America.

Description: Adults (*C. duodecimpunctata*) are orange beetles, with black spots, to 8mm (⅓in) long. *C. asparagi* adults are metallic blue-black. The females lay their shiny black eggs on young asparagus spears or stems. Larvae are grey or greenish. Adults and larvae eat leaves and the outer bark of spears. There are two to four generations per year, depending on the climate.

Damage: Spears dry out and turn yellow-brown. In cases of severe infestation, plants can be defoliated.

Plants affected: Asparagus.

Prevention and control: *Chemical*: Spray with permethrin or bifenthrin. *Non-chemical/organic:* Substitute pyrethrum. Pick off beetles and larvae by hand. Cover young spears with a floating mulch.

Below: The colourful adult spotted asparagus beetle is clearly visible.

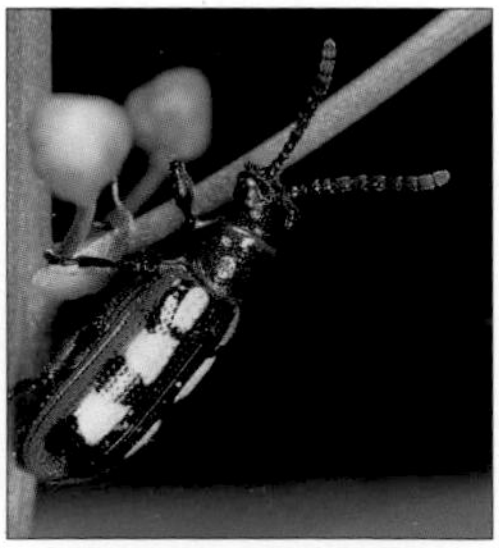

CURRANT BLISTER APHID

Cryptomyzus ribis

Range: Europe.

Description: This light yellow aphid feeds on the leaves of certain bush fruits. Eggs overwinter on the bushes.

Damage: Blisters appear on leaves. Leaves of red currants and white currants often turn red; blackcurrant leaves turn yellowish. Sticky honeydew is deposited on leaves and fruits, attracting *sooty mould*.

Plants affected: Red, white and blackcurrants.

Prevention and control: *Chemical:* Spray with dimethoate, heptenophos or pirimicarb immediately after flowering. *Non-chemical/organic:* Spray bushes with tar oil in midwinter to destroy eggs.

MACADAMIA FLOWER CATERPILLAR

Cryptoblabes hemigypsa

Range: Tropical and subtropical areas.

Description: The adult is a grey moth, about 1.5cm (⅗in) across, with darker grey marks. The larvae initially feed within buds, later emerging to feed on the outsides of buds and on flowers. They grow to 3.2cm (1¼in) long and can be light green, grey or reddish-brown. They produce masses of webbing that traps their excreta and chewed pieces of bud.

Damage: Growth is impeded. Cropping may be severely reduced by heavy infestations.

Plants affected: Macadamias and other members of Protaceae, including grevillea (*Grevillea*).

Prevention and control: *Chemical:* Spray with carbaryl. *Non-chemical/organic:* Choose varieties that flower before larvae are active.

Above: A currant blister aphid attack has caused this blister reaction on a blackcurrant leaf.

MACADAMIA NUTBORER

Cryptophlebia ombrodelta

Range: India to the Philippines, including New Guinea and Australia.

Description: The adult female is a reddish-brown moth, about 2.5cm (1in) across, that lays its eggs on soft nuts. The larvae, pink and up to 2cm (⅘in) long, are active in early to midsummer, feeding on the nuts. If the shells are soft, they feed on the kernels; if they have hardened, they can get to the kernels only if the nut has already been damaged, for instance by fruitspotting bugs (*Amblypelta nitida*).

Damage: Nuts or seeds are eaten.

Plants affected: Macadamias; also lychees and ornamentals such as golden-rain trees (*Koelreuteria*).

Prevention and control: *Chemical:* Spray with carbaryl around the time fruit is being set. Repeated applications may be necessary. *Non-chemical/organic:* Look for eggs on developing nuts and squash them.

HAZELNUT WEEVIL

Curculio nucum

Range: Central and northern Europe.

Description: The adult weevil is 6–9mm (¼–½in) long, and lays its eggs in the developing nuts in late spring. Emerging grubs feed on the kernels.

Damage: Nuts are spoilt

Above: An emerging hazelnut weevil has damaged the shell of this nut.

Above: A pea moth larva has fed inside this pea pod.

Above left and right: Gall wasp damage can appear in different manifestations as these two damaged leaves indicate. Raised swellings and rust spots are both indicative that gall wasps are active in the area.

(though generally only a small proportion of the crop).
Plants affected: Hazelnuts.
Prevention and control: None available.

PEA MOTH
Cydia nigricana
Range: Europe.
Description: The adult is a moth that lays its eggs on plants in flower during summer. Larvae are creamy-white caterpillars, up to 6mm (¼in long), with a black head, that feed within developing pods. They are most likely to be a problem on late summer crops.
Damage: Peas are eaten.
Plants affected: Peas.
Prevention and control: *Chemical*: Spray in the evening with fenitrothion, bifenthrin, pirimiphos-methyl or permethrin at the start of flowering. *Non-chemical/organic*: Choose early or late varieties that flower outside the period when the adults are active.

Below: The male pea moth is olive brown and has a wingspan to 1.5cm (⅝in).

CODLING MOTH
Cydia pomonella
Range: Cosmopolitan.
Description: The adult is a grey-brown moth, to 2cm (⅘in) across, that lays its eggs singly on or near small fruits. The larvae are white to pale pink caterpillars, to 2cm (⅘in) long. They tunnel into fruits (usually at the blossom end), pushing out a crumbly, brown excrement as they feed. They exit to pupate, leaving a characteristic mark on the fruit surface. There are up to three generations per year. The codling moth is a serious garden pest.
Damage: Fruits are tunnelled.
Plants affected: Apples and pears (including ornamentals); sometimes other fruit trees.
Prevention and control: Pheromone traps can be used to establish the presence of fertile

Below: The codling moth can do more damage to apples than any other garden pest.

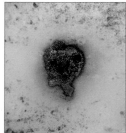

adults. *Chemical*: Spray with fenthion, carbaryl, permethrin, bifenthrin, fenitrothion or pirimiphos-methyl. Timing is critical in order to kill larvae before they have entered the fruits. *Non-chemical/organic*: Remove any infested fruits shed on to the ground near the tree. Remove loose bark (in which cocoons can overwinter) from the tree in late winter. Special bands tied around tree trunks can deter crawling larvae.

GALL WASPS (oaks)
Cynipidae
Range: Europe.
Description: Gall wasps are black or brown, up to 5mm (⅕in) long. They cause galls to form on the leaves (including the undersides), stems, roots and acorns of oak trees.
Damage: Galls are unsightly, but cause no lasting damage.
Plants affected: Oaks (*Quercus*).
Prevention and control: None necessary.

GRAPE PHYLLOXERA
Daktulosphaira vitifolii
Range: Widespread where grapes are grown.
Description: This aphid affects plants both above and below ground. Its activity causes fleshy, yellow galls to form on fine roots, which then stop growing. Sometimes galls also appear on the underside of leaves. Vines grown in heavy soils suffer more damage than those in light, sandy soils.

Warning: in some areas, control of the pest is a legal requirement.
Damage: Growth is weakened. Fruiting is severely impaired.
Plants affected: Grapevines.
Prevention and control: *Non-chemical/organic*: If the pest is known to be prevalent in your area, plant only vines that are grafted on resistant rootstocks.

VIOLET LEAF MIDGE
Dasineura affinis
Range: Europe.
Description: The adult is a gnat-like fly that lays its eggs among developing leaves. Orange-white maggots, up to 3mm (⅛in), feed on the leaves, making them curl and thicken.
Damage: If severe, plants die.
Plants affected: Violets (*Viola*).
Prevention and control: *Chemical*: Spray with dimethoate or pirimiphos-methyl as soon as any symptoms are noticed. *Non-chemical/organic*: Pick off and burn any affected leaves.

Below: These violet leaf midges are at the larval stage.

ONION FLY MAGGOT, Onion Maggot (alliums)
Delia antiqua

Range: Europe; introduced into north USA.
Description: The adult is a bristly grey fly, to 7mm (⅓in) long, which lays its eggs on decaying organic matter. Maggots, white and 8mm (⅜in) long when fully grown, feed on plant roots in summer, either destroying plants or tunnelling into bulbs and allowing harmful rots to enter. There may be two generations per year.
Damage: Young plants can be killed. Older plants that survive produce inedible crops.
Plants affected: *Allium*, especially onions.
Prevention and control: *Chemical:* Protect late spring plantings by treating the bed with lindane or pirimiphos-methyl.

BEAN SEED FLY, Onion Maggot
Delia platura

Range: Europe, North America, Australia.
Description: The adult resembles a house fly. Females lay their eggs in soil, especially that soil that contains fresh organic matter. The maggots are white and up to 5mm (⅓in) long. They feed on emerging seedlings and young shoots. Plants are most vulnerable during cold, wet weather that slows down germination and subsequent growth.
Damage: Seedlings are

Below: Onion fly larvae cause serious damage.

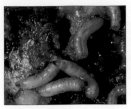

Above: Bean seed fly larvae feed on a field bean seed.

completely destroyed. Young plants suffer distorted growth.
Plants affected: Beans.
Prevention and control: *Chemical:* Dust with pirimiphos-methyl. *Non-chemical/organic:* Protect seedlings with cloches and water well.

CABBAGE ROOT FLY, Cabbage Root Maggot, Cabbage Maggot
Delia radicans

Range: Europe; introduced into north USA.
Description: The adult is a grey fly, to 6mm (¼in) long, that lays its eggs in soil. The larvae are white maggots, to 6mm (¼in) long. Maggots tunnel into roots and stems, allowing diseases to take a hold, or in severe cases causing the plant to die. There can be two to four generations per year.
Damage: Plants wilt and growth slows down; severely affected plants can die.
Plants affected: All brassicas, such as broccoli, Brussels sprouts, cabbages, cauliflowers, radishes and turnips (transplant seedlings are especially vulnerable). Related ornamentals are also susceptible to attack.
Prevention and control: *Chemical:* Dust planting rows or the roots of transplants with lindane or pirimiphos-methyl. *Non-chemical/organic:* Protect growing plants by surrounding them with discs or squares of tar paper (or stiff cardboard), 15cm (6in) across. (Females will lay their eggs on the card

Above: All brassicas are prone to attack by the cabbage root fly.

surface rather than on the soil.) Destroy the roots of all brassica plants after harvesting. Practise crop rotation.

PRIVET THRIPS
Dendrothrips ornatus

Range: Europe.
Description: This thrips is a thin, black or yellow insect, up to 2mm (½in) long, that sucks sap from the upper surface of leaves. It is prevalent during warm, dry summers.
Damage: Leaves turn dull green/silvery brown.
Plants affected: Privets (*Ligustrum*) and lilacs (*Syringa*).
Prevention and control: *Chemical:* Spray with dimethoate, permethrin, pirimiphos-methyl or fenitrothion as soon as damage is noticed.

CORN ROOTWORMS (Northern and Western)
Diabrotica spp.

Range: USA and southern Canada.
Description: The adults are yellowish-green beetles, up to

Below: A leaf covered in thrips.

9mm (⅓in) long, that lay their eggs near corn roots in autumn. The larvae are thin, white grubs, up to 1.25cm (½in) long, with brown heads. They are active underground from spring to early summer. Adults chew on developing corn cobs. Larvae tunnel into corn roots.
Damage: Larval activity stunts growth and can introduce bacterial and mosaic diseases. Adult activity can affect pollination.
Plants affected: Sweet corn; also grains and grasses.
Prevention and control: *Chemical:* Spray with bifenthrin. *Non-chemical/organic:* Practise crop rotation. Dig up and destroy corn roots that may harbour eggs in autumn. Plant fresh crops early in the season so they are well established before the larvae become active.

SPOTTED CUCUMBER BEETLES, Southern Corn Rootworms
Diabrotica undecimpunctata howardi and related species

Range: Throughout North America.
Description: The adult is a greenish-yellow beetle, up to 7mm (¼in) long, with black spots, that lays its eggs in the soil around the base of plants. The larvae are thin, white worms, up to 2cm (⅘in) long. There are up to three generations per year, depending on the local climate.
Damage: Larvae feed on the roots and crowns of plants, weakening or sometimes killing

Above: This beetle belongs to the genus *Diabrotica*.

them. Adults chew holes in leaves and the skins of fruit. They can also transmit *cucumber mosaic virus* and bacterial diseases.

Plants affected: Cucumbers and other cucurbits; also peanuts, potatoes, sweet corn and other plants.

Prevention and control: *Chemical:* Spray with bifenthrin. *Non-chemical/organic:* Rotate crops. Spray with kaolin or canola oil. Grow seedlings on under floating mulches or cloches. (Larvae can be controlled with the parasitic nematode *Heterorhabditis bacteriophora*.)

RHODODENDRON WHITEFLY
Dialeurodes chittendeni

Range: Europe and North America.

Description: The adult is a tiny, white, moth-like insect, often seen on the underside of leaves in summer. The nymphs are pale green. Both adults and nymphs suck sap from leaves and excrete honeydew.

Damage: Honeydew attracts *sooty mould*.

Plants affected: Rhododendrons (*Rhododendron*).

Prevention and control: *Chemical:* Spray with permethrin or pirimiphos-methyl as soon as the adults are observed. Repeated applications are usually necessary. *Non-chemical/organic:* Spray with pyrethrum.

PICKLEWORM (cucurbits)
Diaphania nitidalis

Range: Mainly south-eastern USA. Adults move northwards as temperatures rise through the year.

Description: The adult is a yellowish-brown moth, up to 2.5cm (1in) across, that lays its eggs in late spring on plants. The larvae are pale yellow with dark spots initially; they turn green or pink, without spots, reaching a length of 2cm (⁴⁄₅in). There are up to four generations per year.

Damage: Developing larvae eat leaf and flower buds, moving on to fruits and stems.

Plants affected: Cucurbits, including cucumbers, melons, pumpkins and squashes.

Prevention and control: *Chemical:* Spray with fenitrothion, bifenthirin or pirimiphos-methyl. *Non-chemical/organic:* Plant crops as early as possible, before the adult moths are active. Cover developing plants with a floating cloche. Destroy plant debris after harvesting, if the pest has caused damage.

HARD SCALES, Armoured Scales
Diaspididae

Range: Tropical areas; they also occur on plants under glass in temperate zones.

Description: A number of scale insect species can be referred to as hard scales. The wax coating with which they cover themselves grows bigger as the insects feed (by sucking sap). Even where present in small numbers, they can cause considerable damage. Hard scales do not excrete honeydew. Species with a specific host range, and those that cause specific problems, have their own entries.

Damage: Yellow blotches appear on leaves, which can then be shed by the plant. Stems and even branches can die back.

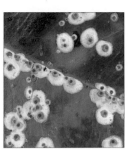

Above: This coffee leaf has a severe hard scale infestation.

Plants affected: A range of plants; citrus fruits are commonly affected by a number of hard scale species.

Prevention and control: *Non-chemical/organic:* Spray with white oil (deciduous trees and shrubs in winter).

ORCHID SCALE (orchids, palms)
Diaspis boisduvalii

Range: Tropical areas; it also occurs on plants under glass in temperate zones.

Description: This scale is roughly circular, the females (1.2–2.25mm (¹⁄₂₀–¹⁄₁₁in)) being larger than the males (1mm (¹⁄₂₅in)). They are found towards the basal sheaf of orchids and often go unnoticed until plant growth is affected.

Damage: Leaves turn yellow and growth is retarded or stops altogether.

Plants affected: Orchids; also palms and some other plants.

Below: Orchid scales on this palm leaf have caused it to turn yellow.

Prevention and control: *Non-chemical/organic:* Spray with white oil. Pick off scales by hand if the infestation is minor.

PINEAPPLE SCALE
Diaspis bromeliae

Range: Widespread in areas where pineapples are grown.

Description: The adult female scale is about 2mm (¹⁄₁₀in) in diameter and dull white. It is prevalent on the shaded parts of plants and appears initially at the base of leaves, eventually forming a greyish, scurfy covering on leaves and fruit.

Damage: Yellow spots appear on leaves.

Plants affected: Pineapples; also agaves (*Agave*), billbergias (*Billbergia*) and bromeliads (*Bromelia*).

Prevention and control: *Non-chemical/organic:* Remove and burn affected leaves. Destroy heavily infested plants.

SOUTHWESTERN CORN BORER
Diatraea grandiosella

Range: Southern USA.

Description: The adult is a beige moth (the females lighter than the males), around 3cm (1¼in) across. Eggs are laid in overlapping rows on leaves. The caterpillars are white with black dots and brown heads. There are two or more generations per year.

Damage: First-generation caterpillars attack emerging leaves, then bore into stalks, sometimes killing the growing points of plants. Second-generation caterpillars bore into husks and stalks.

Plants affected: Sweet corn, grasses and sorghum.

Prevention and control: *Chemical:* Spray with pyrethrins. *Non-chemical/organic:* Choose strong-stalked varieties. Spray with canola oil to control first-generation larvae. Destroy affected crops at the end of the season to prevent larvae overwintering.

JUNIPER WEBBER MOTH
Dichomeris marginella

Range: Europe, North America, northern Asia.

Description: The adult is a small brown moth. The larvae are brown caterpillars, up to 1.2m (½in) long, that feed in groups on foliage, binding leaves and branches together with silk. This webbing protects them from chemical sprays. They are active from late spring. There is one generation a year.

Damage: Leaves turn brown, leading to unsightly patches on the tree.

Plants affected: Junipers (*Juniperus*); compact, upright varieties are susceptible.

Prevention and control: *Chemical:* Spray with permethrin, pirimiphos-methyl or fenitrothion as soon as the caterpillars are seen, and before their webbing is fully formed. *Non-chemical/organic:* Cut out infested growth. Use the bacterial control *Bacillus thuringiensis.*

MILLIPEDES
Diplopoda

Range: Cosmopolitan.

Description: Millipedes are soil-dwelling, slender, many-jointed, cylindrical animals, to 7.5cm (3in) long (depending on the species), with two pairs of legs per segment. They feed on decaying organic matter, but can also attack plant tissue, sometimes enlarging wounds made by other pests. They often feed on strawberry fruits.

Below: An adult black millipede.

Damage: Holes are eaten in strawberries and other fruits. Soft seedlings and plant roots can also be eaten.

Plants affected: Strawberries, tomatoes, and other soft-fleshed fruits that rest on the ground. Seedlings are also at risk of attack.

Prevention and control: Not usually necessary: where millipedes merely extend the damage caused by other pests, those pests should be controlled first. *Chemical:* Dust with lindane, if necessary. *Non-chemical/organic:* Keep strawberries and the ripening fruits of other plants clear of the ground. Spread straw under the fruit, or stake the plant as necessary.

NARCISSUS EELWORM,
Onion Eelworm, Phlox Eelworm
Ditylenchus dipsaci

Range: Cosmopolitan, in temperate regions.

Description: A devastating nematode that is introduced into gardens on infected plants. It can be dormant during frost and drought. Various forms are host specific. In some countries, the local government agriculture department should be made aware of it.

Damage: *Daffodils and narcissi:* New leaves are distorted, with raised sections that can be yellow in colour. Late flowering can also be an indicator. The nematodes also feed within the bulb; brown rings are seen if these are cut in half. *Phlox:* Stems become swollen and split. Growth is stunted. Severely infested plants can die.

Plants affected: Daffodils and narcissi (*Narcissus*); onions and phlox (*Phlox*).

Prevention and control: *Non-chemical/organic:* Lift and destroy damaged bulbs. Destroy affected phlox (it is possible to propagate fresh stock from root cuttings, since the nematode does not attack the roots).

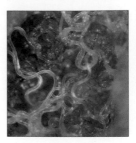

Above: This stem is infested with stem and bulb eelworms.

HARLEQUIN BUG
Dindymus versicolor

Range: Eastern Australia.

Description: The adult is a black and red bug, about 1.2cm (½in) long. The bugs suck sap from young plants and their excrement ("frass") disfigures fruit. They are also to be found on fences, wood piles and tree trunks and often overwinter in such places.

Damage: Plants wilt and can die. The fruit is damaged.

Plants affected: A range of crops, including apples, figs, grapes, melons, oranges, rhubarb and tomatoes; also dahlias (*Dahlia*) and violets (*Viola*).

Prevention and control: *Chemical:* Spray the plants and anywhere where the insects may be hiding with dimethoate, carbaryl or maldison. *Non-chemical/organic:* Spray with pyrethrum.

CUP MOTHS
Doratifera spp.

Range: Australia.

Description: The adults are moths that lay groups of eggs on plant leaves and cover them with hair, making furry patches about 1cm (⅜in) across. The larvae are generally green, some with red, yellow or blue markings, and about 2.5cm (1in) long. Spines on the body carry stings. Droppings indicate their activity. Their cocoons are cup-shaped.

Damage: Larvae eat the surfaces of leaves. Larger ones chew the edges of leaves.

Above: If unchecked, cup moths can strip large portions of certain trees.

Plants affected: Eucalyptus (*Eucalyptus*); also brush boxes (*Tristania conferta*), Sydney red gums (*Angophora costata*); apricots, guavas.

Prevention and control: *Chemical:* Spray with maldison where practical. *Non-chemical/organic:* Remove eggs by hand.

APPLE LEAFHOPPER,
Canary Fly
Edwardsiana australis

Range: Europe, New Zealand, Australia, North America, Chile and Argentina.

Description: The adult is a greenish-yellow, cicada-like insect, about 4mm (⅛in) long. Populations are greatest in warm weather.

Damage: Leaves are mottled with grey. The insects' sticky excreta spoils fruit.

Plants affected: A range of fruiting trees, especially apples but also plums. Neglected trees, crab apples and young trees that have yet to bear fruit are particularly vulnerable.

Prevention and control: *Chemical:* Spray with carbaryl or dimethoate. *Non-chemical/organic:* Use sticky whitefly traps.

ROSE LEAFHOPPER
(roses, apples)
Edwardsiana rosae

Range: Eurasia and North America.

Description: The adult is a pale yellow insect about 3mm (⅛in) long that sucks sap from the

Above: The pale green mottling on this leaf indicates an infestation by rose leafhoppers.

underside of leaves. The nymphs are creamy white. Plants grown in warm, dry conditions (such as against a sunny wall) are especially vulnerable to attack. There are usually two or three generations per summer.

Damage: Leaves are mottled with white or pale green. In severe cases, almost the entire leaf surface is discoloured.

Plants affected: Roses (*Rosa*); also apples.

Prevention and control: *Chemical*: Spray with dimethoate, fenitrothion, malathion, pirimiphos-methyl or permethrin. *Non-chemical/organic*: Subsitute pyrethrum.

SMALL CITRUS BUTTERFLY, Dingy Swallowtail

Eleppone anactus, other spp.

Range: Southern Australia.

Description: The adult is a black butterfly, about 7.5 cm (3 in) across, with predominantly grey and white markings (the hindwings are also marked with red and blue). It lays its eggs singly on citrus trees and other related plants. The caterpillars, which are green with brown spines, grow to 4.5 cm (1¾ in) long and feed on the leaves. They emit a strong smell when disturbed. (A number of species of butterfly are referred to as citrus butterflies; they cause similar damage to that described here.)

Damage: Leaves are eaten.

Plants affected: Citrus; also Mexican orange blossom (*Choisya ternata*) and long-leaf wax flower (*Eriostemon myoporoides*).

Prevention and control: *Chemical*: Spray with carbaryl. *Non-chemical/organic*: Pick individual caterpillars off the plants by hand.

POTATO LEAFHOPPER

Empoasca fabae

Range: Eastern North America.

Description: The adult is a winged, green insect, about 3 mm (⅛ in) long. The nymphs are paler and lack wings. There are two to four generations per year. In warm areas, adults are capable of overwintering.

Damage: Both adults and nymphs suck sap from leaves. Brown spots appear on leaves, the veins can be distorted and the edges are rolled (known as "hopper burn"). Leafhoppers are also vectors of certain viral diseases.

Plants affected: Potatoes, aubergines (eggplants), beans, apples, alfalfa, citrus, rhubarb.

Prevention and control: *Chemical*: Spray with demethoate, fenitrothion, malathion, pirimiphos-methyl or permethrin. *Non-chemical/organic*: Spray with kaolin to prevent attack. Cover vulnerable plants with a floating cloche. Spraying with the fungus *Beauveria bassiana* can also be effective.

Below: The winged adult potato leafhopper lays its eggs on the undersides of leaves.

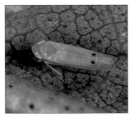

ROSE SLUGWORM LARVA

Endelomyia aethiops

Range: Europe; introduced into North America.

Description: The adult is a sawfly that resembles a bee or wasp. The larvae are pale green caterpillars, up to 1.4 cm (⅝ in) long, with a brown head, feeding on the underside of leaves and eventually skeletonizing them. In shaded areas they may also appear on the upper surface. There are usually two generations per year.

Damage: Leaves dry out and turn white or brown as the lower surface is eaten away. The second generation, in mid- to late summer, is usually more numerous and therefore causes more damage.

Plants affected: Roses (*Rosa*).

Prevention and control: *Chemical*: Spray with fenitrothion, pirimiphos-methyl, bifenthrin or permethrin when the pests are active (late spring and mid- to late summer). *Non-chemical/organic*: Substitute derris or pyrethrum.

LEAFEATING LADYBIRDS

Epilachna spp.

Range: Australia.

Description: The adult is a spotted, orange-yellow beetle, about 6 mm (¼ in) long, that feeds on the upper surface of leaves. It bears a superficial resemblance to the common

Below: These rose leaves have been damaged by rose slugworm larvae, which eat the lower surface.

spotted ladybird (*Harmonia conformis*), which is a beneficial garden insect. The larvae, about 6 mm (¼ in) long, are greenish-yellow with black spines and are active on the lower surface of leaves.

Damage: Leaves become brown and papery as a result of adult activity. The larvae skeletonize patches on leaves.

Plants affected: Cucurbits; also beans, potatoes and tomatoes.

Prevention and control: *Chemical*: Dust or spray with carbaryl or maldison. *Non-chemical/organic*: Dust plants with derris or pick individual insects off by hand.

BLISTER BEETLES

Epicauta spp.

Range: Throughout North America.

Description: Adult beetles vary in size (most are 9–19 mm/ ⅜ in–¾ in), with colours ranging from blue-black or dark brown to yellow with black stripes. They are active in summer. Larvae grow into fleshy, white grubs.

Damage: Adults eat leaves and fruits.

Plants affected: Beans, beetroot (beet), melons, peas, potatoes, tomatoes and some other vegetable plants.

Prevention and control: *Chemical*: Spray with bifenthrin. *Non-chemical/organic*: Pick beetles off plants by hand (wearing gloves to protect against their toxic secretions) or spray with canola oil.

Below: The leafeating ladybird damages the leaves of a number of vegetable crops.

Above: This adult Mexican bean beetle is feeding on a leaf.

Above: This lightbrown apple moth caterpillar is in the process of rolling a leaf with its webbing.

Above: A mottled umber moth caterpillar loops itself towards its food.

MEXICAN BEAN BEETLE
Epilachna varivestis
Range: USA (except West Coast states).
Description: The adult is an oval beetle, up to 7mm (¼in) long, yellowish-brown with black spots, that lays its eggs in clusters on the underside of leaves. The fleshy larvae, up to 8.5mm (⅜in) long, are yellow. Up to four generations can occur per year. Adults and larvae feed on the underside of leaves.
Damage: Leaves are skeletonized. Sometimes plants are entirely defoliated.
Plants affected: Alfalfa, cowpeas, lima beans, snap beans and soya beans.
Prevention and control: *Chemical:* Spray with bifenthrin. *Non-chemical/organic:* Pick off individual beetles, eggs and larvae by hand. Spray with insecticidal soap, kaolin or canola oil. Make early or late sowings to avoid population peaks. Protect crops with floating mulches or cloches.

WASP GALLS
Epimegastigmus spp.
Range: Australia.
Description: The common name refers to the galls produced by the pests. These wasps are tiny, and so usually go undetected. They lay their eggs in young leaves. The larvae feed within the leaves, and their activity causes galls to form.
Damage: Leaves are disfigured.
Plants affected: Wattles (*Acacia*), bottlebrushes

(*Callistemon*), eucalyptus (*Eucalyptus*) and other Australian natives.
Prevention and control: *Non-chemical/organic:* Prune off affected growth.

LIGHTBROWN APPLE MOTH
Epiphyas postvittana
Range: Australia; introduced into Europe.
Description: The adult is an orange-brown moth. The green larvae can be up to 2cm (⅘in) long. They either roll leaves around themselves or web two together. Young larvae feed on the leaf surface. Older larvae chew the edges of leaves and also eat into fruits. They are more prevalent in cool areas than in hot, dry ones.
Damage: Holes are chewed in leaves and fruits. Grapes can be rendered inedible by webbing or larval droppings, and yield can also be reduced.
Plants affected: Apples and other pome fruits, citrus, grapes and a range of ornamentals.
Prevention and control: *Chemical:* Spray with carbaryl. *Non-chemical/organic:* Remove weeds that may harbour the pest.

MOTTLED UMBER MOTH
Erannis defoliaria
Range: Temperate Europe.
Description: The adult male, about 4.2cm (1¾in) across, is brownish-yellow, with darker mottling and banding on the

wings. The female is drab and wingless and climbs into trees to lay its eggs. Mottled umber moths are active in autumn–winter (and are therefore often referred to as "winter moths"). The larvae are reddish-brown with yellow sides and a dark, wavy stripe. They have often left the host plant by the time their activity has been detected, so preventive control measures are recommended.
Damage: Larvae feed on young leaves as they expand, leaving irregular holes; in cases of severe infestation, large quantities of foliage can be stripped. Rarely, flowers and fruitlets are attacked.
Plants affected: A range of fruit trees, including apples, cherries, plums and pears; woodland trees such as beech (*Fagus*) and oaks (*Quercus*) can also be affected.
Prevention and control: *Chemical:* Spray with pirimiphos-methyl, permethrin or bifenthrin. *Non-chemical/organic:* Place grease bands around tree trunks in autumn to deter egg-laying females. The biological control *Bacillus thuringiensis* can be effective.

GUMTREE SCALE
Eriococcus coriaceus
Range: Australia and New Zealand.
Description: The female scales are about 3mm (⅛in) long,

gradually turning a dark reddish-brown; they crowd together on stems, petioles and leaf veins. Male scales are much smaller. The scales produce large quantities of sticky honeydew.
Damage: The upper surfaces of leaves are covered in honeydew, which attracts *sooty mould*. Branches of young trees can die back.
Plants affected: Many species of eucalyptus (*Eucalyptus*), especially *E. glaucescens*, *E. haemastoma*, *E. linearis*, *E. perriniana*, *E. pulverulenta* and *E. smithii*.
Prevention and control: *Chemical:* Spray with dimethoate in early or mid-spring as the eggs are hatching. *Non-chemical/organic:* Rub off the scales by hand or spray the branches with white oil, though several applications may be necessary.

Below: The presence of gumtree scale on the stems of eucalyptus trees is an early indication of a potential problem.

MACADAMIA FELTED COCCID
Eriococcus ironsidei
Range: Australia (areas where macadamias are grown).
Description: The adult is a white to yellowish-brown insect, about 1mm (¹⁄₂₅in) long, sheltering in the axils of leaves, in bark splits, between buds and under leaves.
Damage: Young growth is distorted or stunted. Yellow spots appear on older leaves. Cropping is reduced.
Plants affected: Macadamias (*Macadamia integrifolia* and *M. tetraphylla*).
Prevention and control: *Chemical:* Spray with malathion. *Non-chemical/organic:* Ladybirds and wasps can help control the pest. Spray with white oil or summer oil.

MANUKA BLIGHT (manukas)
Eriococcus orariensis
Range: Australia; New Zealand.
Description: The common name of this problem refers not to the insect itself – a scale – but to the damage it creates: the copious honeydew that the pest excretes leads to heavy infestations of *sooty mould*. In severe cases, bushes look as though they have been burnt. (In Australia, natural predators generally keep numbers low; it is more of a problem in New Zealand.)
Damage: Plants lose vigour. Twigs die and are blackened with mould.
Plants affected: Manukas (*Leptospermum scoparium*).
Prevention and control: *Chemical:* Spray with malathion. *Non-chemical/organic:* Spray with white oil.

GALL MITES, Rust Mites
Eriophydae
Range: Cosmopolitan.
Description: Gall mites, or eriophyds, are microscopic creatures that attack a range of plants, especially deciduous trees and shrubs. Feeding within leaves and buds, they stimulate the plant to put out abnormal growths ("galls"). These can take the form of raised, blister-like areas on leaves, thickened or curled leaf margins, or small, cauliflower-like structures on stems. Some common gall mites that produce characteristic symptoms are dealt with in specific entries.
Damage: Affected plants usually continue to grow normally, but the affected areas can be unsightly.
Plants affected: A range of trees and shrubs (mainly deciduous), including pears, plums, various soft fruit bushes, maples (*Acer*) and limes (*Tilia*).
Prevention and control: *Chemical:* Chemical control is usually unnecessary. *Non-chemical/organic:* Cut off affected leaves.

WALNUT BLISTER MITE
Eriophyes erineus
Range: Common where walnuts are grown.
Description: The mites feed on the underside of leaves, causing raised areas to appear on the upper surfaces.
Damage: Leaves are topped with oval blisters about 2cm (⁴⁄₅in) long.
Plants affected: Walnuts.
Prevention and control: None necessary.

Above: The raised areas on these leaves were caused by walnut blister mites.

ERINOSE MITE (lychees)
Eriophyes litchii
Range: Western Australia.
Description: The mite is microscopic. Eggs are laid on leaves (sometimes while they are still in bud); the mites feed on young leaves, shoots, flower buds and fruits (preferring young leaves). The damage they cause is characteristic: areas where they are feeding show a soft, velvety appearance.
Damage: Leaves blister on the upper surface, and can twist and curl. Velvety areas, initially yellowish, turn red-brown, then black.
Plants affected: Lychees.
Prevention and control: *Non-chemical/organic:* Spray with wettable sulphur just before new leaves appear (repeated applications may be necessary).

Below: A severe infestation of pearleaf blister mites.

PEARLEAF BLISTER MITE
Eriophyes pyri
Range: Europe, North America, Australia, South Africa.
Description: Adult overwinters inside buds, where it lays its eggs. Emerging mites feed on the underside of the new leaves. Yellow or reddish pustules appear on the upper surface, with blisters on the underside, swelling to 3mm (¹⁄₈in) across. There can be several generations in a season, though activity decreases during hot summers.
Damage: Trees lose vigour and cropping is reduced. Depressed spots appear on fruits and there can be other signs of distortion.
Plants affected: Pears; also apples and quinces, and cotoneasters (*Cotoneaster*), hawthorns (*Crataegus*) and rowans (*Sorbus*).
Prevention and control: *Chemical:* Dicofolor carbaryl. *Non-chemical/organic:* Spray with lime sulphur in spring.

Below: Blisters caused by the pearleaf blister mite turn black or brown with age.

Below: Galls can look unsightly, but the plants suffer little harm.

CITRUS BUD MITE
Eriophyes sheldoni
Range: Australia; the pest may also be present in other areas where citrus are grown.
Description: This mite is microscopic, feeding mainly on unopened flower and leaf buds, but is also found where fruits touch. The most striking evidence of its presence is the appearance of severely distorted fruits. The citrus bud mite is present on plants throughout the year, but its activity decreases during hot, dry periods.
Damage: Depending on where on the plant the mites are present, buds blacken and can be completely destroyed; skins of fruits can also blacken. Leaves distort in a variety of ways: some are cupped and/or have irregular margins, or emerge in a rosette from shoot tips. Flowers are deformed, and fruits are lobed or otherwise distorted.
Plants affected: Mainly lemons; also oranges and other citrus.
Prevention and control:
Chemical: Spray with difocol in midwinter and summer or early autumn. *Non-chemical/organic:* Substitute wettable sulphur.

Below: Lime leaves can be severely disfigured by an infestation of nail gall mites.

NAIL GALL MITE (limes)
Eriophyes tiliae
Range: Widely distributed.
Description: Red, finger-like galls appear on the upper surfaces of leaves.
Damage: Damage is slight, but is unsightly.
Plants affected: Limes (*Tilia*).
Prevention and control: *Non-chemical/organic:* Cut off affected leaves.

WOOLLY APHID, Woolly Apple Aphid
Eriosoma lanigerum
Range: North America (native); distributed worldwide.
Description: The adult aphid is purplish-brown. Nymphs are reddish-brown. As the aphids feed, they cover themselves with masses of waxy, white threads. They are often found in the cracks in tree bark, in pruning scars or on new growth. Their activities stimulate the production by the tree of soft, knobbly galls that split open when frosted. Honeydew excreted by the aphids attracts *sooty mould*. They feed above ground mainly between spring and autumn; they feed on plant roots throughout the year. Woolly aphids prefer cool, damp areas.
Damage: The waxy substance produced by the pest is

Above: This distorted apple twig shows damage caused by woolly aphids.

unsightly. In cases of severe infestation, growth is distorted because buds have been destroyed. Fruits can be shed prematurely. The aphids' excreted honeydew (on leaves) attracts *sooty mould*.
Plants affected: Mainly apples, occasionally pears; also ornamentals including hawthorns (*Crataegus*), firethorns (*Pyracantha*) and cotoneasters (*Cotoneaster*).
Prevention and control:
Chemical: Spray with pirimicarb, dimethoate, heptenophos with permethrin or pirimiphos-methyl. Where the infestation is on the roots, chemical control can be difficult. *Non-chemical/organic:* Spray vulnerable trees with canola oil in late spring to early summer. Prune out affected shoots. Some rootstocks show resistance to the pest.

FRUITPIERCING MOTHS
Eudocima spp., see under *Othreis* spp.

FROSTED SCALE
Eulecanium pruinosum
Range: Australia.
Description: The adult scale is oval, about 5mm (⅛in) long, and brown with a white, powdery coating. The scales are clustered on small twigs in spring. Crawlers emerge in late spring and feed on the underside of leaves, moving to the twigs in autumn. Honeydew produced by the scales attracts *sooty mould*.
Damage: *Sooty mould* disfigures plants.

Plants affected: Many woody ornamental plants; also apricots, nectarines, peaches and plums.
Prevention and control:
Chemical: Spray with malathion.
Non-chemical/organic: Spray with white oil when plants are dormant, paying particular attention to lateral branches.

CELERY LEAF MINER
Euleia heraclei
Range: Europe.
Description: The adult is a fly. The larvae are small white maggots that live inside leaves, tunnelling as they feed. There are usually two generations per year (in late spring and from midsummer to early autumn), the second more numerous but the first causing more harm, since tender young plants are attacked.
Damage: Irregular pale blotches appear on leaves, which later turn brown. In some cases, nearly all the foliage is destroyed and plants have a scorched appearance. Celery stalks are bitter and stringy. The first generation can stunt the root growth of root crops.
Plants affected: Celery, lovage, parsnips, annual spinach and other related vegetables.
Prevention and control: *Chemical:* Spray with malathion. *Non-chemical/organic:* Pick off and burn leaves that show signs of infestation.

Below: This leaf, disfigured by the celery leaf miner, shows white and pale brown blotches.

LESSER BULB FLY

Eumerus tuberculatus

Range: Europe; introduced into North America and Australia.
Description: The adult is a black fly, about 8mm (⅜in) long, that lays its eggs in the necks of bulbs (if damaged) or in their vicinity, usually at the end of the season. The yellowish larvae grow to 8mm (⅜in) long and feed around the top of the bulb.
Damage: Partially eaten bulbs produce only a few thin leaves and no flowers, or may not grow at all. Larval activity can cause entire bulbs to rot.
Plants affected: Mainly daffodils (*Narcissus*); also hippeastrums (*Hippeastrum*), hyacinths (*Hyacinthus*), irises (*Iris*) (bulbous varieties) and onions.
Prevention and control: *Non-chemical/organic:* Either make sure the necks of bulbs are well covered with soil after the leaves have died down, or lift bulbs and treat with hot water.

GUMTREE HOPPERS

***Eurymela* spp.**

Range: Australia.
Description: The adults vary in colour, but are all generally about 1cm (⅖in) long and lay their eggs in twigs. They suck sap from plants and their honeydew attracts ants and *sooty mould*.
Damage: Growth is distorted.

Below: Gumtree hoppers are sap-sucking insects.

Sooty mould disfigures plants.
Plants affected: Wattles (*Acacia*), she oaks (*Casuarina*) and eucalyptus (*Eucalyptus*).
Prevention and control: *Chemical:* Spray with dimethoate or omethoate.

GALL WASPS

Eurytomidae (see also *Bruchophagus fellis*)

Range: Widely distributed.
Description: The adult wasps are inconspicuous and lay their eggs into young plant tissue. Larvae feed on leaves, causing galls to form. Most species cause only minor damage.
Damage: Galls disfigure the plant.
Plants affected: Wattles (*Acacia*), bottle-brushes (*Callistemon*), eucalyptus (*Eucalyptus*) and some others.
Prevention and control: *Non-chemical/organic:* Prune off any affected growth if necessary.

GARDEN SOLDIER FLY, Garden Maggot

Exaireta spinigera

Range: Northern-west Australia.
Description: The adult is a slender black fly, about 1.2cm (½in) long. It is often found indoors near windows. The larvae, which are about 1.5cm (⅗in) long, have brown, flattened bodies.
Damage: Live plant tissue is generally unharmed. Larvae feed on rotting organic matter, such as is sometimes found around the base of plants.
Plants affected: Any type of soft, decaying plant material.
Prevention and control: Not usually necessary. *Chemical:* Heavy infestations of larvae may be controlled with kerosene.

EARWIG, European Earwig

Forficula auricularia

Range: Europe; introduced into other areas.
Description: The adult is a reddish-brown insect, about

Above: Like many pests, earwigs are hard to detect because they are active at night.

2cm (⅘in) long; young earwigs are smaller and paler. They feed at night.
Damage: Holes are eaten in the leaves and flowers of a range of plants.
Plants affected: Many plants, especially dahlias (*Dahlia*), clematis (*Clematis*) and chrysanthemums (*Chrysanthemum*).
Prevention and control: *Chemical:* Spray plants at dusk with pirimiphos-methyl, fenitrothion, permethrin or bifenthrin. *Non-chemical/organic:* Trap the pests overnight in upturned pots filled with straw and placed on canes planted in the soil. Dispose of the earwigs each morning.

ANTS

Formicidae

Range: Cosmopolitan
Description: Ants are black, red or brown insects, 4–20mm (⅙–⅘in) long, that live in colonies. Some species are winged. Ants are attracted by the honeydew excreted by aphids, scale insects and other sap-suckers and their presence can deter some of these pests' natural predators.
Damage: The soil thrown up by nesting can bury small plants and, on lawns, interfere with mowing. An ants' nest around the roots can render some plants susceptible to drought.
Plants affected: Potentially all garden plants, though damage is rarely serious.
Prevention and control: *Chemical:* Treat the sites of nests with a proprietary ant killer.
Non-chemical/organic: Where practical, pour boiling water over the sites of nests.

OLIVE LACE BUG

Froggattia olivinia

Range: Australia.
Description: The adult is a brown bug, about 3mm (⅛in) long, with lacy wings. Both the adults and nymphs suck sap from the underside of leaves.
Damage: Leaves are mottled with yellow and eventually turn brown. In severe cases, a whole tree can be defoliated.
Plants affected: Olives.
Prevention and control: *Chemical:* Spray with dimethoate or maldison. *Non-chemical/organic:* Use a soap-based spray or set sticky traps.

SNAILS AND SLUGS

Gastropoda

Range: Cosmopolitan.
Description: A number of species of slug and snail occur in gardens. They feed at night, at or near ground level, but some snails are capable of ascending tree trunks to feed on leaves. They hide by day under stones or under ground. Some slugs live mainly undergound, feeding on the roots of plants. Snails tend to be more numerous on alkaline soils. A slimy, silvery deposit ("trail") indicates the activity of slugs and snails – that and the often serious damage they cause.
Damage: Irregular holes are eaten in foliage. In severe cases, plants are completely defoliated. Bulbs and tubers are eaten.

Below: Slugs are a common and persistent garden pest.

Above: Snails are instantly recognizable.

Above: This cotton semi-looper is feeding on a cotton leaf.

Below: Rhododendron leafhoppers have distinctive reddish markings on their backs.

Plants affected: A wide range, especially seedlings and soft-leaved plants such as lettuces and hostas (*Hosta*). Potato tubers and bulbs such as tulips (*Tulipa*) can be attacked. All seedlings are vulnerable.
Prevention and control: *Chemical:* Kill the pests with poison baits (usually based on metaldehyde). NB Some slug and snail poisons may be toxic to dogs, cats and garden wildlife. *Non-chemical/organic:* Patrol the garden at night with a torch (flashlight), and pick off slugs and snails by hand. Treat with the parasitic nematode *Phasmarhabditis hermaphrodita* (usually effective on slugs only). Surround vulnerable plants with copper strips, which deliver an electric shock to the pests. Various other products are available that are claimed to deter slugs and snails. *Potatoes:* Look for varieties that show some resistance.

LOOPERS AND SEMI-LOOPERS
Geometridae and Noctuidae
Range: Cosmopolitan.
Description: Loopers and semi-loopers are the caterpillars of certain moths. The arrangement of the legs on their bodies causes them to move with a characteristic "looping" action, the middle, legless part of the body forming an upturned U-shape. When disturbed, they often rear up or project outwards on the legs towards the rear of their bodies. Young loopers and semi-loopers feed on the undersides of leaves, creating a window-pane-like effect. Older caterpillars can also chew holes in leaves and damage flowers. Some species are entered under their own entries.
Damage: Holes are chewed in leaves. Flowers can be damaged.
Plants affected: Geometridae: Wattles (*Acacia*), banksias (*Banksia*) and some others are susceptible. Noctuidae: A wide range, including potatoes, beans and tomatoes; plants under glass can also be attacked.
Prevention and control: *Chemical:* Spray with carbaryl. *Non-chemical/organic:* Pick off caterpillars by hand.

AUSTRALIAN FLATWORM
Geoplana sanguinea
Range: Australasia, Africa and Israel; introduced into Europe.
Description: The Australian flatworm is an orange-brown, leech-like creature, 3–8cm (1¼–3¼in) long. They are mainly nocturnal, and can be found beneath stones, logs and other objects that are in contact with the soil. Flatworms are often unwittingly introduced into gardens in the roots of bought container-grown plants. They prey on earthworms and so are a very serious pest.
Damage: Reduction of earthworm activity results in poor drainage and aeration of the soil, and plant growth suffers.
Plants affected: Potentially all garden plants.

Prevention and control: None possible. Soak newly purchased container-grown plants in water to encourage any flatworms to emerge. Wash the roots carefully before planting out (egg capsules are black). Contact your local agriculture office for further advice.

POTATO CYST EELWORMS
(potatoes, tomatoes)
Globodera rostochiensis, G. pallida
Range: Europe.
Description: Cyst eelworms spend most of their lives feeding within plant roots. Mature females burst through the root walls, creating characteristic cysts. The cysts of *Globodera rostochiensis* are white initially, turning yellow then brown; those of *G. pallida* are white, then brown. Eelworm cysts lie dormant in the soil and can affect subsequent plantings of vulnerable plants.
Damage: Leaves turn yellow and dry out, from the base of the stem upwards. Plants die prematurely and cropping is poor.
Plants affected: Potatoes; tomatoes can also be attacked.
Prevention and control: *Non-chemical/organic:* Practise crop

Below: This potato root has gold and brown potato cyst eelworm cysts on it.

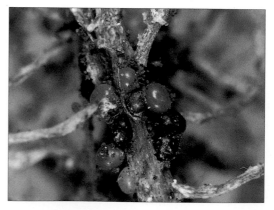

rotation (effective only where eelworm numbers have not been allowed to build up). Plant potato varieties known to be resistant to the eelworm.

RHODODENDRON LEAFHOPPER
Graphocephala coccinea
Range: North America; introduced into Europe.
Description: The adult is a turquoise insect, up to 9mm (⅜in) long, with orange-red markings, active from late summer into autumn. Nymphs are yellow-green and are found on the underside of leaves. They suck sap from leaves but cause little harm. However, the wounds in plants made by adult females for egg-laying are thought to contribute to *rhododendron bud blast*.
Damage: The plant may develop rhododendron bud blast disease.
Plants affected: Rhododendrons (*Rhododendron*).

Above: Adult whitefringed weevils chew foliage. They do little damage individually but a severe infestation can cause plants to wilt.

Prevention and control: *Chemical:* Spray with fenitrothion, permethrin or dimethoate when the adults are active, late summer to autumn.

WHITEFRINGED WEEVIL
Graphognathus leucoloma
Range: Australia and New Zealand.
Description: The adult is a dark grey to brownish-black weevil, about 1.2cm (½in) long, with white bands along its body. It chews leaves. Although unable to fly, it can walk long distances and is long-lived. More damage is caused by the larvae, which are whitish with a brown head and can grow to 1.2cm (½in) long. They are most common in spring, feeding below ground on plant roots and tubers.
Damage: Plants are weakened. Root vegetables are spoilt.

Below: A damaged shoot shows signs of gum, an indication of oriental fruit moth activity.

Plants affected: Root crops such as carrots, potatoes and turnips; beans, broccoli, cabbages, strawberries and tomatoes can also be attacked. Both woody and soft-stemmed ornamentals are also vulnerable. Prevention and control: *Non-chemical/organic:* Keep beds free of tap-rooted weeds that may harbour the pest. Leave infested areas bare for a while, and fork over the soil to bring larvae to the surface for birds to eat.

ORIENTAL FRUIT MOTH
Grapholita molesta
Range: Cosmopolitan.
Description: The adult is a grey moth, to 1.25cm (½in) across, with brown markings, that lays its eggs on the undersides of leaves or on stems near young shoots or fruits. The larvae are white to pink caterpillars, to 1.25cm (½in) long. They tunnel into shoots (sometimes producing gum) or fruits. There can be up to seven generations per year (later generations attack fruits).
Damage: Affected shoots turn brown and die. Tunnels are eaten in fruits.
Plants affected: Mainly peaches and nectarines; also almonds, apples, pears and quinces.
Prevention and control: *Chemical:* Spray with carbaryl or fenthion. *Non-chemical/organic:* Cut off and burn stems that are affected early in the season. Destroy any fruits shed prematurely by the plant. Spray eggs and larvae on leaves with canola oil.

FIELD CRICKET
Gryllus assimilis
Range: Throughout North America.
Description: The adult is a winged brown or black insect, 1.9–2.5cm (¾–1in) long. Nymphs are smaller and lack wings. In warm climates, adults are capable of overwintering; in cool climates, the crickets are

Above: Field crickets produce one to three generations per year.

active in summer. Damage is usually slight, though plagues can occur in favourable conditions, which can cause serious problems.
Damage: Both adults and nymphs chew seedlings, leaves, flowers and fruits.
Plants affected: Beans, cucumbers, melons, peas, squashes, strawberries and tomatoes.
Prevention and control: *Non-chemical/organic:* Protect crops where possible with a floating cloche when the crickets are active.

STAGHORN FERN BEETLE
Halticorcus platycerii
Range: Tropical areas.
Description: The adult is a rounded, bluish-black beetle, about 3mm (⅛in) long, with orange-red spots, that lays its eggs at the growing points of certain ferns. Its chewing creates small dents in the frond surface. The larvae tunnel into the new growth.

Below: The strawberry seed beetle damages strawberries by eating the seeds.

Damage: Fronds develop brown marks, spoiling the overall appearance.
Plants affected: Staghorn fern (*Platycerium*).
Prevention and control: *Non-chemical/organic:* Remove new fronds as soon as any evidence of damage is noticed. Pick off adults by hand.

STRAWBERRY SEED BEETLES
Harpalus rufipes, Pterostichus spp.
Range: Central Europe to the British Isles.
Description: The adults are shiny black beetles, about 1.5cm (⅛in) long, that feed on weed seeds and the seeds on the outside of strawberries (sometimes also the flesh). They are mainly nocturnal.
Damage: Fruits discolour where the seeds have been removed.
Plants affected: Strawberries.
Prevention and control: Owing to the risk of fruit contamination, non-chemical methods of control are preferable. *Chemical:* Spray unripe fruits with bifenthrin at dusk, just before the beetles become active. *Non-chemical/organic:* Keep strawberry beds weed-free. Set traps for the beetles by sinking jam jars into the ground around plants.

GRAPELEAF SKELETONIZERS
Harrisina spp.
Range: USA and southern Canada.
Description: The adults are blue or dark grey moths, about 2.5cm (1in) across, that lay their eggs on the leaves of grapevines. The larvae, up to 1.9cm (¼in) long, are cream to yellow, with purple or black bands. There are two or three generations per year.
Damage: Larvae eat leaves from the underside; in cases of severe infestation (for example, by the Western grapeleaf skeletonizer, *Harrisina brillians*), plants can be

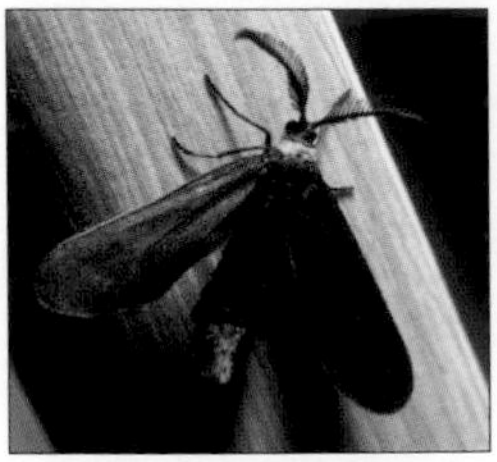

Above: The grapeleaf skeletonizer is a large moth; its larvae can cause serious damage.

defoliated. The fruits can also be attacked.
Plants affected: Grapes.
Prevention and control: *Chemical:* Spray with fenitrothion. *Non-chemical/organic:* Larvae numbers can be controlled with the bacterium *Bacillus thuringiensis* var. *kurstaki*. Alternatively, spray with canola oil or kaolin.

GLASSHOUSE LEAFHOPPER
Hauptidia maroccana
Range: Europe.
Description: The adult is a pale yellow insect, about 3mm (⅛in) long. The nymphs are creamy white. Their shed skins adhere to the underside of leaves. Adults and nymphs suck sap from leaves, living on the underside. The adults breed continuously throughout the year.
Damage: White dots appear on the upper surface of leaves. In severe cases, these merge and the leaves lose almost all their green colour.
Plants affected: A range of ornamentals under glass; garden plants such as foxgloves (*Digitalis*), tobacco plants (*Nicotiana*) and primulas (*Primula*) are also vulnerable.
Prevention and control: *Chemical:* Spray with bifenthrin, pirimiphos-methyl or permethrin. Alternatively, use an insecticidal smoke.

Below: Glasshouse leafhopper damage shows on the surface of a leaf, while the pests live and feed on the underside

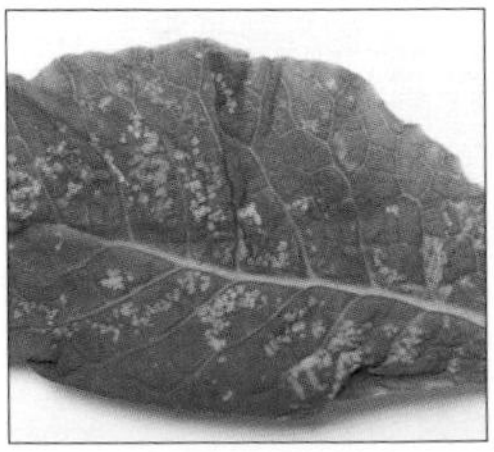

BUDWORMS
***Helicoverpa* spp.**
Range: Eurasia and Australia.
Description: Budworms are the larvae of certain moths. Moths lay their eggs singly on the young growth of a range of plants. Depending on the species, they grow to 4cm (1⅝in) long, and can be yellow-green, buff or reddish-brown, marked or striped with darker colours.
Damage: Holes are eaten in leaves. Flowers and fruits are damaged.
Plants affected: A wide range, including tomatoes, sweet corn, peas, beans and strawberries. Apples, pears, stone fruits (those with pits) and lettuces can also be attacked. Vulnerable ornamentals include gardenias (*Gardenia*), roses (*Rosa*) and carnations (*Dianthus*).
***Prevention and control*:** Sprays should be used before the larvae have entered fruits. *Chemical:* Spray with carbaryl. *Non-chemical/organic*: Substitute pyrethrum. Pick off caterpillars by hand.

Below: Newly hatched budworm caterpillars feed on young leaves, before moving on to blossoms and fruits.

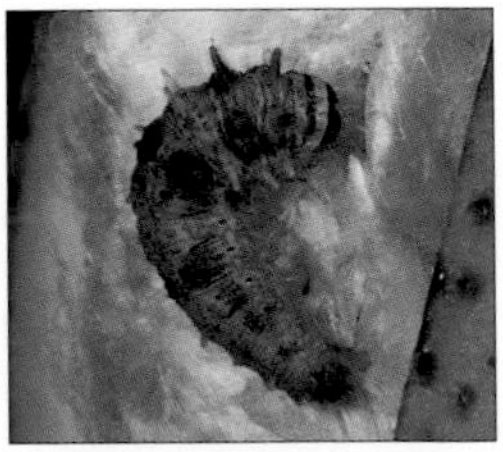

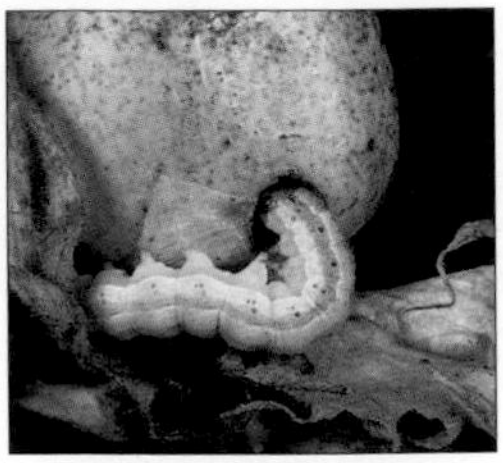

Above: The corn earworm caterpillar feeds by boring into fruits and vegetables. The affected fruit may appear to go on developing normally.

CORN EARWORM
***Helicoverpa armigera*; for other related species see *Helicoverpa* spp.**
Range: Eurasia and Australia.
Description: The adult is a moth that lays its eggs either on the silks of sweet corn cobs or at the tip of the cob, as well as on other fruits. The larvae, up to 4cm (1½in) long, are variable in colour: they can be green, fawn, yellow or reddish-brown.
Damage: Caterpillars enter fruits and vegetables as they are developing and feed on the insides, sometimes damaging them severely (though from outward appearances they seem to continue to develop normally). The caterpillars also tunnel through bean pods to feed on them from the outside. Affected crops, if not destroyed completely, become susceptible to disease and attack from other pests.
Plants affected: A range of fruiting plants, including beans (as well as their flowers), strawberries, sweet corn and tomatoes.
Prevention and control: Difficult. *Chemical:* Dust the vulnerable parts of plants (including young growth) with carbaryl. *Non-chemical/organic:* On sweet corn, cut off the tips of the husks and the silks (once these have turned brown) to prevent damage.

CORN EARWORM, Tomato Fruitworm
Heliocoverpa zea
Range: North America (especially southern states).
Description: The adult is a tan to brown moth, up to 4cm (1½in) across, that lays its eggs singly on leaves. Larvae, 2.5–5cm (1–2in) long, can be yellow to green, pink or dark red-brown. There can be four or more generations per year.
Damage: Larvae feed on plants.
Plants affected: Peppers, sweet corn and tomatoes; also beans, cabbages, peas, potatoes, squashes and some other vegetables.
Prevention and control: *Non-chemical/organic:* Pick off larvae by hand. Spray tomatoes with kaolin to prevent females from laying eggs. The bacterium *Bacillus thuringiensis* var. *kurstaki* provides some control. *Sweet corn:* Choose varieties with tight husks and aim to plant as early in the season as possible, so the cobs develop before the adults are active.

GLASSHOUSE THRIPS, Greenhouse Thrips
Heliothrips haemorrhoidalis, Frankliniella occidentalis
Range: Cosmopolitan.
Description: Despite their common name, these pests can also attack plants outdoors during warm periods. Glasshouse thrips are yellow or dark brown insects, to 2.5mm (⅒in) long, that suck sap from the leaves of plants. They also feed on the flowers of a number of ornamentals commonly grown under cover. Tiny black spots that appear on plants are the thrips' excrement. There are many generations throughout the year. They are also vectors of *tomato spotted wilt virus*.
Damage: Upper leaf surfaces show a dull green or silver discolouration. Petals of flowers show pale flecking. Flowers fail to open or deteriorate rapidly.

Above: Attack by glasshouse thrips has caused the discolouration on these cacti.

Plants affected: A range of plants under glass, including tomatoes, cucumbers, passion fruits and grapes; vulnerable ornamentals include African violets (*Saintpaulia*), Cape primroses (*Streptocarpus*), gloxinias (*Gloxinia*), cyclamen (*Cyclamen*) and busy Lizzies (*Impatiens*).
Prevention and control: Insecticidal sprays are often ineffective against this pest. *Chemical*: Spray with maldison, pirimiphos-methyl or permethrin. *Non-chemical/organic*: Substitute pyrethrum. The predatory mite *Amblyseius degenerans* can help to control the pest.

LATANIA SCALE
Hemiberlesia lataniae
Range: Cosmopolitan.
Description: The adult female scale is pale grey, and about 2mm (¹⁄₁₀in) across; the males are smaller. The scales are found on branches and fruits, including nuts. In warm areas, there can be several generations per year.
Damage: Pitting appears on fruits. Heavy infestation can result in leaf fall.
Plants affected: A wide range of plants including king palms (*Archontophoenix*), avocados, brush boxes (*Tristania conferta*) and macadamias.
Prevention and control: *Non-chemical/organic*: Spray plants with white oil in early summer.

SWIFT MOTH CATERPILLARS
Hepialus spp., including *H. humili* and *H. lupinus*
Range: Europe.
Description: The adults are moths that vary in size and colour. Caterpillars are up to 5cm (2in) long and are white with sparse dark hairs and a red-brown head. Found among the roots of certain herbaceous perennials, they are detected if plants are lifted for division or transplanting. (The larval stage of some species lasts for two years, so caterpillars can be found all year; older larvae cause more damage.)
Damage: Growth is impaired; in severe cases, plants can die.
Plants affected: A wide range, including Michaelmas daisies (*Aster*), chrysanthemums (*Chrysanthemum*), delphiniums (*Delphinium*), peonies (*Paeonia*), phlox (*Phlox*) and some other ornamentals; bulbs, corms and rhizomes are also susceptible.
Prevention and control: *Chemical*: Apply a root drench of pirimiphos-methyl (older larvae show more resistance to

Right: Swift moth caterpillars have burrowed into this carrot.

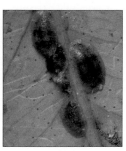

Above: Adult scale insects are covered in armour.

chemicals than younger ones). *Non-chemical/organic*: Lift affected plants and pick out and destroy any caterpillars found.

SCALES
Hermiptera
Range: Cosmopolitan.
Description: Adult scale insects appear on the stems and leaves of plants and are hidden beneath waxy scales (or shells) that are usually either round or oval, and 1–6mm (¹⁄₂₅–¹⁄₄in) long, depending on the species. Newly hatched scales (crawlers) move about until they find a suitable place from which to suck sap. Besides the damage (sometimes considerable) they cause by feeding, many species excrete honeydew, which attracts *sooty mould*.
Damage: Plants are weakened. Honeydew attracts *sooty mould*.
Plants affected: A wide range, including plants under glass and house plants.
Prevention and control: *Chemical*: Spray crawlers with malathion. *Non-chemical/organic*: Spray with white oil. Cut back seriously affected growth. Some scales can be controlled with parasitic wasps.

AFRICAN BLACK BEETLE
Heteronychus arator; see also under Scarabaeidae
Range: Australia, Brazil, Africa.
Description: The adult is a black beetle, about 1.2cm (¹⁄₂in) long, active from spring to summer.

The larvae are white curl grubs (see under Scarabaeidae), about 2.5cm (1in) long, and damage lawns. Adults eat stems below ground, burrowing into the soil and becoming semi-dormant in cold weather. Numbers are highest after a long dry spell.
Damage: Plants attacked underground wilt and fall over. Eyes of seed potatoes are damaged. Holes are eaten in strawberries.
Plants affected: Many vegetables (but not legumes); also bananas, grapes, tomatoes and sweet corn; ornamentals such as dahlias (*Dahlia*) and petunias (*Petunia*); lawns.
Prevention and control: *Chemical*: No control is available, but treating young larvae on lawns in spring will prevent their spread (*see* Lawns). *Non-chemical/organic*: Fork over the soil in spring to expose young larvae to birds.

GRAPEVINE HAWK MOTH
Hippotion celerio
Range: Africa, migrating to temperate zones in both hemispheres.
Description: The adult is a pale brown moth, about 7.5cm (3in) across, with black markings. The larvae, about 7.5cm (3in) long, are green or brownish-black and chew leaves. Their droppings sometimes betray their presence.
Damage: Leaves are chewed; in severe cases, plants are completely defoliated.

Below: The African black beetle has a shiny metallic appearance.

Above: A grapevine hawk moth.

Plants affected: A broad range, including fruiting grapes, rhubarb and sweet potatoes, as well as callas (*Calla*), Virginia creeper (*Parthenocissus quinquefoia*), Boston ivy (*Parthenocissus tricuspidata*) and ornamental vines (*Vitis*).
Prevention and control: *Chemical:* Spray with carbaryl. *Non-chemical/organic:* Pick the caterpillars off by hand.

APPLE SAWFLY, European Apple Sawfly
Hoplocampa testudinae
Range: Europe; introduced into northern USA.
Description: The adult, 5mm (¼in) long, is a sawfly similar in appearance to a wasp. It lays its eggs on flowers. The larvae are white maggots with a dark brown head that tunnel through the developing fruit, leaving a scar on the skin. Sometimes the maggots die within the fruit, in which case it develops normally apart from the outer scarring.
Damage: Fruits are scarred.

Some fall prematurely, in early to midsummer.
Plants affected: Apples; some varieties are more susceptible than others.
Prevention and control: *Chemical:* Spray with pirimiphos-methyl, permethrin or fenitrothion within seven to ten days after most of the flower petals have been shed. *Non-chemical/organic:* Where practical, pick affected fruit from the tree and destroy it to eliminate the next generation.

PLUM SAWFLY
Hoplocampa flava
Range: Europe. The pest tends to be localized.
Description: The adult is a brown sawfly that lays its eggs on plum blossom in spring. The creamy white larvae, up to 1cm (⅜in) long, tunnel into developing fruits. Sometimes their presence is indicated by pellets of black excreta on the surfaces of fruits.

Below: The scars on these apples were caused by apple sawflies.

Damage: Fruits are dropped prematurely.
Plants affected: Plums; some varieties (e.g. 'Victoria' and 'Czar') are more susceptible than others.
Prevention and control: *Chemical:* Spray with pirimiphos-methyl, permethrin or fenitrothion seven to ten days after petal fall. *Non-chemical/organic:* Gather shed fruit and destroy it to eliminate the next generation of sawfly.

BEET WEBWORM
Hymenia recurvalis
Range: Native to Hawaii, migrating into both hemispheres.
Description: The adult is a brown moth, about 2.5cm (1in) across, that lays its eggs in groups under leaves. The caterpillars are initially cream, turning green and reaching 2cm (⅘in) in length.
Damage: Young caterpillars remove patches of tissue from the underside of leaves, creating "windows". Older caterpillars chew holes through leaves and sometimes attack protruding beetroots at ground level.
Plants affected: Beetroot (beet) and related plants; also love-lies-bleeding (*Amaranthus*), purslane and moss roses (*Portulaca*) and others. Weeds such as salt bush and fat hen can also harbour the pest.
Prevention and control: *Chemical:* Spray or dust with carbaryl. *Non-chemical/organic:* Pick off young larvae from the underside of leaves by hand. Remove weeds that attract the pest and avoid growing related host plants nearby.

FALL WEBWORM
Hyphantria cunea
Range: USA and southern Canada.
Description: The adult is a white moth, 5–6.5cm (2–2½in) across, that lays its eggs on host plants. Larvae, up to 2.5cm (1in) long, are creamy

white and hairy, with dark spots. They spin webs over leaves and the tips of branches, feeding within the webs. There are one or two generations per year.
Damage: Leaves are eaten. On large plants such as trees, the damage is rarely serious, but the webs are unsightly.
Plants affected: A wide range, including many fruit trees and shrubs.
Prevention and control: Sprays are of limited value, since the feeding larvae are protected by their webs. *Non-chemical/organic:* Prune back growth on which webs have been spun. The bacterium *Bacillus thuringiensis* var. *kurstaki* provides some control.

COTTONY CUSHION SCALE
Icerya purchasi
Range: Australia, New Zealand; introduced into California.
Description: The female scale is oval, about 5mm (⅛in) long and reddish-brown. It produces a waxy white egg sac containing bright red eggs. The ladybird (ladybug) *Rodolia cardinalis* usually keeps the pest under control.
Damage: The scale itself causes little damage, but its honeydew attracts *sooty mould*.
Plants affected: A wide range of plants, including pittosporums

Below: Cottony cushion scales tend to congregate in rows on leaf midribs and on twigs. They also attract sooty mould.

Above: Cottony cushion scale does most damage in its young stages.

(*Pittosporum*), wattles (*Acacia*), laburnums (*Laburnum*), magnolias (*Magnolia*), roses (*Rosa*); various fruit trees.
Prevention and control: *Non-chemical/organic:* Spray with white oil in late summer to early autumn, or any time when the scales are noticed. Repeat sprayings may be necessary to kill emerging crawlers. Encourage ladybirds.

TERMITES
Isoptera
Range: Mainly tropical; some termite species occur in temperate zones.
Description: Termites are white or cream insects, 4–10mm (¼–⅖in) long, that live in colonies. They build nests in a variety of places, depending on the species. Some are underground; but nests may also appear at the base of trees, on tree branches or as mounds above the ground. Termites chew wood (live trees, fallen

logs or fences), sometimes causing considerable damage. They may be undetected until a tree branch breaks off.
Damage: Trees are weakened; branches can break off.
Plants affected: A range of trees.
Prevention and control: Contact your local forestry office in the first instance. Once the species of termite has been identified, it is usually advisable to employ a registered pest control officer.

PEA THRIPS
Kakothrips robustus
Range: Europe.
Description: The adult is a thin black insect, up to 2mm (¹⁄₁₀in) long. The nymphs are yellow. They feed on developing pods, causing them to turn silvery brown, and are most prevalent during hot, dry summers.
Damage: Pods discolour and are distorted. Cropping is reduced.
Plants affected: Peas.
Prevention and control: *Chemical:* Spray with permethrin, dimethoate, or pirimiphos-methyl when damage is noticed.

NATIVE FIG MOTH
Lactura caminaea, syn. Eustixis caminaea
Range: Eastern Australia.
Description: The adult is a moth. The creamy white larvae, up to 2cm (⅘in) long, feed on leaves, usually during late winter or spring.
Damage: Leaves are skeletonized or chewed. In severe cases,

entire trees can be defoliated.
Plants affected: Figs, especially Moreton Bay (*Ficus macrophylla*) and Port Jackson (*F. rubiginosa*).
Prevention and control: *Chemical:* Spray with maldison. *Non-chemical/organic:* Feed and water vulnerable plants well.

MUSSEL SCALE, Oystershell Scale
Lepidosaphes ulmi
Range: Europe; also North America.
Description: The adult scale, up to 3mm (⅛in) long, is roughly pear-shaped and grey-brown. It sucks sap. Nymphs hatch from mid-spring to the end of summer. There is one generation per year. In severe cases, bark is covered by scales.
Damage: Plants lose vigour and can suffer die-back.
Plants affected: Woody plants such as apples (including crabs), box (*Buxus*), Scotch heathers (*Calluna*), ceanothus (*Ceanothus*), dogwoods (*Cornus*), cotoneasters (*Cotoneaster*) and heathers (*Erica*).
Prevention and control: *Chemical:* Spray with malathion in late spring/early summer. *Non-chemical/organic:* Spray affected plants with tar oil when dormant in winter.

COLORADO BEETLE, Colorado Potato Beetle
Leptinotarsa decemlineata
Range: North America; introduced into Europe.
Description: The adult is a yellow-orange beetle, to 1cm

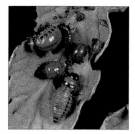

Above: Colorado beetle larvae have damaged this tomato leaf.

(⅖in) long, striped with black, that lays oval, yellow eggs on the undersides of leaves of suitable host plants. Larvae are orange with black heads. There are two or three generations per year. NB In the UK, the Colorado beetle is a notifiable quarantine pest. Introduction is prohibited under the European Community Single Market Protected Zone Arrangements.
Damage: Both adults and larvae attack leaves, in severe cases causing extensive defoliation.
Plants affected: Potatoes, tomatoes, aubergines (eggplants) and other Solanaceae (including weeds).
Prevention and control: *Chemical:* Spray with permethrin, pirimiphos-methyl or fenitrothion. *Non-chemical/organic:* Pick off eggs or larvae by hand. Young larvae can also be controlled with *Bacillus thuringiensis tenebrionis*. Protect vulnerable plants with a floating mulch.

Below: Some mussel scales on an apple.

Below: Termite workers digesting a piece of timber.

Below: A single termite mound in woodland savanna.

WHITE CEDAR MOTH (bead trees)
Leptocneria reducta

Range: Australia.
Description: The adult is a grey moth. The larvae, up to 4.5cm (1¼in) long, are dark brown with a yellow head, and are covered in grey or black hairs that are irritating to the touch. They cluster near the base of trees by day, scaling the trunk and feeding on the leaves by night. Once a tree has been defoliated, they march in single file to the next tree. There are usually two generations during the year, one in spring and one in autumn.
Damage: Leaves are eaten; trees can be completely defoliated by severe infestations.
Plants affected: Bead tree (*Melia azedarach*).
Prevention and control:
Chemical: Spray tree trunks and lower leaves with maldison.
Non-chemical/organic: Tie a length of hessian or sacking around the base of the tree trunks and collect and dispose of any caterpillars that congregate there during the day.

FRUIT-TREE ROOT WEEVIL
Leptopius squalidus

Range: Southern Australia.
Description: The adult weevil climbs the trunks of woody plants, reaching the top of the crown and chewing on young leaves and new growth. Eggs are laid in folded-up leaves. The larvae feed on the roots of trees and shrubs. They pupate in the soil.
Damage: Adults chew young leaves and stems. Larvae feed on roots; in cases of severe infestation, plants can be seriously weakened.
Plants affected: A large range of ornamental and fruit trees, including apples, citrus, figs and pears.
Prevention and control: *Non-chemical/organic:* Band the trunks of vulnerable plants with grease

or an adhesive to discourage adults. Ensure that overhanging branches of trees do not touch each other (thus allowing the weevil to spread).

LILY BEETLE, Lily Leaf Beetle
Lilioceris lilii

Range: Eurasia; introduced into North America.
Description: The adult is a conspicuous brilliant red beetle, to 7mm (¼in) long, that lays its eggs on the undersides of leaves. Larvae are orange-red, to 9mm (⅜in) long, and carry a layer of excrement on their backs. There is usually one generation per year.
Damage: Adults and larvae eat leaves, flowers and seed cases. Entire plant parts can be consumed. (Larvae cause more damage than adults.)
Plants affected: Lilies (*Lilium*); also fritillaries (*Fritillaria*). Potatoes and other plants are also occasionally attacked.
Prevention and control:
Chemical: Spray with bifenthrin, heptenophos with permethrin or pirimiphos-methyl. *Non-chemical/organic*: Spray with pyrethrum. Pick the adult beetles and larvae off the plants by hand.

Below: Lily beetles wreak havoc on lilies and fritillaries, eating leaves and stalks and leaving larvae indiscriminately over the surface of the plants.

Above: Holly leaf miners burrow under the surface of the leaves, creating discoloured patches. They have little impact on the general health of the plant.

LEAF MINERS
Liriomyza spp., other species

Range: Cosmopolitan.
Description: "Leaf miner" is a generic term that is applied to the larvae of certain flies, moths, sawflies, beetles and other insects. They mine through leaves to produce a range of symptoms. (In some cases, it is possible to see larvae by holding affected leaves up to the light.) Many leaf miners are specific to certain plants and have their own entries.
Damage: Straight or wavy lines or round or irregular blotches appear on leaves.
Plants affected: A range of plants, including celery, beets, beans, cabbage, potatoes, spinach and other vegetables; beech (*Fagus*), chrysanthemums (*Chrysanthemum*), hollies (*Ilex*), laburnums (*Laburnum*), firethorns (*Pyracantha*) and other ornamentals.
Prevention and control:
Chemical: Spray with malathion or pirimiphos-methyl. *Non-chemical/organic*: Cut off affected leaves or squash the mining larvae within leaves.

BEET LEAFMINER
Liriomyza chenopodii

Range: Parts of Australia and New Zealand.
Description: The adult is a grey and yellow fly, about 1mm (⅟₂₅in) long, that lays its eggs in leaf stalks. The larvae are white maggots; they tunnel through stalks and leaves.

Damage: White lines appear on leaf surfaces. Affected leaves are rendered unpalatable.
Plants affected: Beetroot (beet), Swiss chard; also related weeds.
Prevention and control:
Chemical: Spray with dimethoate.
Non-chemical/organic: Remove affected leaves as soon as white lines start to appear. Alternatively, squash the larvae within the leaf.

VEGETABLE WEEVIL
Listroderes difficilis

Range: Australia and North America (subtropical areas).
Description: The adult is a grey to brown beetle, about 8mm (⅓in) long, that lays its eggs on the stems and crowns of plants. The larvae, to 1.2cm (½in) long, are cream initially, turning green. Both adults and larvae cause damage. There is one generation per year. Damage tends to occur in cool weather (usually in spring and autumn).
Damage: Small, irregular holes are eaten around the base of plants. Whole leaves can be removed and holes eaten in fleshy parts around the crown of the plant. Root crops can also be eaten underground. Small plants and seedlings can be killed outright.
Plants affected: Fleshy-rooted vegetables such as carrots, radishes, beetroots (beets) and parsnips; cabbages, lettuces and spinach are also vulnerable. Weeds can also be attacked.

Below: The larva of the vegetable weevil in its second phase.

Prevention and control:
Chemical: Spray with carbaryl.
Non-chemical/organic: Remove
weeds. Practise crop rotation.
Spray with pyrethrum.

CARROT WEEVIL
Listronotus oregonensis
Range: Eastern and central
North America.
Description: The adult is a dark
brown to black insect, 5mm
(⅛in) long, that lays its eggs in
leaf stalks. Larvae are curving
white grubs that tunnel through
roots and crowns of plants.
Their activity lays plants open
to disease. One or two
generations per year are
possible.
Damage: Young plants collapse
and may die. The crops of some
vegetables are spoilt.
Plants affected: Carrots and
celery.
Prevention and control:
Chemical: Dust planting rows
with lindane or pirimiphos-
methyl before sowing. *Non-
chemical/organic:* Make late
sowings of carrots to miss the
first generation. Practise crop
rotation. Protect seedlings with
a floating mulch or cloche.
After harvesting, remove all
traces of plant debris, which
could provide shelter for
overwintering adults.

GRASSHOPPERS,
Locusts
Locustidae
Range: Africa, Australasia,
North America, Asia, southern
Europe.
Description: Depending on the
species, adults are brown,
reddish-yellow or green winged
insects, up to 5cm (2in) long.
Eggs are laid in late summer to
early autumn. Nymphs are
smaller, and lack wings. There is
one generation per year. In
favourable conditions, plagues
can occur. Commercial crops are
more at risk than those in the
garden.
Damage: Stems and leaves are
eaten. Where plagues occur,

Above: A desert locust.

whole fields of sweet corn can
be defoliated.
Plants affected: A wide range,
especially sweet corn and some
other commercial crops; weeds
are also attacked.
Prevention and control:
Chemical: Poison baits or traps
can be effective in controlling
swarms. *Non-chemical/organic:*
Cover vegetable plants with a
floating mulch where locusts
occur in high numbers.

CALLISTEMON
SAWFLIES
Lophyrotoma spp.
Range: Australia.
Description: The adult is a
sawfly. Larvae are bright green,
with tapering bodies. They feed
on leaves.
Damage: Leaves are
skeletonized. Entire plants can
be defoliated.
Plants affected: Bottlebrushes
(*Callistemon*).
Prevention and control:
Chemical: Spray with maldison.
Non-chemical/organic: Cut back
affected growth.

Below: Capsid bugs damage leaves
at the shoot tips.

CAPSID BUGS
Lygocoris pabulinus, other
species
Range: Europe.
Description: The adult is a
green insect, about 6mm (¼in)
long. Capsid bugs suck sap
from plants and also secrete a
toxic saliva that can kill plant
cells. They are active between
late spring and late summer.
Damage: Holes are eaten in soft
leaves growing at shoot tips.
Flowers open unevenly or can
be aborted. The bugs also feed
on developing fruitlets.
Plants affected: A wide range,
including bluebeards
(*Caryopteris*), dahlias (*Dahlia*),
forsythias (*Forsythia*),
chrysanthemums
(*Chrysanthemum*), fuchsias
(*Fuchsia*), hydrangeas
(*Hydrangea*) and roses (*Rosa*).
Prevention and control:
Chemical: Spray with dimethoate,
fenitrothion or pirimiphos-
methyl as soon as any damage
is noticed.

KURRAJONG
LEAF-TIER
Lygropia clytusalis
Range: Parts of Australia.
Description: The adult is a pale
orange moth, about 2.5cm
(1in) across. The larvae are
light green and feed in groups,
webbing leaves together into
distinctive protective "tents".
Damage: The rolled-up leaves
are unsightly rather than
detrimental.
Plants affected: Kurrajongs
(*Brachychiton populneus*) and

Illawarra flame trees
(*B. acerifolius*).
Prevention and control: *Non-
chemical/organic:* Cut off and burn
affected parts.

TARNISHED
PLANT BUG
Lygus lineolaris
Range: North America.
Description: The adult is a
green-yellow to brown winged
bug, about 6mm (¼in) long,
that lays its eggs in the tissue
of stems, buds and leaves.
Nymphs are wingless and
yellowish, with black dots on
their bodies. Adults and
nymphs suck sap from stem
tips, buds and fruits, and
produce a toxic saliva.
Damage: Buds and leaves are
blackened and distorted. Fruits
fail to reach full size and are
puckered or pitted.
Plants affected: A wide range
of ornamental, fruiting and
vegetable plants; weeds can also
harbour the pest.
Prevention and control:
Chemical: Spray with dimethoate,
fenitrothion or pirimiphos-
methyl. *Non-chemical/organic:*
Spray with canola oil or kaolin.
The fungus *Beauveria bassiana* can
provide some control. Cover
developing plants with a
floating mulch in early spring
before the pest becomes active,
and keep the kitchen garden
weed-free.

Below: Tarnished plant bugs
produce between three and five
generations per year.

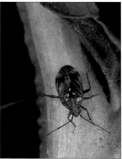

GYPSY MOTH
Lymantria dispar

Range: Europe; introduced into eastern USA and southern Canada.

Description: The adult male is a grey moth, up to 5cm (2in) across, with a thick, hairy body. The female is white and flightless and lays its eggs in masses on tree trunks, with a yellow coating of hairs. The grey larvae, up to 5cm (2in) long, have tufts of brown hairs and are spotted blue and red; they hatch in late spring. There is one generation per year.

Damage: Young larvae feed on the leaves of deciduous trees; the older larvae are capable of chewing conifer needles. In cases of severe infestation, entire trees can be defoliated, making this a serious pest.

Plants affected: A range of ornamental shrubs, trees and conifers; also soft fruit bushes.

Prevention and control: *Chemical:* Spray larvae with permethrin, biferthrin, pirimiphos-methyl or femitrothion. *Non-chemical/organic:* Scrape off overwintering eggs from the bark of trees, shrubs and conifers in autumn/winter. Tying hessian bands around trunks can deter the pest. Destroy cocoons and

Below: An apple tree provides food for a gypsy moth caterpillar.

larvae as seen. Young larvae can be controlled with the bacterium *Bacillus thuringiensis* var. *kurstaki*.

PERIODICAL CICADA
Magicicada septendecim

Range: Eastern USA.

Description: The adult is a brown to black insect, up to 4cm (1½in) long, with transparent wings. Eggs are laid in summer in slits in tree bark. As they hatch, nymphs fall to the soil, which they burrow into, spending up to 17 years underground before emerging for the final moult. The shrill buzzing that cicadas make during hot weather generally betrays their presence. Both adults and nymphs suck sap from plants. (Owing to the cicada's long life cycle, it is possible to predict the next wave of attack, dating from the previous emergence of adults. Check with your local pest control officer or government agriculture department.)

Damage: The sap-sucking activities of nymphs and adults cause little damage. More damage is caused during the egg-laying process, as tree bark is slit and holes are drilled in the underlying tissue. In cases of severe infestation, branch tips can be killed.

Plants affected: Many deciduous trees and shrubs, especially hickory (*Carya*), oak (*Quercus*), apples, peaches, pears and grapes.

Prevention and control: *Non-chemical/organic:* Net vulnerable young trees and shrubs from late spring in those years when adults are predicted to emerge.

TENT CATERPILLARS
Malacosoma spp.

Range: North America.

Description: Depending on the species, adults are yellowish to reddish-brown moths, 2.5–4cm (1–1½in) across. Eggs are laid

around small branches. Caterpillars, up to 5cm (2in) long, are black with a white stripe or row of dots along their backs; they are also patterned with brown, blue, red or yellow. The larvae spin webs between branches, from which they emerge at night to feed. There is one generation per year.

Damage: Larvae eat leaves; in cases of severe infestation, trees and shrubs can be defoliated. The webs they spin are unsightly.

Plants affected: A range of ornamental and fruiting deciduous trees and shrubs, including apples and pears.

Prevention and control: *Chemical:* Spray with fenitrothion. *Non-chemical/organic:* Scrape off eggs when noticed. Prune back and destroy any growth bearing webs. Spray young foliage with canola oil or use the bacterium *Bacillus thuringiensis* var. *kurstaki*.

LEAFHOPPERS
Macropsis spp.

Range: Europe.

Description: The adults are pale yellow insects, 2–3mm (1/10–1/8in) long. Nymphs are creamy white. Leafhoppers suck sap and also transmit viral diseases. Many leafhoppers are specific to one plant and have separate entries.

Damage: Small green or white dots appear on the upper surface of leaves. In severe cases, nearly all the leaf's colour may be lost. Viruses may take hold.

Plants affected: Cane fruit,

Below: This tent caterpillar is feeding on a beech leaf.

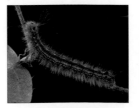

Above: Cabbage moth eggs are grouped in rafts of 20–30 eggs on the undersides of leaves.

especially blackberries; also mints and plums; beeches (*Fagus*), phlomis (*Phlomis*) and sages (*Salvia*) are also susceptible.

Prevention and control: *Chemical:* Spray with a systemic insecticide as soon as evidence of activity appears.

CABBAGE MOTH
Mamestra brassicae

Range: Europe and North America.

Description: The adult is a light brown to greyish moth with a wingspan up to 4.5cm (1¾in). Caterpillars, up to 4cm (1½in) long, are green or brown and feed on plant leaves. There are one or two generations per year, with most damage occurring from mid-spring to early autumn.

Damage: Irregular holes are eaten in leaves. *Cabbages:* Caterpillars work their way to the plant's heart. *Onions:* Eaten leaves can fall over.

Plants affected: Cabbages and other brassicas; onions can also be attacked.

Prevention and control: Inspect

Below: Leafhoppers vary in colouring and body size.

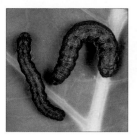

Above: Cabbage moth caterpillars can be up to 4cm (1½ in) long, and damage all types of brassicas.

Above: Cabbage moth caterpillars pupate approximately two months after hatching.

plants regularly and deal promptly with any caterpillars. *Chemical:* Spray with permethrin, fenitrothion, pirimiphos-methyl or bifrenthin. *Non-chemical/organic:* Spray with pyrethrum. Pick off caterpillars by hand. The bacterium *Bacillus thuringiensis* can also be used.

TOMATO HORNWORM
Manduca quinquemaculata
Range: North America.
Description: The adult is a grey moth, with zigzag patterns on the wings, which are up to 10–12.5cm (4–5in) across. Eggs are laid on the underside of leaves. Larvae, up to 10cm (4in) long, are pale green, with diagonal marks on their sides and a prominent black "horn" at the end of their body. There are one or two generations per year, depending on the climate. They seldom occur in sufficient numbers to cause major problems. The related tobacco hornworm has a red horn.
Damage: Larvae eat leaves and make holes in developing fruits. In cases of severe infestation, plants can be defoliated.
Plants affected: Tomatoes; also aubergines (eggplants), peppers and potatoes.
Prevention and control: *Chemical:* Spray with fenitrothion. *Non-chemical/organic:* Pick off caterpillars by hand. The bacterium *Bacillus thuringiensis* var. *kurstaki* can be effective. Larvae can also be paralysed by braconid wasps.

PRAYING MANTIDS
Mantidae
Range: Mainly tropical and subtropical areas; some species are native to, or have been introduced into, North America and Europe.
Description: The size of praying mantids varies depending on the species, but adults are 5–7.5cm (2–3in) long and green or brown, with papery wings. Eggs are laid in large numbers on stems and twigs, and are enclosed in light brown cases. The nymphs are similar to the adults but are smaller and lack wings.
Damage: No direct damage to plants, but praying mantids feed on a range of beneficial insects, such as bees, butterflies and wasps.
Plants affected: Potentially all plants; the activity of these pests has an impact on the ecology of the garden.
Prevention and control: *Non-chemical/organic:* Scrape egg cases off the plants.

FRUIT-TREE BORER
Maroga melanostigma
Range: Australia.
Description: The adult is a white moth that lays its eggs at the junctions of tree trunks, branches and twigs. Larvae tunnel into the wood, emerging at night to feed on bark and leaves. They retreat into their tunnels by day, sealing the entrance with chewed wood, bark, webbing and droppings.
Damage: Branches can be ringbarked. Cherries and some other trees exude gum from damaged areas.
Plants affected: Wattles (*Acacia*), jacarandas (*Jacaranda*), crape myrtles (*Lagerstroemia indica*) and other ornamentals; also some fruit trees.
Prevention and control: *Chemical:* Spray with carbaryl, wetting trunk, branches and leaves. *Non-chemical/organic:* Remove the protective covering from entrance holes and inject kerosene into them. Severely damaged plants are best replaced.

BEAN PODBORER
Maruca testualis
Range: Throughout Australia.
Description: The adult is a predominantly brown moth, about 3cm (1¼ in) across, with translucent patches on its wings. The caterpillars, about 2.5cm (1in) long, are bright

Below: Praying mantids may disturb the garden's ecological balance.

green or greenish-yellow with black or dark brown spots down their backs. They feed on flowers and stems and within pods, their presence betrayed by webbing or droppings at the union with stalks or where pods are touching. Damage is likely to be worst in warm, humid conditions.
Damage: Plants and crops are eaten.
Plants affected: Beans (but not soya beans) and some other Leguminosae.
Prevention and control: *Chemical:* Spray with carbaryl or trichlorfon; weekly applications may be necessary. *Non-chemical/organic:* Catch the adults on sticky traps hung among developing plants. In areas where summers are humid, sow crops as early in the season as possible.

MACADAMIA CUP MOTH
Mecytha fasciata
Range: Northern and eastern Australia.
Description: The adult is a black and white moth, about 4cm (1½ in) across. The larvae are roughly oval in shape, up to 3.5cm (1¼ in) long and 2cm (⅘ in) across. A yellow stripe along their backs provides effective camouflage as they lie along leaf veins. They feed principally on mature leaves.

Below: Larvae of the macadamia cup moth are well camouflaged.

Damage: Leaves are eaten. In severe cases, whole plants can be defoliated.
Plants affected: Macadamias, waratahs (*Telopea*) and other members of Protaceae.
Prevention and control: *Chemical:* Spray with maldison or carbaryl. *Non-chemical/organic:* Pick off caterpillars by hand, or prune off affected growth.

LEAF-CUTTING BEES
Megachile spp.
Range: Europe, Australia, North America.
Description: Adults are 6–16mm (¼–⅔in) long, depending on the species. They resemble honeybees but are stouter. Leaf-cutting bees are solitary, and can be important pollinators. They cause little damage and are usually best left alone.
Damage: Circular to oval holes are removed from the edges of leaves.
Plants affected: Roses (*Rosa*), lilacs (*Syringa*), camellias (*Camellia*), wisterias (*Wisteria*) and other plants.
Prevention and control: Unnecessary. Swat bees from plants as they are seen, if the damage is considered unsightly.

Below: Leaf-cutting bees take neat pieces from leaves, which they use to build their nests.

BEAN BLOSSOM THRIPS
Megalurothrips usitatis
Range: Warm, humid areas of Australia.
Description: The adult thrips is dark brown and about 1.5mm (¹⁄₁₆in) long. Immature thrips are pale yellow or orange-red. They feed on leaves and on the inner parts of flowers.
Damage: Young leaves are puckered, with downturned edges. Beans are twisted or distorted, and can also be lumpy, with rusty marks near the stalk.
Plants affected: Dwarf French beans and climbing beans.
Prevention and control: *Chemical:* Spray with dimethoate or maldison or dust with maldison at flowering time, paying particular attention to the flowers; or treat as for bean fly (*Ophiomyia phaseoli*). *Non-chemical/organic:* Destroy bean plants as soon after cropping as possible. Separate new crops from old ones or sow only one bean crop per year.

WATTLE MEALYBUG
Melanococcus albizziae
Range: Eastern Australia.
Description: These scales, 3–4mm (⅛–¹⁄₆in) long, are oval and dark purple to black, banded with white wax. They occur in groups on stems and feed on soft new growth.
Damage: The scales themselves cause little damage, but their honeydew attracts *ants*.
Plants affected: Wattles (*Acacia*) and some *Albizia* species.
Prevention and control: *Non-chemical/organic:* Prune off affected growth.

SQUASH VINE BORER
Melittia cucurbitae
Range: Eastern USA and southern Canada.
Description: The adult is an olive-brown moth, 2.5–4cm (1–1½in) across, which lays its

eggs singly on plant stems near the base. Larvae, up to 2.5cm (1in) long, are white with a brown head. They eat into stems, pushing out a green excrement. There is one generation per year, two in warm climates.
Damage: Larvae chew the bases of stems, which suddenly collapse.
Plants affected: Cucurbits such as cucumbers, gourds, melons, pumpkins and squashes.
Prevention and control: *Chemical:* Spray with carbaryl or trichlorfon. *Non-chemical/organic:* Spray or wipe the lower portion of stems with insecticidal soap. Cover young plants with a floating mulch (choose self-fertilizing varieties). Collapsed stems can be layered to promote rooting; slit the stem near the base to locate and remove the borer.

LARGE NARCISSUS BULB FLY
Merodon equestris
Range: Europe.
Description: The adult is a bumblebee-like hoverfly that lays its eggs from early to mid-summer near the necks of certain bulbs. The dull-cream maggots grow to about 2cm (⅘in) long.
Damage: Bulbs fail to flower, or produce only a few leaves. Often bulbs are destroyed.
Plants affected: Daffodils (*Narcissus*); also snowdrops

Below: The maggots of the large narcissus bulb fly tunnel into the bulbs. There is usually only one maggot per bulb.

Above: Katydid species have adapted to resemble the leaves on which they feed.

(*Galanthus*), bluebells (*Hyacinth-oides*) and some Amaryllidaceae.
Prevention and control: *Non-chemical/organic:* Rake up the soil around bulbs after flowering to deter flies from egg-laying. Tent bulbs with a floating mulch when the adults are active.

KATYDIDS (citrus, willows)
Microcentrum spp.
Range: North America.
Description: The adults are winged, green, grasshopper-like insects, up to 5cm (2in) long, that lay their eggs in double rows on twigs. Nymphs are smaller and lack wings. There is one generation per year.
Damage: Adults and nymphs eat leaves, but are seldom present in sufficient numbers to cause serious damage.
Plants affected: A wide range, including citrus and willows (*Salix*).
Prevention and control: These are not usually necessary.

CRUSADER BUG
Mictis profana
Range: Australia.
Description: The adult is a light brown bug, about 2cm (⅘in) long, with a yellow cross on its back. On nymphs, the marking appears as two dots. Nymphs are easier to control.
Damage: The bugs suck sap causing plants to wilt. Young shoots and flower heads die.
Plants affected: A wide range, most commonly wattles (*Acacia*) and cassias (*Cassia*); also citrus and grapes.

Above: Katydid camouflage is able to match leaf colour, markings and common blemishes.

Prevention and control:
Chemical: Spray with dimethoate or fenthion. *Non-chemical/organic:* Wearing gloves, pick off bugs by hand. Prune back any damaged growth.

AUTUMN GUM MOTH
Mnesampela privata
Range: Australia.
Description: The adult is a dark brown moth, about 4cm (1½in) across. The grey-green to black caterpillars feed in small groups, attacking young leaves and webbing them together.
Damage: Leaves are chewed at the edges. Leaves can be entirely skeletonized if the infestation is severe.
Plants affected: Eucalyptus (*Eucalyptus*), mainly *E. cinerea* and forms of *E. globulus*.

Below: Crusader bugs suck sap, but may not cause damage every year in every area.

Above: The autumn gum moth caterpillar can cause severe damage to leaves.

Prevention and control:
Chemical: Spray with maldison. *Non-chemical/organic:* Prune off and destroy any webbed leaves.

REDSHOULDERED LEAF BEETLE, Monolepta Beetle
Monolepta australis
Range: Mainly tropical areas.
Description: The adult beetle is about 6mm (¼in) long and yellow with red markings. It forms swarms in spring and late summer and is a particular pest of fruit trees, attacking leaves, flowers and fruits.
Damage: Holes are chewed in leaves. Sometimes leaves are completely eaten, exposing twigs to excess sunlight and causing die-back. Eaten flowers have a scorched appearance and fail to set fruit. The fruit skins are eaten. Small injuries to the skin result in scarring and cracking, but in severe cases all the skin is stripped off and the pulp is also eaten. Sweet corn attacked before pollination will not produce cobs. If the grain has been set, the pest's activity exposes the cob tip, rendering it susceptible to disease or attack from pests.
Plants affected: A wide range of fruiting plants, including avocados, citrus, figs, grapes, macadamias, mangoes, mulberries, peaches, plums and strawberries; vulnerable vegetable crops include beans, pumpkins and sweet corn. Dahlias (*Dahlia*), roses (*Rosa*) and other ornamental plants are also attacked.

Prevention and control:
Control is difficult. *Chemical:* Spray swarms with carbaryl. *Non-chemical/organic:* Knock the beetles from the trees into buckets containing an insecticidal soap solution.

CALICO BACK BUG, Harlequin Bug
Murgantia histrionica
Range: Eastern North America.
Description: The adult is a bright, shiny, red and black winged beetle, up to 1cm (⅜in) long. It lays its eggs in double rows on the underside of leaves. The nymphs are oval and wingless, and are also red and black. Both nymphs and adults suck sap from leaves. There are three or four generations per year (sometimes more in warm climates).
Damage: White or yellow blotches appear on leaves. In the case of severe infestation, plants wilt and die.
Plants affected: Many brassicas, such as Brussels sprouts, cabbages, kohlrabi and turnips; radishes, fruit trees, ornamentals and weeds can also be attacked.
Prevention and control:
Chemical: Spray with dimethoate or fenthion. *Non-chemical/organic:* Plant resistant varieties. Remove eggs by hand from the underside of leaves. Control weeds. Spray plants with an insecticidal soap or canola oil.

BRONZE ORANGE BUG (citrus fruits)
Musgraveia sulciventris
Range: Tropical and subtropical areas.
Description: The adult is a shiny brown to black bug, about 2.5cm (1in) long, that lays its eggs in midsummer to autumn in rows under leaves. The nymphs hatch in winter. Although they are initially green, they show considerable variation in colour as they age, varying from green or grey to orange or pink. They cluster

around the new shoots. Both adults and nymphs suck sap from stalks, and their presence is sometimes betrayed by their evil-smelling secretions. High temperatures and low humidity can kill them, so they often migrate to the base of trees on hot days.
Damage: Flowers and fruits are shed. New shoots wilt and turn brown.
Plants affected: Citrus, especially strong-growing plants.
Prevention and control:
Chemical: Spray foliage with maldison or dimethoate (but do not use dimethoate on Seville oranges, kumquats or Meyer lemons). *Non-chemical/organic:* Spray young nymphs in winter with an insecticidal soap. Later, larger bugs can be picked off the plants by hand.

FIG PSYLLID
Mycopsylla fici
Range: Tropical and subtropical areas.
Description: This tiny insect sucks sap from the underside of fig leaves, covering itself with the sap that the plant exudes when it is injured.
Damage: Affected leaves are shed by the plant.
Plants affected: Figs, especially Moreton Bay figs (*Ficus macrophylla*).
Prevention and control:
Chemical: Spray with maldison. *Non-chemical/organic:* Keep plants well fed and watered to maintain their leaf production and help recovery.

CHERRY APHID, Black Cherry Aphid
Myzus cerasi
Range: Europe; introduced into North America, Australia and New Zealand.
Description: These aphids damage soft new growth of plants from spring to autumn. Young aphids are brown, maturing black. The adults lay their eggs near growth buds in

Above: A mass of black cherry aphids clustering on a leaf.

late autumn. Many young aphids are found on the new growth in spring; as it matures, they move on to suckers and seedlings. Ladybirds (ladybugs) are a predator.
Damage: New growth turns yellow and curls. Honeydew attracts *sooty mould*.
Plants affected: Cherry trees.
Prevention and control: *Chemical:* Spray with dimethoate, but take care not to use close to fruiting. *Non-chemical/organic:* Spray with an insecticidal soap. Remove suckers from established trees and dig up unwanted seedlings.

PEACH-POTATO APHID, Green Peach Aphid, Spinach Aphid
Myzus persicae
Range: Cosmopolitan.
Description: This aphid is a

Below: Peach-potato aphids sucking sap from a leaf.

species of greenfly that sucks sap from the underside of leaves and also from stems and shoot tips. Its activity is often indicated by the whitish skins that it sheds and the presence of *sooty mould* growing on its honeydew. It sometimes occurs on plants in association with the mottled arum aphid. The peach-potato aphid can also transmit viruses. It thrives in humid conditions.
Damage: Leaves are puckered and plants grow slowly. Leaves and fruits are shiny with honeydew, then blacken with *sooty mould*.
Plants affected: A range of plants under glass.
Prevention and control: *Chemical:* Spray with pirimicarb or permethrin. *Non-chemical/organic:* Substitute pyrethrum.

LETTUCE APHID
Nasonovia ribisnigri
Range: Europe; also North America, Australia and New Zealand. The pest is rapidly extending its range.
Description: The lettuce aphid is a species of greenfly, active from mid-spring until the end of summer. Once the aphids take hold, they increase rapidly.
Damage: Growth is stunted and leaves are unpalatable.
Plants affected: Lettuces.
Prevention and control: *Chemical:* Spray with pirimicarb or heptenophos. *Non-chemical/organic:* Substitute derris.

Below: A colony of lettuce aphids will stunt the growth of this lettuce.

Above: A yellowish prepupa larva and a gooseberry sawfly caterpillar.

GOOSEBERRY SAWFLY CATERPILLARS (gooseberries, red and white currants)
Nematus ribesii, N. leucotrochus, Pristiphora pallipes
Range: Europe.
Description: The adults are sawflies that lay their eggs on the underside of leaves towards the centre of certain fruit bushes – where the first signs of damage appear. The caterpillars, up to 2cm (⅘in) long, and usually found in groups, are pale green with black spots. Several generations

Below: The underside of this gooseberry leaf reveals some sawfly eggs.

can occur between mid-spring and the end of summer.
Damage: Leaves are eaten. In cases of severe infestation, an entire bush can be defoliated. The fruit is not damaged, but the plant's future fruiting potential is reduced.
Plants affected: Gooseberries; also red and white currants.
Prevention and control: *Chemical:* Spray with permethrin, bifenthrin, pirimiphos-methyl or fenitrothion. *Non-chemical/organic:* Substitute derris or pyrethrum.

GREEN VEGETABLE BUG
Nezara viridula
Range: Cosmopolitan.
Description: The adult is a predominantly green, or sometimes predominantly black, bug, about 1.5cm (⅗in) long, that lays its eggs in spring. Nymphs have yellow, red, orange, green and black markings. Both adults and nymphs suck sap. Nymphs feed on new shoots, but older bugs prefer fruits and seeds.
Damage: Young bean pods are dried out and become distorted. Older pods are pale, with blotches. Tomatoes show mottled areas.

Below: A green vegetable bug nymph sucks sap from a soya bean leaf.

Above: The Rutherglen bug damages leaves by sucking sap.

Plants affected: Beans and tomatoes; also passion fruit, peas, peppers, potatoes, pumpkins and spinach, as well as certain ornamentals and some weeds.
Prevention and control: *Chemical:* Spray with fenthion or dimethoate. *Non-chemical/organic:* Pick off bugs by hand. Keep the vegetable garden free of weeds and remove plants promptly once they have finished cropping.

RUTHERGLEN BUG
Nysius vinitor
Range: Throughout Australia.
Description: The adult bug, about 5mm (⅕in) long, is greyish-brown with silvery wings. Rutherglen bugs suck the sap of a range of plants, but tend to enter gardens only during hot weather when the plants of their natural habitat – weeds and grasses on uncultivated ground – have dried off. Nevertheless, they can cause considerable damage.
Damage: Leaves wilt, stone fruits (those with pits) develop holes and beans shrivel. Clear gum is exuded from the holes made in peaches. The pest's excrement also causes blemishes on plants.
Plants affected: Beans, grapes, lettuces, peaches and other stone fruit; potatoes, tomatoes and other edible crops.
Prevention and control: *Chemical:* Spray with dimethoate, carbaryl or maldison. *Non-chemical/organic:* Substitute pyrethrum.

GOLDEN MEALYBUG
Nipaecoccus aurilanatus
Range: Throughout Australia.
Description: These bugs are black, but coat themselves with a mealy white wax. The golden mealybug tends to cause damage only in spring, since populations are later controlled by certain ladybirds (ladybugs) and their larvae (which are similarly coated with wax but are faster moving).
Damage: Honeydew excreted by the pest attracts *sooty mould,* which disfigures the plant. Growth may slow down and needles become discoloured.
Plants affected: *Araucaria bidwillii* and Norfolk Island pine (*A. heterophylla*).
Prevention and control: This is not usually necessary, provided natural predators are present. Small infestations can be removed from the trees by hand.

BAG-SHELTER MOTH (wattles)
Ochrogaster lunifer
Range: Australia.
Description: The adult is a furry, brown moth, about 5cm (2in) across, that lays its eggs in trees in yellow, ball-like clusters about 2cm (⅘in) across. Larvae grow to 5cm (2in) and have long red-brown hairs that are an irritant to the touch. They make "bags" where branches fork, in which they shelter during the day, emerging to feed on leaves by night. The bags can reach up to 25cm (10in) in length.
Damage: Trees can be completely defoliated. The bags are also unsightly.
Plants affected: Wattles (*Acacia*), especially *A. pendula*.
Prevention and control: *Chemical:* Spray with maldison. *Non-chemical/organic:* Look for and carefully remove egg clusters or bags while these are still small.

Below: This cluster of bag-shelter moth caterpillars will cause considerable damage to the tree.

GREVILLEA LOOPER
Oenochroma vinaria
Range: Australia.
Description: The adult is a pinkish-purple moth, up to 5cm (2in) across. The green caterpillars move with a looping action; they feed on leaves.
Damage: Caterpillars eat leaves; in severe cases, plants can be completely defoliated.
Plants affected: Banksias (*Banksia*), grevilleas (*Grevillea*), hakeas (*Hakea*) and some other ornamentals. Geebungs (*Persoonia*) can be attacked by similar species of looper.
Prevention and control: *Chemical:* Spray with carbaryl. *Non-chemical/organic:* Pick off the loopers by hand.

CONIFER RED SPIDER MITE, Spruce Spider Mite
Oligonychus ununguis
Range: Cosmopolitan.
Description: A tiny yellow-green mite that lays red eggs among silk threads with which it covers stems and leaves. Attacks are worst during hot, dry summers.
Damage: Leaves discolour and may be shed.
Plants affected: Mainly spruce (especially selections of *Picea albertiana*); also junipers (*Juniperus*) and thujas (*Thuja*).
Prevention and control: *Chemical:* Spray with bifenthrin, dimethoate or pirimiphos-methyl as soon as an infestation is noticed. Repeated applications may be necessary to control the mites effectively.

HIBISCUS FLOWER BEETLE
Olliffura concolor* see *Aethina concolor

WOODLICE, Common Slater, Sowbug, Pillbug
Oniscidae, including *Oniscus asellus, Porcellio scaber* and *Armadillidium vulgare*
Range: Europe, introduced into North America (*Oniscus asellus*); some species are cosmopolitan.
Description: Woodlice are grey or brown crustaceans with segmented bodies, 6–16mm (¼–⅔in) long, depending on the species. They are found in damp places, under stones and bark. They usually feed on decaying plant material (and hence are sometimes seen in compost heaps) and cause little damage to growing plants, but can attack soft seedlings.
Damage: Seedlings are eaten.
Plants affected: A range of seedlings; also soft fruits lying on the ground that are already damaged by birds or insects.
Prevention and control: Control is usually unnecessary, and is likely to be unsuccessful, owing to the large numbers of such creatures that are present in most gardens. *Chemical:* Dust vulnerable seedlings with lindane or bendicarb dust.

Below: Woodlice thrive in damp areas of the garden.

WINTER MOTH
(fruit trees)
Operophtera brumata
Range: Central and northern
Europe; parts of Asia.
Description: The adults are
active from mid-autumn to early
spring. Only males, light brown,
to 2.8cm (1⅛in) across, are
capable of flight; the wingless
females crawl up tree trunks to
lay their eggs in the branches.
The caterpillars, which move
with a looping action, feed on
the new growth (leaves, flower
buds and developing fruits),
binding leaves together with silk
threads. They grow to 2.5cm
(1in) long and are yellow-green
with pale lines.
Damage: Holes are eaten in
leaves (only seen once these are
fully unfurled). Leaves are also
bound together with silk
threads. Blossom can be eaten
and fruits are misshapen.
Plants affected: Fruit trees.
Prevention and control:
Chemical: Spray with permethrin,
bifenthrin, pirimiphos-methyl or
fenitrothion when new growth
emerges in spring. *Non-chemical/
organic:* Prevent egg-laying by
binding tree trunks with grease
bands over winter to trap
the females.

BEAN FLY
Ophiomyia phaseoli
Range: Australia; also found in
tropical and subtropical Asia.
Description: The adult is a
sturdy, shiny black fly, 2–3mm
(¹⁄₁₀–⅛in) long, that lays its
eggs in leaves (indicated by
small, yellow spots). The larvae
tunnel through the leaf stalks

Below: A winter moth caterpillar.

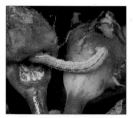

Above: The emperor gum moth has
conspicuous markings.

and main stems and so are never
seen. The pest is most
troublesome in areas prone to
warm, humid weather.
Damage: Stems and stalks are
swollen and crack and turn
reddish. Young plants wilt and
can collapse if the larvae reach
the base; infested parts of older
plants break off easily. Cropping
is reduced.
Plants affected: French and
climbing beans.
Prevention and control:
Chemical: Spray plants weekly
from the seedling stage until
flowering time with dimethoate
or similar.

EMPEROR
GUM MOTH
Opodiphthera eucalypti
Range: Australia.
Description: The adult is a
moth. The bright green
caterpillars, which grow to
12cm (4½in) long, are thick
and fleshy and hang upside
down from twigs to feed.
Damage: Rarely severe. Leaves
are chewed.
Plants affected: Eucalyptus
(*Eucalyptus*) and Californian
pepper-trees (*Schinus molle*); also
apricots, birch (*Betula*), sweet
gums (*Liquid-ambar*) and
Monterey pines (*Pinus radiata*).
Prevention and control:
Chemical: Spray with maldison, if
necessary.

ELEPHANT WEEVIL
Orthorhinus cylindrirostris
Range: Eastern Australia and
New Zealand.
Description: The adult weevil
can be grey or black and vary in

size (1–2cm/½–¾in). Eggs are
laid beneath the bark of weak-
growing trees, shrubs and vines.
Larvae, which cause more severe
damage, bore down into trunks
and roots, filling their tunnels
with their droppings ("frass").
They double back on themselves
and emerge from the bark
through a round hole, which can
be anything up to 1m (3ft)
from ground level. Elephant
weevils are active in spring.
Damage: Affected plants can be
seriously weakened.
Plants affected: Apples,
apricots, citrus, grapes and
peaches; ornamentals such as
eucalyptus (*Eucalyptus*) and
some others are also vulnerable
to the pest.
Prevention and control:
Chemical: In spring, spray the
trunks of trees from the base up

Below: Frit fly larvae have damaged
the heart of these barley shoots.

with carbaryl; repeated
applications are advisable. *Non-
chemical/organic:* Keep vulnerable
plants growing strongly.

FRIT FLY
Oscinella frit
Range: Europe.
Description: The adult is a
minute, black fly that lays its
eggs on sweet corn seedlings.
The larvae are small white
maggots that eat shoots from
the inside.
Damage: Main shoots die,
causing side shoots to be
produced. Young leaves are
tattered and growth is generally
weakened.
Plants affected: Seedling sweet
corn up to the five-leaf stage
(older seedlings are not
attractive to the pest); ryegrass
and barley.
Prevention and control:
Chemical: Not usually practical.
Non-chemical/organic: Keep
seedlings under cover until past
the five-leaf stage. Water
seedlings outdoors well to keep
them growing rapidly during
the period when they are
susceptible to attack.

EUROPEAN
CORN BORER
Ostrinia nubilalis
Range: Continental Europe;
introduced into north and

Below: A frit fly larva feeding on a
ryegrass stem.

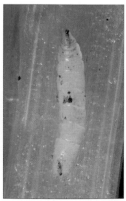

central USA and southern Canada.
Description: The adult is a yellowish-brown moth, 2.5cm (1in) across, that lays its eggs on the underside of leaves around midsummer. The larvae are grey-pink caterpillars, up to 2.5cm (1in) long. There are one to three generations per year.
Damage: Young larvae chew leaves and enter corn husks. Older larvae bore into stalks, sometimes causing them to break.
Plants affected: Mainly sweet corn; also beans, peppers, potatoes, tomatoes and some ornamental plants.
Prevention and control: *Chemical:* Spray with femtrothion. *Non-chemical/organic:* Pick off larvae by hand. Cut back and destroy damaged stalks. Treat developing sweet corn ears with *Bacillus thuringiensis* var. *kurstaki.* Choose corn varieties with strong stems and tight heads.

FRUITPIERCING MOTHS
Othreis spp., *Eudocima* spp.
Range: Tropical regions, especially rainforest areas and along creek banks.
Description: The adults are moths, up to about 10cm (4in) across, that are active at night, sucking the juice from fruit.
Damage: Holes are drilled in fruits; there can be either a soft, sunken area or a dry area around and beneath the hole. Damaged

Below: A European corn borer in a damaged potato stem.

fruits are susceptible to rotting.
Plants affected: Tropical fruits such as bananas, citrus, guavas, mangoes and papayas; tomatoes can also be attacked.
Prevention and control: *Non-chemical/organic:* Pick fruit before fully ripe in areas where the moths are common. Set pheromone traps for the moths.

STRAWBERRY ROOT WEEVILS
Otiorhynchus ovatus,
O. rugostriatus
Range: USA and southern Canada.
Description: The adults are brown to black insects, 6.5mm (¼in) long, that lay their eggs around the crowns of plants towards midsummer. The larvae, dirty white, up to 6.5mm (¼in) long, feed on plant roots and overwinter within them. There is one generation per year.
Damage: Adults eat holes in leaves and cut off flower stalks, reducing crops. Larvae feed on roots crowns, stunting the plant and making it vulnerable to disease. Plants may die.
Plants affected: Raspberries, strawberries, and other soft fruit; tree fruit, seedlings and some ornamentals are also vulnerable.
Prevention and control: *Chemical:* Treat with lindane. *Non-chemical/organic:* Control larvae with the parasitic nematode *Heterorhabditis bacteriophora.* Spray with pyrethrin. Protect young plants with a floating cloche or mulch.

Below: Fruitpiercing moths are large with distinctive markings.

Above: The larvae (left) of the vine weevil (right) can cause significant damage to a plant by feeding on its roots. Check the roots of container-grown plants before planting.

WINGLESS WEEVIL GRUBS
Otiorhynchus spp.
Range: Europe.
Description: These fleshy grubs are white with a brown head and grow up to 1.2cm (½in) long. They feed on plant roots, sometimes also burrowing into the crown. Infestations often go unnoticed.
Damage: Plants wilt, by which time most of the roots will have been destroyed.
Plants affected: Strawberries.
Prevention and control: *Chemical:* Dust areas where the pest is known to be active with lindane in late summer (when the new generation of grubs is hatching). *Non-chemical/organic:* Water in the parasitic nematode *Heterorhabditis* sp. Dig up and burn affected plants.

VINE WEEVIL, Black Vine Weevil
Otiorhynchus sulcatus
Range: Europe; introduced into North America and Australia. It tends to be localized.
Description: The adult is a black weevil, to 9mm (⅜in) long, that lays its eggs in the

Above: The notches in these rhododendron leaves are signs of attack by adult vine weevils.

soil around host plants. Larvae, which cause the most damage, are white grubs, to 1.25cm (½in) long. They feed on plant roots (especially those that have already been damaged), as well as tunnelling into corms and tubers. Adults eat notches in the leaves of plants, often attacking woody ornamentals such as rhododendrons (*Rhododendron*) and hydrangeas (*Hydrangea*). There is usually one generation per year (larvae overwinter in the soil; adults are active between spring and autumn). Vine weevil is a serious pest in gardens, especially affecting pot plants. Damage caused by the grubs is often only apparent once the plant has collapsed.
Damage: Plants grow slowly, then can wilt and die. Other diseases can sometimes take a hold in the wounds caused by the pest.
Plants affected: A wide range, including soft fruits, blueberries, grapes, hops and apples; also cyclamen (*Cyclamen*), fuchsias (*Fuchsia*) and other plants grown in containers.
Prevention and control: *Chemical:* Usually not practical. *Non-chemical/organic:* Control larvae with parasitic nematodes (either *Heterorhabditis megidis* or *Steinernema carpocapsae*). Check carefully for the presence of larvae on purchased container-grown plants and when repotting plants, and repot into fresh compost (soil mix).

COTTONSEED BUG
Oxycarenus luctuosus
Range: Central and eastern Australia.
Description: The adult is a black and grey bug, up to about 3mm (⅛in) long. Both adults and nymphs suck sap from buds and flowers, and juice from fruits.
Damage: Parts of the plant are distorted or wilt; discoloured areas appear on fruits.
Plants affected: *Hibiscus rosa-sinensis*, Norfolk Island hibiscus (*Lagunaria patersonii*) and other members of Malvaceae; other plants are also occasionally attacked.
Prevention and control: *Chemical:* Spray with dimethoate or fenthion. *Non-chemical/organic:* Control the pest with a soap spray.

FRUIT TREE RED SPIDER MITE, European Red Mite
Panonychus ulmi
Range: Europe; introduced into other countries.
Description: This tiny mite is black-red. Its presence is sometimes betrayed by the eggs that are laid on the undersides of branches in autumn, showing red in winter.
Damage: Leaves are finely mottled with yellow; they turn pale, then show a bronze tinge. In cases of heavy infestation, leaves turn brown prematurely and are shed (if this occurs early in the growing season, trees can lose vigour and cropping is affected).
Plants affected: Apples, plums,

Below: An adult cottonseed bug.

Above: This black swallowtail caterpillar has clear yellow and black markings, making it conspicuous on plants.

pears, quinces, grapes and raspberries; also hawthorns (*Crataegus*), roses (*Rosa*) and other members of Rosaceae.
Prevention and control: It is best to avoid spraying to kill other insect pests, since they often prey on this mite. *Chemical:* If necessary, spray with bifenthrin, pirimiphos-methyl or fenitrothion. *Non-chemical/organic:* Spray eggs in late winter with white oil.

BLACK SWALLOWTAIL BUTTERFLY, Western Parsleyworm, Parsleyworm
Papilio polyxenes, P. zelicaon, other related species
Range: North America.
Description: The adults are black or black and yellow butterflies, up to 7.6cm (3in) across. Eggs are laid singly on leaves. Young larvae are brown or black with white marks on their back; older larvae, up to 3.8cm (1½in) long, are green with black bands. Damage caused by their feeding is rarely severe. There are two to four generations per year.
Damage: Leaves are eaten.
Plants affected: Carrots, celery, fennel, lovage, parsley and parsnips; certain weeds can also act as hosts.
Prevention and control: *Non-chemical/organic:* Remove the caterpillars by hand and transfer them to other parts of the garden.

Above: The adult swallowtail butterfly is a beneficial insect in the garden.

BROWN SCALE
Parthenolecanium corni
Range: Europe; introduced into parts of North America and Australia.
Description: The adult scale is oval, about 5mm (⅕in) long, and reddish-brown; it sucks the sap from plants. Brown scale is seen on many ornamental shrubs and fruit bushes, especially when they are wall-trained. There is one generation per year.
Damage: Older stems are encrusted by the pest and the plants lose vigour. Honeydew excreted by brown scale attracts *sooty mould*.
Plants affected: Many woody plants, including outdoor fruiting vines.
Prevention and control: *Chemical:* Spray with malathion in midsummer, when the nymphs are active. *Non-chemical/organic:* Scrape away any loose bark in winter; or spray with tar oil.

GRAPEVINE SCALE
Parthenolecanium persicae
Range: Australia and New Zealand.
Description: Mature scales are dark brown, oval and 7mm (¼in) long. They are found in winter on older stems of the vine. Crawlers hatch from the eggs in late spring and feed on

leaves, moving to the canes in autumn. The scales do not cause harm in themselves, but their honeydew attracts *sooty mould* – a good indicator of their activity.
Damage: Vines are weakened. Where honeydew created by the scales falls on grapes, *sooty mould* spoils the fruit.
Plants affected: Fruiting vines.
Prevention and control: *Non-chemical/organic:* Spray affected areas with white oil in summer, paying particular attention to the underside of leaves where the eggs are laid. Prune out infested canes in winter.

AZALEA WHITEFLY (rhododendrons)
Pealius azaleae
Range: Cosmopolitan
Description: The adult is a tiny, white, moth-like insect, 2mm (½₁₂in) long, often seen on the underside of leaves in summer. The nymphs are pale green. Both adults and nymphs suck sap from leaves and excrete honeydew.

Below: The stems of this viburnum are encrusted with brown scales.

Above: Adult azalea whiteflies cover the underside of this azalea leaf.

Above: Lettuce root aphids seen through a microscope.

Above: An adult large mango tipborer.

Damage: Honeydew attracts *sooty mould*.
Plants affected: Rhododendrons (*Rhododendron*).
Prevention and control:
Chemical: Spray with permethrin, bifenthrin or pirimiphos-methyl as soon as the adults are observed. Repeated applications are usually necessary. *Non-chemical/organic:* Spray with pyrethrum or an insecticidal soap.

BEET LEAF MINER MAGGOT, Spinach Leaf Miner
Pegomya hyoscyami
Range: Europe; introduced into North America.
Description: The adult is a grey fly, 5mm (¼in) long. The maggots live in groups within the leaf tissue, which they mine. They are active from mid-spring to the end of summer.
Damage: Irregular blotches appear on the leaves, at first yellow-green, then turning brown as the leaves shrivel. Early attacks are more damaging than later ones.
Plants affected: Beetroot (beet) and spinach beet.

Prevention and control:
Chemical: Spray with malathion. *Non-chemical/organic:* Pick the affected leaves off the plants or squash the maggots as soon as they are noticed.

LETTUCE ROOT APHID, Poplar Gall Aphid
Pemphigus bursarius
Range: Widely distributed where lettuces are grown.
Description: This aphid is pale yellow and sucks sap from the roots of plants. Both pests and plant roots are covered with a white, waxy, mould-like secretion. The pest is active from mid-spring to midsummer.
Damage: Plants grow slowly and/or wilt. Heavily infested plants may die.
Plants affected: Lettuces. Some varieties are resistant to the pest.
Prevention and control:
Chemical: Drench affected plants with heptenophos. To prevent renewed infestation the following year, plant in a different site and dust the sowing area with pirimiphos-methyl.

LARGE MANGO TIPBORER (mangoes and cashews)
Penicillaria jocosatrix
Range: South-east Asia to the Pacific Islands including northern Australia.
Description: The adult is a moth that lays its eggs near new growth. Larvae are yellow-green dotted with red. They feed on the new growth initially, but eventually start boring into twigs.
Damage: Leaves pale and die; shoots die back.
Plants affected: Mangoes and cashews.
Prevention and control:
Chemical: Spray with Dipel. *Non-chemical/organic:* Feed and water the plants well to maintain their vigour.

STINK BUGS, Earth Mites
Pentatomidae
Range: Cosmopolitan.
Description: Adults are green, brown or grey bugs, with shield-like bodies (when the wings are folded), 1.25–1.6mm (½–⅝in) long, depending on the species. Eggs are laid on the undersides

of leaves. There can be two or more generations per year. Stink bugs emit an unpleasant smell when disturbed.
Damage: Adults and nymphs suck sap from stems, buds and leaves, and juice from fruit. Damaged fruits show a puckered appearance.
Plants affected: A wide range, including beans, soft fruits, sweet corn, okra, peas, squashes and tomatoes; weeds can harbour the pest.
Prevention and control:
Chemical: Spray with dimethoate or fenthion. *Non-chemical/organic:* Knock feeding bugs off plants and check for eggs on the undersides of leaves.

GREVILLEA LEAFMINER (grevillea and silky oaks)
Peraglyphis atimana
Range: Australia.
Description: The adult is a moth. Larvae, which grow to 1cm (⅜in) long, feed by mining leaves.
Damage: Brown blisters appear on leaves. Regular yearly attacks can severely weaken affected plants.
Plants affected: Grevilleas (*Grevillea banksii*) and silky oaks (*G. robusta*).
Prevention and control:
Chemical: Spray with fenthion. *Non-chemical/organic:* Feed and water plants well to maintain their vigour.

Below: Stink bugs have distinctive shield-like bodies.

Below: Spinach leaf miners cause brown withered patches on leaves.

Below: A lettuce root aphid attack has caused this lettuce to wilt.

Below: Stink bug nymphs resemble adults but lack wings.

STEELBLUE SAWFLIES (eucalyptus)
Perga spp.

Range: Mainly South Amercia and Australia.
Description: Adults are sawflies that lay eggs in slits in leaves. Larvae, brownish initially but ageing darker, cluster together by day, but spread out to feed at night. They exude a yellow fluid when disturbed.
Damage: Leaves are eaten, causing serious damage on small trees.
Plants affected: Eucalyptus (*Eucalyptus*).
Prevention and control: *Chemical:* Spray with maldison. *Non-chemical/organic:* Prune off branches on which larvae are clustered.

GRAPEVINE MOTH (vines, Boston ivy and fuchsias)
Phalaenoides glycinae

Range: South-eastern Australia and Tasmania; introduced into other areas (including parts of North America).
Description: The adult is a black moth, about 5cm (2in)

Below: The grapevine moth is more like a butterfly with its highly visible markings.

Above: The caterpillars of steelblue sawflies cluster together on eucalyptus leaves.

across, with yellow markings and an orange tuft of hairs at the end of its body. Caterpillars, about 5cm (2in) long, have white and pink markings.
Damage: Leaves are eaten from the underside, sometimes leading to complete defoliation of a vine. Small grapes are also sometimes eaten.
Plants affected: Vines, and Boston ivy (*Parthenocissus tricuspidata*); fuchsias (*Fuchsia*).
Prevention and control: *Chemical:* Spray with carbaryl. *Non-chemical/organic:* A predatory shield bug (*Oechalia schellembergii*) and certain birds feed on the pest.

WINGLESS GRASSHOPPER
Phaulacridium vittatum

Range: Australia.
Description: The adult is a grey-brown to dark brown grasshopper (darker where populations are largest). Females are up to 1.8cm (¼in) long, the males somewhat

Below: The wingless grasshopper causes the most damage when it is looking for a place to lay eggs.

smaller. Despite the common name, wings are present, but they do not enable the insect to fly. In hot, dry weather in summer, large numbers move into gardens, often causing considerable damage. One generation is produced per year.
Damage: Adults chew fruit and leaf edges. Young nymphs feed on low-growing plants, while older nymphs feed on a wider range of plant material.
Plants affected: Many plants, especially fruit trees and vegetables.
Prevention and control: *Chemical:* Spray with dimethoate, carbaryl or fenthion.

BRAMBLE SAWFLY
Philomastix macleaii

Range: Eastern Australia.
Description: The adult is a yellow-brown sawfly, 1–1.5cm (⅖–⅗in) long, with greyish-yellow wings. The larvae emerge from eggs laid in leaf tissue.
Damage: Larvae defoliate plants.
Plants affected: Mainly loganberries and blackberries.
Prevention and control: *Chemical:* Spray with maldison. *Non-chemical/organic:* Remove affected leaves before the pest has a chance to spread.

WHITE PALM SCALE
Phenacaspis eugeniae

Range: Australia and New Zealand.
Description: These are hard scales, generally found on the lower surface of leaves, but extending to the upper surface in severe cases. Females are white and about 2.5mm (¹⁄₁₀in) long; males are smaller. Several generations per year are possible. The insects suck sap from the plant.
Damage: Yellow blotches appear on leaves, which eventually wither and die.
Plants affected: Palms, magnolias (*Magnolia*) and viburnums (*Viburnum*); some

other woody plants are also susceptible.
Prevention and control: *Chemical:* Spray with maldison or dimethoate. *Non-chemical/organic:* Spray with white oil.

CYPRESS BARK BEETLE (cypresses and other conifers)
Phloeosinus cupressi

Range: California (native); recorded in parts of Australia and New Zealand.
Description: The adult is a dark brown or black beetle about 3mm (⅛in) long. Eggs are laid beneath tree bark and the larvae tunnel into the wood, making holes about 2mm (¹⁄₁₆in) across. Severely affected trees may need to be destroyed.
Damage: Upper branches die, followed by side branches. Leaves turn reddish and/or wilt. Small twigs can break off completely.
Plants affected: Cypresses (*Cupressus*) and the Lawson cypress (*Chamaecyparis lawsoniana*); some other conifers.
Prevention and control: *Non-chemical/organic:* Remove affected branches and feed the tree to keep it growing strongly.

ANGLE SHADES MOTH
Phlogophora meticulosa

Range: Northern Europe.
Description: The adult is a yellowish-green to olive brown

Below: An adult angle shades moth's wings show delicate patterning in shades of brown.

Above: An angle shades moth caterpillar feeds on a chrysanthemum leaf.

moth. The larvae are green or brown caterpillars, and are active at night at any time of year (mild nights only during the winter).

Damage: Caterpillars eat flowers and leaves.

Plants affected: A range of ornamentals under glass; also birches (*Betula*), oaks (*Quercus*) and other trees, shrubs and low-growing garden plants. Common weeds such as nettles and docks can also harbour caterpillars.

Prevention and control: *Chemical:* Spray with pirimiphos-methyl or permethrin. *Non-chemical/organic:* Hunt for caterpillars at night and pick them off by hand.

POTATO MOTH, Potato Tuberworm (potatoes and tomatoes)
Phthorimaea operculella

Range: Cosmopolitan.

Description: The adult is a small moth, active at dusk and so rarely seen. Larvae mine leaves initially, then leaf stalks and stems. They can also make their way into tubers and fruits, particularly those that touch.

Damage: Brown blisters appear on leaves. Tunnels are made in potato tubers and fruits, which then often rot. Stored potatoes are also vulnerable.

Plants affected: Potatoes, tomatoes and other members of Solanaceae.

Prevention and control:

Chemical: Spray with dimethoate. *Non-chemical/organic:* Keep plants well watered and remove any nearby weeds, particularly those belonging to Solanaceae. Dust stored potatoes with derris and keep the storage temperature as low as possible.

LEAFBLISTER SAWFLIES (eucalyptus)
Phylacteophaga spp.

Range: Australia and New Zealand.

Description: The adults are sawflies that look like orange wasps. They lay their eggs within 4m (13ft) of the ground. The larvae are active within leaves.

Damage: Blister-like patches, turning brown and papery, appear on leaves. Lumps harden when the larvae pupate.

Plants affected: Eucalyptus (*Eucalyptus*) and some other trees, especially when young and/or in exposed situations.

Prevention and control: *Chemical:* Spray with dimethoate or fenthion. *Non-chemical/organic:* Prune off affected branches.

Below: Leafblister sawflies create blisters by mining leaves.

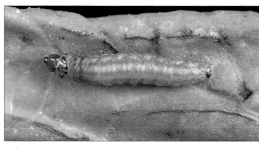

Above: Potato moth larvae are off-white with a darker head. They tunnel into plants from the family Solanaceae.

CITRUS LEAFMINER (citrus)
Phyllocnistis citrella

Range: Asia; also some parts of Africa, America and Australia.

Description: The adult is a white moth, about 5mm (¼in) across, with yellowish markings, and is active at night. The larvae tunnel through leaves, then pupate at the leaf edges. Populations are at their greatest in summer to autumn.

Damage: Silvery white lines appear on leaves, leading to distortion. Leaf margins are curled by the pest during the chrysalis stage.

Plants affected: Citrus; young plants are the most vulnerable.

Prevention and control: *Non-chemical/organic:* Spray leaves with white oil. Withhold water and fertilizer from summer to autumn, to avoid a flush of new growth that will support the pest.

Below: A citrus leafminer larva tunnels through a lemon leaf.

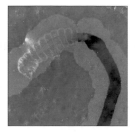

LEAF AND BUD MITE (raspberries and blackberries)
Phyllocoptes gracilis

Range: Europe.

Description: The pest is microscopic, feeding on the underside of leaves. Damage is similar (but less detrimental) to that produced by *mosaic virus*.

Damage: Yellow blotches appear on the upper surface of leaves.

Plants affected: Mainly raspberries; also blackberries and certain hybrid berries.

Prevention and control: None.

OAK LEAFMINER
Phyllonorycter messaniella

Range: Europe; introduced into Australia.

Description: The adult is a tiny moth that lays its eggs on the underside of leaves. Larvae feed inside the leaf. The damage they cause is extremely unsightly.

Damage: Fine lines appear on leaves, and, as the activity of the larvae continues, blisters appear.

Plants affected: Oaks (*Quercus*); also sweet chestnuts (*Castanea sativa*), beeches (*Fagus*) and sweet gums (*Liquidambar*), as well as apples and stone fruits.

Prevention and control: *Chemical:* Spray small trees with dimethoate at regular intervals as soon as the lines are noticed. Control on mature trees is possible only by injection – a seriously damaging procedure.

Below: Leaf and bud mites have created yellow blotches on these raspberry leaves.

Above: Tarsonemid mites have toxic saliva, which causes leaves to crinkle and buds to harden.

JUNE BEETLES, May Beetles
Phyllophaga spp.
Range: Northern hemisphere.
Description: Adult beetles, up to 2.5cm (1in) long, are reddish-brown or black. Eggs are laid in spring. The larvae, active in summer, are greyish-white grubs, up to 4cm (1½in) long, with a brown head.
Damage: Larvae feed on plant roots, and can also damage lawns. Adults eat the leaves of deciduous trees and shrubs.
Plants affected: A wide range, including potatoes, strawberries and many ornamental plants and grasses.
Prevention and control:
Chemical: Treat with fenamiphos. *Non-chemical/organic:* Apply the parasitic nematodes *Heterorhabditis bacteriophora* and *Steinernema glaseri* or the fungus *Beauveria bassiana*.

FLEA BEETLES
Phyllotreta spp., other species (including *Altica lythri* and *Psylliodes affinis*)
Range: Europe.
Description: Adults are blue, brown or, usually, black beetles, about 2mm (⅒in) long (sometimes up to 4mm/⅛in, depending on the species). They feed on the surface of leaves. Flea beetles are active between mid-spring and late summer.
Damage: Areas of leaf attacked by the beetles dry up. In cases of severe infestation, growth is

Above: Solomon's seal sawfly larvae can eat large sections of leaves.

checked; seedlings can be killed.
Plants affected: Brassicas, including swedes (rutabagas) and turnips; radishes, potatoes and other members of Solanaceae; vulnerable ornamentals are attacked by *Altica lythri* include alyssums (*Alyssum*), aubretias (*Aubrieta*), fuchsias (*Fuchsia*) and wallflowers (*Cheiranthus*).
Prevention and control:
Chemical: Control the pests with bifenthrin, lindane or pirimiphos-methyl. *Non-chemical/ organic:* Treat with derris. Protect seedlings and keep them growing strongly. Water young plants well in dry periods to avoid a check in growth.

SOLOMON'S SEAL SAWFLY
Phymatocera aterrima
Range: Europe.
Description: The adult is a black sawfly, 1cm (⅜in) long, which lays its eggs on plants of Solomon's seal around flowering time. The larvae, which grow up to 2.5cm (1in) long, are greyish-white with a black head. They overwinter in the soil around plants.
Damage: The larvae eat sections from leaves, sometimes completely defoliating a plant (though plants usually survive an attack).
Plants affected: Solomon's seal (*Polygonatum x hybridum*).

Prevention and control:
Chemical: Spray with permethrin or pirimiphos-methyl as soon as the larvae are active. *Non-chemical/organic:* Substitute derris or pyrethrum.

HAZEL BIG BUD MITE
Phytocoptella avellanae, syn. *Phytoptus avellanae*
Range: Europe; reported in Tasmania.
Description: These microscopic white mites live inside buds.
Damage: Buds are enlarged and rounded and fail to develop normally. There is no long-term damage to the plant.
Plants affected: Hazelnuts.
Prevention and control: *Non-chemical/organic:* If necessary, remove the affected buds and burn them.

CHRYSANTHEMUM LEAF MINER GRUB
Phytomyza syngenesiae
Range: Europe.
Description: The adult is a grey fly, 2.5mm (⅒in) long. Maggots tunnel through the leaves of chrysanthemums creating whitish-brown lines. Outdoors, there are usually two generations per year, but the pest is able to reproduce throughout the year in greenhouse conditions.

Below: A chrysanthemum leaf miner larva in its mine.

The whole life cycle lasts no more than 40 days and females can lay 60 eggs per week.
Damage: White or brown discoloured areas appear on leaf surfaces. Leaves lose some of their green pigment (sometimes totally, in the case of a severe infestation).
Plants affected: Gerberas (*Gerbera*), cinerarias (*Senecio*) and Chrysanthemums (*Chrysanthemum*).
Prevention and control:
Chemical: Spray with pirimiphos-methyl or malathion. Repeated applications may be necessary. *Non-chemical/organic:* Pick off infested leaves or crush the maggots at the ends of their tunnels.

TARSONEMID MITES, Thread-footed Mites, Michaelmas Daisy Mites, Strawberry Mites,
Phytonemus pallidus, other species
Range: Cosmopolitan.
Description: These mites are microscopic, creamy white creatures that live in the leaf and flower buds of a range of ornamentals that are grown under cover in cool climates; they are also found on some outdoor plants.
Damage: Stems and leaves are scarred. Growth is distorted. Growing tips are killed and flowers are either distorted or fail to open.
Plants affected: A range of glasshouse ornamentals, including begonias (*Begonia*),

Above: The characteristic scarring of tarsonemid mite damage is visible on this leaf.

Above: Young pearleaf blister mites have damaged these newly emerged pear leaves. Mites are too weak to move between trees but are carried on the wind.

Above: A cabbage white caterpillar.

cyclamen (*Cyclamen*), gloxinias (*Gloxinia*), ivies (*Hedera*) and African violets (*Saintpaulia*); Michaelmas daisies (especially *Aster novi-belgii* types) and strawberries.
Prevention and control: There is no form of chemical control. All affected plants should be burned to prevent the spread of the problem.

CYCLAMEN MITE
Phytonemus pallidus
Range: Cosmopolitan.
Description: This mite is microscopic and lives inside leaf and flower buds. As these open, the mites move to unopened buds, and sometimes also feed on the under surface of more mature leaves. They also feed on cyclamen corms in storage.
Damage: Flowers are flecked with dark spots or otherwise discoloured. In severe cases, flower buds wither and drop. Adult leaves curl.
Plants affected: Many flowering tender plants, including azaleas (*Rhododendron*), begonias (*Begonia*), cyclamen (*Cyclamen*), fuchsias (*Fuchsia*), gerberas (*Gerbera*), gloxinias (*Gloxinia*) and African violets (*Saintpaulia*); also some foliage plants such as ivies (*Hedera*) and leopard lilies (*Dieffenbachia*).
Prevention and control: *Chemical*: Spray with difocol or omethoate, especially young growth. *Non-chemical/organic*: Remove all the young leaves as they open over a 3- to 4-week period if you suspect an infestation.

PEARLEAF BLISTER MITE
Phytoptus pyri
Range: Europe; also areas of North America where pears are grown.
Description: This mite is white or pale brown, to 2mm (¹⁄₁₂in) long. Eggs are laid at the base of swelling new buds in spring. Adults and young feed on developing leaves, causing blisters to form. From petal fall onwards the mites live and breed in the blisters.
Damage: Pinkish-red pustules develop on unfurled pear leaves at flowering time. Subsequently, yellow, red or green blisters can be seen on both surfaces of infested leaves, either scattered randomly over the leaf, or in a band each side of the midrib. The blisters turn brown then

Below: The pupae of the cabbage white butterfly are large and clearly visible.

black, and the leaf dies. In cases of severe attack, fruit can be distorted and fall early.
Plants affected: Pears.
Prevention and control: *Chemical*: None available. *Non-chemical/organic*: Pick off affected leaves as soon as any blisters are noticed.

CABBAGE WHITE BUTTERFLY, Large White Butterfly
Pieris brassicae
Range: Europe; also North Africa and parts of Asia.
Description: The adult is a white butterfly, to 6.5cm (2¼in) across. Larvae, to 4cm (1⅗in) long, are yellow with black markings. They feed on the leaves of brassicas. Depending on the climate, there can be up to five generations per year, with population explosions in some years.
Damage: Irregularly shaped holes are eaten in outer leaves.
Plants affected: Cabbages, turnips and other brassicas; nasturtiums (*Tropaeolum*) can also be attacked.
Prevention and control: *Chemical*: Spray with permethrin, bifenthrin, fenitrothion or pirimiphos-methyl. *Non-chemical/organic*: Substitute pyrethrum. Use the bacterium *Bacillus thuringiensis*.

Below: An adult cabbage white butterfly lays its eggs on a range of host plants.

SMALL CABBAGE WHITE BUTTERFLY, Cabbage White Butterfly, Imported Cabbageworm
Pieris rapae
Range: Europe; introduced into North America and Australia.
Description: The adult is a creamy white butterfly, to 5cm (2in) across. Larvae, to 3cm (1⅓in) long, are pale green with yellow lines. They feed mainly at night. Population explosions can occur.
Damage: Holes are eaten in outer leaves; the hearts of leafy vegetables are eaten.
Plants affected: Brassicas, including cabbages, cauliflowers, broccoli and turnips; radishes; some weeds; ornamentals such as nasturtiums (*Tropaeolum*) and spider flowers (*Cleome*).
Prevention and control: *Chemical*: Spray with permethrin, bifenthrin, fenitrothion or pirimiphos-methyl. *Non-chemical/organic*: Substitute pyrethrum. Use the bacterium *Bacillus thuringiensis*. Keep the vegetable garden weed-free.

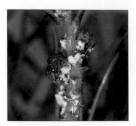

Above: This young shoot has been infested with pine adelgids.

PINE ADELGID, Woolly Pine Aphid (pines)
Pineus pini

Range: Cosmopolitan.
Description: The pest is a sap sucker, common on trees that are under stress or planted too close together. A woolly secretion at the base of needles betrays its activity.
Damage: Shoots die back.
Plants affected: Pines (*Pinus*).
Prevention and control: *Chemical:* Spray with dimethoate. *Non-chemical/organic:* Use a soap-based product or rely on the pest's natural predators, such as lacewings.

APPLE CAPSID
Plesicoris rugicollis

Range: Europe.
Description: The adult is a pale green insect, about 7mm (¼in) long. It sucks juice or sap from developing fruits and leaves. Mild infestations can be tolerated, since neither the flavour of the fruit nor its keeping ability is adversely affected by the capsid.

Below: Apples affected by capsids show dimple-like patches on their surface.

Damage: Corky scabs or raised lumps appear on the surface of fruits, and holes appear in the foliage.
Plants affected: Apples, especially the 'James Grieve' variety.
Prevention and control: *Chemical:* Spray as the new growth emerges with fenitrothion, dimethoate, pirimiphos-methyl or permethrin.

CABBAGE MOTH, Diamond-back Moth (cabbages, other crucifers and annuals)
Plutella xylostella

Range: Eurasia to Australia (especially in hot, dry areas).
Description: The adult is a small, greyish-brown moth, about 1cm (⅜in) across. Larvae, about 1.2cm (½in) long, are green. They are especially prolific in summer.
Damage: Larvae tunnel through leaves, then remove sections within leaves (known as the "windowpane" effect). Later, leaves are scattered with small holes. Larvae gradually work their way to the heart of the plant.
Plants affected: Cabbages and other crucifers; some annuals.
Prevention and control: *Chemical:* Dust or spray with

Below: A cabbage moth pupa is enclosed in its cocoon on a brassica leaf.

Above: This cabbage moth will lay its eggs on a Chinese cabbage leaf.

carbaryl. *Non-chemical/organic:* Use derris dust. Make sure that both surfaces of each leaf are treated.

BROAD MITE
Polyphagotarsonemus latus

Range: Cosmopolitan.
Description: These tiny mites cannot be seen with the naked eye. They feed on the lower surfaces of leaves.
Damage: Leaf edges curl. Leaves can become brittle or curled. Some bronzing occurs. Growth is stunted and buds can be shed from the plant. Flowers can be distorted or discoloured. *Lemons:* Fruits can show silver or grey discolouration.
Plants affected: French beans, peppers, aubergines (eggplants), some citrus; also camellias (*Camellia*), gerberas (*Gerbera*), begonias (*Begonia*), hibiscus (*Hibiscus*) and other ornamentals. (Plants under

Below: This leaf from a rubber tree has been damaged and distorted by broad mites.

glass are also susceptible to the mite.)
Prevention and control: *Non-chemical/organic:* Spray or dust with sulphur. Remove and destroy affected shoots as soon as any damage is noticed.

FIGLEAF BEETLE (figs)
Poneridia semipullata

Range: Eastern Australia.
Description: The adult is a dull brown beetle, about 1cm (⅜in) long, that feeds on leaves and fruit. Eggs are laid in groups of about 50 on leaves. The larvae, which grow to 1.2cm (½in), are initially yellowish, later becoming dark brown to black. They feed in trees, then move to the ground to pupate. In warm weather there may be several generations during the year.
Damage: Larvae skeletonize leaves, which then fall from the plant.
Plants affected: Figs.
Prevention and control: *Chemical:* Spray both adults and larvae from early summer with carbaryl. *Non-chemical/organic:* Remove the eggs by hand.

JAPANESE BEETLE
Popillia japonica

Range: Japan; introduced into eastern USA and southern Canada.
Description: The adult is a blue or black beetle, 1.2cm (½in) long, active in summer, laying its eggs in the soil around grasses in late summer. The larvae, which grow to 2cm (⅘in) long, are fleshy and greyish-white. (See also *lawns*.)
Damage: Larvae chew grass roots. Adults skeletonize leaves and eat flowers, sometimes completely defoliating plants.
Plants affected: A wide range of fruit and vegetables, as well as ornamentals.
Prevention and control: *Chemical:* Spray with fenitrothion or other insecticide. *Non-chemical/organic:*

Pick off adult beetles by hand in the early morning. Protect vulnerable crops using floating mulches or cloches. Spray crops with kaolin or canola oil.

LARGE CITRUS BUTTERFLY (citrus and Mexican orange blossom)
Princeps aegus
Range: Eastern Australia.
Description: The adult is a butterfly. Males are black, about 12cm (4½ in) across, with pale yellow and red markings. Females are brownish, with their hindwings marked with reddish-orange and blue. Eggs are laid singly on citrus branches. Larvae initially resemble bird droppings; later they are fat and fleshy and are olive green, marked with three brown bands that are edged with white.
Damage: Larvae eat quantities of leaves.
Plants affected: All kinds of citrus; also Mexican orange blossom (*Choisya ternata*), long-leaf wax flower (*Eriostemon myoporoides*) and some other plants.
Prevention and control:
Chemical: Spray with carbaryl.
Non-chemical/organic: Pick off individual caterpillars by hand.

RASPBERRY SAWFLY (raspberries and blackberries)
Prioborus morio
Range: South-eastern Australia.
Description: The adult is a black sawfly, about 6mm (¼ in) long, that lays its eggs in the canes and leaf stalks of certain soft fruits. The larvae, which grow to 1.2cm (½ in), are yellowish with a band of dark brown down the back and a central white line. They pupate between leaves or in the soil.
Damage: Larvae chew on leaves between the main veins.
Plants affected: Raspberries and blackberries.
Prevention and control:
Chemical: Spray with carbaryl,

making sure to wet the underside of leaves. *Non-chemical/organic:* Pick off larvae.

PALE GOOSEBERRY SAWFLY
Pristiphora pallipes, see *Nematus ribesii.*

MEALYBUGS
Pseudococcidae
Range: Cosmopolitan.
Description: Depending on species, mealybugs are oval, pale pink, yellow or grey insects, to 4mm (⅛ in) long. The eggs of some species are covered in wax, while others are laid singly. Established colonies, covered in wax, can be mistaken for fungi. They thrive in warm, moist conditions, especially in protected places, and are often found in leaf joints or among twining stems. They are transported between plants by ants attracted to honeydew.
Damage: Growth wilts and new leaves can be distorted. Honeydew attracts *sooty mould*.
Plants affected: A wide range, especially house plants and others grown under glass such as cacti and other succulents, ferns and palms.
Prevention and control: Chemical sprays are repelled by the insects' waxy coating. Controlling ants can help reduce mealybug numbers. *Ferns:* Badly affected plants are best discarded. *Chemical:* Spray with malathion. *Non-chemical/organic:* The biological control *Cryptolaemus montrouzieri* provides some control.

Below: Mealybugs suck sap and excrete honeydew.

Above: The surface tunnels on this carrot are signs of carrot fly activity.

CARROT FLY, Carrot Rust Fly (carrots, celery, parsnips and parsley)
Psila rosae
Range: Europe; also parts of North America, Australia and New Zealand.
Description: The adult is a small fly to 5mm (¼ in) long. Females are attracted by the scent of carrot leaves and lay their eggs on the plants. The larvae are thin, orange-white maggots, up to 1cm (⅜ in) long, active below ground. There are usually two generations per year, with maggots active from early to midsummer, and from late summer through autumn.
Damage: Growth of young plants is stunted. Maggots tunnel into roots, turning them brown and adversely affecting their flavour. Their activity can cause carrots to rot both in the ground and where stored.
Plants affected: Mainly carrots; also celery, parsley and parsnips.

Prevention and control:
Chemical: Dust seed drills prior to sowing with pirimiphos-methyl. Water plants in late summer with pirimiphos-methyl if crops are not to be lifted until autumn. *Non-chemical/organic:* Take care not to bruise leaves when thinning, since this releases the scent that attracts the egg-laying females.

AUSTRALIAN PRIVET HAWK MOTH
Psillogramma menephron subsp. *menephron*
Range: Eastern Australia.
Description: The adult is a grey moth, about 10cm (4in) across. The caterpillars are light green, with diagonal lilac and white bands, and a stiff spine at the end of the body.
Damage: Leaves are chewed.
Plants affected: Jasmines (*Jasminum*), privets (*Ligustrum*), pandoreas (*Pandorea*), lilacs (*Syringa*) and some others.
Prevention and control: *Non-chemical/organic:* Pick off individual caterpillars.

APPLE SUCKER
Psylla mali
Range: Europe.
Description: The adult is a pale green or yellow-brown, aphid-like insect, up to 2mm (¹⁄₁₆ in) long. Nymphs suck sap from blossom and young leaves. Adults, active in late summer, cause little damage. There is only one generation per year.

Below: Australian privet hawk moth caterpillars are camouflaged by foliage.

Eggs overwinter and hatch from late winter to spring. **Damage:** Petals turn brown (a symptom easily mistaken for frost damage). In severe cases, blossom is killed and fruit is not set. **Plants affected:** Apples. **Prevention and control:** *Chemical:* Kill nymphs with dimethoate, heptenophos with permethrin, pirimiphos-methyl or fenitrothion as buds are beginning to show green. *Non-chemical/organic:* In winter, wash trees with a tar oil to prevent eggs from hatching.

PEAR SUCKER
Psylla pyricola
Range: Europe.
Description: The adult is a pale green or yellow-brown insect. Nymphs are about 2mm (1/10in) long, and suck sap from blossom and young leaves. At least two generations are produced per year, and adults can overwinter.
Damage: Petals turn brown (a symptom easily mistaken for frost damage). In severe cases, blossom is killed. The honeydew on the foliage and fruits attracts *sooty mould*.
Plants affected: Pears.
Prevention and control: *Chemical:* Spray with dimethoate, pirimiphos-methyl or fenitrothion at or within three weeks of petal fall.

PAPERBARK SAWFLIES
Pterygophorus spp.
Range: Australia.
Description: The adult is a sawfly. The larvae feed on tree leaves, but also cause damage by burrowing into tree bark, where they pupate.
Damage: Trees are defoliated and can be ringbarked if there are enough pests.
Plants affected: Paperbarks (*Melaleuca*), especially *M. armillaris*, and tea trees (*Leptospermum*).
Prevention and control:

Above: Apple sucker nymphs have sucked the sap from these stems.

Non-chemical/organic: Prune off branches as soon as an infestation is apparent.

STRAWBERRY SEED BEETLES
Pterostichus **spp., see under** *Harpalus rufipes.*

HYDRANGEA SCALE (hydrangeas and camellias)
Pulvinaria hydrangeae
Range: South-eastern Australia, New Zealand.
Description: Females are oval, about 3mm (1/8in) long. In spring they lay eggs in waxy white ovisacs, usually up to 1cm (3/8in), though occasionally 1.6cm (5/8in), long. Emerging scales suck sap from the underside of leaves or from stems. Hydrangea scales are dormant in winter and become active in spring.
Damage: Plants are disfigured and weakened.
Plants affected: Mainly hydrangeas (*Hydrangea*) and also camellias (*Camellia*).
Prevention and control: *Non-chemical/organic:* In early summer, spray with white oil, wetting all the surfaces of the plant. Repeat at intervals if necessary.

SAN JOSE SCALE (fruit trees)
Quadraspidiotus perniciosus
Range: China; introduced into other countries.
Description: This tiny scale is purplish-grey and well camouflaged against woody

plant material. It can multiply rapidly – several generations per year – building up large colonies mainly on the trunks and branches of deciduous trees, but also on fruits. It can appear on evergreens. The scales suck sap. They are surrounded by a reddish "halo". In some areas, the control of this pest is a legal requirement.
Damage: Stems and branches develop a roughened texture as colonies build up. Fruits are damaged at the calyx end. Trees supporting large colonies lose vigour and may even die.
Plants affected: Almonds, apples, apricots, peaches, pears and plums; also cotoneasters (*Cotoneaster*), hawthorns (*Crataegus*), firethorns (*Pyracantha*), willows (*Salix*) and ornamentals.
Prevention and control: *Non-chemical/organic:* Spray thoroughly with oil making sure that the spray penetrates cracks in bark. Spray heavily affected deciduous trees in winter and again in spring (a single application in winter may be sufficient for light infestations). Spray evergreens in spring.

WOOLLY VINE SCALE
Pulvinaria vitis
Range: Europe; Australia and New Zealand.
Description: The adults are oval, about 6mm (1/4in) long, with wrinkled, dark brown shells. Woolly vine scales can encrust the stems of a range of woody plants.
Damage: In cases of severe infestation, plants lose vigour. There can be secondary occurrences of *sooty mould*.
Plants affected: Fruiting vines, currants, gooseberries and others; susceptible ornamentals include alders (*Alnus*) and firethorns (*Pyracantha*).
Prevention and control: *Chemical:* Spray newly hatched nymphs in midsummer with

Above: Woolly vine scale insects attach themselves in rows to twigs.

malathion. *Non-chemical/organic:* Scrape off any loose bark in winter. Apply a tar oil to the bark of plants in the dormant period. Spray with an insecticidal soap in midsummer.

ACACIA SPOTTING BUG (wattles)
Rayiera tumidiceps
Range: South-eastern Australia.
Description: This inconspicuous bug has a slender body about 1cm (3/8in) long, and is yellowish-brown with brown wings. It injects saliva into plants and sucks sap.
Damage: Leaves are spotted with brown and drop off in severe cases.
Plants affected: Wattles (*Acacia*).
Prevention and control: *Chemical:* Spray with omethoate.

CHERRY FRUIT FLIES
Rhagoletis **spp., including** *R. cingulata* and *R. fausta*
Range: North America; related species occur in other temperate areas.
Description: Adults are shiny black flies, about 5mm (1/5in) long, or more, depending on the species; they lay creamy white eggs in slits made in fruit. Maggots are yellow-white and grow to around 5mm (1/4in) long; they feed within the fruits in which they hatch.
Damage: Fruits are distorted or can turn red prematurely.
Plants affected: Cherries, plums and pears.

Prevention and control:
Chemical: Spray with fenthion or dimethoate. *Non-chemical/organic:* Spray vulnerable plants with kaolin during the egg-laying period (usually late spring to midsummer). Remove shrivelled fruits and any that turn prematurely red. In areas where the pest is known to cause particular problems, choose early-fruiting varieties.

APPLE MAGGOT
Rhagoletis pomonella
Range: Eastern USA and south-east Canada.
Description: The adult is a black fly, up to 6.5mm (¼in) long, that lays its eggs singly in holes made in the skins of apples. The white or yellow maggots, up to 6.5mm (¼in) long, tunnel into the flesh of the fruit, remaining within it until it falls from the tree. One generation is produced per year.
Damage: Tunnels are excavated in fruits; damaged fruits are shed early and rot.
Plants affected: Apples; also blueberries, cherries and plums.
Prevention and control:
Chemical: Spray with fenthion or dimethoate. *Non-chemical/organic:* Spray vulnerable plants with kaolin before the flowers open (and at intervals thereafter) to discourage egg-laying. Use sticky traps to catch females. Collect and destroy prematurely shed fruits. In areas where the pest is known to be a particular problem, choose late-fruiting varieties.

BULB MITE
Rhizoglyphus echinopus
Range: Cosmopolitan.
Description: This mite has a globular, glistening, yellowish-white body about 3mm (⅛in) long. Bulb mites breed quickly in high humidity at temperatures around and above 23°C (73°F). Besides being the carriers of other harmful organisms, they pass through a stage when they can also attach

themselves to flying pests.
Damage: Bulbs are completely destroyed. If infected bulbs are stored, the mites move from rotting bulbs to attack firm, healthy ones.
Plants affected: Daffodil (*Narcissus*) bulbs and others, including hyacinths (*Hyacinthus*), lilies (*Lilium*) and tulips (*Tulipa*); also garlic, onions and potatoes. Daylilies (*Hemerocallis*) can also be affected by the pest.
Prevention and control:
Chemical: Drench with dimethoate. *Non-chemical/organic:* Check stored bulbs regularly and discard any that show signs of softening.

CHRYSANTHEMUM GALL MIDGE (chrysanthemums)
Rhopalomyia chrysanthemi
Range: Europe; introduced into North America, Australia.
Description: The adult is a reddish-brown fly, about 2.5cm (1in) long. The larvae burrow through young leaves, eventually producing conical galls, 2cm (⅘in) long, protruding from the surface of the leaves. The pest is prevalent in warm, moist conditions but is undetectable in winter.
Damage: Stems are twisted; leaves and flowers are distorted.
Plants affected: Florists' chrysanthemums (*Dendranthema x grandiflora*).
Prevention and control:
Chemical: Spray with a systemic insecticide, such as fenthion, as soon as the infestation is noticed. *Non-chemical/organic:* Lift and destroy any affected plants.

BLACK SCALE, Brown Olive Scale
Saissetia oleae
Range: Temperate areas of the world.
Description: A soft scale, about 3mm (⅛in) across. Young scales excrete honeydew, which attracts *sooty mould* and ants. Eggs hatch in early summer,

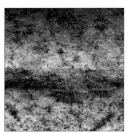

Above: Some sooty mould and young brown olive scale insects can be seen on this olive leaf.

with a second generation possible in autumn.
Damage: Twigs and leaves are covered; *sooty mould* can take hold.
Plants affected: Olives and citrus; also oleanders (*Nerium*), passion flowers (*Passiflora*) and many houseplants.
Prevention and control:
Chemical: Spray with maldison. *Non-chemical/organic:* Spray with solutions of white oil or rub scales off the plants by hand.

HEMISPHERICAL SCALE
Saissetia coffaea
Range: Tropical areas; the pest also appears in enclosed environments in temperate regions.

Below: Hemispherical scales excrete copious amounts of honeydew, which attracts sooty mould.

Description: The adult scale is a dark brown, hemispherical insect, to 4mm (⅙in) long. Immature scales are yellow-brown. In favourable conditions, they are capable of reproducing throughout the year.
Damage: The honeydew secreted by the scales attracts *sooty mould.*
Plants affected: A wide range of greenhouse plants, including ferns and frangipanis (*Plumeria*).
Prevention and control:
Chemical: Spray with malathion or an insecticidal soap. *Non-chemical/organic:* Spray with white oil or rub the scales off with a damp cloth. NB Ferns are sensitive to most insecticides (including white oil); heavily infested ferns are best discarded.

WHITE CURL GRUBS
Scarabaeidae
Range: Cosmopolitan.
Description: The larvae of scarab or cock-chafer beetles, varying in size according to the species. The grubs are white or bluish-white, with an orange-brown head, and curl round.
Damage: White curl grubs feed on the roots of plants, occasionally also around the base near soil level. Some species damage lawns.
Plants affected: A wide range, especially strawberries and all plants in containers.
Prevention and control:
Chemical: Apply fenamiphos.

Below: White curl grubs are the larvae of beetles in the family Scarabaeidae.

Above: Fungus gnat larvae viewed through a microscope.

Above: A fungus gnat is visible in the soil on the right.

Above: This potato crop has been attacked by garden symphylans.

Above: Green treehoppers clasp stems while they suck sap.

FUNGUS GNATS
Sciaridae

Range: Cosmopolitan.
Description: Adults are grey and black flies, about 3mm (⅛in) long, that hover in groups around plants. They are commonly found close to decaying plant material, occasionally near small, tender seedlings. The larvae, about 5mm (⅕in) long, are white with a black head and feed on the roots of seedlings. A slimy trail on the soil sometimes betrays their presence.
Damage: Plants fail.
Plants affected: Seedlings, cuttings and small, soft-leaved plants are all vulnerable.
Prevention and control: *Non-chemical/organic:* Replace infested soil or compost with material containing less organic matter.

PASSIONVINE HOPPER
Scolypopa australis

Range: Temperate areas, including Hawaii and parts of Australia and New Zealand.

Below: Passionvine hoppers feeding on wisteria leaves.

Description: A moth-like insect, about 8mm (⅓in) long, with transparent wings that are mottled with brown. Nymphs are greenish. Both suck sap and excrete honeydew that attracts *sooty mould*.
Damage: Leaves and fruit become shrivelled and can drop off.
Plants affected: Beans, citrus, grapes, peaches, passionfruit, rhubarb; vulnerable ornamentals include dahlias (*Dahlia*) and hydrangeas (*Hydrangea*), as well as others.
Prevention and control: *Chemical:* Spray with maldison or dimethoate, wetting the ground around the plant as well as the plant. *Non-chemical/organic:* Spray with pyrethrum.

GARDEN SYMPHYLAN
Scutigerella immaculata

Range: North America, Hawaii, Europe.
Description: The adult symphylan is white, 6.5mm (¼in) long, and has 12 pairs of legs; eggs are laid in small clusters about 30cm (12in) below the soil surface. Young symphylans are smaller and have fewer legs. Symphylans spend their lives in the soil, usually at a depth of 15–30cm (6–12in); they burrow deeper in periods of hot and cold weather. They feed on plant roots and other underground plant parts, chewing off the fine, hair-like roots and creating small craters in tougher material. There are

one or two generations per year.
Damage: In cases of severe infestation, plants are stunted or can be killed outright.
Plants affected: A wide range, including asparagus, beans, carrots, celery, cucumbers, tomatoes and other vegetables; ornamentals can also be affected.
Prevention and control: *Non-chemical/organic:* The parasitic mite *Pergamasus quisquiliarium* provides some control.

GREEN TREEHOPPER (wattles)
Sextius virescens

Range: Mainly tropical areas.
Description: A green insect, about 9mm (⅜in) long, with horn-like protuberances to each side of the head. Green treehoppers are sap suckers; adults cut slits in twigs for egg-

Below: A young garden symphylan is microscopic in size but destroys plants by feeding on fine roots.

laying. The honeydew excreted attracts ants and *sooty mould*.
Damage: Shoot tips die back; *sooty mould* can take a hold. The slits made for egg-laying can become more noticeable as the plant grows.
Plants affected: Mainly wattles (*Acacia*).
Prevention and control: *Chemical:* Spray with a systemic insecticide such as dimethoate. *Non-chemical/organic:* Cut back damaged growth.

SIREX WASP (pine, larch, spruce)
Sirex noctilio

Range: Eurasia, parts of North America, North Africa and Australia.
Description: Adults vary in length (1–1.4cm/⅖–⅝in) and are metallic blue (males have an orange band on the body). Eggs are surrounded by a mucus that encourages a fungus. This fungus attacks plant tissue and renders it ingestible by the emerging creamy-white larvae. They tunnel initially through young sapwood, then the harder heartwood.
Damage: Resin is exuded from tree bark; needles wilt and turn brown.
Plants affected: Pines (*Pinus*), especially the Monterey pine, larches (*Larix*) and spruces (*Picea*) (particularly if already weakened).
Prevention and control: Inform the local forestry office if an infestation of sirex wasp is suspected.

Above: Pea and bean weevil larvae do not damage their host plants.

PEA AND BEAN WEEVIL
Sitona lineatus
Range: Europe.
Description: The adult, which causes the damage, is a grey-brown beetle around 3–4mm (⅛–¼in) long. It is active from late spring to late summer. Damage is generally serious only on young plants.
Damage: Notches are eaten in leaf margins.
Plants affected: Peas and beans.
Prevention and control:
Chemical: Dust or spray plants with pirimiphos-methyl, malathion or permethrin.

BEAN ROOT APHID
Smynthurodes betae
Range: Europe.
Description: A creamy brown aphid, well camouflaged among soil and roots, that sucks sap from plant roots. A waxy white powder secreted by the aphid on the roots sometimes betrays its presence.
Damage: Growth is poor, stems wilt and crops are reduced.
Plants affected: Beans (mainly French and runner beans, sometimes broad (fava) beans).
Prevention and control:

Below: An adult weevil beetle feeds on a field bean leaf.

Chemical: Treat established plants with a root drench of heptenophos as soon as any wilting has been noticed. Where the pest is well established, dust the seed drill at sowing time with pirimiphos-methyl.

WOOLLYBEAR CATERPILLARS
Spilosoma glatignyi and other members of Arctiidae
Range: Temperate areas.
Description: The adult moths, about 5cm (2in) across, vary in colour, depending on the species. The larvae are banded with dense black and brown hairs that can cause skin rashes.
Damage: Leaves are eaten.
Plants affected: A range of herbaceous plants.
Prevention and control:
Chemical: Spray with carbaryl.
Non-chemical/organic: Wearing gloves, pick off individual caterpillars by hand.

BEET ARMYWORMS
Spodoptera exigua, other species
Range: North America (Spodoptera exigua usually in the southern half only).

Below: Armyworms do not have the hairy bristles of caterpillars.

Above: The adult stage of the woollybear caterpillar is a black-spotted white tiger moth.

Description: The adults are mottled grey moths, about 3.2cm (1¼in) across, that lay their eggs in masses. Larvae are green, up to 3.2cm (1¼in) long, with dark green and yellow stripes along their sides. They spin fine webs on the leaves on which they feed; they pupate just below the soil surface. There may be four or more generations per year, depending on the species and the climate.
Damage: Leaves, stems and roots are eaten.
Plants affected: A wide range, including asparagus, beetroot (beet), lettuce, onions, peas, potatoes, sugar beet and tomatoes; weeds can also harbour the pest.
Prevention and control:
Chemical: Treat with carbaryl.
Non-chemical/organic: Pick off caterpillars by hand. Spray with canola oil or kaolin. The fungus Beauveria bassiana and the bacterium Bacillus thuringiensis var. azaiwi can also provide some control.

Below: A fall armyworm caterpillar feeds on some maize kernels.

FALL ARMYWORM
Spodoptera frugiperda
Range: USA, east of Rocky Mountains.
Description: The adult is a dark grey moth, up to 3.8cm (1½in) across, that lays its eggs on the leaves of host plants. Caterpillars can be green, brown or black, with yellow and black stripes along their body. The moths move north during the growing season. There are one to six generations per year (numbers tend to be higher in late summer). The fall armyworm is a particular pest of sweet corn.
Damage: Larvae eat ragged holes in leaves. Older larvae can virtually destroy sweet corn plants by burrowing into the developing cobs.
Plants affected: Sweet corn; also beans, cabbages, potatoes, spinach, sweet potatoes, tomatoes, turnips; some weeds are also infested.
Prevention and control:
Chemical: Treat with carbaryl.
Non-chemical/organic: Plant early-ripening varieties of sweet corn as early as possible to avoid possible plagues of the pest. Pick off eggs and larvae by hand. Spray with canola oil or kaolin. The fungus Beauveria bassiana and the bacterium Bacillus thuringiensis var. azaiwi can also provide some control.

CLUSTER CATERPILLAR
Spodoptera litura
Range: Cosmopolitan.
Description: The adult is a moth, about 4cm (1½in) across, with whitish wings marked with silvery white. Larvae, which grow to 4.5cm (1½in) long, are green or greenish-brown with two rows of triangular black marks along their backs. They are often a problem during wet weather in late summer.
Damage: Small larvae remove sections from leaves or skeletonize them. Larger larvae,

Above: A cluster caterpillar shows its distinctive triangular black markings.

active during the day, feed on any part of the plant, including flowers and fruits.
Plants affected: A wide range of annuals, including vegetables and weeds.
Prevention and control: *Chemical:* Dust or spray with carbaryl, paying particular attention to the underside of leaves. *Non-chemical/organic:* Remove eggs and larvae from plants by hand.

LILY CATERPILLAR (clivias)
Spodoptera picta
Range: India to Samoa.
Description: The adult is a red and black moth, about 5cm (2in) across. The caterpillars are grey and smooth-skinned.

Below: Lily caterpillars are a serious pest in suburban gardens.

They have black lines along the length of the body, acquiring yellow colouring as they age. Lily caterpillars can grow to 5cm (2in).
Damage: Leaf surfaces are chewed.
Plants affected: Clivias (*Clivia*) and related plants.
Prevention and control: *Chemical:* Spray with carbaryl. *Non-chemical/organic:* Pick off individual caterpillars by hand and remove damaged leaves.

BULB SCALE MITE (daffodils and hippeastrums)
Steneotarsonemus laticeps
Range: Europe.
Description: This tiny mite, less than 1mm (¹⁄₂₅in) long, lives in the neck of certain bulbous plants under glass. It feeds on sap.
Damage: Leaves are unnaturally curved, often with notches along the edges. Flower stems are stunted and distorted, also with notches along the edges.
Plants affected: Mainly daffodils (*Narcissus*) and hippeastrums (*Hippeastrum*) under glass.
Prevention and control: *Non-chemical organic:* Discard all affected plants.

AZALEA LACEBUG (rhododendrons)
Stephanitis pyrioides
Range: Widely distributed.
Description: The adult is a shiny black beetle, about 4mm

(¹⁄₆in) long, with lace-like wings. Eggs are laid on the surface of leaves, and nymphs suck sap from the underside. The pest is active in spring and summer.
Damage: Leaves are disfigured by brown sticky spots of the nymphs' excreta.
Plants affected: Rhododendrons (*Rhododendron*).
Prevention and control: *Chemical:* Spray with a systemic insecticide such as dimethoate.

RHODODENDRON LACEBUG
Stephanitis rhododendri
Range: Widely distributed.
Description: The adult is a dark brown, winged bug, about 4mm (¹⁄₆in) long. Both adults and nymphs live on the underside of leaves, where they suck sap. One generation is produced per year.
Damage: Upper surfaces of leaves are mottled yellow; lower surfaces turn rust brown.
Plants affected: Rhododendrons (*Rhododendron*).
Prevention and control: *Chemical:* Spray with permethrin, fenitrothion or pirimiphos-methyl. *Non-chemical/organic:* Do not site rhodendrons in warm, dry situations.

Below: Azalea lacebug damage is at its greatest in late summer. The damage, caused by the insects sucking sap, is either grey in colour, or on evergreen azaleas, it may be light brown.

Above: Both these rhododendron leaves show the classic signs of a lacebug attack.

ORCHID BEETLE, Dendrobium Beetle
Stethopachys formosa
Range: Eastern Australia (native).
Description: The adult beetle, about 1.2cm (¹⁄₂in) long, is orange with black spots. The pupae are often found around the base of host plants.
Damage: Buds, flowers and leaves are eaten by both larva and beetle.
Plants affected: Orchids, especially *Dendrobium* (mainly *D. speciosum*); also *Cymbidium* and *Cattleya*.
Prevention and control: *Non-chemical/organic:* Pick off individual beetles by hand.

BUFFALO TREEHOPPER
Stictocephalus bisonia
Range: USA and southern Canada; central Europe.
Description: Viewed from above, the adult is a triangular, green insect, up to 6.5mm (¹⁄₄in) long; it presents a domed, buffalo-like profile. Nymphs are paler and lack wings. Yellow eggs are laid in rows in slits made in bark. It is these slits, rather than the feeding activities, that cause damage. There is one generation per year.
Damage: Stems on young trees appear scaly and cracked. Growth can be poor.
Plants affected: A range of fruit trees, such as apples, cherries, peaches and pears; ornamentals can also be affected.
Prevention and control: *Chemical:* Spray with dimethoate.

Non-chemical/organic: Cut out damaged twigs in winter. Overwintering eggs can also be killed by spraying with a petroleum-based oil during the dormant period.

PEACHTREE BORERS

Synanthedon exitiosa and related species

Range: Throughout North America.

Description: The adults are moths, up to 2.5cm (1in) long, with transparent wings. Males have a central yellow band, females an orange one. Eggs are laid in small groups near the base of trees. The larvae, up to 2.5cm (1in) long, are pale yellow or white with a brown head.

Damage: Larvae bore holes at the base of trees or in the roots. Young trees can be seriously damaged by an attack.

Plants affected: Mainly peaches; sometimes also apricots, cherries, nectarines and plums.

Prevention and control: *Chemical:* Not practical, since the caterpillars feed inside plants. *Non-chemical/organic:* In autumn check tree trunks for holes (from 8cm/3¼in below soil level to 30cm/12in up the trunk). Gouge out larvae with a knife, or inject bore-holes with the fungus *Beauveria bassiana* or the parasitic nematode *Steinernema carpocapsae.*

Below: An adult peachtree borer.

CURRANT CLEARWING MOTH, Currant Borer Moth

Synanthedon tipuliformis

Range: Europe; introduced into Australia.

Description: The adult is a moth, about 1.8cm (¾in) across, with clear wings, that lays its eggs on the stems of plants. Larvae feed on the pith inside the stems. Stems infested by the pest produce small, yellow leaves in spring, and are easily identified when the pupal cases appear on the outsides of the stems.

Damage: Stems are weakened and can break easily, or wilt; they eventually die. Fruit crops are reduced.

Plants affected: All currants, especially blackcurrants; also gooseberries and raspberries. Persimmons and junipers (*Juniperus*) can also be attacked.

Prevention and control: *Chemical:* Not practical, since the caterpillars feed inside plants. *Non-chemical/organic:* Cut back and burn stems showing signs of infestation.

COTTON HARLEQUIN BUG (hibiscus)

Tectocoris diophthalmus

Range: Eastern Australia.

Description: The adult is a bug, about 2cm (⅝in) long. Females are yellow to orange-yellow,

Below: A cotton harlequin bug.

with black patches; males are red with dark blue or green patches. They are often metallic in appearance. Both adults and nymphs suck sap.

Damage: Brown, papery patches appear on the leaves. Flower buds may drop.

Plants affected: Hibiscus (*Hibiscus*).

Prevention and control: Usually unnecessary, since the damage caused by the bugs is rarely severe. Wasps are a natural predator, and females guard their eggs from them.

APPLE CURCULIO

Tachypterellus quadrigibbus

Range: Eastern North America.

Description: The adult is a brown-red weevil, 2.5mm (⅒in) long, that lays its eggs in young fruit. Larvae are white and legless.

Damage: Larvae tunnel into fruit, where they pupate. Adults scar fruit through feeding and egg-laying. Infested fruit is shed early.

Plants affected: Apples, pears, quinces and related ornamentals.

Prevention and control: *Chemical:* Spray with fenitrothion, pirimiphos-methyl or bifenthrin. *Non-chemical/organic:* Collect dropped fruit from the ground and dispose of it elsewhere to prevent weevil populations building up.

PAINTED APPLE MOTH, Painted Wattle Moth (apples and wattles)

Teia anartoides

Range: Australia, including Tasmania

Description: The adult is a moth: males, about 2.5cm (1in) across, have brown and yellow wings; females are wingless and are covered in fawn hairs. The caterpillars, up to 3cm (1¼in) long, have four tufts of hair on their backs and tufts of black hair that extend forwards like

Above: The male painted apple moth is attracted to the female, who is wingless, by the emission of pheromones.

horns. They can be all colours. Infestations tend to be localized.

Damage: Caterpillars chew leaves.

Plants affected: A range of plants, especially apples and wattles (*Acacia*).

Prevention and control: *Chemical:* Spray with carbaryl. *Non-chemical/organic:* Remove caterpillars, or their cocoons, by hand.

BLACK FIELD CRICKET

Teleogryllus commodus

Range: Eastern Australia.

Description: A black or dark brown cricket, about 2.5cm (1in) in length when fully grown, with strong back legs for jumping. It is prevalent in autumn. Both adults and nymphs chew leaves, sheltering by day and emerging to feed at night. They may occasionally enter houses.

Damage: Leaves (sometimes at ground level), growing tips of plants and some fruits are chewed.

Plants affected: Young plants, including trees, and some fruits such as strawberries.

Prevention and control: *Chemical:* Spray with fenthion. *Non-chemical/organic:* Pick the pests off the plants by hand when noticed.

Above: False wireworm larvae (*Tenebrio molitor*) are shiny brown.

FALSE WIREWORMS
Tenebrionidae

Range: Cosmopolitan.
Description: Wireworms (Elateridae) and false wireworms are the larvae of certain beetles. They are shiny brown or yellow, growing to 2–3.5cm (⅘–1¼in) long, with legs near the head. They attack the roots of plants and other parts below ground level. They can cause damage to *lawns*.
Damage: Holes are bored in underground organs and also fleshy stalks near ground level. Plants can wilt and die.
Plants affected: Cabbages, carrots and potatoes; also grasses, including weeds.
Prevention and control: *Non-chemical/organic:* Control weeds that may harbour the pest, and keep plants growing strongly.

Above: The flesh of this peach has been damaged by a larva of *Ceratitis capitata*.

FRUIT FLIES
Tephritidae (including *Ceratitis capitata, Dacus cucumis* and *D. tryoni*)

Range: Cosmopolitan.
Description: Fruit flies are serious pests. Depending on the species, adults are around 7mm (¼in) long; they become active in warm weather, increasing in numbers and reaching a peak by late summer. They feed on honeydew and other sweet deposits. Eggs are laid just beneath the skin of fruits. Larvae, usually 7–9mm (¼–⅜in) long and creamy white, feed within the fruits. (If the fruits are immature at the time of egg-laying, the eggs may not hatch, and damage is restricted to a patch of woody tissue.) Secondary rots can also take hold, leading to complete destruction of the fruits. Warning: in some areas, control of fruit flies is a legal requirement.
Damage: Infested fruits can ripen prematurely and be shed by the plant. *Avocados:* Star- or T-shaped cracks appear on the surface of fruits. *Tomatoes:* The surface of fruits can show tiny green spots, while the rest of the fruit ripens.
Plants affected: A wide range of fruiting plants, including aubergines (eggplants), avocados (especially 'Fuerte' and 'Rincon'), bananas, citrus, cucumbers (and other cucurbits), figs, grapes, guavas, passion fruits, papayas, persimmons, tomatoes; stone fruits (those with pits) and pome fruits.
Prevention and control: Measures to control fruit flies may need to be taken throughout the season. Contact your local agriculture office for advice. *Chemical:* Spray with fenthion or dimethoate. Adults can be trapped by painting leaves and smooth parts of vunerable trees with a sweet, sticky solution containing maldison. *Non-chemical/organic:* Gather infested fruits from the ground and destroy them.

SPIDER MITES
Tetranychidae

Range: Cosmopolitan.
Description: Spider mites are tiny, barely visible to the naked eye. They breed rapidly in warm weather. Depending on the species, adults can be green or red (some change colour as they overwinter). Nymphs are paler than the adults. Both adults and nymphs suck sap from the undersides of leaves. Generations overlap; in favourable conditions, new generations can appear year round. Spider mite activity is often, though not invariably, indicated by the presence of fine webbing. Some particularly troublesome species are described in separate entries.
Damage: Affected leaves are speckled with yellow, then bronze or silver. Leaves can turn yellow or brown and can be shed by the plant.
Plants affected: A wide range, including apples, citrus fruits, beans, cucumbers and other cucurbits, aubergines (eggplants) and tomatoes; also houseplants and other plants grown under glass.
Prevention and control: *Chemical:* Chemical control is often ineffective, since the mites are capable of developing immunity. *Non-chemical/organic:* Remove mites (and webs) with a spray of water. Mist plants regularly to increase humidity (which suppresses reproduction). Biological controls can be effective against some species.

Below: Glasshouse plants are prone to spider mite infestations.

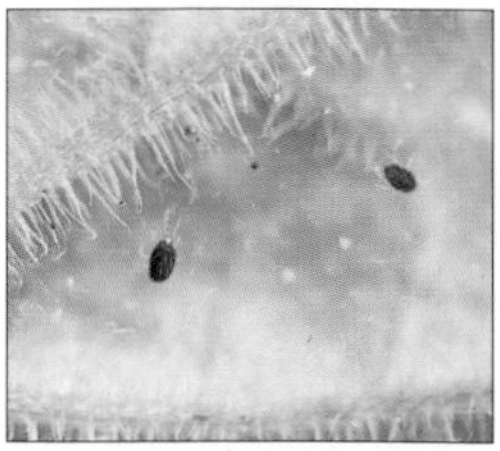

GLASSHOUSE RED SPIDER MITE, Red Spider Mite, Two-spotted Mite
Tetranychus urticae

Range: Mainly temperate zones, but also some subtropical areas.
Description: The adult is a yellow-green (turning orange-red) mite, 1mm (1/25in) long, which lays spherical eggs. The mites spin fine, silk webs between leaves and stems.
Damage: Leaves are mottled, then turn dull green to yellow-white. They dry up and can be shed by the plant. Cropping of fruiting plants can be reduced.
Plants affected: A wide range under glass; in warm weather, they appear on outdoor plants such as beans, raspberries, strawberries and roses (*Rosa*).
Prevention and control: *Chemical:* Spray with bifenthin, pirimiphos-methyl or malathion; the species is capable of developing immune forms. *Non-chemical/organic:* Control with the mite *Phytoseiulus persimilis.*

STRAWBERRY SPIDER MITE (bananas, strawberries and beans)
Tetranychus lambii

Range: Australia.
Description: This mite feeds on both leaves and fruits. Its activity is often indicated by its fine webs. Damage tends to be worse in dry weather, especially on plants that receive an irregular water supply.
Damage: Leaves turn yellow, dry out and can be shed.

Below: Spider mites produce very fine webbing.

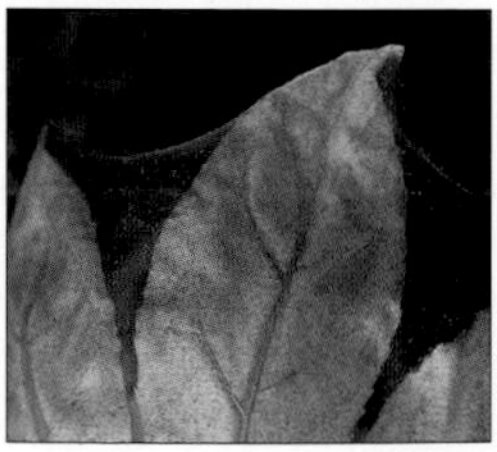

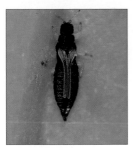

Above: A black adult thrips.

Bananas: Skins turn red, usually in patches. Damage is worst at the stalk end.
Plants affected: Bananas, strawberries and beans; also other plants including weeds.
Prevention and control:
Chemical: Spray with dicofol. *Non-chemical/organic*: Keep down weeds and water plants regularly.

THRIPS
Thripidae
Range: Cosmopolitan.
Description: Adult thrips are winged, black insects, to 2mm (1/12in) long. Nymphs are wingless and creamy yellow. They feed on the upper surfaces of leaves, causing a silvery discoloration (some species also damage flowers). They can spread certain plant viruses. Some have specific host ranges.
Damage: Sap is sucked from leaves and sometimes flowers.
Plants affected: A wide range, including some plants grown under glass.

Below: Rose thrips have made this flower wilt by feeding on its petals.

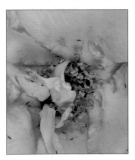

Prevention and control:
Chemical: Spray with malathion, permethrin, pirimiphos-methyl or dimethoate. *Non-chemical/organic*: Substitute pyrethrum. Use sticky traps under glass.

ROSE THRIPS
Thrips fuscipennis
Range: Europe.
Description: Rose thrips live between rose petals, from which they suck sap.
Damage: Petals are streaked with brown. In severe cases, flowers can be distorted.
Plants affected: Roses (*Rosa*).
Prevention and control:
Chemical: Spray with dimethoate or pirimiphos-methyl.
Non-chemical/organic: Substitute pyrethrum.

PLAGUE THRIPS
Thrips imaginis
Range: Oceania; reportedly introduced into Europe on cut flowers.
Description: The adult is an insect, about 1mm (1/25in) long, that lays its eggs in flower stalks. Nymphs are initially colourless, but turn yellow; they feed on leaves and flowers. Adults feed on flowers (especially pollen). Depending on weather conditions, plagues can occur.
Damage: Petals turn brown. The cropping of certain fruiting plants can be reduced.
Plants affected: Many flowering and fruiting plants, especially apples, pears, citrus, grapes, strawberries, plums and raspberries. Weeds can harbour plague thrips.
Prevention and control:
Chemical: Spray with maldison or dimethoate. *Non-chemical/organic*: Substitute pyrethrum.

GLADIOLUS THRIPS
Thrips simplex
Range: Africa (native); widespread where vulnerable plants are grown.

Description: The adult is a brown-black insect, to 2mm (1/12in) long. Nymphs are pale yellow. Adults feed on the outer parts of plants; nymphs live in flower buds and leaf tubes. Hot, dry conditions favour them.
Damage: Leaves are mottled with the thrips' excrement. Flowers show pale flecking (which is especially noticeable on dark-flowered hybrids). In cases of severe infestation, flowers can fail to open. Dormant corms can also be affected while in storage, turning first sticky, then hard and scabby.
Plants affected: Gladioli (*Gladiolus*); also carnations (*Dianthus*), irises (*Iris*), tiger flowers (*Tigridia*) and some other ornamentals.
Prevention and control:
Chemical: Spray with malathion, dimethoate or pirimiphos-methyl. *Non-chemical/organic*: Cut off and burn all affected plant material before the thrips descend to the corms. Store sound corms in a cool but frost-free place.

ONION THRIPS
Thrips tabaci
Range: Cosmopolitan.
Description: The adult is a yellow- to brownish-grey insect, about 1.5mm (1/16in) long. Nymphs are cream to yellow and do not have wings. Nymphs feed at the base of central leaves, eating new leaves as they emerge; adults feed further up the leaves. Besides the damage they cause in their own right by

Above: This mature plant will survive the damage caused by thrips on the leaves at its base.

feeding on the leaves, onion thrips are also the carriers of disease. They usually cause most trouble in hot, dry summers. This is a serious pest of onion and garlic crops in the tropics.
Damage: Leaves are blotched with silver, grey or white. In cases of severe infestation, leaves can be twisted and bent. Often there is insufficient leaf left to photosynthesize. Young plants can be killed outright.
Plants affected: Onions, garlic and leeks; also lettuces, tomatoes, beans, crucifers and potatoes. Ornamentals such as dahlias (*Dahlia*) and Icelandic poppies (*Papaver croceum*) are also vulnerable.
Prevention and control:
Chemical: Spray with malathion, permethrin, pirimiphos-methyl or dimethoate. *Non-chemical/organic*: Substitute pyrethrum.

Below: An onion thrips nymph viewed under a microscope.

Above: Glasshouse whitefly nymphs and honeydew on a tamarillo leaf.

BANANA FRUIT CATERPILLAR

Tiracola plagiata

Range: Tropical areas.

Description: The adult is a brown moth with light and dark patterns on the wings. The larvae are khaki caterpillars that grow to 6cm (2½in) long. Young larvae often begin life on weeds, moving to banana plants as they grow.

Damage: Fruit skins are chewed; larger caterpillars will also eat the flesh.

Plants affected: Bananas and some weeds.

Prevention and control: *Chemical:* Spray with carbaryl. *Non-chemical/organic:* Control weeds and pick caterpillars off the fruit.

ROOT APHID (artichokes)

Trama troglodytes

Range: Europe.

Description: A soil-coloured aphid, to 3mm (⅛in) long, that feeds on the roots of artichokes. A white, waxy powder, which it secretes on roots and surrounding soil particles, betrays its activity.

Damage: Growth is poor and plants can wilt.

Plants affected: Jerusalem artichokes and globe artichokes.

Prevention and control: *Chemical:* Drench the soil with dimethoate, heptenophos with permethrin, pirimicarb or pirimiphos-methyl where the aphid has caused problems. *Non-chemical/organic:* Practise crop rotation.

GLASSHOUSE WHITEFLY

Trialeurodes vaporariorum

Range: Europe.

Description: The adult is a small, white insect, 2mm (¹⁄₁₂in) long. The nymphs are small, scale-like and pale green; they live on the underside of leaves, depositing a sticky honeydew on the upper surface of leaves beneath them. On plants grown under glass, whitefly breed year-round. They can spread outdoors in summer, but cold temperatures in winter will kill them.

Damage: Honeydew excreted by the nymphs encourages *sooty mould*.

Plants affected: Potentially all plants grown under glass (including tomatoes and cucumbers) and houseplants.

Prevention and control: Many strains of whitefly have developed a resistance to insecticides, and chemical controls are unlikely to be successful. *Chemical:* Spray with permethrin, bifenthrin or pirimiphos-methyl. *Non-chemical/organic:* Use the parasitic wasp *Encarsia formosa*, introducing it as soon as any adult flies are noticed, but do not use this wasp in conjunction with chemical insecticides. Whiteflies can also be controlled with insecticidal soaps (which it is possible to use in conjunction with the parasitic wasp).

CABBAGE LOOPER

Trichoplusia ni

Range: Throughout North America.

Description: The adult is a grey-white moth, 3.8cm (1½in) across, active at night, laying eggs singly on leaf surfaces. The larvae, 3.8cm (1½in) long, are green with pale stripes; they are so-named because they curl their bodies into a loop as they move. There can be three or four generations per year, from spring to autumn.

Damage: Larvae chew holes in leaves; small plants and seedlings can be completely destroyed.

Plants affected: Cabbages and other crucifers; beetroot (beets), celery, lettuce, spinach, tomatoes; also some ornamental plants.

Prevention and control: *Chemical:* Spray with carbaryl. *Non-chemical/organic:* Spray with a soap-based product, canola oil or *Bacillus thuringiensis* var. *kurstaki*. Remove larvae by hand and crush eggs.

WHITE LOUSE SCALE (citrus)

Unaspis citri

Range: Widespread in citrus-growing areas.

Description: Male scales are white and 1mm (¹⁄₂₅in) long; females are brown and 2mm (¹⁄₁₂in) long. They are inconspicuous initially, but as colonies build up they cover tree trunks, branches and twigs.

Damage: Weakening of the plant, making it susceptible to die-back and infestation by other pests. Leaves may turn yellow and drop.

Plants affected: Citrus.

Prevention and control: *Non-chemical/organic:* Wash stems and branches with sulphur every two years between late winter and spring.

GUMLEAF SKELETONIZER

Uraba lugens

Range: Australia and New Zealand.

Description: The adult is a grey moth, about 2.5cm (1in) across. The larvae are hairy caterpillars, 2.5cm (1in) long, with a prominent "horn" on their head.

Damage: Young larvae remove the surface of a leaf; older ones chew pieces from leaves.

Plants affected: Mainly eucalyptus (*Eucalytpus*).

Below: A cabbage looper larva.

Below: A cabbage looper moth.

Prevention and control:
Chemical: Spray with maldison.
Non-chemical/organic: Prune off
any branches bearing eggs or
small larvae.

WASPS, Hornets, Yellow Jackets
Vespidae

Range: Cosmopolitan.
Description: Adults are black-
and-yellow striped insects, to
2cm (⅘in) long, depending on
the species. They live in
colonies, building papery nests
that sometimes hang from tree
branches or other supports or
can be located underground.
Larvae are white grubs that live
in the nests. Adults feed on
ripening fruits, often enlarging
damage caused by birds; they
are also attracted to the
honeydew secreted by certain
other insects. NB Wasp stings
can produce allergic reactions.
Damage: Holes are eaten in
fruits.
Plants affected: Apples, pears,
plums and other tree fruits;
also grapes.
Prevention and control: To
prevent and control wasp
damage it is necessary to
locate the nest. *Chemical:* Place
bendiocarb, pirimiphos-methyl
or other insecticidal dust in the
nest entrance at dusk (when the
adults are no longer active).
Non-chemical/organic: Enclose
ripening fruits (or fruit
trusses) in muslin bags. Wasps'
nests can also be physically
removed (in cases of severe
infestation, contact your local
pest control officer).

MACADAMIA TWIG-GIRDLER
Xylorycta luteotactella

Range: Mainly tropical and
subtropical areas.
Description: The adult is a
white moth, about 2.5cm (1in)
across, that lays its eggs on
young leaves and nuts. It is
active at night. The larvae, also
up to 2.5cm (1in) in length,
have pale, mottled brown bodies

Above: The larvae of the cypress
pine sawfly will eat large quantities
of leaves.

and darker heads. They create
webbed shelters or web leaves
together. The pest causes most
damage in summer to autumn.
Damage: Bark is eaten from
twigs near forks; damaged twigs
can snap off, leading to die-
back. Leaves are skeletonized.
Tunnels can be drilled in nuts.
In cases of severe infestation,
young trees can be defoliated.
Plants affected: Macadamias;
also banksias (*Banksia*),
grevilleas (*Grevillea*) and other
members of Protaceae.
Prevention and control:
Chemical: Spray with carbaryl.
Non-chemical/organic: Encourage
wasps, which prey on the pest.

CYPRESS PINE SAWFLY (cypresses and cypress pines)
Zenarge turneri

Range: South-eastern Australia
(native).
Description: The adult is a
sawfly. The larvae, which grow
to 2.5cm (1in) long, are bright
green and well camouflaged
among leaves and stems.
Damage: Larvae defoliate plants
and shoot tips die back.
Plants affected: Cypresses
(*Cupressus*) and cypress
pines (*Callistris*).
Prevention and control:
Chemical: Spray with maldison.
Non-chemical/organic: Cut back
affected branches.

LEOPARD MOTH
Zeuzera pyrina

Range: Europe and Asia;
introduced into North America.
Description: The adult is a
moth, up to 3.5–6cm
(1¼–2½in) across (females
are larger than males), with
white wings spotted with black.
Eggs are laid in bark crevices.
Larvae, up to 5.5cm (2¼in)
long, are creamy yellow or
white, spotted with black. They
burrow into trunks and
branches, often causing
considerable damage (even if
only a single caterpillar is
present). Their activity can
sometimes be detected by the
presence of compacted sawdust-
like excrement at the entry to
each tunnel. The life cycle takes
two years.
Damage: Burrowing larvae
weaken branches, which can
snap off in strong winds.
Young trees can be killed
outright if tunnelling takes
place in the trunk.
Plants affected: A range of
woody plants, especially crab
apples (*Malus*); also maples

Below: The adult leopard moth has
distinctive markings on its wings.

Above: The grass blue butterfly is a
beneficial insect, but the
caterpillars are destructive.

(*Acer*), birch (*Betula*), chestnuts
(*Castanea*), pears, mountain
ashes (*Sorbus*), lilacs (*Syringa*)
and other fruit trees.
Prevention and control: *Non-
chemical/organic:* Prune out
affected branches. Alternatively,
kill larvae by skewering them
with lengths of stout wire
pushed into their tunnels.

GRASS BLUE BUTTERFLY
Zizina labradus labradus

Range: Throughout Australia.
Description: The adult is a blue
butterfly that lays its eggs
singly on leaves, stems and
flower heads. The larvae, which
are usually active in summer, are
white initially, later becoming
green, pink or brown and with a
white stripe down each side of
the body.
Damage: Leaves are eaten.
Plants affected: Peas and beans;
also other members of
Papilionaceae.
Prevention and control:
Chemical: Spray with carbaryl.
Non-chemical/organic: Pick off the
larvae by hand.

Below: A leopard moth larva has
burrowed into this apple branch.

Fungal, Bacterial and Other Diseases

The following directory lists plant pathogens (fungi, bacteria and viruses) in Latin name alphabetical order. It describes the conditions favourable to the pathogens and the damage to plants that can occur. Susceptible plants are listed, followed by suitable methods of prevention and control.

Left: Toadstools are the fruiting body of fungi.

Fungal and bacterial diseases

The entries that follow are in Latin name alphabetical order. To locate a problem by common name entry, use the index.

CROWN GALL

Agrobacterium spp. and
A. tumefaciens

Definition: Apparently benign bacteria that enter plants through wounds to lower stems and roots, though the effects are unsightly. Crown gall, a very widespread disease, is associated with wet soils.

Symptoms and damage: Large galls appear on roots, but otherwise the shrub grows normally. On cane fruits, roses, daphnes and viburnums, small, soft galls appear on the shoots, at ground level or further up the stems, sometimes in chains. Plants can wither and growth can be affected if the galls interfere with take-up of nutrients. Galls can also be affected by secondary rots.

Plants affected: Raspberries, blackberries, brambles, grapes, rhubarb, carrots and other vegetables. Roses (*Rosa*), daphnes (*Daphne*), viburnums (*Viburnum*) and ornamentals.

Prevention and control: Cut off and burn diseased roots if necessary. Cut out and destroy affected growth above ground level. Dig up and destroy severely affected plants. Check the roots of newly purchased stock for any signs of the disease. Avoid injuring the roots of any replacement shrub to minimize the risk of

Below: Close-up view of a crown gall formed on a loganberry stem.

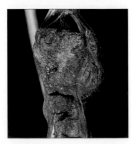

Above: The white blisters on this cabbage leaf may spoil the plant's appearance but will not affect its taste.

reinfection. Improve the drainage on wet soils by digging in grit and adding humus prior to planting; alternatively, after pruning out affected growth, transfer plants to better-drained ground. Avoid over-watering susceptible plants. *Roses:* Dig up and destroy badly affected plants and do not replace with roses. *Vegetables:* Practise crop rotation.

WHITE BLISTER, White Rust

Albugo candida, A. tragopogonis

Definition: Unsightly fungal diseases of brassicas and some other crucifers (including ornamentals) that distort growth but do not affect vegetable crops, which remain edible. They occur most commonly on overcrowded plants. These diseases are spread by wind or by insects, and tend to be prevalent in cool, damp conditions. *See also* White rust (gerberas), below.

Symptoms and damage: Glistening white masses of fungal spores appear on leaves, sometimes in concentric rings. Growth is stunted and root development can be poor. Heads of broccoli and cauliflower can also be distorted.

Plants affected: Many cruciferous vegetables, including

brassicas, radishes, horseradish, swedes (rutabagas) and turnips, salsify and scorzonera. Ornamental plants include aubretia (*Aubrieta*), alyssum (*Alyssum*), rock cress (*Arabis*) and honesty (*Lunaria*).

Prevention and control: Cut off and dispose of affected leaves. Thin the remaining plants to prevent overcrowding. Control weeds, since these too can harbour the disease. Rotate crops to prevent further occurrences of the disease.

WHITE RUST (gerberas)

Albugo tragopogonis

Definition: A fungal disease of gerberas (in climates where they can be grown as perennials). It can spread rapidly in spring, but slows down in summer.

Below: The margins of this sugar beet leaf are weakened by leaf spot.

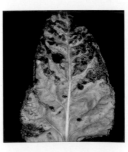

Symptoms and damage: Whitish pustules appear on lower leaf surfaces, with corresponding yellowish blotches on the upper surfaces.

Plants affected: Gerbera (*Gerbera*).

Prevention and control: Cut off affected leaves. If the disease has struck in previous years, spray gerberas in late winter with zineb. Avoid excessive use of nitrogen-high fertilizers.

LEAF AND STEM ROT

Alternaria spp., including *A. tenuis; Heteropatella valtellinensis*

Definition: A fungal disease of seedling lobelias (*A. tenuis*). Carnations and pinks (*Dianthus*) are also vulnerable. (*Heteropatella valtellinensis* is localized in certain areas.)

Symptoms and damage: Leaves show pale spots, giving a scorched appearance. Flower buds can also be affected. Affected parts can rot. Seedlings can be subject to damping off.

Plants affected: Lobelia (*Lobelia*) seedlings, carnations and pinks (*Dianthus*).

Prevention and control: Destroy affected seedlings. On mature plants, cut off the affected parts and spray with mancozeb.

LEAF SPOT

Alternaria brassicicola, Cercospora beticola, Coniothyrium hellebori (**hellebores**), *Drepanopeziza ribis, Glomerella cingulata* (**syn.** *Gloeosporium rhododendri; rhododendrons*), *Heterosporium variabile, Mycosphaerella brassicicola, M. macrospora, Phyllosticta* spp., *Ramularia beticola, R. rhei, Septoria anemones* var. *coronariae* (**bulbs, corms and rhizomes**), *S. apiicola*

Definition: Leaf spots, common

on many plants, can be caused by a range of fungi. *Glomerella cingulata*, *Ramularia rhei* and *Septoria apiicola* also have their own entries. Leafy plants grown soft (as with nitrogen-high fertilizers) are vulnerable in wet seasons, especially if overcrowded. Leaf spots typically occur in spring and autumn.
Symptoms and damage:
Brassicas: Older leaves show brown spots, with concentric rings of tiny fungal bodies, which carry the spores. Sometimes, these leave holes in leaves. On spinach, the spots are light brown or grey, with brown or purple edges. *Ornamental bulbs, corms and rhizomes:* Dry, dark, sunken spots appear on leaves; sometimes the whole leaf turns brown (especially in winter). If spots merge (for instance on irises), leaves can be killed. *Hellebores:* Black blotches appear on buds and petals. *Rhododendrons:* Circular purple patches, which turn brown, appear on leaves. Weak specimens are at risk.
Prevention and control:
Vegetables: Cut off and dispose of affected leaves. Thin plants to minimize the risk of further infection. Practise crop rotation. Spraying affected plants with a foliar feed can boost recovery. Adding potash to the soil before sowing spinach can reduce the plants' susceptibility to disease. *Ornamentals:* Cut off affected leaves and spray the plant with mancozeb. *Rhododendrons:* Boost

Below: These wisteria leaves have leaf spot.

recovery (especially if the plant has been severely affected) with a foliar feed and check that the soil type is appropriate (i.e. of a low enough pH and with an adequate humus content).

BROWN SPOT
Alternaria citri
Definition: A fungal disease of some citrus. It most commonly occurs during cool, damp weather in early spring, late summer and early autumn.
Symptoms and damage: Brown spots appear on leaves, fruits and young stems. Young leaves can be shed from the plant. Badly affected fruits can be shed, but are sometimes retained. In this case, the spots enlarge and become paler.
Plants affected: Mandarins (especially 'Emperor'), tangelos (some varieties), calamondins and some grapefruits.
Prevention and control: Spray with copper oxychloride or zineb. Prune off and destroy all affected parts of the plant.

LEAF BLIGHT, Alternaria Blight (carrots and cucurbits)
Alternaria dauci, *A. cucumerina*
Definition: Fungal diseases affecting a range of vegetables and ornamentals, favoured by warm, damp weather.
Symptoms and damage: *Carrots:* Dark brown, yellow-edged spots

Below: Brown spot on an orange.

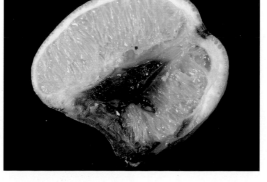

appear on leaf edges. The spots grow larger, and the leaves turn brown and die. Leaf stalks can also be affected, and in severe cases the whole plant dies. *Cucurbits:* Small, round, brown spots appear on the upper surfaces of older leaves, which curl and can die. The fruits show sunken spots, which sometimes develop a velvety dark brown or black mould.
Plants affected: Carrots, cucurbits, parsley, beans, onions and many ornamentals.
Prevention and control: Remove affected plants. Grow disease-resistant varieties. Practise crop rotation. Spray with copper oxychloride. Add grit or humus to poorly drained soil.

LEAF BLIGHT
Alternaria panax
Definition: A fungal disease that affects members of Araliaceae, principally *Schefflera*.
Symptoms and damage: Dark brown to black patches appear on leaves, which can then be shed. On *Schefflera arboricola*, the spots are smaller and paler and young leaves are distorted.
Plants affected: Scheffleras (*Schefflera arboricola* and *S. actinophylla*). Aralias (*Aralia*), false aralia (*Dizygotheca*), tree ivy (x *Fatshedera*), ivies (*Hedera*), and polyscias (*Polyscias*) are also vulnerable to leaf blight.
Prevention and control: Spray with copper oxychloride. Remove affected leaves.

Above: Leaf blight has caused these leaves to discolour and curl.

BROWN SPOT (passion fruits)
Alternaria passiflorae
Definition: A fungal disease of passion fruit and related plants. It is encouraged by warm, humid conditions.
Symptoms and damage: Brown spots appear on all parts of the plant above ground. These become paler as they dry out. Infected leaves are shed; in severe cases, whole plants can be defoliated. Circular, dark green spots appear on fruits, later turning light brown. Fruits then shrivel and are shed.
Plants affected: Passion fruit and other species of *Passiflora*.
Prevention and control: Spray monthly with copper oxychloride in winter. In spring, spray monthly with mancozeb (more frequently if the weather is damp). Thin congested plants to improve air circulation and do not plant fruiting vines too close together.

Below: The pale edges to the brown spots on these leaves show that the leaves are drying out.

Above: Leaf lesions on a potato leaf show early signs of target spot.

Above: The dead and dying roots of this pea plant have been infected by foot rot.

Above: Root rot is killing these conifers from the crown downwards.

TARGET SPOT (potatoes and tomatoes)

Alternaria solani

Definition: A fungal disease of members of Solanaceae, including weeds. It is favoured by warm, moist conditions.

Symptoms and damage: Brown to black spots appear on leaves, sometimes in concentric rings. Signs of disease normally occur on older leaves first. *Potatoes:* Leaves normally show symptoms around flowering time. Small sunken pits appear on tubers. These can enlarge, until whole areas are sunken. *Tomatoes:* Seedlings show dark, sunken lesions at the soil line ("collar rot"). They can be killed outright. Stems of affected older plants show elongated marks. Fruits rot to one side of the stalk, the infection showing as a brown or black sunken area. The rotting extends down into the fruit.

Plants affected: Members of Solanaceae, especially tomatoes, aubergines (eggplants), capsicums and weeds such as nightshades.

Prevention and control: Spray with copper oxychloride, copper hydroxide, zineb or mancozeb. Sow guaranteed disease-free seed of resistant varieties. Practise crop rotation. Remove and destroy related weeds (such as deadly nightshade) growing near the plot. Feed and water plants well to keep them growing strongly. Avoid wounding plants when transplanting. Allow potato crops to mature fully before harvesting.

SEEDLING BLIGHT (zinnias)

Alternaria zinniae

Definition: A fungal disease of zinnia seedlings.

Symptoms and damage: Leaves show reddish-brown spots with grey centres; brown cankers appear on stems. Seedlings collapse and then die.

Plants affected: Zinnias (*Zinnia*).

Prevention and control: Remove and destroy affected zinnia seedlings.

BLACK ROOT (radishes)

Apanomyces raphani

Definition: A fungal disease that is commonest during warm, damp weather.

Symptoms and damage: Black patches appear on the roots, and these can split. Secondary infections can then take a hold.

Plants affected: Radishes. Long varieties of radish are more susceptible to the disease than the round ones.

Prevention and control: This fungus lives in the soil. Improve drainage on ground where radishes are to be grown by adding grit and humus and practise crop rotation.

FOOT AND ROOT ROT, Black Root Rot

Aphanomyces euteiches, Fusarium spp., *Phytophthora* spp., *Pythium spp., Thanatephorus cucumeris* (syn. *Corticium solani, Rhizoctonia solani*), *Thielaviopsis basicola*, other fungi

Definition: A range of soil-borne fungi that attack plants, usually killing roots and causing stems to rot. Such rots are likely to occur where the same crops are grown year on year. Outdoor tomato plants that have not been regularly watered or potted on properly are particularly susceptible. Root rots can also result from irregular watering and may affect plants under glass. These soil-borne fungi can also cause other problems, such as storage mould, stem canker and damping off.

Symptoms and damage: Stem bases turn brown or black. The leaves discolour and shoots die back. In severe cases of rot, plants can collapse.

Plants affected: A huge range of shrubs and perennials, especially Michaelmas daisies (*Aster*), chrysanthemums (*Chrysanthemum*), delphiniums (*Delphinium*), heathers (*Erica*), gentians (*Gentiana*), lupins (*Lupinus*), primulas (*Primula*); tomatoes, peas and beans.

Prevention and control: If the plants are only lightly affected, water with a solution of Cheshunt compound. Alternatively, lift plants, cut out diseased tissue and replant in fresh soil. Boost recovery with a foliar feed. Destroy severely affected plants. *Woody plants:* If the disease is not severe, cut back damaged shoots to some healthy material. Badly affected plants are best dug up and destroyed. To minimize risk of reinfection, replace the soil before replanting to a depth of 30cm (12in) for heathers, 60cm (2ft) for larger shrubs. *Vegetable garden:* Practise crop rotation. Seeds can be dressed

Below: This pumpkin shows signs of storage mould caused by a soil-borne fungus (*Fusarium* spp.).

Below: These seedlings in a seed tray show signs of damping off (*Pythium* spp.).

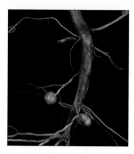

Above: Lesions on this potato plant stem indicate stem canker (*Rhizoctonia solani*).

with a product containing captan prior to sowing. *Under glass:* Replace or sterilize the soil every three years if growing in the open ground; use fresh, sterilized compost (soil mix) in containers. Water with care, since these rots often take hold as a result of *faulty root action*.

LEAF NEMATODES
Aphelenchoides spp.
Definition: These nematodes attack a wide range of plants. Although they attack moist plant parts, they are capable of surviving in dead plant material that has dried out.
Symptoms and damage: Yellow patches on leaves, turning brown, which can be extensive.
Plants affected: A wide range of ornamentals, including anemones (*Anemone*), begonias (*Begonia*), fuchsias (*Fuchsia*),

Below: Many rots look similar but may be caused by different species of fungi.

gloxinias (*Gloxinia*) and African violets (*Saintpaulia*); also blackcurrants and strawberries. Some chrysanthemum (*Chrysanthemum*) varieties are more susceptible than others.
Prevention and control: Spray with fenthion as soon as damage appears. Cut back and destroy affected growth.

BACTERIAL CANKER OF POPLARS
Aplanobacter populi
Definition: An unsightly bacterial disease that affects poplars.
Symptoms and damage: Large cankers appear on shoots and branches, sometimes also on trunks. Affected new shoots can die back in summer. On one-year-old growth, a dull creamy slime oozes out from cracks in the wood.
Plants affected: Poplars (*Populus*); *P. nigra* and some trees of hybrid origin are immune.
Prevention and control: Cut back and destroy diseased growth. In severe cases, dig up and destroy the whole tree. Replace with resistant varieties.

ARMILLARIA ROOT ROTS, Honey Fungi
Armillaria spp.
Definition: A serious disease caused by a number of related species of fungi that often

Below: An attack by eelworms (nematodes) has badly damaged these leaves.

Above: White mycelium is clearly visible on this tree bark.

results in the death of plants. It can affect plants such as vines grown in greenhouse borders. The disease is often undetected until the affected plant dies. It is the commonest cause of die-back of woody plants, especially privet hedges. Soft-stemmed plants are also vulnerable.
Symptoms and damage: Stems die back and leaves discolour and wither (they are often not shed, but cling on). New buds may fail to open in spring. The plant itself can suddenly die. Fan-shaped, honey-coloured fungal growths appear on roots and at the base of trunks or stems around soil level, as well as bootlace-like rhizomorphs on the roots, which spread laterally and affect plants nearby. Creamy-white mycelium is seen under the bark at soil level or extending higher.
Rhododendrons: Death usually occurs within a week. *Conifers:* Needles discolour and wither but are not shed by the plant. *Citrus:* Trees may set a heavy crop, then collapse and die. *Herbaceous plants:* Death is usually swift.

Below: Fungi have many different appearances.

Above: Evidence of *Armillaria* can be seen beneath this willow bark.

Plants affected: Trees, shrubs, conifers, vines and bush fruit; plants such as delphiniums (*Delphinium*), lupins (*Lupinus*) and peonies (*Paeonia*).
Prevention and control: Prevention is difficult, since no outward signs are visible until the plant is already dying. The problem is often associated with dead roots left in the ground after trees and shrubs have been felled or moved. Try to trace the original dead plant that first harboured the fungus and destroy any of its remaining debris in the soil. Dig up and dispose of newly affected plants with as much of the root mass as possible. Treat the soil with a fungicide, or replace it to a depth of up to 1m (3ft) before replanting with fresh material. In the greenhouse, after removing all affected plants, sterilize the soil with a tar acid or replace all the soil before replanting. *Herbaceous plants:* Dig up and destroy affected plants, and either change the soil before replanting or replace with annuals until you are sure that the disease is eradicated.

Below: *Armillaria* fruiting bodies often appear on the trunks of trees.

Above: This maturing pea shows characteristic tan spots of ascochyta blights.

ASCOCHYTA BLIGHTS
Ascochyta spp., *Mycosphaerella pinodes*

Definition: A disease affecting members of Solanaceae and Leguminosae. High humidity and rainfall encourage attack.
Symptoms and damage: *Peas:* Small, round, tan spots appear on leaves, stems and pods. These enlarge, merge and darken; the pods may wither. Lesions can also appear on stems from ground level up. *Tomatoes and related crops, okra and beans:* Dark spots appear on leaves and stems.
Plants affected: Tomatoes and other Solanaceae; okra and beans; Leguminosae; many ornamentals.
Prevention and control: Sow disease-free seed. Do not replant affected areas with susceptible crops for at least four years.

CLEMATIS WILT
Ascochyta clematidina
Definition: A fungal disease of clematis.
Symptoms and damage: Shoots wither and die back. Sometimes all the topgrowth is affected. The fungus attacks plants, often just before flowering. Lesions girdle the stems, killing everything above them, although not necessarily the entire plant.
Plants affected: Clematis (*Clematis*), especially large-flowered hybrids.

Prevention and control: Cut back affected growth, to below ground level if necessary. Destroy all removed foliage to prevent spread of the fungus. Apply a foliar feed to boost recovery. Plant new specimens 10cm (4in) below ground, as they are more likely to produce healthy new growth if attacked.

PEA POD SPOT (peas and beans)
Ascochyta pisi
Definition: A seed-borne fungal disease that affects certain leguminous crops, particularly troublesome in wet seasons.
Symptoms and damage: Sunken dark brown patches appear on leaves and stems, followed by similar marks on the pods. Fruiting bodies form on these, and the disease is then spread to healthy plants. The fungus grows through the pods and affects the seeds, which then display purple or brown spots.
Plants affected: Peas and beans.
Prevention and control: Lift and destroy affected plants. Do not grow susceptible crops in the same site for at least three years. Sow fresh seed, guaranteed disease-free.

LEAF SPOT (rhubarb)
Ascochyta rhei
Definition: A fungal disease of rhubarb. Wet conditions are favourable to it.

Below: These black-rimmed lesions are caused by pea pod spot.

Symptoms and damage: Small, round, brown spots appear on leaves. The spots enlarge, and affected tissue falls away. Leaves can be shed and the edible stalks are sometimes also affected.
Plants affected: Rhubarb.
Prevention and control: Spray with copper oxychloride or zineb. Cut off and dispose of affected leaves. Feed plants well.

BLACK MOULD (onions)
Aspergillus niger
Definition: A long-lived fungus that can attack a wide range of plant material, but causes most problems on onions in storage.
Symptoms and damage: Black powdery masses appear on the outsides of bulbs, then between sections. Affected sections dry out and become brittle.
Plants affected: Mainly onions in storage.
Prevention and control: Harvest onions at the correct time, dry them adequately and store carefully in dry, well-ventilated conditions.

CORN LEAF BLIGHT (SOUTHERN)
Bipolaris maydis, Cochliobolus heterostrophus
Definition: A wind-borne, fungal disease of sweet corn. Symptoms can be mistaken for frost or drought damage.
Symptoms and damage: Small, pale spots appear on lower leaves. These quickly turn into narrow lesions, which can measure up to 20cm (8in) long and are bordered with brown. Entire leaves, ears, husks and stalks can turn tan-coloured and dry out. In warm, damp weather, black spores can appear on the kernels and on the lesions.
Plants affected: Sweet corn, sorghum and some other grasses.
Prevention and control: Practise crop rotation where the disease is known to occur. Plant resistant varieties.

STEM GALL, Dingley Branch Gall (wattles)
Botryosphaeria acaciae
Definition: An unsightly fungal disease of wattles (*Acacia*).
Symptoms and damage: Small, cushion-like galls appear on branches, sometimes crowded together.
Plants affected: Acacias (*Acacia*), especially the Cootamundra wattle (*A. baileyana*).
Prevention and control: Prune off and dispose of affected branches. Badly affected plants are best replaced.

NECK ROT (onions)
Botrytis allii
Definition: A fungal disease that affects onions in storage. Other *Botrytis* species can cause similar problems.
Symptoms and damage: Grey furry mould appears on or near the necks of stored onions, which then soften. Later, black resting bodies develop.
Plants affected: Onions in storage.
Prevention and control: Practise good cultivation to ensure onions are firm and well ripened before lifting. (Do not apply fertilizers late in the growing season, which encourages soft growth.) Lift at the correct time, dry the onions well, and store them in well-ventilated, cool conditions. Inspect them regularly and remove any that show signs of rotting. Buy guaranteed disease-free onion seed or sets.

Below: Root ginger with black mould.

Above: A cross-section of an onion suffering from neck rot.

GREY MOULD
Botrytis cinerea

Definition: A very common and widespread air-borne fungus that can prove fatal to plants. It can enter through cracks in bark caused by frost, or through flowers. It can also appear on frosted (or otherwise damaged) leafy material. It is also troublesome on greenhouse crops, such as grapes, tomatoes and cucumbers, as well as ornamentals, especially where

Below: The lower leaves on this hellebore show signs of grey mould.

high temperatures are associated with high humidity. Grey mould is easily spread from plant to plant, making early detection and treatment essential; it causes particular problems in wet seasons. Grey mould on wallflowers is sometimes referred to as "winter killing". (Other species of *Botrytis* can produce similar symptoms to those detailed below; *Botrytis* species that are host-specific have their own entries.)
Symptoms and damage: *Woody plants:* Plants die back branch by branch until succumbing entirely. Cracks develop in bark to reveal grey pustules of spores. Black fungal threads may also be present. The stems of cane fruits turn pale or silvery, developing velvety grey growths in wet weather. A grey-brown fluff covers the fruits of affected plants, as well as appearing on stems and leaves. *Figs:* Fruits dry on the branch, but are not shed. *Strawberries:* The first sign of disease is usually the appearance of the characteristic fluff on fruits,

stems and leaves. *Vegetables.* Crops wilt. *Tomatoes:* The fungus is sometimes seen on fruits as spots surrounded by a green ring ("water spots"). *Ornamentals:* Summer flowers can rot. *Roses:* Partially open flowers can succumb to *Botrytis* in wet weather. *Plants under glass:* Petals of ornamentals can show small red or brown spots.
Plants affected: Potentially all garden plants, especially where growing conditions are poor. Plants grown in nitrogen-rich soil and seedlings are especially vulnerable.
Prevention and control: Cut back and destroy affected growth. Infections can be spread by contact, so cut out any affected growth that might touch healthy material. Space plants correctly and prune woody plants to improve air circulation. Regularly improve the soil to maintain good drainage. If the whole plant is affected, dig it up and destroy it. Cut off damaged flowers, and prevent later damage by spraying with carbendazim at two-weekly intervals when flowering. Take care when watering plants that have soft fruits (for example, strawberries and cucurbits), as a sharp jet of water can injure these, opening them up to disease. *Strawberries:* Remove affected berries before the fungus has a chance to spread. Make sure any straw mulches around strawberries are not too thick, and watch ripening fruit for any sign of fungus. *Figs:* Remove affected fruits. *Vegetables:* Spray

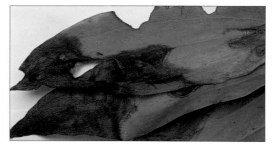

Above: Lily disease causes browning and rotting of the leaves.

overwintering crops with carbendazim. Remove all dead leaves and over-ripe fruits. *Plants under glass:* Ventilate greenhouses carefully to reduce humidity. Overwintering plants under glass can be sprayed with carbendazim. Grapes and strawberries under cover can be sprayed with carbendazim when the first flowers open, repeating as the later flowers emerge. (NB Regular applications of carbendazim are not advisable as the fungus is capable of developing resistant strains.)

LILY DISEASE, Leaf Blight (lilies)
Botrytis elliptica

Definition: A fungal disease of lilies that can cause problems during humid weather.
Symptoms and damage: Oval spots appear on leaves, which spread in humid conditions, turning brown and causing the leaves to rot. Stems and leaves can also suffer damage.
Plants affected: Lilies, most commonly *Lilium candidum* and *L. x testaceum*, and occasionally *L. regale*. All seedling lilies are vulnerable.
Prevention and control: Cut off and destroy affected leaves. Evidence of the disease can also be observed on overwintering rosettes of *L. candidum*, so check these during the dormant season and remove any affected leaves. Grow lilies in well-drained soil in a site that has good air circulation.

CHOCOLATE SPOT (broad (fava) beans)
Botrytis fabae
Definition: A disease of certain legumes. It is troublesome during a wet spring (especially on winter-sown crops), or where plants are grown in too acid a soil or have been given an excess of nitrogen-high fertilizer.
Symptoms and damage: Chocolate brown spots or streaks, which can merge into larger patches, appear on leaves and stems. Affected plants may turn black and die.
Plants affected: Broad (fava) beans; other related plants can also be vulnerable.
Prevention and control: At the end of the season, burn affected plants to prevent the disease overwintering in the soil. The following spring, spray seedlings regularly with carbendazim between germination and flowering. Prepare the soil well. Lime acid soils, to raise the pH to 7. Sow seed thinly.

BOTRYTIS LEAF AND FLOWER SPOT (gladioli)
Botrytis gladiolorum
Definition: A fungal disease of gladioli, favoured by misty or rainy weather.
Symptoms and damage: Symptoms can occur on one plant part or several. *Flowers:* Small, white to brown water-soaked spots appear at the petal edges, enlarging quickly in

Below: Chocolate spot damage on a bean. To help prevent chocolate spot sow seeds thinly to prevent overcrowding and weak growth.

humid weather. Petals can turn slimy. *Leaves:* Small, red-brown spots appear, then enlarge. They can be covered with a furry grey mould. If the infection is near ground level, the fungus can penetrate through to the stem ("neck rot"), and the plant turns yellow and falls over. *Corms:* Damage to the corms usually occurs when they are lifted. Spores germinate on the husk and the fungus spreads down through the corm. Rotted areas shrivel.
Plants affected: Gladioli (*Gladiolus*); some varieties are more susceptible than others.
Prevention and control: Spray with mancozeb at weekly intervals. Remove affected parts. If the whole plant is affected, dig it up and destroy it. Lift corms for storage during dry weather, dry them carefully, then store in well-ventilated, dry conditions.

PEONY WILT
Botrytis paeoniae
Definition: A fungal disease of peonies; it is favoured by damp conditions.
Symptoms and damage: The shoot bases turn brown, wilt and die back. Grey velvety mould can sometimes be observed on affected growth. Leaf tips can also show brown patches, and flower buds fail to open, turn brown and die.
Plants affected: Peonies (*Paeonia*).
Prevention and control: *Herbaceous peonies:* Cut back diseased growth below ground

Below: Peony wilt has caused this leaf to develop a brown patch.

Above: Tulip fire has caused this leaf to rot.

level. Lift and divide congested clumps, which are prone to the disease. *Tree peonies:* Cut back to healthy growth.

TULIP FIRE
Botrytis tulipae
Definition: A serious fungal disease of tulips. It can persist in the soil for long periods.
Symptoms and damage: Tips of young leaves have a scorched appearance. In wet weather these show a grey mould and can rot. Small brown spots appear on leaves and flowers. Severely affected plants collapse. The fungus produces black resting bodies on the bulbs, which can also rot. Affected bulbs produce pale, stunted topgrowth.
Plants affected: Tulips (*Tulipa*).
Prevention and control: Spray regularly with mancozeb. Dig up and destroy affected plants. After lifting bulbs, dust them with sulphur before storing in cool, dry conditions. Do not replant diseased bulbs; remove the tulips prior to planting to check for sclerotia (small black fungal resting bodies). Do not grow tulips in the same soil each year.

DOWNY MILDEW (lettuces and radishes)
Bremia lactucae, Peronospora spp., *Phytophthora phaseoli, Pseudoperonospora cubensis*
Definition: A fungal disease that affects both mature plants and seedlings, usually associated with damp, overcrowded conditions.
Symptoms and damage: White

Above: The effect of tulip fire on a flower petal.

mealy or furry growths appear on the undersides of leaves. The growth of seedlings can be checked. On older plants, usually only the outer leaves are affected. Pale green to yellow patches appear on the upper surfaces, which later turn brown. Secondary bacterial infections can occur.
Plants affected: Lettuces and radishes.
Prevention and control: Thin seedlings as early as possible. Remove affected leaves and spray with mancozeb or copper oxychloride.

DUTCH ELM DISEASE (elms)
Ceratocystis ulmi
Definition: A fatal fungal disease of elms. In Europe, the disease has caused the death of a huge number of trees.
Symptoms and damage: Trees die rapidly.
Plants affected: Elms (*Ulmus*).
Prevention and control: None possible. Breeding programmes are being focused on producing varieties of elm that are resistant to the disease.

Below: The upper surface of this leaf shows greenish-yellow and brown patches.

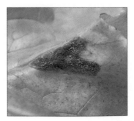

Above: Dutch elm disease has caused the stems and foliage of this elm to wither.

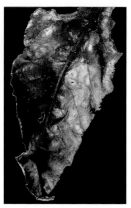

Above: Fungal lesions on a beetroot leaf indicate an attack of cercospora leaf spot.

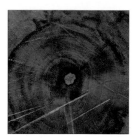

Above: Silver leaf has stained this *Prunus* wood a mid-brown colour.

EARLY BLIGHT OF CELERY

Cercospora apii

Definition: A fungal disease of celery and celeriac that greatly reduces yields. Its spread is encouraged by warm, wet weather, and it is most likely to occur in warm areas.

Symptoms and damage: Small round spots appear on the leaves of young plants, first on outer leaves, then spreading inwards. The spots turn brownish and dry. Later, brown lesions appear on stems.

Plants affected: Celery and celeriac.

Prevention and control: Lift and destroy affected plants and apply recommended spacing to seedling crops. Practise crop rotation. Look for disease-free seed of disease-resistant varieties.

CERCOSPORA LEAF SPOT, Leaf Spot (beetroot and spinach beet)

Cercospora beticola

Definition: A fungal disease, prevalent during wet weather, especially where plants are grown too close together and/or if the temperature is high.

Symptoms and damage: Brown spots appear on leaves (the oldest first), which then fall away to leave holes. Spots can appear on other parts of the plant.

Plants affected: Beetroot (beets) and spinach beet; related weeds are also vulnerable.

Prevention and control: Grow susceptible crops on a fresh site each year. Dress the soil with potash before sowing to firm growth. Thin out seedlings to prevent the overcrowding that encourages the disease. Cut off and destroy affected leaves. *Spinach beet:* After cropping, lift and destroy the old roots. Seedling plants can be sprayed with copper oxychloride. (Plants should not be sprayed prior to harvest.)

LEAF SPOT (violas)

Cercospora violae

Definition: A serious fungal disease of *Viola*.

Symptoms and damage: Leaves show brown spots. The disease spreads from leaf to leaf.

Plants affected: Pansies, violets, violas (*Viola*).

Prevention and control: Spray with zineb. Cut off and dispose of affected leaves. Thin plants if necessary to relieve congestion.

SILVER LEAF

Chondrosternum purpureum, syn. *Stereum purpureum*

Definition: A fungal disease that enters plants through wounds, sometimes following pruning. It is commonest in areas with mild, wet winters.

Symptoms and damage: Leaves turn silver then brown. Shoots die back. Mauve fruiting bodies (brackets), which later turn white or brown, appear on dead wood. The extent to which the disease has penetrated the plant's tissue can be determined by cutting off a branch (at least 2.5cm (1in) in diameter on trees, 2cm (⅘in) on rhododendrons) and wetting the cut surface. Affected tissue shows as a brown or purple stain. *Rhododendrons:* Leaves do not turn silver, but shoots die back. If they are then cut back, the inner tissues can sometimes be seen to be stained purple or brown.

Plants affected: Tree fruits, especially plums ('Victoria' is vulnerable); red and black-currants; hydrangeas (*Hydrangea*), poplars (*Populus*), rhododendrons (*Rhododendron*) and willows (*Salix*).

Prevention and control: Cut back all of the affected growth to about 15cm (6in) beyond the point where the brown or purple staining ceases. Recurrence of further infection will be reduced by performing this procedure during dry weather in summer. Sterilize all tools before and after use. Feed, water and mulch the affected plants to promote their recovery from the disease. Where fruiting bodies have appeared on the main trunk of a tree or shrub, it is best to dig up the plant and destroy it.

Below: The first signs of Dutch elm disease are browning and shrivelling of the leaves.

Below: The small circular brown lesions on these pansy leaves are signs of leaf spot.

Below: These apple leaves are at an early stage of silver leaf infestation.

Below: The silvery leaves later turn brown.

TOMATO LEAF MOULD
Cladosporium fulvum; see *Fulvia fulva.*

LEAF SPOT (irises)
Cladosporium iridis
Definition: A fungal disease of irises that is particularly troublesome in warm, wet weather conditions.
Symptoms and damage: Small brown spots appear on leaves. They enlarge and turn grey. In severe cases, the spots merge to form dead areas, following which, the leaves die back, the plant is weakened and flowering is impaired.
Plants affected: Irises (*Iris*); rhizomatous varieties are more at risk than bulbous ones.
Prevention and control: Spray with copper oxychloride. Repeated applications may be necessary in a wet season.

BACTERIAL CANKER (tomatoes)
Clavibacter michiganensis subsp. *michiganensis*
Definition: A widespread bacterial disease of tomatoes (and other members of Solanaceae), spread by seed, in rain and in soil. It can spread rapidly in wet weather.
Symptoms and damage: Lower leaves wilt, then the disease moves up the plant. Edges of leaves turn brownish-black; later the whole leaf turns brown and dies. Usually, one side of a plant is affected, then the other. In damp weather, small, raised, white spots appear on fruits,

Below: These iris leaves show the effects of leaf spot.

which may also be stunted or distorted. Infected seed can produce stunted seedlings, but sometimes these develop normally, showing signs of disease as they reach maturity.
Plants affected: Tomatoes. The disease can also appear on daturas (*Brugmansia*) and related weeds such as deadly nightshade.
Prevention and control: Spray with copper hydroxide. Lift and destroy any infected plants. Keep the site free of related weeds. Do not grow tomatoes in the same site for at least three years.

BACTERIAL RING ROT OF POTATO
Clavibacter sepedonicus
Definition: A serious bacterial disease of potatoes that is widespread in North America. It enters plants through wounds and can be difficult to detect.
Symptoms and damage: Late in the growing season, foliage (usually only a proportion) wilts. Lower leaves on wilted stems turn yellow. Cut stems exude a cream liquid. Evidence of infection can also appear later in stored tubers, which, when cut, show ragged cracks beneath the skin. Infected tubers can be subject to rot.
Plants affected: Potatoes.
Prevention and control: Plant guaranteed disease-free tubers. Ideally, plant whole tubers, rather than cutting them. Practise crop rotation. Control Colorado beetles and aphids, which can spread the disease.

CANKER (roses)
Clethiridium (syn. *Griphosphaeria*) *corticola*, *Leptosphaeria coniothyrium*
Definition: A fungal disease that causes damage to roses, sometimes arising from poor pruning and other wounds. Infection can take hold at any time of year and is likely to be worse on plants that are lacking in strength and vigour.

Above: The stem of this mature rose exhibits both healthy and infected wood.

Symptoms and damage: Shoots have brown patches and die back. Cankers can develop near the ground in serious cases; stems swell and the bark cracks. In summer, each canker forms white pustules of fungal spores; later, overwintering red fruiting bodies form.
Plants affected: Roses (*Rosa*).
Prevention and control: Cut out affected wood. Practise good cultivation and cut out any dead or damaged material as a matter of course. Use sharp tools and cut cleanly just above a bud. Improve the cultivation of weak-growing plants by feeding, watering and mulching, and improving drainage if necessary.

CORN LEAF BLIGHT (SOUTHERN)
Cochliobolus heterostrophus
For symptoms and control, see under *Bipolaris maydis.*

ANTHRACNOSE
Colletotrichum spp., *Gloeosporium* spp.
Definition: Fungal diseases affecting a range of crops (some species are crop-specific and have their own entries below). Spores need wet conditions to germinate, so spread is favoured by damp weather. Severity of attack can vary widely.
Symptoms and damage: Yellow, brown or purplish spots appear on stems, leaves or fruit. The spots expand and darken. The fruiting bodies are pinkish. The fruits of cucurbits have dark, sunken lesions; tomatoes have dark, depressed spots, sometimes with pinkish-orange spores at the centre. Potatoes have small black sclerotia on the skins of tubers and lesions that appear on stems. (On potatoes, the disease is sometimes referred to as "black dot".)
Plants affected: Beans, brambles, cucumbers, melons,

Below: Courgette (zucchini) leaves severely infected with anthracnose.

peas, peppers, strawberries, tomatoes and turnips as well as many garden weeds.

Prevention and control: Lift and destroy any affected plants. Sow disease-free seed. Avoid watering susceptible plants from overhead and handle them only when the leaves are dry, in order to prevent spreading the disease to other plants. Keep the vegetable plot weed-free.

BLACK SPOT (strawberries)
Colletotrichum aculatum
Definition: A disease of strawberries that is harboured by dead leaves and rotting berries. Occurring in subtropical to tropical areas, it is encouraged by humid weather.
Symptoms and damage: Round black spots appear on ripening fruits. These enlarge and produce a white fungal growth.
Plants affected: Strawberries.
Prevention and control: Pick plants carefully; discard any overripe or rotting berries.

SMUDGE (onions)
Colletotrichum circinans
Definition: A fungal disease of onions that attacks bulbs both in the field and in storage. It is encouraged by damp conditions.
Symptoms and damage: Small green dots appear on the outside of bulbs. The fungus continues to grow on onions in storage, making the bulb shrink and sprout new leaves.
Plants affected: Onions. White varieties are more susceptible than brown ones.
Prevention and control: Lift and destroy diseased bulbs. Practise crop rotation. Where the problem has been known to occur, restrict choice to brown varieties.

ANTHRACNOSE (fruit)
Colletotrichum gloeosporioides
Definition: A fungal disease of fruit that is particularly troublesome during very hot,

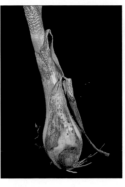

Above: Anthracnose lesions on an onion.

humid weather. It most commonly occurs on fruit near or on the soil.
Symptoms and damage: Small, depressed spots appear on fruits, later enlarging and developing concentric rings. Dark specks are fungal fruiting bodies. In hot, humid conditions, entire fruits can rot, and seed can also be infected.
Plants affected: A wide range of fruiting plants, especially tomatoes.
Prevention and control: Spray with zineb or copper hydroxide once the fruits start to ripen. Sow only healthy seed and practise crop rotation in order to minimize any chances of reinfection.

ANTHRACNOSE (beans)
Colletotrichum lindemuthianum
Definition: A seed-borne fungal disease of certain legumes that can be particularly troublesome during cold, wet weather and on plants forced under glass.
Symptoms and damage: Black or reddish- brown patches appear on pods, also on the stems. Leaf veins turn black (the symptom appears most clearly on the lower leaf surface). Under glass, the spots can also be encrusted with white. The fungus passes into the seeds.
Plants affected: Beans,

Above: This guava shows a rotting lesion caused by anthracnose.

especially dwarf, French, mung and Lima beans.
Prevention and control: Spray with mancozeb or zineb. Destroy all seriously affected plants, and do not take seed from diseased crops. The following year, sow in a fresh site, since the fungus can overwinter on decaying material. Spray with mancozeb or zineb. Plant disease-free seed of resistant varieties.

ANTHRACNOSE (cucurbits)
Colletotrichum orbiculare
Definition: A fungal disease of certain cucurbits. Symptoms sometimes appear on fruits only after harvesting.
Symptoms and damage: Rounded, brown to black spots

Below: Anthracnose has infected this watermelon plant.

appear on leaves and stems. In damp conditions, runners can die. Spots can also appear on fruits, sometimes with masses of pink spores.
Plants affected: Watermelons, cantaloupe melons and cucumbers.
Prevention and control: Spray affected plants with mancozeb. Remove and destroy affected leaves as soon as damage is noticed. Do not save seed from affected crops. Practise crop rotation, and do not grow cucurbits in the same site for at least four years.

LEAF SPOT (ivies)
Colletotrichum trichellum
Definition: A fungal disease of ivies. Damage is worst in a cool spring, especially if the plants are grown in a cool, moist position.
Symptoms and damage: Leaves turn yellow and are shed from the plant. On English ivies, brown lesions form. The aging lesion surfaces are the host for structures to form, which produce thousands of spores. The spores are then carried by rain and wind and spread to the next plant.
Plants affected: Ivies (*Hedera helix* and its various forms).
Prevention and control: Spray affected plants with fungicide. Cut off and dispose of any affected leaves.

Below: The raised brown markings of leaf spot on an English ivy plant.

ANTHRACNOSE
(mangoes)
Colletotrichum gloeosporioides
var. *minor*

Definition: A fungal disease of mangoes; the fungus lives in dead parts of the plant and is capable of remaining dormant.
Symptoms and damage: Leaves show black spots, which enlarge to form extensive areas that can crack. Small black spots can appear on flowers, which then die and are shed by the plant. Young fruits can be dropped. On older affected fruits, black spots appear, which then enlarge into brown or black, irregularly shaped patches. The crop yield is often reduced as a result of infection by this fungus.
Plants affected: Mangoes.
Prevention and control: Spray with mancozeb from blossom time until harvest. Cut back all affected growth.

ROSE CANKER
(roses)
Coniothyrium fuckelii

Definition: A fungal disease of roses that enters plant tissue through wounds (often as a result of pruning).
Symptoms and damage: The fungus grows down stems from the cut edge, resulting in die-back. On strong-growing roses, stems do not die back far and the plant grows and flowers

Below: A mango with necrotic lesions and weeping exudation caused by anthracnose.

normally. Where wounds are caused by thorns on branches that rub against each other, pale yellow to red spots, which enlarge, appear on the stems. Stems can crack.
Plants affected: Roses (*Rosa*).
Prevention and control: Cut back affected stems to healthy growth. Prune to relieve congestion, especially on thorny varieties. Feed plants well to encourage vigorous growth.

WIRESTEM FUNGUS
Corticium solani, see
Thanatephorus cucumeris.

LEAFY GALL
Corynebacterium fascians

Definition: A bacterial disease of ornamentals, mainly those grown under glass (most commonly pelargoniums and chrysanthemums). Some outdoor plants are also vulnerable to this disease.
Symptoms and damage: A mass of abortive shoots appear at the base of the plant, which are often fused together or flattened in shape. Affected plants will not flower normally.
Plants affected: Several ornamentals under glass. Snapdragons (*Antirrhinum*), dahlias (*Dahlia*), coral flowers (*Heuchera*), sweet peas (*Lathyrus odoratus*) and phlox (*Phlox*).

Below: These fused, imperfectly developed shoots are signs of leafy gall.

Above: The swollen shoot of this juniper has pronounced orange-brown aecia – gelatinous spores – caused by a conifer rust.

Prevention and control: Destroy affected plants. Grow snapdragons, sweet peas and dahlias in a fresh site each year. Do not replant with anything known to be susceptible in the same soil. Under glass, sterilize the area in which the affected plants were grown before replanting.

CONIFER RUSTS
Cronartium spp. (pines),
Gymnosporangium spp.
(junipers)

Definition: Fungal diseases of conifers. Their life cycle involves a number of host plants. The disease can occur annually until shoots die.
Symptoms and damage: *Junipers*: Horn-like aecia – gelatinous masses of orange spores – emerge from swollen parts of shoots in mid- to late spring. *Pinus sylvestris*: Swollen sections of the stem bear yellow blisters in late spring to early summer. (On *P. ayacahuite*, *P. monticola* and *P. strobus* the blisters release powdery orange spores.) The blisters dry up after the spores have been released, leaving scarring and some residual resin.
Plants affected: Junipers (*Juniperus*) and pines (*Pinus*).

Juniper rusts also occur on hawthorns (*Crataegus*) and rowans (*Sorbus*); *Pinus sylvestris* rust can occur on peonies (*Paeonia*); and rusts affecting five-needled pines can also occur on blackcurrant bushes.
Prevention and control: Cut back affected branches to well behind any swollen tissue (at least 15cm (6in)). However, other parts of the plant can be affected in following years. Avoid planting vulnerable plants near each other to minimize the risk of reinfection.

MELANOSE
Diaporthe citri

Definition: A fungal disease of citrus. Hot, humid conditions favour the development of this disease.
Symptoms and damage: Small red-brown to dark brown spots appear on fruits. They can be crowded together, so appearing as patches. Skins can crack. Severely affected fruits can be distorted or may fail to grow to their full size.
Plants affected: Citrus; oranges, sour oranges, mandarins and lemons are more susceptible to the disease than grapefruit and 'Valencia' oranges.

Above: The fruits of this lemon tree have been severely affected by melanose.

Prevention and control: Spray with copper oxychloride when half the petals have fallen and again six to 12 weeks later. Cut off and dispose of dead material from the tree; collect and dispose of dead material from the ground.

BLACK KNOT (cherries and plums)
Dibotryon morbosum
Definition: An unsightly fungal disease of certain *Prunus*.
Symptoms and damage: Infection occurs in spring and develops one year later in the following spring. Large, knot-like swellings appear on stems and branches. These are olive green in spring, later turning black as they harden. Spore-bearing fruiting bodies form below the surface of the

swellings. Severely affected trees are stunted, and whole branches can die, although the disease is rarely fatal to the tree. The swellings are most easily seen in winter when the trees are out of leaf.
Plants affected: Cherries (including wild cherries) and plums; some varieties are known to be resistant.
Prevention and control: Cut out affected growth at least 15cm (6in) below the swelling. Burn the prunings. Plant resistant varieties in areas where the disease is known to cause problems.

THUJA BLIGHT (western red cedars)
Didymascella thujina, syn. *Keithia thujina*
Definition: A fungal disease of the western red cedar (*Thuja plicata*). It can become a serious problem where this conifer is used as a hedging plant.
Symptoms and damage: Individual needles turn brown, particularly towards the base of the plant. Later, blackish-brown or black fruiting bodies of the fungus appear on the needles, leaving holes as they fall. If a majority of needles are affected,

Below: The dark fruiting bodies of thuja blight may be seen on the needles of this conifer.

Above: Raspberry canes affected by spur blight.

die-back can occur.
Plants affected: Western red cedars (*Thuja plicata*).
Prevention and control: Cut back affected shoots promptly, before the fruiting bodies are formed.

SPUR BLIGHT (raspberries and loganberries)
Didymella applanata
Definition: A fungus that attacks some soft fruits, usually where growth is overcrowded.
Symptoms and damage: Dark purple to reddish-brown blotches appear on canes in late summer. They turn silver, with tiny black fungal growths, which affect the emerging buds.

Below: This courgette (zucchini) shows an early sign of gummy stem blight.

These either die immediately or die back when they develop as new shoots the following spring. The canes normally survive.
Plants affected: Raspberries; loganberries.
Prevention and control: Cut out and destroy affected canes as soon as any infection is seen. Spray plants with copper oxychloride.

GUMMY STEM BLIGHT (cucurbits)
Didymella bryoniae
Definition: A troublesome fungus that attacks certain cucurbits. It is likely to be worst in moist conditions.
Symptoms and damage: Water-soaked areas appear on stems, developing as sunken cankers. Girdled stems wilt and die. Leaves and fruits can also show black spots.
Plants affected: Cucurbits, most commonly watermelons; also cantaloupe melons, cucumbers and pumpkins.
Prevention and control: Spray with copper oxychloride. Plant disease-free seed and practise crop rotation.

RAY BLIGHT (chrysanthemums)
Didymella ligulicola
Definition: A fungal disease of chrysanthemums; it strikes during periods of warm, humid weather, especially during autumn.
Symptoms and damage: Dark pink spots appear on petals, which then quickly turn brown and rot. Florets fall from the plant and stem lesions form. The disease spreads down the flower stem, which can droop.
Plants affected: Chrysanthemums (*Chrysanthemum*).
Prevention and control: Spray plants with zineb. Dig up and destroy any severely affected plants. Deadhead plants regularly. Do not feed plants with nitrogen-high fertilizers which encourage soft growth.

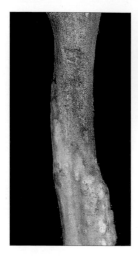

Above: This tomato stem shows the black cankers that result from infection by tomato stem rot.

Above: The red spots produced by strawberry leaf spot.

Above: These pears show the dark spots characteristic of leaf blight.

TOMATO STEM ROT (tomatoes)
Didymella lycopersici

Definition: A fungal disease of tomatoes that usually affects mature plants only.

Symptoms and damage: Plants suddenly wilt. Brown or black cankers appear on the stems, usually towards the base, and black dots are visible and characteristic. The fungal spores can overwinter to affect crops the following season. The plant may wilt and wither. It survives in the soil and is spread by the tools used in the soil, by wind and by watering. Regular trimming of plants can cause the disease, if already present, to spread.

Plants affected: Tomatoes that are grown under cover.

Prevention and control: Destroy seriously affected plants. On less severely damaged plants, cut out all affected growth and spray with carbendazim (spray healthy plants also). At the end of the season, destroy all tomato plant remains and thoroughly disinfect the greenhouse. Always grow stock from healthy seeds and avoid excessive watering.

STRAWBERRY LEAF SPOT (strawberries)
Diplocarpon earlianum, Mycosphaerella fragariae and *Stagonospora fragariae*

Definition: Fungi that attack older leaves of strawberry plants or plants lacking in vigour, usually during wet spells in late spring.

Symptoms and damage: Small, red or purple spots, sometimes turning grey or brown with red or purple margins, appear on leaves. In severe cases, the spots can merge, and leaves turn yellow, wither and disintegrate.

Plants affected: Strawberries.

Prevention and control: Cut off and destroy affected leaves. Spray new growth with a foliar feed. Spray with copper oxychloride or mancozeb when cutting back and again in autumn. Grow in an open, sunny spot.

QUINCE LEAF BLIGHT, Fleck
Diplocarpon mespili, syn. *Fabraea maculata*

Definition: A fungus of certain fruit trees that is spread by wind and rain. It can survive for a time on diseased growth and shed material.

Symptoms and damage: Leaves show small, irregular spots, initially red, turning black; leaves then turn brown and can be shed from the plant. Leaf fall is often heavy on quinces. Sometimes, shoots die back and fruits are spotted or misshapen.

Loquats: The spots are round and red-brown. The fruits show dark brown spots that age black.

Plants affected: Quinces, pears and loquats.

Prevention and control: Dispose of affected leaves (including those shed by the plant in autumn). Cut back dead shoots in winter. The following spring, spray with copper oxychloride as the leaves open; repeat the spraying in summer, if necessary. (Spray programmes for pear scab can also help to control this disease.)

BLACK SPOT (roses)
Diplocarpon rosae, Marssonina rosae

Definition: A disease of roses that are lacking in vigour (usually as a result of inadequate cultivation), though some varieties are known to be susceptible. Black spot varies in its impact, and varieties that succumb in one area may not in another. The weather has an impact.

Symptoms and damage: Round brownish to black spots, with feathery or ragged margins, appear on leaves. The area around the spots turns yellow. Eventually, the whole leaf discolours and is shed. In severe cases, complete defoliation occurs. Spotting can occasionally appear on petals, hips and stems.

Plants affected: Roses (*Rosa*).

Prevention and control: Cut off and destroy affected growth. (Remove all fallen leaves and other debris from the soil surface around the plants.) Spray with mancozeb, myclobutanil, penconazole, triforine with bupirimate or triforine with sulphur. Preventive practices are necessary if fungicidal applications are to be effective. Applications of a foliar feed can boost recovery. In areas where black spot is a problem, look for resistant varieties, but note that some varieties known to be resistant in one area can be susceptible in another, since different strains of the fungus can occur.

SHOOT BLIGHT (pines)
Diplodia pinea

Definition: A disfiguring fungal disease of pines. It tends to strike plants that are already under stress, which can be caused by poor siting of the tree, drought, hail and snow damage, or by insect attack or pruning damage.

Symptoms and damage: Needles turn yellow, then brown. Dead patches appear at the ends of branches. Shoots behind the dead areas grow unnaturally long, destroying the natural habit. New growth is attacked in consecutive years, leading to stunting, deformed growth and even the eventual death of the tree. Older trees are more susceptible, but very young specimens growing near infected trees could be killed outright by the first infection. The disease spreads in rainy weather.

Below: Black spot is the most common fungal disease of roses.

Above: This section of field bean stem reveals nematode infestation.

Plants affected: A wide range of pines (*Pinus*), especially *P. radiata*.
Prevention and control: Keep trees well watered during dry spells to reduce the risk of infection. Removing affected branches will improve the tree's appearance but will not stop the spread of the fungus. Select trees with higher levels of resistance. Do not prune trees in wet weather.

BULB AND STEM NEMATODE
Ditylenchus dipsaci
Definition: A devastating nematode that is often introduced into gardens on infected bulbs. It is capable of becoming dormant during periods of frost and drought. Various forms exist that are host-specific.
Symptoms and damage: New leaves are distorted, with raised sections that can be yellow in colour. The nematodes also feed within the bulbs underground, and brown rings are seen if these are cut in half. Sometimes, grey to brown spongy patches appear on the outsides of bulbs. Pale streaks can appear on stems and flowers; flowers may also be distorted. *Daffodils and narcissi:* Rough yellow swellings ("spickels") can appear on leaves. Late flowering can also be an indicator. Bulbs show spongy areas, which turn

orange- to grey-brown. *Tulips:* White or purplish marks can be seen at the tops of stems just before flowering. Bulbs develop grey or shiny brown patches on the outer scales. *Onions and related plants:* Affected seedlings may fail to emerge above ground level. Older plants will be stunted and will wilt.
Plants affected: Onions, shallots, chives, garlic and leeks; ornamental bulbs such as hyacinths (*Hyacinthus*), daffodils (*Narcissus*) and tulips (*Tulipa*). Beans, peas and strawberries are also vulnerable.
Prevention and control: Lift and destroy damaged bulbs. Practise crop rotation. In some countries, signs of this virulent organism should be reported to the local government agriculture department.

STEM-END ROTS (avocados)
Dothiorella spp.
Definition: A fungal disease of avocados. Affected fruits are inedible. It is likeliest to strike during wet weather.
Symptoms and damage: The disease is generally undetected until it enters the fruits. A blackish-brown or black rot appears at the stem end, then progresses down the fruit.
Plants affected: Avocados.
Prevention and control: Avoid damage to the stem end of fruits when harvesting. Store in cool, well-ventilated conditions.

INK DISEASE (irises)
Drechslera iridis
Definition: A soil-borne fungal disease of bulbous irises that causes particular damage during a wet season.
Symptoms and damage: Bulbs show black patches and become hollow inside. Badly infected bulbs may rot and never flower. If the growing period is wet, inky black, irregular patches can appear on leaves and even flowers. Dark spores may be visible to the naked eye within

the lesions. Otherwise reddish-brown spots develop on leaves. The disease can pass from infected to sound bulbs. The plants yellow and die early.
Plants affected: Irises (*Iris*) (bulbous varieties).
Prevention and control: Prior to planting, cut off and destroy any black outer scales. Discard those that show damage beneath this outer layer. If the disease has occurred before, spray new plantings with mancozeb. At the end of the season, remove and destroy infected leaves. The fungus survives within infected bulbs only and spreads in humid conditions. Dig up bulbs every few years and replant in a different location.

LEAF BLIGHT (sweet corn)
Drechslera turica
Definition: A fungal disease of sweet corn.
Symptoms and damage: Thin, grey-green patches appear on leaves. Badly affected leaves can wither and die. If many leaves are affected, cobs will be small.
Plants affected: Sweet corn.
Prevention and control: Sow resistant varieties. Where wet autumns are likely, sow as early as possible. Rotate crops.

Below: Damage in avocados caused by stem-end rot.

Above: This grapevine shows signs of black rot. *Elsinoe tristaniae* has an almost identical appearance, but the spots are different in colour.

BLACK ROT (grapes)
Elsinoe ampelina
Definition: A fungal disease of grapes that is most likely to occur in damp, cool weather in spring.
Symptoms and damage: Brown-black spots appear along stems. Flowers and young fruits can wither and fall from the plant. Grey spots can appear on leaves, turning black; the affected tissue then falls away to leave holes in the leaves. Spots can also appear on the fruits.
Plants affected: Grapes, especially sultana grapes.
Prevention and control: Spray vines with mancozeb at bud burst and again 10–14 days later. A further application may be necessary if the weather is cool and damp. Cut back infected growth as soon as it is seen.

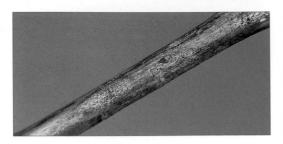

Above: An affected raspberry stem shows signs of anthracnose.

LEAF SPOT, Yellow Leaf Spot (brush box)

Elsinoe tristaniae

Definition: A fungal disease of brush box. It is more common in certain areas.

Symptoms and damage: Dull yellowish spots appear on leaves.

Plants affected: Brush box (*Tristiana conferta*).

Prevention and control: None necessary.

CANE SPOT, Anthracnose (raspberries)

Elsinoe veneta

Definition: A fungus that overwinters on the stems of certain cane fruits, causing some distortion of the fruits if untreated.

Symptoms and damage: Small purple spots appear on canes in late spring, becoming oval with a purple border. They split,

either to form shallow pits or small cankers, and large areas of bark can be killed. Spots may also occur on leaves and fruits (especially of loganberries). In severe cases, shoots die back and crops will be much reduced.

Plants affected: Raspberries (especially 'Lloyd George'), loganberries and other hybrid berries (rarely blackberries).

Prevention and control: In autumn, cut out and destroy canes showing spotting. Badly infected young canes should also be removed as they appear. Spray with copper oxychloride or carbendazim.

INDIAN HAWTHORN LEAF SPOT (Indian hawthorns)

Entomosporium mespili

Definition: A widespread fungal disease of *Rhaphiolepis*, symptoms of which are most prevalent in

winter and early spring.

Symptoms and damage: Grey spots with brown edges appear on leaves; older leaves turn yellow, orange or red and can be shed from the plant.

Plants affected: *Rhaphiolepis x delacourii* and *R. indica*; mature specimens are most likely to be affected.

Prevention and control: Spray with copper oxychloride. Feed plants well to promote vigorous growth.

SMUT, LEAF SPOT (dahlias)

Entyloma dahliae

Definition: A fungal disease of dahlias. It is worst in humid weather.

Symptoms and damage: Brown spots appear on the lower leaves. As the disease spreads up the plant, whole leaves wither. Sometimes, holes appear in leaves.

Plants affected: Dahlias (*Dahlia*).

Prevention and control: Spray with copper oxychloride. Repeated applications may be necessary. Cut off and dispose of any affected leaves.

FIREBLIGHT

Erwinia amylovora

Definition: A common bacterial disease that affects certain members of Rosaceae. It

Above: The withered, wrinkled apples and leaves on this tree indicate a fireblight infection. The length of infected stem should be destroyed.

normally enters plants through the blossom when open during warm weather in late spring or summer and can spread rapidly. It can also enter plants through mechanical damage and insect damage to roots. In some countries, fireblight is a notifiable disease.

Symptoms and damage: Leaves turn brown and wither, but are not shed by the plant. Shoots die back. Flowers wilt and young shoots wither and die. Cankers appear around the base of dead shoots in autumn. On some hosts, there is a reddish-brown discoloration of tissue just beneath the bark. The cankers exude droplets in spring. Trees whose roots are affected by fireblight can wilt and die.

Plants affected: Japonica (*Chaenomeles*), hawthorns (*Crataegus*), photinias (*Photinia*), pyracanthas (*Pyracantha*), rowans (*Sorbus*) and other members of Rosaceae.

Prevention and control: Cut back and destroy affected wood, cutting at least 60cm (2ft) behind the diseased material. Remove whole trees, if necessary. Disinfect tools after use. Plant disease-resistant varieties. During flowering,

Below: These leaves exhibit varying signs of Indian hawthorn leaf spot.

Below: Smut on a dahlia leaf.

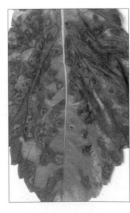

plants can be sprayed with copper or Bordeaux mixture. Organic sprays based on *Pseudomonas* bacteria can also help to combat the disease.

BACTERIAL SOFT ROT (potatoes), Blackleg
Erwinia carotovora subsp. *atroseptica*

Definition: A bacterial disease of members of Solanaceae (mainly potatoes). It is spread by contact and is associated with cool, wet, poorly drained soil, where the disease can spread rapidly. It can also enter plants through wounds caused by pest activity occurring underground.

Symptoms and damage: *Potatoes:* Stems show inky black lesions at or near soil level (sometimes only a single stem is affected). Lower leaves turn yellow and curl at the edges before turning brown and falling from the plant. Affected stems can collapse and sometimes have a dark slime on their outer surface. Plant growth tends to be more erect than normal. Any tubers that have formed are affected by a brown or grey slime inside or can rot completely. *Tomatoes:* Water-soaked or dark spots appear on fruits, which quickly rot.

Plants affected: Potatoes (tomatoes only rarely); some varieties are more susceptible than others.

Prevention and control: Not generally necessary, since only isolated plants are likely to be affected. The disease does not spread from plant to plant and does not persist in the soil. Destroy affected plants. When lifting potatoes for storage, check them carefully for signs of disease and do not store any tubers that appear to be affected. Healthy tubers can be infected by contact with a diseased tuber. Plant disease-resistant varieties.

BACTERIAL SOFT ROT
Erwinia carotovora var. *carotovora*

Definition: A widespread soil-borne bacterial disease that affects some root crops and a few ornamentals with fleshy tissue. It can affect root crops in storage. Bacterial soft rot can be troublesome during warm, wet weather, especially on plants that have suffered pest damage. The bacterium can also enter the flowers of hyacinths if growth has been checked by some physiological factor. Soft rot is commonly a problem on over-manured, poorly drained

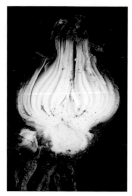

Above: The withered leaves of a potato plant with bacterial soft rot.

Above: This *Hippeastrum* bulb shows signs of bacterial soft rot.

soil where crop rotation is not practised, especially during a wet season. (This form of *Erwinia* is also the cause of other host-specific problems, and these are entered separately overleaf.)

Symptoms and damage: Small, water-soaked spots appear on leaves or roots or on stored crops. These enlarge: underlying tissue on roots goes soft and the lesions themselves turn slimy. Liquefied tissue can be exuded from cracks in the roots. The affected roots will be vulnerable to rotting.

Plants affected: Root crops, including carrots, swedes (rutabagas), turnips and

potatoes; irises (*Iris*); some other ornamentals such as dahlias (*Dahlia*); some ornamental bulbs.

Prevention and control: Dig up and destroy all affected plants and those that are next to them. Lift roots for storage with care and check them for signs of disease. Allow soil clinging to them to dry before cleaning off, and store healthy roots at the lowest recommended temperatures. Do not grow vulnerable crops in the same ground for three years. Control other diseases and pests such as slugs that can open up wounds on plants, rendering them susceptible to the bacterium.

Below: The surface of this potato shows some symptoms of soft rot.

Below: Rot affects potatoes in many ways; this one is rotting from within.

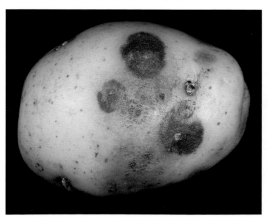

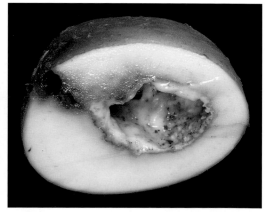

Above: This cactus plant is showing severe signs of rotting caused by infection by an *Erwinia* bacterium.

ARUM CORM ROT (arum lilies)
Erwinia carotovora var. *carotovora*

Definition: A bacterial disease that affects *Zantedeschia* grown under glass.
Symptoms and damage: Plants wither and collapse. The corms display brown patches and the roots rot. The disease can lie dormant in resting corms that are stored dry.
Plants affected: Arum lilies (*Zantedeschia*).
Prevention and control: Destroy seriously affected plants and disinfect the greenhouse. Sterilize the soil if the plants were grown in beds. Check stored corms before replanting and cut out any brown patches. Store in a cold and dry environment.

HEART ROT (celery)
Erwinia carotovora var. *carotovora*

Definition: A bacterium that enters celery plants through wounds, typically those caused by slugs.
Symptoms and damage: A brown slimy mass develops in the centre of a plant, rendering it inedible.
Plants affected: Celery.
Prevention and control: Control slugs early in the season. When earthing up, take care not to damage plant tissue, and dust plants with dry Bordeaux mixture to kill any bacteria. Protect young growth against frost. Change the site where celery is grown periodically to prevent a build-up of bacteria in the soil.

RHIZOME ROT (irises)
Erwinia carotovora var. *carotovora*

Definition: A bacterial disease of rhizomatous irises. It is particularly troublesome during a wet season.
Symptoms and damage: Rhizomes rot, producing a yellow slime. Leaves turn brown and die back.
Plants affected: Irises (*Iris*) (rhizomatous varieties).
Prevention and control: Cut out diseased material. Grow irises in well-drained soil in a sunny site and control slugs (which expose plant tissue to disease), if necessary.

CROWN ROT (rhubarb)
Erwinia rhapontici, various fungi

Definition: A soil-borne disease of rhubarb (caused by a fungus or bacterium) that is particularly troublesome on wet soils. Crown rot enters plants through wounds.
Symptoms and damage: Terminal buds rot, and a soft brown rot also appears in the crown of the plant. Affected plants gradually deteriorate, producing only a few stems, which also rot.
Plants affected: Rhubarb.
Prevention and control: Lift and destroy affected plants. Replant on a fresh site, making sure the soil is well drained.

BACTERIAL WILT (cucurbits)
Erwinia tracheiphila

Definition: A bacterial disease that is spread by cucumber beetles (*Diabrotica* spp.).
It develops most quickly during dry weather, when these pests are active.
Symptoms and damage: Large, dull, irregularly shaped patches appear on leaves. Branches wilt until the plant dies. Infected stems exude a white "milk" when cut.
Plants affected: Cucumbers; occasionally other cucurbits.
Prevention and control: Control cucumber beetles with chemical or non-chemical sprays. Cover young plants with a floating mulch when the pests are active. Practise crop rotation. Plant seed of resistant varieties.

POWDERY MILDEW
Erysiphe spp., *Oidium* spp. (cucurbits, grapes, papayas, strawberries and roses), *Podosphaera leucotricha* (apples and other pome fruits), *Sphaerotheca fuliginea* (cucurbits), *S. pannosa* var. *persicae* (peaches), *S. macularis* (strawberries), *Uncinula necator* (vines, tomatoes), other fungi

Definition: Powdery mildew is a white, powder-like coating of fungal spores on leaves, which can be caused by a number of related fungus species. The problem is usually associated with humid conditions and dryness at the roots; some species of powdery mildew are capable of reproducing even at

Above: These young apple leaves have been distorted by powdery mildew.

low temperatures. Once the fungus has taken hold, it can continue to grow even in dry conditions. Some powdery mildew species are host-specific (or affect only a small range of plants); others can affect a larger number of plant species.
Symptoms and damage: Developing leaves in spring and summer are coated with powdery, greyish-white spores and are shed by the plant (some distortion of the leaves can also occur), leading to a general debility. Sometimes, leaves are attacked when fully developed, and no change in shape occurs. Whole leaves can be covered, and the powder can also appear on other parts of the plant. *Strawberries:* Leaves turn purple and curl upwards, showing grey undersides. (This can be the first symptom.) Cropping can be reduced, and fruits that are produced can be

Below: This oak leaf shows the greyish-white spores of powdery mildew.

small and fail to ripen. *Fruiting vines (including those grown under glass):* Grapes can be shed when young or harden and split, making them susceptible to other fungal infections such as grey mould. All parts of the plant can show a floury coating of white fungal spores. Black varieties may colour unevenly. *Apples (red-skinned varieties):* Thin yellowish lines appear on the fruits. *Cucurbits:* White spots appear first on the lower surface of leaves. Growth is checked and cropping is reduced. *Papayas:* Grey blotches appear on fruits, though these will still be edible. *Roses:* If plants are affected early in the season, growth can be checked and the flowering performance will be poor. Flowers that do open may be distorted.

Plants affected: A large range of plants: apples (some varieties are more susceptible than others), quinces, occasionally pears; peaches; strawberries; cucurbits; vines, tomatoes and other crops under glass; brassicas, beans, and ornamentals including hollyhocks (*Alcea*), delphiniums (*Delphinium*) and roses (*Rosa*) (some varieties are more susceptible than others).

Prevention and control: Keep plants well watered. Cut off and dispose of affected shoots.

Below: The terminal leaf on this camellia stem has been grossly distorted by leaf gall.

Above: Azalea gall has turned this young leaf pale green.

Clear up plant debris from around neighbouring plants. Avoid overcrowding plants. Spray affected plants with a systemic fungicide. Choose plant varieties known to have some resistance. *Strawberries:* Cut off old leaves (on which the spores can overwinter) after harvesting. Dust with sulphur at the first sign of disease, or spray with myclobutanil when the flowers open. *Grapes:* Thin the stems carefully to prevent the overcrowding that leads to stagnant air through the plant. Keep plants well watered during drought and mulch to conserve soil moisture. *Cucurbits:* Spray with carbendazim or dust with sulphur when the first symptoms appear, and repeat as necessary. *Papayas:* Light infections can be left untreated. *Roses:* Prune to encourage open growth and improve air circulation. Begin spray programmes on susceptible varieties early on. *Under glass:* Water plants evenly to avoid dryness at the roots and

Above: This flowering azalea has a gall on one of its leaves.

ventilate carefully. Thin the growth to prevent overcrowding. Use sprays once a problem is seen.

LEAF GALL (camellias)
Exobasidium camelliae

Definition: An unsightly fungal disease of certain camellias.

Symptoms and damage: Small leaves at the ends of branches grow unnaturally large and are thickened. The leaves can have a dark pink or red appearance. Inside these leaves the mycelium develops. At maturity the underside of the leaves breaks off to expose the mycelium, resulting in dried and shrivelled leaves.

Plants affected: *Camellia sasanqua*; occasionally also *C. reticulata*.

Prevention and control: Cut off and dispose of affected growth.

Below: These young maize plants have been severely infected with corn leaf blight.

AZALEA GALL, Leaf Gall (azaleas)
Exobasidium vaccinii

Definition: A fungal disease that affects the new growth of some evergreen azaleas and related species.

Symptoms and damage: Young leaves and flower buds appear pale green (occasionally turning red), then swell and produce small galls (most commonly on leaves). Fungal spores develop on these, which then turn white and waxy, before turning brown and shrivelling.

Plants affected: Some evergreen azaleas (*Rhododendron*) (including indoor varieties), blueberries and rhododendrons (*Rhododendron*).

Prevention and control: Remove and destroy the galls before they turn white as the fungal spores are produced. Spray plants with Bordeaux mixture or copper oxychloride. Plants should also be sprayed the following year as they come into growth.

CORN LEAF BLIGHT (NORTHERN)
Exserohilum turcicum, syn. *Setosphaeria turcica*

Definition: A fungal disease of sweet corn that occurs in North America; it can be mistaken for damage caused by frost or drought. Fungal spores are wind-borne.

Symptoms and damage: Long, greyish-green lesions, up to 15cm (6in) long, appear on lower leaves, spreading up the plant. The lesions turn tan and the plant tissues dry out. Lesions can also appear on husks, though the ears are unaffected. In damp weather, dark green to black spores form on the lesions.

Plants affected: Corn, sorghum, other grasses.

Prevention and control: Practise crop rotation in areas where the disease is known to occur. Plant seed of resistant varieties of sweet corn and other crops.

Above: Bracket fungi growing on the trunk of a cherry tree.

BRACKET FUNGI, Wood Rots

Fistulina hepatica, Ganoderma spp., *Innonotus hispidus, Laetiporus sulphureus, Meripilus giganteus, Phaeolus schweinitzi, Phellinus pini, Piptoporus betulinus, Sparrisis crispa,* **other fungi**

Definition: These fungi produce fruiting bodies on the trunks of a variety of trees.

Symptoms and damage: Bracket-like growths, which may become very large, sometimes more than 30cm (12in) across, appear on tree trunks. They are often near ground level, but sometimes grow further up the trunk or on higher branches. These growths either disintegrate after shedding their spores or persist as hard lumps. Severely affected trees are weakened and become unstable.

Plants affected: A range of trees, especially birch (*Betula*), and shrubs.

Prevention and control: Cut back branches bearing brackets to healthy wood. Gouge out brackets on trunks, removing any rotting wood beneath the bracket. A severely affected tree may need to be completely removed.

QUINCE LEAF BLIGHT, Fleck

Fabraea maculata, see *Diplocarpon mespili.*

FOMES ROOT and Butt Rot

Fomes annosus, see *Heterobasidion annosum.*

Above: These tomato leaves show yellow patterns above and brown mould below.

TOMATO LEAF MOULD (tomatoes)

Fulvia fulva, syn. *Cladosporium fulvum*

Definition: A fungal disease of tomatoes grown under glass; it is encouraged by humid conditions.

Symptoms and damage: The undersides of the leaves show patches of purple-brown mould, with corresponding yellow blotches appearing on the upper surfaces. This is often followed by an attack of grey mould (*see Botrytis cinerea*).

Plants affected: Tomatoes grown under cover.

Prevention and control: Maintain a temperature below 21°C (70°F) and ventilate well to avoid a build-up of humidity. Spray affected plants with

Below: This ornamental sedge has lesions on its leaves caused by fusarium wilt.

carbendazim or mancozeb. Grow varieties that are known to be resistant. Disinfect the greenhouse thoroughly at the end of the season.

FOOT AND ROOT ROT

Fusarium spp., see under *Aphanomyces euteiches.*

FUSARIUM WILT

Fusarium spp.

Definition: Fusarium wilt, a widespread problem, covers a huge range of fungal diseases. *Fusarium* comprises a large number of species and strains, many specific to certain plants. (Details of some of these appear below and overleaf.) Usually, crop-specific forms of *Fusarium* do not spread to unrelated plants, which helps when planning crop rotation in the garden. The disease can strike at seedling stage or at any point thereafter.

Symptoms and damage: Older leaves generally wilt first. Yellow patches can appear on leaves, later turning brown. Plants generally have brown or black lesions on the lower stem and upper parts of the roots. *Tomatoes:* Seedlings show a downward curling of the oldest leaves. *Beets and chard:* Outer leaves wilt and younger leaves tend to curl inwards.

Plants affected: Beetroot (beet), cucurbits, brassicas, tomatoes and related crops, onions, Swiss chard and a range of ornamentals.

Prevention and control: Keep young plants growing vigorously and take care not to damage their roots or leaves when transplanting them. Practise crop rotation. Grow resistant or tolerant varieties.

FUSARIUM BULB ROT (lilies)

Fusarium oxysporum, forms

Definition: A fungal disease of lilies that is likeliest to occur on damaged bulbs.

Above: This ornamental gourd is covered with mould.

Symptoms and damage: Scales separate from the base of the bulb. Leaves turn yellow or purple and die. Flowering, if it occurs at all, is impaired.

Plants affected: Lilies (*Lilium*).

Prevention and control: Check lilies for signs of damage before planting. Plant new bulbs in an area where lilies have not been grown before.

FUSARIUM WILT (cucurbits)

Fusarium oxysporum, forms

Definition: A fungal disease that affects certain cucurbits.

Symptoms and damage: Growth is slow, and stems can wilt and die. Affected seedlings are prone to damping off, especially in cold weather.

Plants affected: Cantaloupe melons, watermelons and other cucurbits.

Prevention and control: Do not grow susceptible plants in the same ground each year.

Below: This cauliflower displays the later stages of cabbage yellows.

Above: This greenhouse-grown carnation has collapsed with fusarium wilt.

CABBAGE YELLOWS (brassicas)

Fusarium oxysporum f. sp. *conglutinans*
Definition: A disease of brassicas, associated with hot, dry weather.
Symptoms and damage: Lower leaves turn dull green, then yellow. The disease spreads upwards through the plant. Affected leaves turn brown and are shed. Plants develop a bitter taste.
Plants affected: Cabbages, broccoli, cauliflowers and other brassicas.
Prevention and control: Irrigate crops well and mulch to maintain soil moisture. Grow varieties known to be resistant, though even these can succumb during hot, dry seasons.

FUSARIUM WILT (carnations)

Fusarium oxysporum f. sp. *dianthi, Phialophora cinerescens* (syn. *Verticillium cinerescens*)
Definition: Soil-borne fungi that attack carnations and pinks, commonly introduced into gardens on infected cuttings. They can remain dormant in the soil for some length of time.
Symptoms and damage: Leaves turn yellow and wither and the whole plant wilts. Cut stems show brown streaks.
Plants affected: Carnations, pinks (*Dianthus*).

Prevention and control: Dig up and destroy affected plants. Replant with healthy stock in fresh soil.

YELLOWS, Dry Rot (gladioli)

Fusarium oxysporum f. sp. *gladioli, Sclerotinia gladioli*
Definition: A soil-borne fungal disease of gladioli, usually introduced into gardens on infected corms. It can remain dormant in the soil for several years and can also affect corms in storage.
Symptoms and damage: Yellow stripes appear between the veins of leaves, which then turn yellow and die back. The plants can collapse. Severely affected corms can rot underground without producing any growth above ground level. If infected corms are cut across they reveal a dead area with brown strands radiating from it. (Although usually called "basal brown rot" rather than "yellows", this condition is caused by the same fungus.)
Plants affected: Gladioli (*Gladiolus*).
Prevention and control: Destroy affected plants. Next year, grow gladioli from fresh corms in a new site (a four-year cycle provides good protection). When lifting corms for storage,

Above: The yellow leaves indicate that these tomatoes are suffering from fusarium wilt.

discard any that show black patches. Dust the remainder with sulphur and store in cool, dry conditions.

FUSARIUM WILT (tomatoes)

Fusarium oxysporum f. sp. *lycopersici*
Definition: A soil-borne disease of tomatoes that enters plants through the roots and blocks the vascular tissues. It develops in warm weather.
Symptoms and damage: Plants wilt rapidly on hot days, as if suffering drought. Lower leaves turn yellow, and plants can die.
Plants affected: Tomatoes.
Prevention and control: Practise crop rotation and sow resistant varieties.

Above: A daffodil with stunted growth displays the symptoms of basal rot.

BASAL ROT (narcissus)

Fusarium oxysporum f. sp. *narcissi*, other *Fusarium* spp.
Definition: A soil-borne fungal disease affecting daffodils and narcissi. It is most commonly a problem during warm weather, when roots are dying back and the bulb is entering its period of dormancy. It is therefore difficult to spot unless bulbs are lifted for storage. Where bulbs are left in the ground, affected bulbs will fail and the disease can be passed to other bulbs nearby. Affected bulbs can die.
Symptoms and damage: The basal plate of a bulb turns brown; later the bulb shrivels and hardens. Bulbs that appear healthy after lifting can show symptoms of rot after about a month.
Plants affected: Daffodils (*Narcissus*).
Prevention and control: If basal rot is known to be a problem in your garden, lift bulbs soon after the foliage has died down and dust them with sulphur, allow to dry, then store them in cool, airy conditions until the following autumn. Check regularly and discard any that show symptoms of the disease. Replant in fresh soil in autumn. If an area of the garden is known to harbour the disease, do not replant with daffodils for five years.

Below: Gladioli corms infected with yellows, which can remain dormant in soil and affect the corms while in storage.

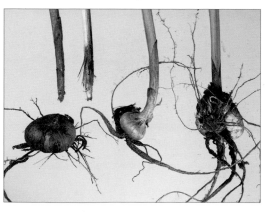

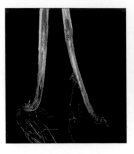

Above: These bean stems have fusarium wilt damage at the base.

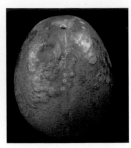

Above: The scab lesions on this plum indicate a case of freckle.

FUSARIUM WILT (beans)

Fusarium solani f. sp. *phaseoli*
Definition: A common fungal disease of peas and beans.
Symptoms and damage: Plants wilt and leaves turn yellow. Sometimes, a pink layer of fungal growth on reddish-brown sunken lesions can be seen at the base of stems. Cutting the stem near ground level reveals reddish-brown streaks inside.
Plants affected: Dwarf and runner beans.
Prevention and control: Destroy affected plants. Rotate crops to prevent infection in subsequent years. Choose disease-resistant varieties of peas and beans.

SOOTY BLOTCH and Fly Speck

Gloeodes pomigena (sooty blotch) *and Leptothyrium pomi* (fly speck)
Definition: Fungal diseases of fruit. Both mark fruits, but they remain edible (though unsuitable for storing). These diseases are favoured by damp conditions and often appear together, developing after cold, wet springs. Their effects become visible in autumn.
Symptoms and damage: *Sooty blotch:* Dark, circular, cloudy patches of fungi appear on the skins of fruits. Their outlines are indefinite and they enlarge, so that whole areas of fruit are blackened. *Fly speck:* Small circular specks appear on the skins of fruits at around harvest

time. The disease affects only the appearance and not the taste quality of the fruit.
Plants affected: Apples, pears and citrus. Peaches and wattles (*Acacia*) also occasionally show signs of infection.
Prevention and control: Either ignore the problem, or treat outbreaks of both diseases as for black spot or other fungal diseases.

ANTHRACNOSE

Gloeosporium spp., see under *Colletotrichum* spp.

FRECKLE

Fusicladium carpophilum
Definition: A fungal disease of stone fruits (US: those with pits) that is most common on apricots and peaches.
Symptoms and damage: Clearly defined, cream, pale green or black spots appear on fruits, usually near the stalk, where the fruit may crack. Spotting occurs less commonly on leaves. Twigs show black lesions and leaves can be affected.
Plants affected: Stone fruits, especially apricots, peaches and nectarines.
Prevention and control: Prune off and destroy affected twigs. Spray with copper oxychloride and white oil as the flowers start to open. Spray again at petal fall (using mancozeb for apricots and zineb for peaches and nectarines, both plus white oil). Further applications may be necessary.

BITTER ROT (apples)

Glomerella cingulata
Definition: A fungal disease that affects apples, especially in hot, humid weather. The fungus also causes die-back on camellias (see below).
Symptoms and damage: Small brown spots appear on the skins of maturing fruits. The rot spreads rapidly in sunken, concentric rings, and fruits can wrinkle and dry out.
Plants affected: Pome fruits (apples and pears). All apples, but especially 'Willy Sharp', 'Gravenstein' and 'Granny Smith'.
Prevention and control: Spray with zineb in late spring; further applications may be necessary if the weather is humid. Remove all affected fruits promptly. Prune trees to improve air circulation through the crown. Some varieties of apple are more resistant to bitter rot than others.

DIE-BACK (camellias)

Glomerella cingulata
Definition: A fungal disease of camellias that enters plants through wounds (including natural wounds such as those that are caused by leaf scars).
Symptoms and damage: The tissue surrounding a leaf scar is killed. Unchecked, the fungus can girdle the stem, causing the portion above the girdling to die back. The fungus spreads when water carrying the disease splashes on a plant wound.

Below: Bitter rot is spreading across the surface of this Bramley apple.

Plants affected: Camellias (*Camellia*). Varieties with large leaves are more susceptible than those with small leaves.
Prevention and control: Cut off and destroy affected stems, sterilizing the pruners after each cut to prevent spread of the fungus.

ANTHRACNOSE (avocados)

Glomerella cingulata var. *minor*
Definition: A fungal disease of avocados that is spread during warm, wet weather. Spores are usually dormant, but they will grow on fruits as these ripen or if the fruits become damaged.
Symptoms and damage: Small, circular, light brown spots appear on the skins of fruits. These enlarge and darken. The flesh beneath the spots rots. In damp conditions, pink powdery spores appear on the skin.
Plants affected: Avocados.
Prevention and control: Spray with copper oxychloride monthly from flowering until harvest time. (More frequent applications may be necessary in a wet season.) Handle fruits carefully to avoid damage. Store fruits in a well-ventilated place.

STRAWBERRY LEAF BLOTCH, Gnomonia Fruit Rot (strawberries)

Gnomonia fructicola, syn. *Zythia fragariae*
Definition: A fungal disease of strawberries that shows various

Below: These strawberry leaf stalks have large reddish-brown blotches.

Above: This leaf shows the brown patches of walnut leaf blotch.

symptoms. It is most likely to occur in warm, humid weather.
Symptoms and damage: Large, brown blotches bordered with yellow or purple can appear on leaves. Alternatively, leaves turn black and rot, and leaves and fruits wither. Flowers and young fruit can shrivel.
Plants affected: Strawberries.
Prevention and control: Cut off and dispose of all parts of the strawberry plant showing signs of disease. The following season, spray with mancozeb to prevent reinfection. Alternatively, spray with copper oxychloride in spring and summer. (More frequent applications may be needed in warm, wet weather.)

WALNUT LEAF BLOTCH
Gnomonia leptostyla, syn. *Marssonina juglandis*
Definition: A fungal disease of walnuts.
Symptoms and damage: Yellowish-brown patches appear on upper leaf surfaces, with corresponding grey patches on the undersides that then turn dark brown. Leaves wither and are shed by the tree. Sunken black or dark brown blotches also appear on the developing nuts.
Plants affected: Walnuts.
Prevention and control: Collect and dispose of all affected leaves shed by the tree. The disease can be prevented by spraying walnut trees in spring with copper oxychloride or mancozeb.

ANTHRACNOSE (plane)
Gnomonia platani, syn. *Gloeosporium nervisequum,* see under *Marssonina salicicola.*

CANKER (roses)
Griphosphaeria corticola, see *Clethiridium corticola.*

CONIFER RUSTS
Gymnosporangium spp. (junipers), see under *Cronartium* spp. (pines).

VIOLET ROOT ROT
Helicobasidium purpureum
Definition: A soil-borne fungus that affects the crown roots of asparagus and certain root vegetables underground. The disease may strike individual plants but then spreads outwards, affecting entire beds if not treated. Symptoms and damage: Violet, web-like strands appear on the crown roots of asparagus or the surface of

Below: A potato with violet root rot.

carrots, sometimes with masses of fungal threads. Roots die, and topgrowth turns yellow and dies. Beetroot (beet) leaves turn yellow or become stunted; the roots become webbed with violet or purple fungal strands.
Plants affected: Asparagus, carrots, beetroot, potatoes, turnips, swedes (rutabagas).
Prevention and control: *Asparagus:* If only individual plants are affected, contain the spread of the fungus by sinking thick plastic sheeting around them to a depth of at least 30cm (12in). If a majority of the plants fail, make a new asparagus bed. *Carrots and beetroot:* Destroy affected crops. Do not replant the affected area with asparagus or any root crop for at least three years.

FOMES ROOT and Butt Rot (conifers)
Heterobasidion annosum, syn. *Fomes annosus*
Definition: A fungal disease of conifers. It is damaging and hard to detect, but relatively rare, since the fungus is spread by root contact.
Symptoms and damage: Shoots die back and the heartwood can rot. Roots can also die. While this does not necessarily kill the plant outright, it makes it less stable and more likely to blow over in strong winds. Fruiting bodies of the fungus, which vary in shape and size, are reddish-brown above, white beneath; they appear at ground level but are often hidden by soil or fallen leaves.
Plants affected: Most conifers.
Prevention and control: Dig up or cut down and destroy affected plants.

SHOT HOLE BLIGHT (snapdragons)
Heteropatella antirrhini
Definition: A fungal disease of snapdragons, particularly favoured by cool, damp weather.
Symptoms and damage: Yellow spots appear on leaves and stems; affected tissue falls away to leave characteristic holes. Young shoots can be destroyed. Leaves and stems can turn brown, and the plant has a scorched appearance.
Plants affected: Snapdragons (*Antirrhinum*).
Prevention and control: Spray regularly with zineb or copper oxychloride. Lift and destroy affected plants. Sow disease-free seed.

Below: These reddish-brown fruiting bodies indicate fomes root and butt rot.

LEAF AND STEM ROT

Heteropatella valtellinensis, see under *Alternaria* spp., including *A. tenuis*.

PETAL BLIGHT

Itersonilia perplexans

Definition: A fungal disease affecting a range of ornamentals and globe artichokes. It can be especially troublesome during a wet season. (It also causes parsnip canker, *see below*.)

Symptoms and damage: *Globe artichokes:* Before the heads mature, light brown round spots appear. The whole head then turns brown and can rot. *Cormous anemones:* Small, translucent spots appear on the outer petals. *Dahlias:* Brown spots appear on the outer petals, and the rot gradually spreads inwards. Grey mould (*Botrytis cinerea*) then usually takes a hold. *Chrysanthemums:* Outer florets show small oval spots and can later develop a white bloom. In wet weather, plants may contract grey mould.

Plants affected: Globe artichokes, cormous anemones (*Anemone*), dahlias (*Dahlia*) and chrysanthemums (*Chrysanthemum*).

Prevention and control: Avoid growing vulnerable plants together, since the disease is easily spread by contact. Cut off flowerheads as soon as signs of the disease are seen.

PARSNIP CANKERS

Itersonilia perplexans, other fungi

Definition: A fungal disease of parsnips and some other umbellifers, caused mainly by *Itersonilia perplexans*. Unsuitable soil conditions make it more likely. Outbreaks are worst in a wet season and/or poorly drained ground.

Symptoms and damage: Roots show cankers and horizontal cracks, usually around the widest part. These develop as red-brown or black lesions; in

Above: Dark lesions of parsnip canker on an infected root.

severe cases, the rot extends down into the flesh of the parsnip. Small spots can appear on leaves and stems.

Plants affected: Parsnips; chrysanthemums (*Chrysanthemum*) and sunflowers (*Helianthus*).

Prevention and control: Not possible. Grow parsnips on a fresh site each year. Prepare the soil carefully before planting. Add lime to acid soils. Some varieties are resistant.

THUJA BLIGHT

Keithia thujina, see *Didymascella thujina*.

CANE BLIGHT (raspberries)

Leptosphaeria coniothyrium

Definition: A fungal disease of raspberries that enters canes usually through cracks caused by frost. Where the fungus enters at ground level, the soil itself can become infected. The fungus can also cause canker on roses: *see under Clethiridium* (syn. *Griphosphaeria*) *corticola*.

Symptoms and damage: Canes show dark patches just above ground level and become brittle, snapping in severe cases. Leaves wither in summer.

Plants affected: Raspberries (some cultivars are particularly susceptible).

Prevention and control: Cut

affected stems right back to soil level and destroy them. Spray any new shoots appearing from ground level with copper oxychloride. Look for disease-resistant cultivars.

BLACK LEG (crucifers)

Leptosphaeria maculans

Definition: A fungal disease of crucifers that is most serious in wet weather.

Symptoms and damage: Plants wilt and the edges of leaves may turn reddish. Cracks can appear in stems and plants can fall over. The roots of root crops can also crack and show a brownish dry rot. Seedling stems have a brown sunken area at soil level, which gradually blackens. Seedlings then die.

Plants affected: Crucifers such as cabbages, turnips and swedes (rutabagas).

Prevention and control: Remove and destroy all diseased material. Sow disease-free seed and practise crop rotation.

FLY SPECK

Leptothyrium pomi (fly speck), see under *Gloeodes pomigena* (sooty blotch) and *Leptothyrium pomi* (fly speck).

WALNUT LEAF BLOTCH

Marssonina juglandis, see *Gnomonia leptostyla*.

Below: The brown area on this plane leaf indicates anthracnose.

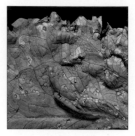

Above: The characteristic spots of anthracnose on a lettuce leaf.

ANTHRACNOSE (lettuces)

Marssonina panattoniana

Definition: A fungal disease of lettuces, favoured by cool, wet weather.

Symptoms and damage: Small spots appear on leaves. Initially yellow, they enlarge and turn brown. Growth can be stunted.

Plants affected: Lettuces.

Prevention and control: Spray with mancozeb. Plant disease-free seed and practise crop rotation.

ANTHRACNOSE (weeping willows, poplars and planes)

Marssonina salicicola (willows and poplars), *Gnomonia platani* (syn. *Gloesporium nervisequum*; planes)

Definition: A fungal disease of certain ornamental trees that tends to be prevalent during wet springs. On planes, the symptoms are easily confused with frost damage.

Symptoms and damage: *Planes:*

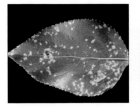

Above: The pustules on this white poplar leaf are due to poplar rust.

Above: These peony leaves have been turned reddish-brown by rust.

Above: This hollyhock leaf is pitted with tiny yellow rust markings.

Above: These euphorbia leaves are covered in yellow rust patches.

emerging leaves and developing shoots turn brown; sometimes buds fail to open at all. Later in the season, leaf veins show brown banding and leaves are then shed prematurely. Small cankers appear on shoots, which then die back. *Willows:* Leaves are distorted and marked by small brown spots; they are shed prematurely. Masses of small dark cankers appear on shoots, which then die back. In severe cases, the tree's weeping habit is lost.

Plants affected: Weeping willows (particularly *Salix babylonica* and its selections), poplars (*Populus*), and planes (*Platanus*).

Prevention and control: Collect and destroy fallen leaves. Promote recovery of affected trees by feeding, watering and mulching.

POPLAR RUST
(poplars)
Melampsora medusae,
M. larici-populina

Definition: A serious fungal disease of some poplars.

Symptoms and damage: The lower surface of leaves is flecked with yellow. Leaves turn brown and are shed prematurely from the tree in late summer and early autumn. Large trees suffer die-back. Young trees can be seriously weakened and may die in severe cases.

Plants affected: *Populus nigra* 'Italica' and *P. deltoides*; other poplars can also be affected by the disease.

Prevention and control: Spray with sulphur (not practical on

large specimens). Plant varieties that are known to be resistant to the disease.

RUSTS
Melampsoraceae,
Puccininaceae

Definition: A huge range of diseases caused by a number of related fungi are classified as rusts. Most are specific to one or a few host plants and cannot be transferred from one group of plants to other unrelated plants. Troublesome/common rusts that affect particular plants have their own entries.

Symptoms and damage: Rusty red, brown or yellow patches appear on leaves, and sometimes on flowers and fruits. Some rusts result in galls or other swellings. Growth can be affected, and in extreme cases of

Below: Brown and yellow patches show that this pear tree has rust.

infestation, the plants can die.

Plants affected: A huge range of plants, including ornamentals, are susceptible to rust diseases.

Prevention and control: Cut off and destroy affected leaves. Pull up and destroy any severely affected plants (including weeds). In some cases, spraying with sulphur is helpful, though this is not effective on all rusts. Prune woody plants to improve air circulation and avoid overcrowding other plants. Plant disease-resistant varieties.

WITCHES' BROOMS
Melampsorella caryophyllacearum,
Taphrina spp.

Definition: A condition of trees and shrubs (including some conifers) that can be caused by

a number of fungi (sometimes also by the activities of certain invertebrates, such as mites). In conifers other than firs (*Abies*), it generally arises as the result of a mutation.

Symptoms and damage: A mass of erect shoots emerges from a single point, giving the appearance of an upended broom.

Plants affected: Many broad-leaved trees and shrubs; firs (*Abies*).

Prevention and control: Cut back affected growth to at least 15cm (6in) behind the broom. Further control is not possible.

Below: This maple tree has been severely deformed by the growth of witches' brooms.

ROOT KNOT NEMATODES
Meloidogyne spp.

Definition: Nematodes (or eelworms) that attack the roots of plants (some species of nematode are host-specific). Secondary infections by *Fusarium* spp. and other pathogens can follow. They are most troublesome in light soils and warm climates and can also appear in greenhouses. These nematodes can be spread by running water and by means of soil stuck to garden implements and to the soles of shoes.

Symptoms and damage: Growth is stunted and plants wilt. Leaves can be paler than normal. Affected roots or tubers have galls, scabby lesions or other swellings.

Plants affected: A wide range of plants, including potatoes, ornamentals such as roses, and greenhouse crops (though grasses are immune).

Prevention and control: Intercropping susceptible plants with marigolds (*Tagetes patula* or *T. erecta*) can provide some control over most nematodes. Grow nematode-resistant varieties where these are available. Improving the soil with garden compost can increase the range of soil-borne organisms that attack nematodes. Practise crop rotation. Leaving infected soil

Below: The swellings on this lettuce root are root galls caused by eelworms.

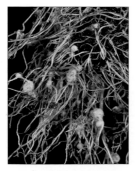

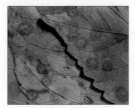

Above: Yellowed leaves from a hibiscus suffering from flyspeck.

fallow for a season can decrease nematode populations. (Sweet corn, onions, cabbages and cauliflowers are tolerant of these nematodes.)

FLYSPECK (hibiscus)
Microthyriella hibisci

Definition: A fungal disease of hibiscus that tends to occur in areas where the weather is often humid. It is rarely serious.

Symptoms and damage: Leaves turn yellow and are shed from the plant. Black spots are sometimes seen on the leaves.

Plants affected: Hibiscus (*Hibiscus*), especially if grown in shady conditions.

Prevention and control: Spray with zineb, if necessary. Grow hibiscus in sunny sites.

BLOSSOM WILT (tree fruits)
Monilinia spp.

Definition: A number of related fungi that can cause particular problems to tree fruit during wet springs.

Symptoms and damage: Flower trusses wither but are not shed by the plant. Leaves can also shrivel and there may be some die-back at the shoot tips.

Plants affected: All tree fruit. Ornamental cherries (*Prunus*) are also vulnerable.

Prevention and control: Cut back and dispose of affected growth. The following year, spray with copper oxychloride (or benomyl on ornamentals) as the flowers begin to open, repeating the application one week later. Alternatively, spray trees with tar oil in late winter.

Above: These withered leaves are caused by blossom wilt.

BROWN ROTS (various tree fruits)
Monilinia fructicola,
M. fructigena, M. laxa

Definition: A disease of top fruits that can be particularly troublesome during a wet season. It can be caused by a number of related fungi that can enter plant tissue through wounds made by birds, wasps or caterpillars.

Symptoms and damage: Small brown spots appear on petals, spreading quickly to stems. A soft brown mould covers affected tissues. Sunken brown cankers appear on twigs, and fruits show small, brown, round spots, which spread rapidly. Fruits turn brown, become soft and rot. They can also be covered with rings of buff or grey fungal spores. Affected fruits can shrivel and become mummified. They are either shed by the tree or remain on the branches over winter. Shoots affected by cankers can die back.

Plants affected: Stone fruits (US: those with pits) such as almonds, apricots and other members of *Prunus*; quinces; occasionally also apples and pears. These fungi can also affect fruits in storage.

Prevention and control: Spray with sulphur when the blossom shows pink, before petals fall

and again before harvesting fruits. In autumn to early winter, collect and destroy all mummified fruits (both from the tree and on the ground). Look for cankers on stems and cut back affected growth in winter to healthy wood. Prune to improve air circulation through the crown. Store only perfect, dry, undamaged fruits and keep the storage area clean. Avoid fertilizing with nitrogen-high fertilizers that promote sappy growth (which will be more susceptible to infection). Plant resistant varieties.

LEAF SPECKLE (bananas)
Mycosphaerella musae

Definition: A fungal disease of bananas.

Symptoms and damage: Undersides of leaves show

Below: This apple has turned brown and is covered with buff fungal spores of brown rot.

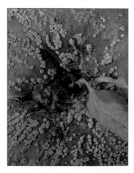

MYCOPLASMAS

These unclassified bacterial parasitic organisms are responsible for the following serious conditions. All those described here are spread by leafhoppers. These insects tend to migrate to cultivated plants during hot, dry weather, when the weeds in uncultivated ground, on which they have been feeding, are drying off.

BIG BUD, Greening, Virescence

Symptoms and damage: Shoots proliferate and plants develop an unnaturally bushy habit. In tomatoes, the stems are thickened and cropping is reduced.

Below: Big bud, spread by a leafhopper, on the stem of a plant.

Plants affected: Tomatoes, potatoes, lettuces, chrysanthemums (*Chrysanthemum*), dahlias (*Dahlia*), zinnias (*Zinnia*); weeds.
Prevention and control: Keep garden borders and the vegetable patch weed-free. Control leafhoppers with a suitable insecticide.

PURPLE TOP WILT (potatoes)

Symptoms and damage: Young leaves are curled at the edges. Stems collapse. Tubers produced are small.
Plants affected: Potatoes.
Prevention and control: Keep the vegetable patch weed-free. Control leafhoppers with a suitable insecticide.

Below: The yellowing leaves of this papaya indicate the plant has yellow crinkle.

Above: This potato plant has died from purple top wilt.

STRAWBERRY GREEN PETAL (strawberries)

Symptoms and damage: Young strawberry leaves are small and yellow, then turn red and wilt. The petals of the flowers are small and green, while the sepals are enlarged. Edible fruits are not produced. In cases of severe infestation the plants die.
Plants affected: Strawberries.
Prevention and control: Keep the strawberry patch free from clover, which can harbour the mycoplasma. Control leafhoppers with a suitable insecticide.

YELLOW CRINKLE (papayas)

Symptoms and damage: Older leaves turn yellow, and their stalks bend downwards at the union with the trunk. Leaves at the top of the plant fail to develop fully and show a claw-like appearance. Older leaves are shed from the plant. Affected plants fail to recover.
Plants affected: Papayas.
Prevention and control: Dig up and destroy the affected plants.

---

discoloration. Affected areas turn yellow and dark brown spots or speckles appear.
Plants affected: Bananas.
Prevention and control: Spray with mancozeb or copper oxychloride (but not on fruiting plants). Cut off and dispose of diseased material and feed plants well to keep them growing strongly.

BANANA LEAF SPOT, Sigatoka Disease (bananas)

Mycosphaerella musicola
Definition: A widespread fungal disease of bananas.

Symptoms and damage: Pale yellow streaks appear on young leaves. These enlarge to brown oval spots that then turn grey. In severe cases, entire leaves can turn brown with black and grey streaks.
Plants affected: Bananas.
Prevention and control: Spray in spring with mancozeb or copper oxychloride. (It may be necessary to continiue spraying all year round in tropical areas.) Do not spray fruiting plants. Cut off and dispose of any damaged material and feed plants well to maintain their vigour.

LEAF SPOTS (eucalyptus)

Mycosphaerella spp.
Definition: Many different fungi can cause spotting on eucalyptus leaves, but only a few cause unsightly damage to the tree (usually to the juvenile leaves). Fungal infection is commonest during warm, humid weather.
Symptoms and damage: Young leaves are marked with irregular brownish patches.
Plants affected: Eucalyptus (*Eucalyptus*), especially forms of *E. globulus*.
Prevention and control: Not

usually needed. Stems on which leaves are damaged can be cut from the plant.

Below: This diseased young banana tree shows the leaf lesions caused by banana leaf spot.

Above: The pinkish pustules of coral spot.

CORAL SPOT
Nectria cinnabarina
Definition: A troublesome fungus affecting broad-leaved trees and shrubs, which enters through small wounds, often as a result of careless pruning.
Symptoms and damage: Shoots die back and show a quantity of pink to coral red, cushion-like pustules of spores. In severe cases, the whole plant dies.
Plants affected: Red currants and figs. Ornamentals such as maples (*Acer*), Judas trees (*Cercis*), eleagnus (*Elaeagnus*) and magnolias (*Magnolia*) are especially vulnerable.
Prevention and control: Cut back affected stems to healthy growth well behind the point of infection. Dispose of all other woody material (such as support canes), since this can harbour fungal spores. When pruning, use clean, sharp tools that will not snag the wood (this is a common cause of infection) and disinfect the blades between cuts.

STEM CANKER (spruce)
Nectria cucurbitula, other fungi
Definition: A fungal disease of spruces, usually caused by *Nectria cucurbitula*, though other fungi can cause similar symptoms. The disease enters through wounds, generally caused by frost damage.
Symptoms and damage: Red fruiting bodies of the fungus appear on dead wood. Shoots die back.
Plants affected: Spruces (*Picea*).
Prevention and control: Take off dead growth, cutting back to healthy wood.

APPLE CANKER (apples)
Nectria galligena
Definition: A serious fungal disease of pome fruits. It can occur at any time of year, and the fungus enters plants through wounds caused by pruning, leaf scars or pest damage. The damage is worst on weak-growing fruit trees.
Symptoms and damage: Sunken, elliptical patches appear on tree bark. Girdled shoots can die back. White fungal spores appear on the cankers in summer, followed by small, red fruiting bodies.
Plants affected: Apples; pears can also be vulnerable to the disease.
Prevention and control: Cut back severely affected branches to healthy growth. If thick branches have not suffered die-back, cankers can be gouged out with a pruning knife. Spray with Bordeaux mixture or other copper fungicide after harvesting but before leaf fall. Improve the vigour of weak-growing trees by applying an appropriate fertilizer during the growing season, and improve the drainage if necessary.

PETAL BLIGHT (rhododendrons)
Ovulinia azaleae
Definition: A fungal disease of rhododendrons.
Symptoms and damage: White spots appear on affected petals (brown on white flowers); the flowers then turn slimy and collapse, but are not shed from the plant (sometimes persisting until the following spring). They become dry and papery.
Plants affected: Rhododendrons (*Rhododendron*), especially deciduous types, Kurume and Indian (*Indica*) hybrids; also calico bushes (*Kalmia latifolia*).
Prevention and control: Control is difficult: remove all affected flowers to prevent the disease passing to any later-flowering rhododendrons growing near the diseased shrub.

BLUE MOULD, Soft Rot (onions, carrots, ornamental alliums)
Penicillium spp.
Definition: A bacterial infection that causes vegetables in storage to rot. It mainly affects onions that have not been grown or harvested correctly as well as carrots that have been damaged. Blue mould can also affect gladioli corms and tulip bulbs in storage, especially if these have been damaged (slugs are a common culprit for this). A damp atmosphere encourages the mould to grow. *Erwinia carotovora* var. *carotovora* can also cause blue mould.
Symptoms and damage: *Onions:* Stored bulbs turn soft, becoming slimy and smelly; blue-green fungal growths appear between the outer scales. *Carrots:* Stored roots turn soft and slimy. *Gladioli:* Stored corms develop reddish-brown sunken patches. Blue mould develops where conditions are damp, and the corms rot.
Plants affected: Onions and carrots in storage; ornamental bulbs in storage.
Prevention and control: Cultivate onions well to produce firm, ripe bulbs. Dry them correctly before storing in cool, well-ventilated conditions. Check them regularly and remove any that show signs of rotting. Store undamaged carrots only, since the disease enters through wounds. Lift bulbs (including gladioli) with care to prevent damage. Store only healthy specimens, and dry them off properly. Examine them regularly through the winter and discard any that show signs of rotting.

Below: The white fungal spores of apple canker surround the sunken patches on this branch.

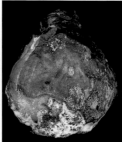

Below: This infected blue hyacinth bulb is suffering from a severe growth of blue mould.

Above: An attack of downy mildew on salad onions.

Above: A calabrese leaf infected with downy mildew of brassicas.

Above: This rose shoot shows many of the symptoms of downy mildew.

DOWNY MILDEW (onions)
Peronospora destructor

Definition: A fungal disease that is especially troublesome in wet weather. In some gardens it can be a recurring problem.

Symptoms and damage: Leaves turn grey, wither and fall over; sometimes, a purple fungal growth can be observed. Bulbs turn soft and cannot be stored. The disease can also grow into seedheads, affecting the seed.

Plants affected: Onions, garlic, shallots, leeks.

Prevention and control: Spray with mancozeb, copper hydroxide or zineb at the first sign of infection, or before, in areas where the disease is known to occur. Weed the onion bed to prevent stagnant conditions that encourage the spread of the

Below: The dried brown patches on the upper surfaces of these rhubarb leaves are symptomatic of downy mildew on rhubarb.

fungus. Plant onions on a fresh site each year, in well-prepared, well-drained soil.

DOWNY MILDEW (rhubarb)
Peronospora jaapiana

Definition: A fungal disease of rhubarb that is worst during cool, wet weather.

Symptoms and damage: Upper leaf surfaces show irregular light brown patches. These can spread and tear. (The furry growth typical of downy mildew appears under the leaves.)

Plants affected: Rhubarb.

Prevention and control: Spray with copper oxychloride, mancozeb or zineb. Cut back and destroy affected leaves. Feed well to promote recovery.

DOWNY MILDEW (crucifers)
Peronospora parasitica **and strains**

Definition: A fungal disease of crucifer seedlings, encouraged

by a moist atmosphere. Plants that are being grown too close together are particularly at risk. The problem also occurs under glass. The fungus has a number of strains, not all of which attack the same plants.

Symptoms and damage: A white, mealy growth appears on the undersides of leaves, which can discolour. Growth of affected plants is checked.

Plants affected: Brassica seedlings, especially cauliflowers and cabbages. Stocks (*Matthiola*) are affected by a different strain of the fungus.

Prevention and control: Remove all affected leaves and spray with mancozeb, copper oxychloride, zineb or copper hydroxide. Sow seed thinly, rotating the crop, and thin the emerging seedlings at the first opportunity.

DOWNY MILDEW (roses)
Peronospora sparsa

Definition: A fungal disease of roses, favoured by humid weather.

Symptoms and damage: Purplish-red to dark brown spots appear on leaves, sometimes with corresponding furry growth on the underside. Stems and flower stalks can split. Petals can show brown patches. Young shoots can die and infected buds can open as distorted flowers.

Plants affected: Roses (*Rosa*); some varieties are more

susceptible than others.

Prevention and control: Spray with zineb or copper oxychloride. Cut off and destroy all affected growth.

DOWNY MILDEW (peas)
Peronospora viciae

Definition: A fungal disease of peas that is worst in damp weather.

Symptoms and damage: The upper leaf surfaces turn yellow. In humid conditions, a thick, furry, greyish growth appears on the undersides. Pea pods show cream patches and leaves turn brown.

Plants affected: Peas.

Prevention and control: Spray with mancozeb. Grow peas in well-ventilated conditions.

Below: Downy mildew has caused this pea plant to wilt.

Above: The edge of this camellia leaf is severely affected by pestalotiopsis.

PESTALOTIOPSIS (camellias)
Pestalotiopsis spp.

Definition: An unsightly fungal disease of camellias. Symptoms appear on leaves that have already been damaged, usually either as a result of scorch or bad pruning.

Symptoms and damage: Areas of leaf turn silver-grey.

Plants affected: Camellias (*Camellia*), especially forms of *C. japonica*.

Prevention and control: Avoid damaging leaves.

ANGULAR LEAF SPOT (French beans)
Phaeoisariopsis griseola

Definition: A fungal disease of French beans. It can be seed-borne and is favoured by cool,

wet weather. It can spread rapidly among plants.

Symptoms and damage: Angular, rounded spots appear on leaves. Dark sunken patches appear on pods, and the disease penetrates through to the seeds.

Plants affected: French beans.

Prevention and control: Controls for rust can provide some protection. Sow guaranteed disease-free seed of a resistant variety. Remove and destroy all plant debris after harvesting.

MICHAELMAS DAISY WILT (Michaelmas daisies)
Phialophora asteris

Definition: A soil-borne fungal disease that affects certain Michaelmas daisies.

Symptoms and damage: Individual shoots within a clump turn brown, and leaves wither from the base of the stem upwards. Affected plants usually die within two to three years of the attack.

Plants affected: Michaelmas daisies (*Aster*) except varieties of *Aster novae-angliae*.

Prevention and control: Destroy affected plants (it is possible to propagate new stock from healthy shoots of plants that show signs of the disease).

Below: This dying French bean leaf has been badly affected by angular leaf spot.

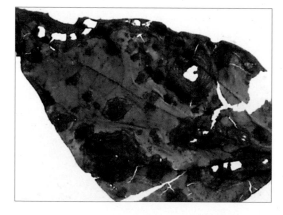

Above: The speckled brown spots on this leaf make mulberry leaf spot easy to identify.

Replant with healthy stock in fresh soil. Look for varieties that are known to be resistant.

CARNATION WILT
Phialophora cinerescens (syn. *Verticillium cinerescens*), see under *Fusarium oxysporum* f. sp. *dianthi*.

MULBERRY LEAF SPOT (mulberries)
Phloeospora maculans

Definition: A fungal disease of mulberries.

Symptoms and damage: Small brown spots appear on leaves. The spots increase in size and become paler, and sections of the leaf can die.

Plants affected: Mulberries.

Prevention and control: Spray leaves with lime sulphur as they emerge in spring. Repeat two weeks later and again after the fruit has set. Collect and dispose of all fallen leaves in the autumn.

GANGRENE (potatoes)
Phoma solanicola f. *foveata*

Definition: A fungal disease, present in most soils, that affects potatoes in storage, particularly damaged tubers. It enters the tubers through wounds made at harvest time.

Symptoms and damage: Rounded, brown depressions appear on the skins of tubers. These then enlarge and the

tissue beneath rots. The affected tubers shrink and become hollow inside.

Plants affected: Potatoes.

Prevention and control: Plant disease-free tubers. Take care not to damage potatoes for storing when lifting. Store tubers in cool, well-ventilated conditions. Destroy badly affected tubers.

FIG CANKER (figs)
Phomopsis cinerascens

Definition: A canker-inducing fungus, spread by rainfall, birds and insects, that enters plant tissue via pruning cuts and other wounds.

Symptoms and damage: Oval cankers (sometimes large) appear on the bark. The fruiting bodies are tiny, producing tendrils of spores in wet weather. In severe cases, whole branches can be killed.

Plants affected: Figs.

Prevention and control: Cut back and dispose of affected growth before the spores that will spread the disease are produced. Make sure pruning tools are clean and sharp, and disinfect blades between cuts.

Below: These gangrene lesions are a result of harvest-time wounds.

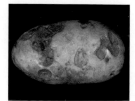

STRAWBERRY LEAF BLIGHT
Phomopsis obscurians
Definition: A fungal disease of strawberries.
Symptoms and damage: Leaves show red-purple spots, which later darken to brown. Sometimes large areas of leaf are covered.
Plants affected: Strawberries.
Prevention and control: Cut off and dispose of affected leaves. Spray with copper oxychloride when cutting back leaves and again in autumn.

PHOMOPSIS DISEASE (Douglas firs)
Phomopsis pseudotsugae
Definition: A fungal disease of Douglas firs. It lives on dead wood and usually enters living plants through wounds (such as can be caused by frost). Other fungi can cause similar problems on cedars and larches.
Symptoms and damage: Shoots die back. In young plants, if the main stem is affected, the top of the tree can die. Older trees can develop cankers. The small black fruiting bodies of the fungus appear on cankers, dead shoots and bark as well as on live shoots.

Below: These strawberry leaf stalks show signs of strawberry leaf blight.

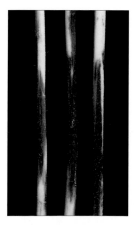

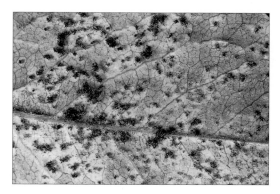
Above: A rose leaf showing signs of rust.

Plants affected: Douglas fir (*Pseudotsuga*), cedar (*Cedrus*) and larch (*Larix*).
Prevention and control: Cut out and destroy damaged and dead plant material.

RUST (roses)
Phragmidium mucronatum, P. tuberculatum
Definition: A fungal disease of roses that is commonest on poorly cultivated, weak-growing plants, particularly where the soil is allowed to dry out and/or when the weather is hot and humid. The spores are spread by the wind.
Symptoms and damage: In spring, orange patches can appear on stems and leaf stalks. A more common sign of infection is the appearance in summer of yellow spots on the upper surfaces of leaves, with powdery orange pustules on the undersides. These turn brown, then black; the leaves crisp and are shed by the plant. Severely affected plants can die back.
Plants affected: Roses (*Rosa*), especially older varieties.
Prevention and control: Cut out affected growth in spring. If the problem appears in summer, spray with mancozeb, myclobutanil, penconazole, triforine with sulphur or triforine with bupirimate or zineb. Spray with a foliar feed to help restore vigour to

weakened plants and mulch to preserve moisture. Dispose of any leaves shed by the plants. Dig up and destroy severely affected plants.

RASPBERRY RUST (raspberries)
Phragmidium rubi-idaei
Definition: A fungal disease of raspberries.
Symptoms and damage: Orange pustules appear on the upper surface of leaves. Later, dull orange patches appear on the undersides.
Plants affected: Raspberries (particularly 'Lloyd George' and 'Neka').
Prevention and control: Spray with copper oxychloride. Grow resistant varieties.

Below: Raspberry rust spores can be seen on the underside of this raspberry leaf.

PHYTOPHTHORA ROOT ROTS
Phytophthora spp.
Definition: A serious fungal disease of roots that develops quickly in moist soils, especially in plants near running water. For other root rots, see under *Aphanomyces euteiches*.
Symptoms and damage: Roots rot (feeder roots first, followed by main roots). Leaves turn yellow and die, and shoots die back. In severe cases, the whole plant dies.
Plants affected: A wide range of trees and shrubs, as well as some herbaceous plants. Some plants are resistant.
Prevention and control: Dig up and dispose of affected plants. Improve the soil well before replanting and mulch new plantings regularly to keep plants growing strongly.

BROWN ROTS (citrus fruit)
Phytophthora spp.
Definition: A fungal disease of citrus. The fungus produces its spores on the soil surface; these are splashed on to lower parts of plants. It commonly occurs in autumn in areas where citrus are grown, but can also occur at other times. Wet weather

Below: Blackened tissue on the stem base and roots of this gerbera indicate phytophthora root rot.

Above: Brown rot has covered the skin of this orange.

provides the fungus with favourable conditions.
Symptoms and damage: *Lemons:* A yellow-brown rot appears on fruits. *Oranges and mandarins:* A firm, grey-brown rot appears on fruits. In wet weather, leaves can be shed from the plant and shoots can die back.
Plants affected: Citrus; grapefruit are rarely affected by the disease.
Prevention and control: Spray trees with copper oxychloride before or immediately after the first rains of autumn. Repeat in late winter or spring if the season continues wet. (The soil surrounding the trees should also be sprayed.) Prune trees so that branches will not come into contact with the soil when

they are laden with fruit, and remove any neighbouring vegetation that increases humidity around the plants.

TOP and ROOT ROTS (pineapples)
Phytophthora spp.
Definition: A fungal disease of pineapples. It is prevalent in wet soils (particularly if alkaline) and tends to attack the soft tissues of the plants.
Symptoms and damage: *Top rot:* Heart leaves turn yellow or pale brown with a reddish tinge. Stems and leaf bases start to rot, and the plant develops an unpleasant smell. *Root rot:* Outer leaves are limp and die back from the tips. Roots rot, and plants can easily be pulled from

Below: These pineapple plants show the reddish tinge of top rot.

the ground. Fruits developing near soil level are also susceptible to rot (the condition is sometimes referred to as "green fruit rot").
Plants affected: Pineapples.
Prevention and control: Drain wet soils or install raised beds that drain more freely. Lower the pH of alkaline soil through the use of flowers of sulphur or another acidifier.

DAMPING OFF
Phytophthora spp, *Pythium* spp, *Rhizoctonia* spp.
Definition: A condition that causes the collapse of a wide range of seedlings, usually as a result of overcrowded, excessively damp conditions. It can be caused by a number of fungi that can be soil- or water-borne. Overwatering can sometimes cause problems of damping off.
Symptoms and damage: Seedlings collapse shortly after germinating (some pathogens can attack seedlings before they emerge from the soil). Stems sometimes blacken and wither.
Plants affected: Many seedlings, especially those of beetroot (beet), celery, lettuce, peas and tomatoes. Ornamentals such as snapdragons (*Antirrhinum*), sweet peas (*Lathyrus odoratus*), lobelias (*Lobelia*), stocks (*Matthiola*) and zinnias (*Zinnia*) are especially vulnerable. Plants raised under glass, where humidity levels can climb steeply, are particularly at risk.
Prevention and control: Make sure the ground is adequately prepared before planting to prevent soil compaction, which commonly leads to damping off. For plants grown under glass, sow seed in trays of fresh, sterilized compost (soil mix). Water carefully with clean water so that the compost does not compact. Sow thinly or thin seedlings as early as possible to prevent overcrowding. Remember that most seedlings do best in good light with only

Above: Some of these cactus seedlings have collapsed, due to damping off.

moderate warmth. Remove dead seedlings and spray or water the remainder with Cheshunt compound or copper oxychloride.

COLLAR ROT (citrus)
Phytophthora citrophthora
Definition: A soil-borne fungal disease of citrus that thrives in damp conditions. Some varieties are more susceptible to the problem than others.
Symptoms and damage: Gum is exuded from the bark near soil level. The bark in this area dries out and splits. The infection can spread round the tree and ringbark it.
Plants affected: Citrus. Some forms and some rootstocks

Below: This citrus fruit is suffering from collar rot.

are resistant to the fungus.
Prevention and control: Cut away damaged bark with a sharp knife. Improve soil drainage prior to planting and plant so that the graft union is well above soil level. Prune off any low branches that might come into contact with the soil and avoid overwetting the trunk when watering. Remove any other plants growing close to the trunk.

RED CORE, Red Stele (strawberries)
Phytophthora fragariae
Definition: A fungal disease of strawberries. It is likely to be a problem on cold, wet, poorly drained soils. The fungus spreads rapidly and is extremely difficult to eradicate.
Symptoms and damage: Plants start to wilt early in the growing season and are stunted. Leaves lose their green colour, turning greyish or purplish. Older leaves turn yellow or red. Fruiting is impaired and plants can die.
Plants affected: Strawberries; occasionally also hybrid berries and potentillas (*Potentilla*).
Prevention and control: Dig up and destroy the affected plants. Do not replant the area with strawberries for at least ten years. Improve drainage prior to planting.

Below: To avoid red core, choose disease-resistant varieties of strawberries.

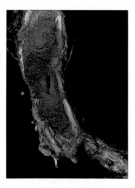

LATE BLIGHT, Tomato Blight (potatoes, tomatoes)
Phytophthora infestans
Definition: A serious and widespread fungal disease of potatoes and other crops belonging to Solanaceae. It is spread both on the wind and through the soil and seems to be more common in some areas than others. It is always more of a problem during humid weather, particularly when warm days follow cool nights. On outdoor tomatoes, it is especially troublesome if the weather in late summer is wet. The disease can also spread on potato tubers in storage.
Symptoms and damage: Yellow-brown patches appear on leaves, usually from mid- to late summer, but sometimes earlier in the season. These spread in wet weather, when leaves and stems blacken and rot. Large numbers of plants can suddenly collapse. White fungal threads that appear on the underside of leaves release spores, which are carried by the wind to other crops or are washed down into the soil where they can infect potato tubers. Affected tubers have red-brown dry rot under the skin, which extends down towards the middle. They are then susceptible to other bacterial infections. Tomato leaves show similar patches, then dry up and curl. Stems can show black patches and can even collapse. Fruits turn brown, shrink, then rot. Apparently

Above: These potato leaves have yellow-brown patches, indicating late blight.

unblemished fruit can also show signs of rot around five days after picking.
Plants affected: Potatoes, tomatoes and related crops. Some potato and tomato varieties show resistance to or tolerance of blight.
Prevention and control: Remove and destroy affected plants. *Potatoes:* Plant healthy tubers only, to the correct depth. Earth up regularly. Maincrop potatoes can be sprayed in early to midsummer with mancozeb, zineb, Bordeaux mixture or other copper fungicide. Repeated applications may be necessary. In areas where the disease is known to be a problem, choose resistant varieties. When lifting potatoes

Below: A severe infection of tomato blight has caused this plant to collapse in late summer.

for storage, inspect the tubers carefully for signs of spots. Do not store affected tubers. *Tomatoes:* Spray against blight, and apply copper fungicide or mancozeb after pinching out the growing tips. Repeated applications (perhaps every two to three weeks) may be necessary if the season is wet.

PHYTOPHTHORA BLIGHT (passion fruits)
Phytophthora nicotianae var. *parasitica*
Definition: A soil-borne fungus that attacks a wide range of plants. It is likeliest to occur during warm, wet weather. The fungus also causes crown rot of rhubarb, some diseases of pineapples and other diseases. The symptoms described here relate to the effects of the fungus on passion fruit.
Symptoms and damage: The lower parts of plants are affected first, then infection spreads upwards. Mature leaves show translucent patches, which then turn brown. Shoots can die back. If the main stem is girdled, the whole plant can die back. Fruits show water-soaked spots, which enlarge to cover most of the surface.
Plants affected: Passion fruit.
Prevention and control: Spray with copper oxychloride, but not if the fruit is maturing. Space vines correctly and prune to relieve congestion among the stems.

BROWN CORE (primulas)
Phytophthora primulae
Definition: A soil-borne fungal disease of primulas.
Symptoms and damage: Roots die back from the tips; topgrowth wilts.
Plants affected: Primulas (*Primula*) (including the bedding types).
Prevention and control: Lift and destroy affected plants. Do not replant the area with primulas unless it is possible to replace or sterilize the soil.

SUDDEN OAK DEATH
Phytophthora ramorum
Definition: A serious fungal disease that affects a range of plants. It is responsible for deforestation in the states of California and Oregon, where outbreaks have reached epidemic proportions.
Symptoms and damage: *Oaks:* Dark red to black sap is exuded from lesions on the lower trunk. *Rhododendrons:* Shoots discolour, leaves are spotted and there is some die-back. *Viburnums:* The disease spreads from the base of stems upwards. Stems wilt and die back.
Plants affected: Oaks (*Quercus*) and other plant species native to California; in Europe, rhododendrons (*Rhododendron*)

and viburnums (*Viburnum*). Other species are also potentially at risk.
Prevention and control: Dig up and destroy affected plants. In some countries, you should notify the local government agriculture department if you suspect an outbreak.

ASTER YELLOWS, Strawberry Green Petal
Phytoplasmas
Definition: Phytoplasmas are organisms intermediate between viruses and bacteria and are spread by insect pests. Aster yellows and strawberry green petal are spread by leafhoppers (*Macrosteles* spp.). Symptoms can vary depending on the strain and the plant affected.
Symptoms and damage: *Carrots:* Growth is stunted and leaves are distorted and yellow, turning red or purple. Roots are thin, with an abnormal number of feeder roots, and bitter to the taste. *Lettuces:* The inner part of the head is pale (a condition sometimes referred to as "white heart"). *Potatoes and tomatoes:* Leaves are rolled and stems are distorted. *Celery:* Stems are stunted and twisted; affected plants are vulnerable to soft rots. *Strawberries:* Flowers have

Below: These discoloured potato leaves are a sign of aster yellows.

Above: These grevillea leaves show symptoms of leaf spot.

green petals and enlarged sepals. They usually wither and fruit is not set. New leaves are smaller than average and turn red. In severe cases, the plants collapse and die.
Plants affected: Many garden crops, including carrots, celery, lettuce and strawberries. Ornamental plants, particularly asters, and some weeds can also be affected.
Prevention and control: Dig up and dispose of affected plants. Spray with a systemic insecticide to kill leafhoppers or cover vulnerable plants with a floating mulch to protect against the pest. Remove host weeds (these include clover, plantain, chicory, knotweed, pineapple-weed, stinkweed, wild asters, ragweed, wild carrot and Kentucky bluegrass) that attract leafhoppers. Grow tolerant varieties.

LEAF SPOT (grevilleas)
Placoasterella baileyi
Definition: An unsightly, though usually not debilitating, fungal disease. Similar symptoms can also be caused by species of *Verrucispora* in hot, humid climates.
Symptoms and damage: Black spots appear on leaves.

(*Verrucispora* causes red-brown spotting.)
Plants affected: Grevilleas (*Grevillea*) and hakeas (*Hakea*).
Prevention and control: Spray with mancozeb. Cut off and destroy all affected growth.

CLUB ROOT
Plasmodiophora brassicae
Definition: A widespread and common soil-borne fungus that thrives in wet, acid soil (though it can cause problems in any soil). It is often unwittingly introduced into gardens on the roots of purchased seedlings. Outbreaks can be mistaken for damage caused by the *cabbage maggot* and/or *root knot nematodes*, and vice versa.
Symptoms and damage: Plants infected at the seedling stage fail to grow. Older plants can be stunted and develop discoloured leaves, which wilt in hot weather. They may die before flowering. The roots thicken and distort and cease to function normally. In severe cases, all the main roots are swollen into a mass of galls.
Plants affected: Brassicas (including swedes [rutabagas] and turnips), seakale and other crucifers; wallflowers (*Cheiranthus*) and stocks

Below: Club root is clearly visible on the root of this brassica.

(*Matthiola*). Weeds such as dock and certain grasses can be hosts. **Prevention and control:** Raise crops from seed of resistant varieties rather than buying in seedling plants. If club root has been a problem, raise seedlings in sterilized compost (soil mix). Treat suspect seedlings before planting by dipping the roots in a solution of thiophanate-methyl. Prior to planting any brassica crop, prepare the soil well and consider liming to raise the pH if necessary. Practise crop rotation so that brassicas and other related plants (including weeds) are kept away from infected land for as long as possible. A seven-year cycle is not excessive if this disease has caused problems. Dig up stunted plants and check the root systems for signs of disease. Top-dress with well-rotted garden compost to increase the range of soil organisms, some of which suppress club root.

DOWNY MILDEW (grapes)
Plasmopara viticola
Definition: A fungal disease that commonly affects grapevines grown in warm, humid weather conditions.
Symptoms and damage: Light green blotches appear on the surface of leaves, answered by downy patches on the underside. These patches dry out, and the leaves curl and are shed by the plant. Severe defoliation can occur. Affected grapes shrivel and turn brown. Shoot tips can also be affected. If the infection occurs at fruiting time, irregular fruit set occurs. Later infections can result in mummified fruits.
Plants affected: Grapevines.
Prevention and control: Cut back and dispose of diseased growth. To prevent a recurrence the next year, spray in spring with mancozeb or copper hydroxide. (On fruiting plants, avoid spraying when the flowers are open or when this could damage developing fruit.)

GREEN ALGAE
Pleurococcus spp.
Definition: Algae are simple organisms that can multiply rapidly, especially in humid weather conditions.
Symptoms and damage: A thick green deposit appears on leaves.
Plants affected: Rhododendrons (*Rhododendron*), especially where crowded together. Other woody plants can also be affected.
Prevention and control: There is no effective control for algal

Below: Downy mildew may cause grapevine leaves to drop.

Above: Green algae is immediately recognizable by its characteristic green colouring and soft texture.

growth on plants. Where possible, wash off with soapy water and rinse well with water. Thin out congested plants and prune the remainder to improve air circulation round the stems.

BLACK BLOTCH (delphiniums)
Pseudomonas delphinii
Definition: A fungal disease of delphiniums. It is difficult to control.
Symptoms and damage: Black blotches appear on leaves, spreading to stems and flowers.
Plants affected: Delphiniums (*Delphinium*).
Prevention and control: Remove affected leaves as soon as they are seen.

SCAB (gladioli)
Pseudomonas marginata
Definition: A soil-borne fungal disease of gladioli; it can cause particular problems in periods of wet weather.

Below: The dark blotches on this delphinium indicate black blotch.

Symptoms and damage: Red-brown specks, which grow bigger and darker, appear on leaves. In wet weather, affected plants can collapse. The base of an affected corm is pitted with circular craters with raised margins.
Plants affected: Gladioli (*Gladiolus*).
Prevention and control: Destroy plants and corms that have been affected. Do not replant the same area with gladioli the next season. If the disease has occurred on only a few plants, dust healthy corms with sulphur prior to storage.

HALO BLIGHT (beans)
Pseudomonas phaseolicola
Definition: A seed-borne bacterial disease that affects certain leguminous crops.
Symptoms and damage: Irregular, angular spots surrounded by a lighter "halo" appear on leaves. Lesions later develop on stems and pods. These turn brown, but are white-encrusted in wet weather.
Plants affected: Dwarf, French and also runner beans.
Prevention and control: Control is not possible. Once it appears, all plants are likely to be infected. At the end of the season, destroy them. To prevent occurrences, buy only disease-resistant seeds.

Below: This French bean shows the characteristic lesions of halo blight.

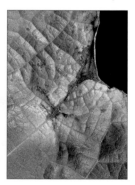

BACTERIAL CANKER
Pseudomonas syringae,
P. mors-prunorum
Definition: A bacterial disease of certain trees and shrubs.
Symptoms and damage: Flat, elongated lesions appear on branches, exuding a sticky gum. Occasionally, no further damage ensues, but typically, the following season, leaf buds on affected branches either fail to open or are narrow, curled and yellow; die-back then follows. Alternatively, leaves are spotted with brown; this tissue then falls away to leave holes as for shot hole (*Stigmina carpophila*).
Plants affected: Flowering almonds and cherries (*Prunus*).
Prevention and control: Cut back affected shoots. Spray with Bordeaux mixture from midsummer to mid-autumn.

ANGULAR LEAF SPOT (cucurbits)
Pseudomonas syringae pv. *lachrymans*
Definition: A widespread bacterial disease, spread by rainfall and in dew, that affects cucurbits. It can be troublesome during warm, wet weather.
Symptoms and damage: Small, angular, water-soaked spots appear on leaves, turning yellow

Above: Angular leaf spot is in an advanced state on these leaves.

to brown. These exude a brown fluid on the undersides of the leaves. The spots then dry out and the affected tissue falls away to leave holes. Spots can also occur on leaf stalks, stems and fruits; the tissue beneath rots deep into the flesh. Immature fruits can be shed.
Plants affected: Cucumbers, melons, summer squash and other cucurbits.
Prevention and control: Spray with copper oxychloride or copper hydroxide. If plants are only lightly affected, remove leaves that show symptoms, preferably before any fluid is released. Dig up and destroy more severely affected plants. Choose disease-resistant varieties and plant in a fresh site each year. Do not save seed from affected crops.

Below: Gumming has appeared on the older stem of this shrub and the leaves have the characteristic signs of bacterial canker

PEPPERY LEAF SPOT
Pseudomonas syringae pv. *maculicola*
Definition: A bacterial disease of brassicas that can be a particular problem with young plants during spells of warm, wet weather.
Symptoms and damage: Small, purplish or brown spots appear on leaves, eventually merging. Leaves turn yellow and can be shed from the plant. They can also become puckered. Cauliflower heads can show small grey or brown spots in cool, damp weather.
Plants affected: Mainly cauliflowers; also broccoli and Brussels sprouts.
Prevention and control: Remove any affected plants as soon as symptoms are noticed. Sow disease-free seed and start seedlings off in a sterile compost (soil mix). Practise crop rotation.

BACTERIAL BLIGHT (mulberries)
Pseudomonas syringae pv. *mori*
Definition: A bacterial disease of mulberries.
Symptoms and damage: Young leaves can turn black as they are emerging in spring. The infected leaves develop small brown or black angular spots and are distorted. Cankers can

Below: This seedling cabbage leaf shows signs of peppery leaf spot.

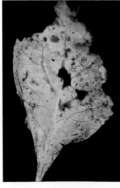

Above: Yellow patches on runner bean leaves indicate halo blight.

appear on young shoots. Die-back occurs.
Plants affected: Mulberries.
Prevention and control: Spray with copper oxychloride just before the leaves emerge, repeating the spraying two weeks later. (Further applications may be necessary.) Prune off and destroy all affected growth as soon as it is noticed. Prune out and destroy dead shoots in autumn.

HALO BLIGHT OF BEANS (beans)
Pseudomonas syringae pv. *phaseolicola*
Definition: A bacterial disease of *Phaseolus* (French, Lima and scarlet runner beans) and other legumes, introduced into gardens on infected seed and spread by wind and rain.
Symptoms and damage: Young plants are yellow and stunted, and the disease spreads to healthy plants. Angular spots appear on leaves. Water-soaked or greasy spots can appear on pods and stems, exuding a white slime in humid conditions. Plants can die.
Plants affected: French beans and other types of bean; other legumes can be affected.
Prevention and control: Spray the plants with copper oxychloride or copper hydroxide. Plant disease-free seed and remove any young plants with signs of infection. Practise crop rotation.

BACTERIAL BLIGHT (peas, sweet peas)
Pseudomonas syringae pv. *pisi*

Definition: A bacterial disease of certain legumes that is most likely to occur in damp weather. It sometimes occurs following frost damage and is introduced on infected seed.

Symptoms and damage: Stems show water-soaked spots near ground level. The spots darken and stems shrivel. Yellow lesions appear on leaflets and stipules, which turn brown and papery. Dark green spots appear on pods, which then turn dark brown. The young pods shrivel.

Plants affected: Peas, sweet peas (*Lathyrus odoratus*) and some related plants.

Prevention and control: Plant disease-free seed; rotate crops.

BACTERIAL GALL (oleanders)
Pseudomonas syringae pv. *savastanoi*, oleander strain

Definition: A bacterial disease of oleanders that apparently enters plants through wounds caused by either pruning or insect activity.

Symptoms and damage: Swellings appear on young stems; they split and develop as rough, irregular cankers. Woody galls appear on midribs or seed pods. Leaves can be twisted and flowers can also be damaged.

Below: Wet lesions on these pea pods are caused by bacterial blight.

Plants affected: Oleanders (*Nerium*).

Prevention and control: Prune damaged stems and destroy the prunings. Disinfect the tools used between each cut to prevent spreading the infection. Water and fertilize plants to keep them growing strongly.

BACTERIAL BROWN SPOT (beans)
Pseudomonas syringae pv. *syringae*

Definition: A bacterial disease that is encouraged by cool, wet weather. It sometimes occurs on plants that have suffered frost damage or have been affected by rust. *Pseudomonas syringae* pv. *syringae* also causes bacterial canker and lilac blight (see individual entries below).

Symptoms and damage: Small, brown-red spots appear on leaves; the spots dry out and fall away. Sunken brown spots appear on pods. The disease can enter seed.

Plants affected: French beans and also kidney beans.

Prevention and control: Spray with copper hydroxide or copper oxychloride. Pull up and destroy affected plants and those close by. Practise crop rotation, and sow disease-free seed of resistant varieties.

BACTERIAL CANKER (stone fruits)
Pseudomonas syringae pv. *syringae*

Definition: A bacterial disease of stone fruits (those with pits) and some other plants. It enters plants through wounds made between autumn and early spring (including scars left from natural occurrences such as leaf fall), particularly during wet, windy weather. Damage is worst on young trees.

Symptoms and damage: New shoots wilt and die back; in severe cases, whole branches can die. Buds can die and leaves show brown spots. Dark, sunken spots appear on fruits.

Plants affected: All stone fruits, especially apricots and cherries; nectarines, peaches and plums are less susceptible.

Prevention and control: Spray with copper or Bordeaux mixture, at leaf fall and then at intervals throughout the dormant season. Prune vulnerable trees only when they are in active growth, so that wounds heal quickly, cutting out all badly affected leaves. Avoid accidental damage to plant tissues from lawnmowers, while mowing around trees, and other garden machinery. Badly affected young trees are best replaced.

LILAC BLIGHT, Bacterial Leaf Spot
Pseudomonas syringae pv. *syringae*

Definition: A fungal disease of lilacs. It can spread rapidly in wet weather.

Symptoms and damage: Angular, brown, water-soaked spots appear on leaves and young stems. Shoots bend, blacken and wither. The symptoms are similar to those caused by frost damage.

Plants affected: Lilacs (*Syringa*), especially white-flowered varieties.

Prevention and control: Cut back diseased wood to healthy growth. Avoid using nitrogen-high fertilizers that encourage soft, sappy growth. Spray with copper oxychloride.

Below: This cherry tree is infected with bacterial canker.

Above: This lilac leaf and stalk have been damaged by lilac blight.

BOX BLIGHT, Cylindrocladium Blight
Pseudonectria rousseliana, other fungi

Definition: A serious disease of box, which can cause the death of established box hedges. The infection is believed to enter plants through pruning wounds. At present, it is localized to certain geographical areas.

Symptoms and damage: Leaves turn brown and are shed by the plant; in severe cases, whole branches can be killed. In wet weather, pinkish or greyish growths may be observed on the undersides of leaves.

Plants affected: Box (*Buxus sempervirens*).

Prevention and control: Cut back all affected leaves and branches, and collect and destroy any fallen leaves from around the plants. Inspect plants in nurseries thoroughly before buying. Some varieties are believed to be immune to the disease.

Below: This box hedge has almost been destroyed by box blight.

Above: Wet and damp have encouraged downy mildew.

DOWNY MILDEW (cucurbits)
Pseudoperonospora cubensis
Definition: A fungal disease of cucurbits that can be severe in moist conditions.
Symptoms and damage: Yellow spots appear on the upper surfaces of leaves. A furry, purplish growth develops beneath each spot. Badly affected leaves can wither and die. (This fungus can also affect lettuces and radishes: *see under Bremia latucae*.)
Plants affected: Cucumbers (many) and cantaloupe melons (most); pumpkins and other squashes are generally affected only in very wet weather.
Prevention and control: Spray with mancozeb, zineb or copper oxychloride. Repeated applications may be necessary, depending on the weather. Remove and destroy affected leaves. Plant resistant cultivars.

ALLIUM RUST (alliums)
Puccinia allii
Definition: A fungal disease affecting members of the onion family (including ornamentals), most often occurring on ground with high nitrogen levels. Affected plants still produce edible crops.
Symptoms and damage: Pustules of bright orange or yellow spores appear on leaves.
Plants affected: Leeks (usually); sometimes chives, shallots and garlic; also ornamental alliums.
Prevention and control: None available. Strip off and destroy affected parts. In the vegetable garden, grow plants in a new site each year. Where nitrogen levels are known to be high, top-dress with potash prior to planting or sowing.

SNAPDRAGON RUST
Puccinia antirrhini
Definition: A fungal disease of *Antirrhinum* that is most likely to occur during periods of cool, damp weather.
Symptoms and damage: Pale raised spots appear on the underside of leaves. These split to release powdery, red-brown spores. If the fungus girdles the plant's stems, the entire plant can be killed.
Plants affected: Snapdragons (*Antirrhinum*).

Above: These snapdragon leaves have pale-coloured pustules on the underside, a sign of rust.

Prevention and control: Spray regularly with zineb. Choose resistant varieties and sow disease-free seed.

CHRYSANTHEMUM RUST
Puccinia chrysanthemi
Definition: A fungal disease of chrysanthemums that is most likely to occur during periods of wet weather.
Symptoms and damage: Blister-like swellings appear on the underside of leaves. Plants wither and growth slows down.
Plants affected: Chrysanthemums (*Chrysanthemum*); some varieties are more resistant than others.
Prevention and control: Dust with sulphur or spray with sulphur or zineb. Cut off and dispose of diseased leaves as soon as they are noticed. Plant resistant varieties.

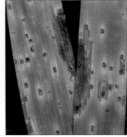

Above: Despite the damage to its leaves from iris rust, this iris will probably survive.

IRIS RUST
Puccinia iridis
Definition: A fungal disease of irises. It is worst in warm, humid weather.
Symptoms and damage: Red, powdery spots appear on leaves; the surrounding tissue then turns yellow. Whole leaves may die back, but plants generally survive.
Plants affected: Irises (*Iris*) (chiefly the rhizomatous varieties).
Prevention and control: Dust with sulphur or spray with sulphur or zineb. Cut back affected leaves. Thin plants to relieve congestion, if necessary.

ENGLISH MARIGOLD RUST
Puccinia lagenophorae
Definition: A serious fungal disease that attacks members of Compositae; it can be difficult

Below: Garlic leaves showing signs of allium rust.

Below: Chrysanthemum rust shows as blister-like swellings on the undersides of the leaves.

Below: This marigold is suffering from a severe attack of rust.

Above: Mint rust pustules can be seen on these mint leaves.

Above: Pelargonium rust has caused the red blisters on this leaf.

Above: The rust pustules underneath this leaf indicate fuchsia rust.

to control once established. It is worst in warm, humid weather.
Symptoms and damage: Pale greenish-yellow spots appear on the upper surface of leaves, and sometimes on stems and flower stalks. Small, cup-like forms appear on leaves.
Plants affected: *Cineraria*, *Lagenophora*, *Senecio* and other members of Compositae, including weeds.
Prevention and control: Spray with zineb or sulphur. Dig up and dispose of affected plants.

MINT RUST
Puccinia menthae
Definition: A fungal disease of mint.
Symptoms and damage: New shoots are distorted and covered in small orange pustules. The infection passes to the leaves, which show spots on the upper surface, wither and are shed. Plants usually recover.
Plants affected: Mint (*Mentha*).
Prevention and control: Cut back affected growth. If the plant is seriously affected, burn off the topgrowth in autumn, and propagate fresh stock from root cuttings that have been washed in cold, then hot (to 45°C/115°F), then cold water.

PELARGONIUM RUST
Puccinia pelargonii-zonalis
Definition: A common fungal disease of some pelargoniums; it can cause serious problems in hot, humid weather.

Symptoms and damage: Small green spots appear on the upper leaf surfaces, with corresponding blisters on the undersides.
Plants affected: Zonal pelargoniums (*Pelargonium*); also ivy-leaved and regal varieties.
Prevention and control: Spray with zineb or sulphur at regular intervals. Cut off and dispose of affected leaves. Do not feed with a nitrogenous fertilizer, which would encourage too much soft, leafy growth.

PANSY RUST
Puccinia violae
Definition: A fungal disease of pansies.
Symptoms and damage: Stems are swollen and have pustules containing spores that are initially yellowish-orange, but later turn brown.
Plants affected: Pansies (*Viola*).
Prevention and control: Destroy all affected plants.

FUCHSIA RUST
Pucciniastrum epilobii
Definition: A fungal disease of fuchsias.
Symptoms and damage: Purplish-red blotches appear on upper leaves. These areas dry out and turn brown.
Plants affected: Fuchsias (*Fuchsia*); some varieties are more susceptible than others.
Prevention and control: Spray with zineb or sulphur. Cut off and dispose of leaves that show signs of disease.

RHODODENDRON BUD BLAST
Pycnostysanus azaleae
Definition: A fungal disease of rhododendrons that is believed to enter plants through wounds caused by rhododendron leafhoppers (*Graphocephala fennahi*).
Symptoms and damage: In spring, flower buds turn brown, black or silver, and are later covered with bristle-like black fungal spores. The flowers fail to open, but the buds remain firm and on the plant for two to three years.
Plants affected: *Rhododendron*.
Prevention and control: Cut off and destroy affected buds. Control the leafhoppers.

Below: This rhododendron bud has turned brown, and has black bristly spores of rhododendron bud blast.

ROOT ROT
Pythium spp., see under *Aphanomyces euteiches*.

BLACK STEM ROTS (pelargoniums)
Pythium spp.
Definition: A soil-borne fungal disease of pelargoniums that is most likely to occur in wet soil conditions.
Symptoms and damage: Stems blacken and wither from the base of the plant upwards. Plants wilt and die.
Plants affected: Pelargoniums (*Pelargonium*) (regal, ivy-leaved and zonal).
Prevention and control: Spray the soil with a suitable fungicide. Pull up and destroy affected plants.

BLACK PSEUDOBULB ROT (orchids)
Pythium ultimum
Definition: A fungus that affects orchids with pseudobulbs.
Symptoms and damage: Either the top or the base of the pseudobulb turns brown or black. If the disease starts at the base, the leaves turn yellow and wilt.
Plants affected: Orchids, especially varieties of *Cymbidium*.
Prevention and control: Drench the pot with furalaxyl. Avoid overwatering and check that the plant has adequate drainage. Discard any plant that is badly affected.

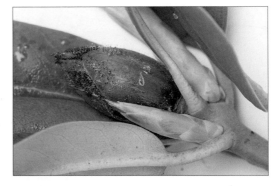

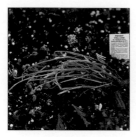

Above: This winter pansy has died after an attack of pansy sickness.

PANSY SICKNESS
Pythium violae; other fungi

Definition: A fungal disease of pansies and violas. The fungus builds up in the soil, where it can persist for several years.

Symptoms and damage: Plants wilt and leaves turn yellow. In severe cases, plants die.

Plants affected: Pansies and violas (*Viola*).

Prevention and control: Dig up and destroy affected plants. Do not replant the same area with pansies or violas. Plant replacements on a fresh site where *Viola* has not been grown before.

SHOOT BLIGHT
(eucalyptus)
Ramularia pitereka

Definition: A fungal disease of eucalyptus and some other related plants. It most

Below: The pale brown spots on these rhubarb stems are caused by rhubarb leaf spot.

commonly occurs in spring and autumn on plants under glass.

Symptoms and damage: Young shoots are whitened and distorted. Brown spots appear on leaves, sometimes merging as irregular patches. Badly affected young plants can die.

Plants affected: Eucalyptus (*Eucalyptus*) such as *E. eximia, E. ficifolia* and *E. maculata*; also *Angophora hispida*.

Prevention and control: Spray with copper oxychloride. Repeated applications may be necessary. Ventilate plants under glass well to improve air circulation.

RHUBARB LEAF SPOT
Ramularia rhei

Definition: An unsightly, though not serious, fungal disease of rhubarb.

Symptoms and damage: Irregular brown spots appear on leaves, which then fall away to leave holes.

Plants affected: Rhubarb.

Prevention and control: Cut off and destroy affected leaves and stems. Apply a foliar feed to boost vigour if the plant is severely affected.

WHITE MOULD
Ramularia vallisumbrosae

Definition: A fungal disease of *Narcissus* that can be particularly troublesome during damp weather. It tends to be localized

Below: These curled *Narcissus* leaves have lesions down one side, indicating white mould.

Above: A bean plant with stem damage due to collar rot.

to specific geographical areas.

Symptoms and damage: Dark greenish or yellowish-brown patches appear on the leaves (especially towards the tips). If the weather is damp, powdery white fungal spores form.

Plants affected: Daffodils (*Narcissus*).

Prevention and control: Dig up and destroy affected bulbs.

COLLAR ROT,
Rhizoctonia Disease
Rhizoctonia solani

Definition: A fungal disease that affects a range of plants, usually in the early stages of growth. It is most likely to occur in warm weather during late spring and autumn. *Rhizoctonia solani* has a number of strains that attack a range of

plants (*see under* rhizoctonia scab). (Collar rots can also be caused by other fungi.)

Symptoms and damage: *Stocks:* Leaves wilt and there are sunken patches at the base of stems. *Beans:* Reddish sunken areas appear just above ground level.

Plants affected: A wide range, including French beans; also seedlings of other vegetables; ornamental annuals and perennials.

Prevention and control: Pull up and discard any badly affected plants.

RHIZOCTONIA SCAB (potatoes)
Rhizoctonia solani

Definition: A fungal disease of potatoes that affects plants in cool, damp conditions.

Below: Black fungal bodies of rhizoctonia scab on potatoes.

Symptoms and damage: Young shoots can rot before they emerge from the ground. On older plants, leaves show red and yellow areas. Leaves can curl, and growth is bunched at the top of the plant. Tubers can show cracks or depressions or be otherwise distorted. Black lumps are fungal resting bodies, capable of persisting in the soil for several years.
Plants affected: Potatoes.
Prevention and control: Plant disease-free tubers. Practise crop rotation.

WIRESTEM FUNGUS
Rhizoctonia solani, see *Thanatephorus cucumeris*.

GREY BULB ROT
Rhizoctonia tuliparum, syn. *Sclerotium tuliparum*
Definition: A soil-borne fungal disease that attacks bulbs.
Symptoms and damage: Bulbs fail to shoot or produce short growth only. A dry, grey rot attacks the bulb from the tip, which then rots completely. The fungus's black resting bodies stay in the soil to infect bulbs the next season.
Plants affected: Hyacinths (*Hyacinthus*); also colchicums (*Colchicum*), crocuses (*Crocus*), fritillaries (*Fritillaria*), gladioli (*Gladiolus*), ixias (*Ixia*), daffodils

(*Narcissus*) and tulips (*Tulipa*).
Prevention and control: Dig up and destroy affected plants. The soil surrounding bulbs, which may harbour the disease, should also be removed and disposed of. Grow susceptible bulbs in a fresh site each season.

CORE ROT (crocus, freesias, gladioli)
Sclerotinia draytonii
Definition: A fungal disease that (usually) attacks corms in storage.
Symptoms and damage: Corms darken and become spongy, and may rot. Less severely affected corms may grow, but are susceptible to *Botrytis* and may produce spotted flowers.
Plants affected: Crocuses (*Crocus*), freesias (*Freesia*) and gladioli (*Gladiolus*).
Prevention and control: After lifting for storage, dust corms with sulphur dust.

BROWN ROT OF STONE FRUIT
Sclerotinia fructicola, *S. laxa*
Definition: Fungal diseases that are favoured by humid or showery weather. Spores can also be spread by the dried-fruit beetle.

Below: This *Prunus* is suffering from an attack of brown rot.

Symptoms and damage: Flowers turn brown and die. The fungi penetrate into the stem, and die-back can occur. Infection can also happen as the fruits are ripening. A small brown spot appears on the skin and the whole fruit rots within a few days. Affected fruits are either shed from the plant or are retained on the stems, shrivelling and becoming mummified.
Plants affected: Stone fruits (US: those with pits); ornamental quince (*Chaenomeles*). Apples and pears can also suffer.
Prevention and control: Spray with copper oxychloride. Remove diseased fruits and pick up shed ones. Prune to improve air circulation.

YELLOWS, Dry Rot
Sclerotinia gladioli, see under *Fusarium oxysporum* f. sp. *gladioli*.

SMOULDER
Sclerotinia narcissicola
Definition: An air-borne fungal disease that affects daffodil and narcissus bulbs, either in storage or when in growth, particularly if the season is cold and wet.
Symptoms and damage: Masses of grey spores appear on the plant, and affected leaves die back. In warm, dry weather, only a few leaves are likely to be affected, and bulbs can flower normally. Flattened black resting bodies of the fungus form on bulbs.
Plants affected: Daffodils (*Narcissus*).
Prevention and control: If the bulb is only lightly affected, cut off damaged leaves. Where the disease is known to be a problem, lift bulbs when dormant. Destroy any that bear the resting bodies of the fungus and dust the remainder with sulphur before storing in cool, dry conditions.

Above: The leaves and stem bases of these narcissi have been affected by smoulder.

WHITE ROT (alliums)
Sclerotium cepivorum
Definition: A troublesome fungal disease that affects *Allium*, both edible and ornamental varieties. The fungus can overwinter in the soil as small black resting bodies, and can persist for many years. It is easily spread on tools and the soles of footwear.
Symptoms and damage: Leaves turn yellow and die back. Bulbs of affected plants have a white, fluffy growth at the base and on the roots. Large numbers of small black sclerotia develop.
Plants affected: Onions, shallots and leeks; ornamental alliums.
Prevention and control: Destroy affected plants before the resting bodies develop. Do not replant

Below: An onion bulb that has been attacked by white rot.

Above: The collapsing stem of this sunflower indicates sclerotinia rot.

an affected area with alliums. Grow crops on a fresh site each year. Clean tools and footwear after use. Raise plants from seed to ensure disease-free stock. The use of carbendazim to control neck rot (*Botrytis allii*) can give some immunity to white rot.

SCLEROTINIA DISEASES, Sclerotinia Rot, Sclerotinia Wilt, White Mould
Sclerotinia sclerotiorum, other *Sclerotinia* spp.
Definition: A soil-borne fungal disease that has a wide host range. It can also affect roots and tubers in storage.
Symptoms and damage: The lower parts of plants are usually attacked first. Stems rot quickly and can show a fluffy white fungal growth. (On Jerusalem artichokes this usually appears on the insides of the stems, and the evidence of the attack is seen only if the stems are broken.) Hard black resting bodies form, which can overwinter in the soil to affect plants the following year. Flowers and buds are often attacked by a wet rot. Affected food plants are inedible. Stored carrots show a white, fluffy fungal growth that then forms hard black resting bodies up to 1cm (⅜in) long. Dahlia and

sunflower stems decay and collapse; fluffy fungal growth develops within the stems rather than appearing outside. The disease can be present in dahlia tubers.
Plants affected: Most garden plants, including ornamentals; susceptible vegetables include celery and celeriac, carrots, cucurbits and Jerusalem artichokes.
Prevention and control: Lift and destroy any affected plants as soon as possible, ideally before the resting bodies form. Crop rotation should still be practised, but it offers limited control because the host range of the disease is so wide. Grow resistant varieties as far as possible. Space plants correctly to improve air circulation. *Jerusalem artichokes:* Watch carefully for any signs of rotting. Grow vulnerable plants on a fresh site the following year, to minimize the risk of reinfection. *Carrots:* Store healthy roots only. *Dahlias:* Do not store tubers if the growing plant succumbed to the disease.

SCLEROTIUM STEM ROT, Southern Blight
Sclerotium rolfsii
Definition: A fungal disease, common in warm climates, that develops most rapidly at temperatures above 27°C

Below: The yellowing leaves on this chrysanthemum indicate the presence of sclerotium stem rot.

(85°F) in soils that are rich in organic matter. Alternate wetting and drying of the soil surface encourages the fungus into growth.
Symptoms and damage: Leaves yellow and wilt. At soil level, water-soaked lesions appear on plants, either girdling stems or progressing up the plant. Later, a white growth covers the infected area of the plant and can spread on to the surrounding soil.
Plants affected: A wide range, including beans, rhubarb, beetroot (beets), melons, carrots, peanuts, peas, peppers, potatoes, sweet potatoes and tomatoes. Susceptible ornamentals include dahlias (*Dahlia*), carnations (*Dianthus*) and irises (*Iris*).
Prevention and control: Pull up and destroy infected plants, and also remove topsoil around the plants (to a diameter of 20cm [8in]). Practise crop rotation and make sure that vulnerable plants are not grown in the same soil for two to three years. (Grasses and corn are known to be immune.)

CYPRESS CANKER (cypresses)
Seiridium spp.
Definition: A fungal disease of cypresses, which usually attacks plants as a result of damage previously caused by insects or other agency.
Symptoms and damage: Splits

Above: The characteristic brown spots of leaf spot have affected this celery plant.

in bark exude resin. If the area of affected bark girdles the stem, the whole branch (or even the whole tree) can die back.
Plants affected: Cypress (*Cupressus* and *Chamaecyparis*). *Cupressus glabra, C. torulosa* and *C. lusitanica* show some resistance.
Prevention and control: If trees are severely affected, dig them up and destroy them. Replace them with different species.

LEAF SPOT, Late Blight (celery)
Septoria apiicola
Definition: A fungus that affects the leaves and (sometimes) stalks of celery plants. Specially treated seed is available to ensure crops that are immune to the disease. The fungus is favoured by cool, moist weather conditions. (If wet weather persists, damage can be severe.)
Symptoms and damage: Small brown spots appear, mainly on the leaves, developing into black fruiting bodies. In severe cases of the disease, whole leaves can wither and die. The yields of affected plants are much reduced.
Plants affected: Celery, especially self-blanching varieties.
Prevention and control: Ideally, raise crops from treated or

Above: Blackcurrant leaf spot appears as light, angular spots with purple edges.

disease-free seed. At the first sign of infection, spray thoroughly with carbendazim, mancozeb or a copper fungicide such as Bordeaux mixture. Repeated sprayings, at two-weekly intervals, may be necessary. The disease is difficult to control with fungicides if the weather is suitable for the fungus. Practise crop rotation.

LEAF SPOT (gerbera)
Septoria gerberae
Definition: A fungal disease of gerberas that is most likely to occur during wet weather in late summer or autumn.
Symptoms and damage: Brown to purple spots on leaves develop purplish rings at their edges. Patches of the leaves can die.
Plants affected: Gerberas (*Gerbera*).
Prevention and control: Cut off affected growth and spray with copper oxychloride.

HARD ROT (gladioli)
Septoria gladioli
Definition: A fungal disease of gladioli that can spread rapidly during wet weather.
Symptoms and damage: Tiny, brown spots appear on both leaf surfaces. Black fruiting bodies appear on the spots.

Plants affected: Gladioli (*Gladiolus*).
Prevention and control: Destroy affected plants. When lifting corms, dust them with sulphur, then store in cool, dry conditions.

SEPTORIA SPOT (passion fruit)
Septoria passifloricola
Definition: A fungal disease of passion fruit.
Symptoms and damage: Spots appear on leaves and/or fruits. Affected leaves can be shed by the plant. Spots on fruits are light brown and can enlarge until they cover a large area. Fruiting is impaired, though affected fruits are still edible.
Plants affected: Passion fruit and granadillas.
Prevention and control: Spray with mancozeb.

Below: These chrysanthemum leaves have been severely affected by chrysanthemum leaf spot.

BLACKCURRANT LEAF SPOT (currants)
Septoria ribis
Definition: A fungal disease that is common when the weather is wet during spring and summer.
Symptoms and damage: Leaves show angular, pale grey spots with purple edges. Leaves can be shed from the plant. Plants lose their vigour and cropping is impaired.
Plants affected: Currants.
Prevention and control: Spray the plants with copper oxychloride as they start into growth. Repeat this spraying treatment when the fruit is half-formed.

CHRYSANTHEMUM LEAF SPOTS
Septoria spp.
Definition: A fungal disease of chrysanthemums that is worst in wet weather.
Symptoms and damage: Yellow areas appear on leaves, often near the edges. These turn brown and merge. Leaves can be shed.
Plants affected: Chrysanthemum (*Chrysanthemum*).
Prevention and control: Spray with zineb or copper oxychloride.

CORN LEAF BLIGHT (NORTHERN)
Setospaeria turcica, see *Exserohilum turcicum*.

Above: Though this fruit has been affected by citrus scab and is visually unappealing, its flavour will not suffer.

CITRUS SCAB
Sphaceloma fawcettii var. *scabiosa*
Definition: A fungal disease of citrus that occurs most commonly during cool, damp weather following a dry spell. Fruits are susceptible only up to about ten weeks after half-petal fall. The flesh of affected fruits is unimpaired, but the disease should be treated because the growth of the tree will also be distorted.
Symptoms and damage: Leaves display brown, pink or grey scabs. Some developing fruits are shed. The remainder grow unnaturally large and develop scabby areas and warty growths on their skins.
Plants affected: Citrus, especially lemons; limes ('Rangpur'), calamondins, some varieties of tangelo and mandarins ('Unshiu') are vulnerable. Sweet oranges are usually immune.
Prevention and control: After half-petal fall in spring, spray the trees with copper oxychloride and white oil. Spray again with zineb towards the end of summer. Prune back all affected growth to healthy wood and destroy the prunings.

Above: Anthracnose is an unsightly condition that affects roses.

ANTHRACNOSE (roses)
Sphaeceloma rosarum
Definition: A fungal disease of roses that is worse during cool, humid weather.
Symptoms and damage: Small black spots appear on leaves. As they enlarge, the centre drops out. Leaves turn yellow (though less than with black spot). Spots occasionally appear on both stems and flowers.
Plants affected: Roses (*Rosa*).
Prevention and control: Spray with copper oxychloride. Sprays for black spot will usually also control anthracnose. Prune plants carefully to improve air circulation through the stems.

VIOLET SCAB (pansies and violets)
Sphaceloma violae
Definition: A fungal disease of violets and pansies. It can be a problem if plants are congested.
Symptoms and damage: Tiny, water-soaked spots appear on stems, leaves and flower stalks. These enlarge into irregularly shaped grey patches; affected tissue becomes scabby and falls off. Growth is distorted. Badly affected plants can die.

Plants affected: Pansies and violets (*Viola*).
Prevention and control: Spray with zineb. Cut off affected plant parts. Thin plants if necessary to improve air circulation around them.

AMERICAN GOOSEBERRY MILDEW (gooseberries and blackcurrants)
Sphaerotheca mors-uvae
Definition: A fungal disease of certain soft fruits, associated with stagnant air.

Below: This gooseberry plant has been damaged by American gooseberry mildew.

Symptoms and damage: A white powdery coating appears in patches on young leaves, shoots and fruits, later turning brown. Affected shoots sometimes become distorted.
Plants affected: Gooseberries and blackcurrants.
Prevention and control: Cut out and dispose of affected material in late summer. Prune to keep the centres of bushes open to improve circulation of air throughout the plant. Avoid nitrogen-high fertilizers that promote sappy growth, which is generally more vulnerable to disease. Look for resistant cultivars. Bushes can be sprayed with copper oxychloride or a systemic fungicide when the flowers open.

Above: These pyracantha berries have sunken areas that are discoloured – the effects of scab.

SCAB (pyracanthas)
Spilocaea pyracanthae
Definition: A fungal disease of pyracanthas.
Symptoms and damage: Olive green or brown blotches appear on leaves, which are then shed by the plant. The surface of fruits is blemished with brown or black scabs, causing cracking in severe cases. Whole clusters of fruits may be blackened.
Plants affected: Firethorn (*Pyracantha*).
Prevention and control: Dispose of shed leaves to prevent spores overwintering. Spray plants with a systemic fungicide or mancozeb. Severely affected plants should be dug up and destroyed. Varieties resistant to scab are available.

Below: Powdery scab has infected this potato, creating brown blisters on its skin.

Above: Fused leaves and flowers with leaf scorch.

POWDERY SCAB, Corky Scab

Spongospora subterranea

Definition: A soil-borne fungal disease that occurs on wet ground and/or during a wet growing season. It is most common where potatoes have been grown in the same ground over a number of seasons.

Symptoms and damage: Scabs (brown, blister-like swellings) appear on the surface of the tubers. When these burst they release brown powdery spores that contaminate the soil. (A canker form of the disease can also occur, resulting in malformed tubers.)

Plants affected: Potatoes; also tomatoes and other members of Solanaceae (including weeds).

Prevention and control: Destroy affected tubers and do not replant the site with potatoes (or any related crops) for at least three years. Plant disease-free tubers.

LEAF SCORCH, Tip Burn

Stagonospora curtisii

Definition: A fungal disease of bulbs (including those grown under cover). It is most likely to develop in warm, humid conditions.

Symptoms and damage: The fungus appears at the tops of the bulb scales and symptoms

appear as growth emerges. Brown blotches appear on the leaves (towards the base on *Hippeastrum*), flower stalks and petals, producing a scorched appearance. Leaves can stick together. Affected parts can turn slimy and rot. Scales can develop dark red-brown spots.

Plants affected: *Hippeastrum, Crinum* and other members of Amaryllidaceae; also snowdrops (*Galanthus*) and daffodils (*Narcissus*).

Prevention and control: Spray with copper oxychloride. Cut out and destroy all affected growth. Dust cut surfaces with sulphur. Dust the bulbs with sulphur when dormant; discard badly affected ones.

STRAWBERRY LEAF SPOT

Stagonospora fragariae, see under Diplocarpon earlianum.

SILVER LEAF

Stereum purpureum, see Chondrosternum purpureum.

SHOT HOLE

Stigmina carpophila

Definition: A fungus that attacks certain poorly growing fruit trees.

Symptoms and damage: Small brown spots appear on leaves,

which later fall away to leave holes. These can be of irregular shape if the spots have merged. On apricot trees, brown scabs appear on fruits and gum is exuded. Fruits can crack. Spotting can also occur on twigs, and gum is exuded. If the infection girdles the stem, die-back can occur.

Plants affected: Cherries, peaches, nectarines, apricots, plums and gages.

Prevention and control: Spray with a foliar feed to promote the plant's vigour at the first sign of disease. Further outbreaks can be treated with Bordeaux mixture. Alternatively, spray with copper oxychloride as the first flowers open. Repeat the application after leaf fall. Maintain the health of fruit trees by feeding, watering and mulching them regularly.

COMMON SCABS, Potato Scabs

Streptomyces spp., including *S. scabies*

Definition: A widespread disease of potatoes and other root vegetables that occurs most commonly on poor, sandy or gravelly soils that are lacking in humus and that tend to dry out. Caused by a bacteria-like organism that is sometimes

present in animal manures, it is encouraged by limy conditions in soil. It can be spread in rain or in wind-blown soil particles, but is sometimes also introduced into gardens on infected tubers. It is worst in dry seasons.

Symptoms and damage: Corky lesions form on the skins of tubers, eventually covering most of the surface, either as raised areas or deep pits. The disease is unsightly, though the crops are still edible. They do not store well, however. *Potatoes:* The outer skin of the tubers is scabby, but this can be peeled off before cooking. *Beetroot (beets):* Sunken or raised scabs appear on the roots, either singly or in patches.

Plants affected: Root vegetables including potatoes, beetroots, carrots, parsnips, radishes, turnips and swedes (rutabagas).

Prevention and control: Improve poor soil by adding plenty of organic matter or sowing green manure. Do not lime the soil, particularly if it is already alkaline. Practise crop rotation. Keep crops well watered during dry spells during the growing season. Look for resistant varieties of root vegetables.

LEAF CURL, Peach Leaf Curl

Taphrina deformans

Definition: A fungal infection of leaves, affecting *Prunus*. It is spread by rain and is a particular problem in areas with wet spring weather.

Symptoms and damage: Leaves become puckered, thickened and curled, showing red blisters that are later covered with pale fungal spores. The leaves later turn white and can be shed by the tree. *Apricots:* whole shoots are affected and leaves bunched together. All severely affected trees are weakened.

Plants affected: Peaches, nectarines, almonds, apricots, including ornamentals; plums can be affected by a similar

Below: The lesion and hole on this plum leaf are signs of shot hole, which attacks trees lacking vigour.

Below: Despite the scabs covering the skin, this potato will be edible when it has been peeled.

Above: Red blisters on leaves are characteristic of peach leaf curl, the spores of which are spread by rain.

disease. Some varieties are more susceptible than others.
Prevention and control: Remove and destroy all affected leaves on small trees as soon as they are noticed. To prevent recurrence of the disease, kill overwintering spores by spraying the whole tree with Bordeaux mixture, lime sulphur, copper or other fungicide in late winter. Repeat the application 10–14 days later and again at the end of the growing season once all the leaves have fallen. The disease does not respond to treatment once symptoms have become evident, so preventive measures should be taken to avoid reinfection the following year. Choose resistant or tolerant varieties. Wall-trained specimens can be covered from autumn (at leaf fall) to early spring with an open-ended plastic shelter to keep the rain off – this effectively prevents the disease, as the spores cannot germinate.

YELLOW LEAF BLISTER (poplars)
Taphrina populina
Definition: A fungal disease of poplars (*Populus*). It is not a serious problem.

Symptoms and damage: Yellow blisters appear on the undersides of leaves.
Plants affected: Poplars (*Populus*).
Prevention and control: No action is necessary.

WITCHES' BROOMS
Taphrina spp., *see under Melampsorella caryophyllacearum.*

WIRESTEM FUNGUS
Thanatephorus cucumeris, syn. *Corticium solani, Rhizoctonia solani*
Definition: A fungal disease of seedlings, both raised in the open and under glass.
Symptoms and damage: The stems of seedlings shrink, and their roots blacken and die. The seedlings collapse. Older plants can also be affected: stems become hard, brown and shrunken at the base, and continued growth is checked.
Plants affected: Brassica seedlings, particularly cauliflowers (other vegetable seedlings can also be susceptible). Affected lettuce seedlings usually then succumb to an infection of grey mould.
Prevention and control: Chemical control is not possible. Make sure the ground is adequately prepared before sowing and avoid overwatering.

Above: This maturing rice plant has been severely infected with wirestem fungus.

Under glass, use fresh, sterilized compost (soil mix). In both cases, sow thinly to avoid overcrowding.

REPLANT DISEASE
Thielaviopsis basicola (**cherries**), *Pythium spp.* (**apples**)
Definition: Fungal diseases that check the growth or even cause the death of trees growing in ground previously planted with a tree of the same kind.
Symptoms and damage: New plantings fail to make good growth and can die.
Plants affected: Cherries and apples. Other fungi may be

responsible for similar problems encountered with other species.
Prevention and control: If a cherry or apple tree has to be replaced, dig out and replace a volume of soil approximately 1m (1yd) across and deep.

ROOT ROT, Black Root Rot, Foot and Root Rot
Thielaviopsis basicola, see Aphanomyces euteiches.

PLUM RUST, Peach Rust
Tranzschelia discolor
Definition: A fungus that attacks some tree fruits. Its spores are easily dispersed on the wind. Most damage is caused when a period of warm, wet weather is followed by hot, dry weather.
Symptoms and damage: Yellow spores appear on the undersides of leaves, spreading to other leaves. If the infection is severe, the leaves will be shed prematurely, leaving the tree vulnerable to sun scorch. Affected trees are weakened, and fruiting can be impaired.
Plants affected: Plums, apricots, peaches, nectarines and other stone fruits.
Prevention and control: Collect

Below: Plum rust has caused mottling on the upper surface of this plum leaf.

Above: This forsythia shoot is covered in disfiguring galls.

and dispose of fallen leaves promptly to prevent spread of the infection and to kill overwintering spores. Spray the trees with mancozeb or copper oxychloride; later sprays of zineb or sulphur may also be necessary. Reduce the likelihood of attack by keeping trees well watered and mulched to make sure the soil does not dry out during periods of hot, dry weather.

LARCH CANKER
Trichoscyphella willkommii
Definition: A fungal disease of larches (*Larix*).
Symptoms and damage: Large, flattened cankers appear on branches and the main stem. Die-back can occur as a result. Orange, saucer-like fruiting bodies appear at the edges of the cankers.
Plants affected: Larches (*Larix*), especially *L. decidua*.
Prevention and control: Cut back all cankered growth to healthy wood. Feed, water and mulch affected trees to promote quick recovery.

FORSYTHIA GALL
unknown
Definition: A common disorder of forsythias, caused by an unidentified agent.
Symptoms and damage: Unsightly galls appear on shoots.
Plants affected: Forsythias (*Forsythia*), especially *F. x intermedia*.
Prevention and control: Cut back the affected growth, pruning to ground level, if necessary. Recovery of the shrubs is usually good.

SMUT
Urocystis anemones, U. violae
Definition: A fungal disease of cormous *Anemone, Trollius* (*Urocystis anemones*) and violets (*U. violae*).
Symptoms and damage: Leaves and stems develop blisters that burst to release powdery black spores.
Plants affected: Anemones (*Anemone*), globe flowers (*Trollius*) and violets (*Viola*).
Prevention and control: Destroy all plants that have been affected by the disease.

BEAN RUST
Uromyces appendiculatus
Definition: A fungal disease of beans, favoured by damp weather and heavy dews.
Symptoms and damage: Pale yellow spots appear on the upper sides of leaves, with corresponding blisters on the undersides. Leaves turn yellow and fall. Blisters can also appear on the pods.
Plants affected: Beans; some varieties are more resistant than others.
Prevention and control: Spray with zineb or sulphur. Dig up and dispose of plants that are badly affected.

BEET RUST
Uromyces betae
Definition: A fungal disease of *Beta*.
Symptoms and damage: Small, reddish-brown spots appear, on the older leaves first, then spreading to the younger ones.
Plants affected: Beetroot (beet), spinach beet, Swiss chard and sugar beet.
Prevention and control: Spray with zineb or wettable sulphur. Remove and destroy any affected leaves. Sow only disease-free seed.

ONION SMUT
Urocystis cepulae
Definition: A fungal disease of onions.
Symptoms and damage: On young plants, blisters appear

Above: This sugar beet leaf shows signs of an infestation of beet rust.

under the skin on new leaves and near the surface of bulbs and roots. A mass of dark spores becomes visible as the galls mature.
Plants affected: Onions.
Prevention and control: Check onion seedlings carefully and destroy affected plants.

CARNATION RUST
Uromyces dianthi
Definition: A common fungal disease of carnations, caused by humid weather. It can sometimes be seen on shop-bought flowers.
Symptoms and damage: Greyish patches appear on leaves, stems and sepals. These burst to release a mass of dark brown

Below: These broad (fava) bean leaves have the yellow spots and blisters of bean rust.

Above: This carnation has rust.

spores. Leaves curl and turn yellow. Flowering can be impaired.

Plants affected: Carnations (*Dianthus*).

Prevention and control: Dust with sulphur or spray with sulphur or zineb.

RUST GALLS (wattles)
Uromycladium spp.

Definition: An unsightly, sometimes fatal, disease of *Acacia*, caused by a variety of related fungi.

Symptoms and damage: Depending on the species, large, woody, red-brown galls or *witches' brooms* appear on stems. The galls are often invaded by insects. Severely affected plants can die.

Plants affected: Wattles (*Acacia*): different species of the fungus attack different species, producing a range of symptoms.

Prevention and control: On slightly diseased plants, prune off affected growth and feed and water well to promote recovery. Dig up and replace badly affected plants.

SMUT (sweet corn)
Ustilago maydis, U. vaillantii

Definition: A fungal disease that occurs usually only in long hot summers. Undamaged parts

of the crop develop normally.

Symptoms and damage: "Smut balls", white galls of varying size, are produced on the ears, tassels, joints, leaves and stems of sweet corn. They split open to release masses of black spores when mature.

Plants affected: Sweet corn.

Prevention and control: Irrigate plants to keep them growing evenly. Check plants regularly for smut balls, and cut them off quickly. Destroy all associated plant debris after cropping and do not replant with sweet corn for at least three years. Plant resistant varieties.

SMUT (winter aconites)
Urocystis eranthidis

Definition: A fungal disease that affects winter aconites.

Symptoms and damage: Blister-like swellings appear on leaves and leaf stalks. These then burst open to release powdery black spores.

Plants affected: Winter aconites (*Eranthis*).

Prevention and control: Destroy plants affected by the disease.

SMUT
Ustilago vaillantii

Definition: A fungal disease of certain spring-flowering bulbs.

Symptoms and damage: Anthers (sometimes also the ovaries) fail to develop normally and are replaced by masses of powdery black spores.

Above: These pears have the characteristic brown blotches of apple scab.

Plants affected: Grape hyacinths (*Muscari*), Glories-of-the-snow (*Chionodoxa*), and bluebells (*Hyacinthoides*).

Prevention and control: Destroy plants.

APPLE SCAB
Venturia inequalis, V. pirina

Definition: A fungal disease that affects certain pome fruits. Wet weather in spring seems to increase the likelihood of attack: spores are rapidly spread by rain and wind. In some countries, the condition is sometimes referred to as "black spot".

Symptoms and damage: Brownish blotches appear on leaf surfaces, and leaves can be shed from the plant. Fruits show rough olive-coloured

Below: Crab apples with apple scab.

patches that crack and become corky. If the fruits are affected when they are virtually fully formed, they will still be edible if only the surface is blemished.

Plants affected: Apples (including crab apples) and pears. 'Granny Smith' and 'Delicious' are the most susceptible.

Prevention and control: Collect and dispose of shed leaves, which can harbour fungal spores. Spray affected plants regularly with mancozeb or a systemic fungicide. Prune trees to ensure good air circulation.

VERTICILLIUM WILT
Verticillium spp., including *V. albo-atrum* and *V. dahliae*

Definition: A widespread fungal disease with a wide host range, which can persist for several years. It is favoured by cool conditions. Verticillium wilt is one of the most common and

Below: The scabbing and cracks on the skin of this apple indicate an apple scab infection.

Above: These leaves have curled and withered as a result of verticillium wilt.

troublesome diseases that affect garden plants. Symptoms vary from plant to plant.
Symptoms and damage: Plants wilt and lose vigour. Leaves curl at the edges, then turn yellow and drop. Sometimes branches die one by one or the whole plant collapses. Fruiting is impaired. *Tomatoes:* Lower leaves wilt and die; the whole plant can die. *Apricots:* Terminal leaves wilt, turn yellow and are shed. *Chrysanthemums:* Lower leaves show a pink or purple cast, turn yellow and wither. The stems are streaked with brown inside.
Plants affected: Members of Solanaceae such as tomatoes, potatoes and aubergines (eggplants), including weeds; also cucurbits, beans and other vegetables; ornamentals, such as chrysanthemums

Below: Some trees are susceptible to verticillium wilt, causing the leaves to wither and drop.

(*Chrysanthemum*) and dahlias (*Dahlia*), and some trees (fruiting and ornamental).
Prevention and control: Dig up infected plants and destroy all debris at the end of the season. Replace with new specimens in fresh soil or sterilize the soil prior to replanting. Rotate crops, though this cannot guarantee protection, since the host range is so diverse. Choose resistant varieties as far as possible. Potato tubers should be disease-free.

LEAF SPOT (grevillea)
Verrucispora spp., see under *Placoasterella baileyi*.

BACTERIAL WILT
Xanthomonas begoniae
Definition: A bacterial disease of some winter-flowering begonia hybrids.
Symptoms and damage: Leaves wilt and show spotting.
Plants affected: Begonia (*Begonia*) hybrids deriving from both *B. socotrana* and *B. dregei* grown under glass.
Prevention and control: Burn

or dispose of severely affected plants. If only lightly affected, cut back and destroy all diseased growth. Lowering the temperature and humidity can reduce risk of the disease spreading. Disinfect the greenhouse after an attack.

BLACK ROT (crucifers)
Xanthomonas campestris pv. *campestris*
Definition: A fairly common bacterial disease of brassicas and related crops. It develops most quickly during warm, wet weather, particularly where the soil is poorly drained. The disease enters plants through pores or small wounds.
Symptoms and damage: V-shaped lesions appear on leaves (usually at the edge on older plants), and leaf veins later turn black. Leaves turn yellow, dry out and are shed by the plant. In some cases, greasy-looking spots are scattered over leaves, which enlarge and tear away. Secondary rots can take hold.
Plants affected: Brassicas, especially cabbages, cauliflowers and broccoli.
Prevention and control: Pull up affected plants (they may be composted provided the resulting material is not used in conjunction with other brassicas). Keep the vegetable plots free of weeds belonging to the brassica family, which can harbour the disease. Practise crop rotation and improve the drainage if necessary on any new site used for vulnerable crops. Sow disease-free seed and/or choose varieties known to be resistant to the disease.

BACTERIAL LEAF SPOT (cucurbits)
Xanthomonas campestris pv. *cucurbitae*
Definition: A bacterial disease of cucurbits, favoured by warm, wet conditions.
Symptoms and damage: Water-soaked areas appear on the

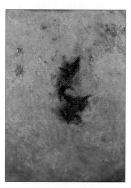

Above: Black rot is a serious disease of crucifer crops worldwide.

undersides of leaves, with corresponding yellow patches on the upper surfaces. These can merge to produce large, dead areas. Spots can also appear on young stems and petioles. Young fruits can show water-soaked spots; as the fruit matures, the flesh beneath can be affected and the disease can spread to the seeds.
Plants affected: Cucumbers, marrows, pumpkins and squashes.
Prevention and control: Spray with copper oxychloride. Sow guaranteed disease-free seed and practise crop rotation.

BLACK ROT (stocks)
Xanthomonas campestris pv. *incanae*
Definition: A bacterial disease of stocks, worst during warm, humid weather. It is introduced on infected seed, but can pass to healthy plants.
Symptoms and damage: Plants grow slowly, and can wilt and die. On older plants, lower leaves turn yellow and drop.
Plants affected: Stocks (*Matthiola*).
Prevention and control: Use guaranteed disease-free seeds. Remove promptly any plant showing signs of disease, together with the soil around the roots. Do not replant the same soil with stocks (or other crucifers) for at least two years.

WALNUT BLIGHT, Walnut Black Spot
Xanthomonas campestris pv. *juglandis*

Definition: A serious bacterial disease of walnuts. It is capable of persisting in dead buds for several seasons, and is easily spread through spring rainfall. Damage by frost and hail can render plants vulnerable to the disease.

Symptoms and damage: Small, round, water-soaked spots appear on leaves and catkins, later enlarging and turning brown. Cropping can be reduced. Infected nuts can be dropped by the tree or can contain shrivelled or rotted kernels. Young shoots can be girdled and killed (older shoots are immune).

Plants affected: Walnuts; some varieties are more susceptible than others. Seedlings are especially vulnerable.

Prevention and control: At bud burst, spray with Bordeaux mixture or copper oxychloride; repeated applications are usually necessary. Pay particular attention to the tree's upper canopy.

BACTERIAL BLACK SPOT (mangoes)
Xanthomonas campestris pv. *mangiferaeindicae*

Definition: A bacterial disease of mangoes associated with low soil nutrient levels. It sometimes appears in association with the fungal disease anthracnose, which can mask it.

Symptoms and damage: Greasy patches appear on leaves; these darken, and eventually turn black. Black, gum-filled cankers appear on stems, and raised, oval black spots appear on fruits.

Plants affected: Mangoes.

Prevention and control: Difficult. In the event of an outbreak, contact your local agriculture department for advice on treatment.

Above: The yellowing pelargonium leaves with their brown marks indicate bacterial leaf spot.

BACTERIAL LEAF SPOT (pelargoniums)
Xanthomonas campestris pv. *pelargonii*

Definition: A bacterial disease of pelargoniums that is a particular problem in warm, wet weather conditions.

Symptoms and damage: Leaves show small brown spots, which gradually increase in size. Leaves turn yellow and are shed from the plant. Brown to black rotting can also affect the stems.

Plants affected: Pelargoniums (*Pelargonium*), especially ivy-leaved forms.

Prevention and control: Remove damaged material. Spray with copper oxychloride. If the base of the plant is affected, destroy the whole plant. Space plants to increase the air circulation.

BACTERIAL SPOT (peppers and tomatoes)
Xanthomonas campestris pv. *vesicatoria*

Definition: A bacterial disease of fruiting plants that can be troublesome during periods of warm, wet weather.

Symptoms and damage: Small, dark, water-soaked spots appear on leaves. Stems show sunken streaks. Developing fruits have small spots that increase in size and darken. These can become

corky or scabby and allow entry of fungal rots.

Plants affected: Peppers and tomatoes.

Prevention and control: Spray plants with a copper fungicide at the first sign of attack; alternatively, pull up and destroy affected plants. Space plants correctly and stake and prune them to improve air circulation around the stems. Do not replant the same area with related plants for at least three years after an attack. Look for resistant varieties.

BACTERIAL LEAF SPOT (lettuces)
Xanthomonas campestris pv. *vitians*

Definition: A bacterial disease of lettuces that is most likely to occur during cool, wet winters.

Symptoms and damage: Translucent spots appear on leaves, sometimes merging and causing whole leaves to collapse. If young plants are affected during a prolonged wet spell, the whole plant can rot.

Plants affected: Lettuces.

Prevention and control: Sow

disease-free seed and cover vulnerable plants with cloches during unfavourable weather.

ANGULAR LEAF SPOT (zinnias)
Xanthomonas campestris pv. *zinniae*

Definition: A seed-borne bacterial disease that affects zinnias. Plant losses can be great in damp conditions.

Symptoms and damage: Growing tips of seedlings can be killed. On older leaves, angular to circular red-brown spots appear. Affected plants lose vigour.

Plants affected: Annual zinnias (*Zinnia*).

Prevention and control: Dig up and destroy plants at the first sign of infection.

STRAWBERRY LEAF BLOTCH, Gnomonia Fruit Rot
Zythia fragariae, see Gnomonia fructicola.

Below: This tomato leaf has separate dark spots on it caused by bacterial spot.

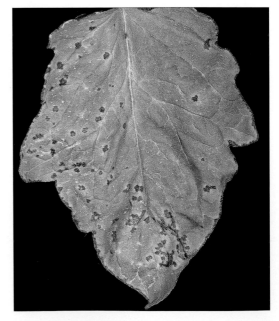

OTHER PROBLEMS

SOOTY MOULDS

Definition: Sooty moulds do not attack plants, but are associated with the activities of insect pests (such as many aphids and scale insects, as well as others) that excrete honeydew. Leaf surfaces covered in honeydew become coated with a secondary, soot-like, black or grey-green non-parasitic fungus.
Symptoms and damage: Affected plants are not damaged directly, but their appearance is spoilt; the growth of severely affected plants is inhibited, because they cannot photosynthesize properly. Cropping of fruiting plants can be reduced.
Plants affected: Any plant attacked by a honeydew-secreting pest, and plants grown in the vicinity on to which honeydew can drip.

Below: Sooty mould has affected the growth of this camellia.

Prevention and control: Cut off badly affected growth or wash off the mould with water. Control insect pests that are the prime cause of the problem.

LICHENS AND MOSSES

Definition: Green or greyish-green (sometimes yellow or orange) growths that appear on the stems of woody plants. Lichens and mosses can also grow on rocks and containers, as well as garden structures such as fences and sheds.
Symptoms and damage: *Mosses:* Cushion-like, tufty growths appear on stems. *Lichens:* Growths are thin, flattish crusts or resemble leafy plants. Lichens and mosses do not cause damage in themselves, but can be an indicator either of high humidity or that the plant is not growing strongly or is suffering die-back from some other cause.
Plants affected: Potentially all woody plants.

Above: Lichens have taken hold of this rhododendron and will need to be removed.

Prevention and control: If necessary, remove any growths with a stiff brush. Prune out badly affected growth; also prune to improve air circulation if growth is congested (and hence encourages high humidity). Feed, water and mulch woody plants well to keep them growing strongly.

SLIME FLUXES, Wetwood

Definition: Watery, sometimes viscous exudations from the stems of affected plants. They are caused by a number of unidentified fungi, yeasts and bacteria. Pathogens can take a hold if sap escapes via a wound or a crack in bark or as a result of frost damage, especially when the injury occurs early in the growing season.
Symptoms and damage: Orange, pink or white fluid (sometimes black in the case of large trees) is exuded from stems. Tissue beneath bark may be killed and the upper part of the stem can wilt and die.
Plants affected: A range of trees and shrubs; clematis (*Clematis*) (especially *C. montana*) are vulnerable to pathogens.
Prevention and control: Cut back affected stems, to below ground level if necessary. If the slime flux is localized, gouge out affected bark and any diseased tissue beneath. Consult a qualified tree surgeon for large trees.

Below: Slime flux is growing on this compostable material.

Viruses and virus-like diseases

Viruses and virus-like organisms are responsible for a range of plant problems. Many are unclassified, and in any case can mutate to produce new strains. They are often spread by aphids and other insect pests ("vectors"), or by contact, entering plants through wounds. Viruses are also often spread during the propagation process. They can be difficult to diagnose, since the symptoms can resemble those caused by recognized fungi or bacteria. Many are host-specific.

POTATO MOSAIC

Definition: A number of viruses are responsible for "potato mosaic"; the disease can also occur on other members of Solanaceae. The viruses are spread by aphids.
Symptoms and damage: The leaves are mottled or spotted (depending on the virus) with yellow or green, and they can also be crinkled. Leaf veins may be blackened. Affected plants can die prematurely.
Plants affected: Potatoes; also related plants, including weeds.
Prevention and control: Plant only guaranteed virus-free material. Control aphids with a suitable insecticide.

ARABIS MOSAIC VIRUS

Definition: A very common virus that can affect many plants. It is spread by eelworms

Below: Potato mosaic virus has had a severe effect on these plants.

Above: These narcissus bulbs and stems have arabis mosaic virus.

active in the soil. The disease is introduced into gardens on the infected rootstocks of roses.
Symptoms and damage: Leaves show mosaic-like marks. Affected plants are often distorted and do not grow to their typical expected size.
Plants affected: A large range of plants, both vegetables and ornamentals.

Above: These apple leaves show the mottling effect of apple mosaic.

Prevention and control: Dig up and destroy affected plants. Make sure that all new plant material brought into the garden is virus-free.

APPLE MOSAIC

Definition: A virus that affects apples. It is spread via the propagation process, rather than by insects.
Symptoms and damage: Leaves show mottled flecks or patches, either light or dark green, or yellow or cream. Affected leaves are shed early. Cropping is reduced, though fruit quality is unimpaired.
Plants affected: Apples, especially older varieties; crab apples are also susceptible.
Prevention and control: None possible. Make sure that any new plant has been propagated from virus-free stock.

SUMMER DEATH OF BEANS

Definition: A disease (caused by a virus or virus-like pathogen) of French beans. It is spread to beans from weeds by the common brown leafhopper.

Damage is most severe if the disease occurs during a period of hot weather.
Symptoms and damage: Plants are stunted and turn yellow and can suddenly die.
Plants affected: French beans; some varieties are more susceptible than others. Other plants can also be affected.
Prevention and control: Sow varieties known to be resistant. Keep the vegetable plot well weeded. Control leafhoppers with an appropriate insecticide.

BEAN MOSAIC, Pea Early Browning Virus (beans, peas, gladioli and freesias)

Definition: A virus that affects a range of plants. It is spread by aphids.
Symptoms and damage: Leaves are mottled with yellow or turn brown; stems can also be streaked yellow. Plants collapse.
Plants affected: Beans and peas; also *Gladiolus* and *Freesia*.
Prevention and control: Dig up and destroy affected plants. Control aphids with an appropriate insecticide.

Below: Bean mosaic virus has caused the mottling and yellowing on these bean leaves.

BEET CURLY TOP

Definition: A virus spread by the beet leafhopper.

Symptoms and damage: Leaves curl upwards and are crinkled; leaf veins are swollen. Leaves turn yellow, then die.

Plants affected: Beetroot (beets); also beans, crucifers, Swiss chard, tomatoes and some ornamental plants.

Prevention and control: Dig up and destroy affected plants. Control leafhoppers with a suitable insecticide.

CARROT MOTLEY DWARF DISEASE, Carrot Red Leaf Virus (carrots and parsley)

Definition: Two viruses that normally occur together to produce the symptoms detailed below. They are both spread by aphids.

Symptoms and damage: Leaves turn yellow and pink and can be twisted. Plants die back prematurely, and cropping may be reduced by the viruses.

Plants affected: Carrots and parsley.

Prevention and control: Dig

Below: A combination of carrot motley dwarf disease and carrot red leaf virus has discoloured these parsley plants.

up and destroy affected plants. Control aphids with an appropriate insecticide.

BROAD BEAN WILT

Definition: A virus spread by certain aphids (including the green peach aphid, *Myzus persicae*). Symptoms are worst in cool weather conditions.

Symptoms and damage: Growing tips of plants blacken and die back. The entire plant may wilt and die. The base of the stems and the roots may be rotted and black. Leaves can be mottled and their edges curved.

Plants affected: Members of Leguminosae, including broad (fava) beans, sweet peas (*Lathyrus odoratus*) and lupins (*Lupinus*); China asters (*Callistephus*) and some weeds.

Prevention and control: Dig up and destroy affected plants. Practise weed control. Avoid planting vulnerable plants during cool weather. Control aphids with a suitable insecticide.

CHRYSANTHEMUM STUNT VIROID

Definition: A serious disease of florists' chrysanthemums. It is caused by a viroid (an RNA molecule, which, unlike a virus, does not have a protein coat). It is spread on contaminated

Above: These field bean leaves have been curled and distorted by clover stunt virus.

propagation tools, and also through plant-to-plant contact. Not all affected plants show symptoms, so the disease can be introduced on apparently healthy plants.

Symptoms and damage: Plants fail to reach their full height and produce brittle stems. Flowers are smaller than usual and open early. Flower colour can be paler than normal. Leaves show yellow spots, flecks or blotches and can be distorted ("crinkled").

Plants affected: Chrysanthemums (*Dendranthema morifolium* and forms);

infections on Surfinia petunias (*Petunia*) and floss flowers (*Ageratum*) have also been reported.

Prevention and control: Dig up and destroy affected plants, as well as plants with which they may have come into contact. Ensure any new plants introduced are viroid free. In some countries, this viroid is a notifiable disease: if you suspect an outbreak, you should contact your local government agriculture department.

CLOVER STUNT VIRUS, Leaf Roll, Top Yellows (beans and peas)

Definition: A virus that affects certain legumes, occurring mostly during cool springs, sometimes also in autumn. It is spread by certain aphids, including the potato aphid and the green peach aphid.

Symptoms and damage: *Peas:* Plants are small and upright and show a yellow cast. Older leaves are thicker than normal. *Beans:* New leaves turn yellow, are thickened and curl downwards. Older leaves can be rolled and pods do not normally develop.

Plants affected: Various beans, including French and broad (fava) beans; peas.

Prevention and control: Sow seed of resistant varieties. Control aphids with an appropriate insecticide.

Above: Blotches on the leaves can indicate cucumber mosaic virus.

CUCUMBER MOSAIC VIRUS

Definition: A virus with a wide host range. It is spread through contact and by insect pests such as aphids. The virus is also responsible for the condition known as "spinach blight".
Symptoms and damage: Plants are stunted; leaves are distorted and show a blotchy, mosaic-like, yellow pattern. Flowering is reduced. Badly affected plants die prematurely. *Marrows, courgettes (zucchini) and cucumbers:* Any fruits produced are small and hard, with yellow blotches. *Spinach:* Leaves turn yellow (young ones first). Central leaves are narrow and puckered.
Plants affected: Cucurbits; also celery, spinach, tomatoes and ornamentals such as petunias (*Petunia*), dahlias (*Dahlia*) and delphiniums (*Delphinium*).

Below: Blotchy rings of cucumber mosaic virus have distorted this begonia leaf.

Prevention and control: Dig up and destroy affected plants. Wash hands carefully after handling diseased plants and do not touch healthy plants immediately afterwards. Keep cultivated areas of the garden weed-free. Control aphids with a suitable insecticide. Grow resistant varieties.

CYMBIDIUM VIRUS

Definition: Several viruses can affect orchids, most producing the symptoms described below. They are spread through the propagation process or through the activities of aphids.
Symptoms and damage: Leaves have a mottled appearance. Black spots can appear on older leaves. Flowering can be impaired.
Plants affected: Orchids (mainly *Cymbidium*).
Prevention and control: Destroy infected plants. Clean tools carefully during the propagation

Below: The markings of cucumber mosaic virus can be clearly seen on this *Epimedium* leaf.

Above: The leaves of this orchid are mottled and wilting as a result of attack by cymbidium virus.

process and control aphids and other insect pests with appropriate insecticides.

INFECTIOUS VARIEGATION (camellias)

Definition: A condition of camellias that is believed to be caused by a virus. It may be transmitted during the process of grafting.
Symptoms and damage: Yellow blotches appear on a few leaves, or just around their margins, and the plant continues to grow normally.
Plants affected: Grafted varieties of *Camellia japonica* and *C. reticulata*.
Prevention and control: Cut back affected growth.

Below: Infectious variegation detracts from the appearance of camellias, but is not fatal.

LEAF ROLL (potatoes), Net Necrosis

Definition: A virus affecting potatoes that is spread by aphids. It reproduces quickly.
Symptoms and damage: Leaf edges curl upwards. Affected plants are stunted, stiff and upright. Tubers are smaller than usual and show a dark brown/black netting when they are cut in half.
Plants affected: Potatoes; also tomatoes and other members of Solanaceae.
Prevention and control: Dig up and destroy affected plants. Buy virus-free tubers.

LETTUCE BIG VEIN

Definition: A virus that affects lettuces, especially where grown on heavy, wet soils.
Symptoms and damage: Plants grow slowly, producing smaller

Below: This potato plant has curled leaves as a result of an attack of leaf roll.

Above: The disintegrating petals suggest that this lily flower is from a plant that has been severely attacked by one of the lily viruses.

hearts with thicker leaves than usual. Tissue is white or yellow on the veins; there may be transparent bands.

Plants affected: Lettuces.

Prevention and control: None possible. Do not replant an area with lettuce crops where the problem has occurred.

LETTUCE NECROTIC YELLOWS

Definition: A virus that affects lettuces. It is spread by aphids that feed on sow thistles (*Sonchus oleraceus*).

Symptoms and damage: Plants are stunted and yellow, with crinkled leaves. Growth can be lopsided.

Plants affected: Lettuces.

Prevention and control: Keep areas where lettuces are grown weed-free.

LILY VIRUSES

Definition: Lilies are prone to a number of viruses, and can also be attacked by the *tulip breaking virus*. They may be spread by aphids and possibly by contact.

Symptoms and damage: Leaves are distorted and are marked with yellow, which appears as mottling, streaking or mosaicing. Flower buds are either not produced or fail to open, turn dry and die off.

Plants affected: Lilies (*Lilium*).

Prevention and control: Dig up and destroy affected bulbs. Wash hands before handling other lilies or tulips. Do not grow lilies and tulips close together. Control aphids with a suitable insecticide.

Below: Iris mosaic is similar in appearance to iris rust, and it is easy to confuse the two.

MOSAIC (irises)

Definition: A viral disease of irises spread by aphids. It is most serious on bulbous irises.

Symptoms and damage: *Rhizomatous irises:* Yellowish streaks appear on leaves, widening and turning brown as the leaves die back. Flowers open earlier than usual, but show a normal appearance. *Bulbous irises:* Leaves are mottled with dark and light green (the mottling is most evident on young leaves and unopened buds). Young plants are streaked yellow. Plants either do not flower or produce flowers marked with streaks.

Plants affected: Irises (*Iris*).

Prevention and control: Dig up and destroy affected plants. Control aphids with insecticide.

MOSAIC (roses)

Definition: A number of viruses can cause mosaic on roses. They are usually spread during the grafting process via infected rootstocks or scions.

Symptoms and damage: Leaves are blotched with yellow or show a variable pattern of yellow lines. Flowering and performance seem unaffected.

Plants affected: Roses (*Rosa*).

Prevention and control: Not necessary, though plants showing signs of virus should not be used for propagation.

MOSAIC (crucifers)

Definition: A viral disease that affects a number of cruciferous plants. It is spread by aphids (including the green peach aphid).

Symptoms and damage: *Cabbages, broccoli and cauliflowers:* Yellow rings appear on young leaves. Leaves are later mottled with varying shades of green. Black rings appear on older leaves in cold weather. *Turnips and swedes (rutabagas):* Veins become transparent and leaves are mottled with dark green. *Stocks:* Plants are stunted and leaves are distorted and mottled. Flowers are streaked with white.

Plants affected: Cruciferous vegetables; also related ornamentals such as stocks (*Matthiola*), alyssum (*Alyssum*) and honesty (*Lunaria*). Cruciferous weeds can also harbour the virus.

Prevention and control: Dig up and destroy affected plants. Keep cultivated areas of the garden free of weeds. Control insect pests with suitable insecticides. Grow resistant varieties and make sure that any seedlings brought into the garden are virus-free.

Below: Mosaic has caused the blotchy yellow colouring on these rose leaves.

PEPINO MOSAIC VIRUS

Definition: A highly contagious disease of tomatoes and other members of Solanaceae. It appears to reproduce quickly at high temperatures. It is spread by contact.

Symptoms and damage: Leaves are distorted, appear chlorotic and show a mosaic pattern. Lower leaves darken, and have angular, yellow spots. Fruits have a marbled appearance.

Plants affected: Tomatoes; potentially other Solanaceae.

Prevention and control: In the event of a suspected outbreak, contact your local government agriculture department.

PLUM POX, Sharka (*Prunus*)

Definition: A serious virus disease of *Prunus*. Symptoms vary, depending on the host species, the locality and the season; the disease is known to occur on wild hosts, such as blackthorn (*Prunus spinosa*). It can be spread through infected propagation material and aphids. The presence of other viruses can greatly increase the damage done by plum pox.

Symptoms and damage: Leaves show diffuse, chlorotic rings, lines and blotches. Fruit symptoms can vary: dark-skinned fruits show bluish, sometimes sunken rings; pale-skinned fruits ripen unevenly and show blotches and rings. Tissue beneath can also be affected, and stones (pits) may be marked. *Peaches:* Affected leaves are distorted as they emerge, with wavy edges. They straighten as they mature. Fruits have paler rings and lines than those found on plums.

Plants affected: Many *Prunus*; cherries are believed immune.

Prevention and control: There are no effective methods of control. In the event of an outbreak, contact your local government agriculture office.

STONY PIT (pears)

Definition: A virus that affects pears.

Symptoms and damage: The bark on affected trees shows cracks and folds. Fruits are distorted and the flesh contains hard, stony areas; they are inedible. Sometimes only one branch of a tree is affected, and the rest of the crop is normal. Equally, the disease can spread to the remaining branches, particularly on old specimens.

Plants affected: Pears; some varieties show more resistance than others.

Prevention and control: Cut back affected branches. Badly affected trees are best dug up and replaced.

TOMATO MOSAIC VIRUS, Bronzing of Tomatoes

Definition: A virus that affects tomatoes. It is spread by contact or by insect pests such as aphids.

Below: This pear has been distorted by stony pit virus and is inedible.

Below: This tomato plant has been attacked by tomato mosaic virus.

Symptoms and damage: Leaves are smaller than usual, and are mottled and distorted. The youngest leaves on plants may curl downwards.

Plants affected: Tomatoes; spread of the virus to other plants is possible.

Prevention and control: Dig up and destroy affected plants. Wash hands carefully afterwards, and before handling other plants. Control aphids with a suitable insecticide. Grow resistant varieties.

TOBACCO RING SPOT, Bouquet Disease (potatoes), Tomato Ring Spot, Bud Blight (soya beans)

Definition: Viruses spread by dagger nematodes (*Xiphinema* spp.), thrips and aphids. Symptoms can vary, depending on the host.

Symptoms and damage: Plants are stunted, with small brown or yellow raised rings or circles on leaves or fruit. *Spinach:* Large, irregular patches turn yellow. *Cucurbits:* Brown dots appear on leaves; fruits show ring spots and are pimpled. *Potatoes:* Leaf stalks are shortened and leaves are bunched together. *Soya beans:*

Above: This rose is showing symptoms of rose wilt, with young shoots dying back.

Plants are stunted and bushy, with crooked shoots.

Plants affected: A wide range, including cucurbits, celery, spinach, tomatoes and other members of Solanaceae, blueberries, beets and grapes; also some ornamentals and fruit trees, as well as weeds.

Prevention and control: Dig up and destroy affected plants. Control insect pests. Keep cultivated areas of the garden free of weeds.

ROSE WILT, Die-back (roses)

Definition: A disease of roses that can be caused by a number of viruses. Symptoms are most pronounced during cool weather in spring and autumn. The viruses can be spread by aphids or during propagation.

Symptoms and damage: Young leaves are curled downwards and can be shed. Older leaves can droop or also turn yellow before being shed. Shoots die back. Older stems can show purplish blotches. Plants can be stunted.

Plants affected: Roses (*Rosa*).

Above: Streaks of colour are one of the effects of tulip breaking virus.

Above: Cauliflower mosaic has twisted and distorted these leaves.

Above: This plant is suffering from woodiness of passion fruit.

WATERMELON MOSAIC VIRUS

Definition: A virus that attacks cucurbits. It is spread by aphids (including the cotton aphid, *Aphis gossypii*, and the green peach aphid, *Myzus persicae*), and can be harboured by weeds belonging to Cucurbitaceae.
Symptoms and damage: Leaves are mottled with lighter and darker green, and can be distorted. Plants fail to reach full size. Fruits can have hollows or be marked by a raised marbled pattern.
Plants affected: Cucurbits, especially pumpkins and courgettes (zucchini).
Prevention and control: Dig up and destroy affected plants. Keep the garden weed-free.

Prevention and control: Dig up and destroy affected plants. Control aphids with an appropriate insecticide.

RINGSPOT (camellias)

Definition: A disease of camellias that is believed to be caused by a virus.
Symptoms and damage: Light green rings on leaves turn into bright green spots with a darker edge; the rest of the leaf turns yellow. Plants flower normally.
Plants affected: *Camellia japonica* and its forms.
Prevention and control: Cut back affected growth. There is no reliable method of eliminating the disease.

TULIP BREAKING VIRUS (tulips, lilies)

Definition: A virus that affects certain bulbs. It is spread by aphids, especially the green peach aphid.
Symptoms and damage: Flowers are streaked with different colours. Leaves may also be streaked with yellow and/or have a tattered appearance. Bulbs are reduced in size.
Plants affected: Tulips (*Tulipa*); lilies (*Lilium*).
Prevention and control: Dig up and destroy affected bulbs. Wash hands carefully before handling other plant material, especially other tulips or lilies. Do not grow tulips and lilies close together. Control aphids with a suitable insecticide.

TURNIP MOSAIC, Cauliflower Mosaic (swedes, turnips and cauliflowers)

Definition: A virus that affects a range of vegetables. It is spread by aphids.
Symptoms and damage: Leaves are twisted and stunted and veins lose their colour. Leaves can also be mottled and blistered. Infected young plants can die; on older plants, leaves die back, exposing the crowns to soft rot.
Plants affected: Swedes (rutabagas), turnips and also cauliflowers.
Prevention and control: Keep the vegetable plot weed-free. Plant resistant varieties.

WOODINESS OF PASSION FRUIT

Definition: A virus that affects passion fruit. It is spread by aphids. Symptoms are most pronounced during periods of cool weather.
Symptoms and damage: Fruit is distorted, and develops a thick rind with reduced pulpy tissue inside. Leaves can be mottled with yellow or be unusually pale. Severely affected plants can die.
Plants affected: Passion fruits, especially *Passiflora edulis* and its varietal forms.
Prevention and control: Destroy affected plants. Grow *Passiflora* in a warm, sheltered site, and keep plants well watered and fed. Look for resistant varieties.

SPOTTED WILT

Definition: The spotted wilt virus affects a range of plants. It is spread by thrips, including onion thrips (*Thrips tabaci*), tomato thrips (*Franliniella schultzei*) and western flower thrips (*F. occidentalis*). All these pests are active during hot, dry periods.
Symptoms and damage: *Tomatoes:* Small, brown spots appear on young leaves. Old leaves have bronze rings. Stems can be streaked brown. Young plants can die. Fruits ripen unevenly and have round blotches. *Potatoes:* Young leaves are spotted brown and tips of shoots can die. Older leaves can also be spotted. *Broad (fava) beans:* Leaves are mottled and the main shoot can die back. Stems are streaked brown and pods have black spots. *Peppers:* Leaves and fruits are marked with yellow. *Dahlias and chrysanthemums:* Leaves are marked with irregular, wavy lines and can turn brown and die. Dahlia stems can be streaked brown or purple.
Plants affected: A wide range of vegetables and ornamentals, including chrysanthemums (*Chrysanthemum*), dahlias (*Dahlia*), poppies (*Papaver*) and zinnias (*Zinnia*); also weeds.
Prevention and control: Dig up and destroy affected plants. Keep cultivated areas of the garden free of weeds. Look for virus-free dahlia tubers. Control thrips with an appropriate insecticide.

SPRAING, Tobacco Rattle Virus, Potato Mop-top Virus (potatoes)

Definition: Viral infections of potatoes. Tobacco rattle virus is spread by eelworms.
Symptoms and damage: Tubers show red-brown lesions when cut in half.
Plants affected: Potatoes; some varieties are more vulnerable than others.
Prevention and control: Do not grow potatoes in a site where the disease has occurred. Remove perennial weeds from the site, because the viruses can overwinter.

Below: The inside of this potato reveals the characteristic brown markings of spraing.

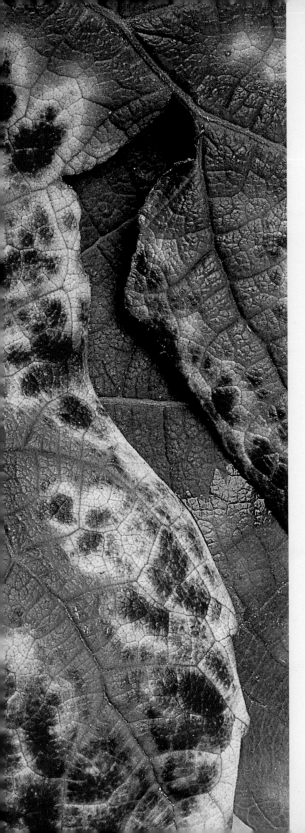

Physiological Problems

Disorders that occur as a direct result of the environment in which a plant lives are usually easier to deal with than those created by invertebrate pests and diseases. Frequently, physiological problems will affect more than one plant growing in a given area at any time. Most commonly, the weather takes its toll on plants – too much heat, humidity, damp, cold, wind, or frost can all have consequences for plants. The site itself may have a detrimental effect – plants that receive more shade than they like will suffer, in the same way that plants can fail to thrive if their nutritional needs are not met. The problems described here are arranged according to the principal factor that is the cause, but physiological problems often occur in combination.

Left: Manganese deficiency.

Adverse weather conditions

Freak weather can wreak havoc in the garden. A heavy frost followed by bright early morning sunshine can scorch and kill young plants or damage tender flower buds, and wild winter gales can tear off branches and even uproot whole trees and shrubs.

SEVERE WEATHER INJURIES

How to identify: Parts of the plants are ripped off; leaves are torn by wind or pitted by driving hail.

Damage: Natural injuries frequently result in ugly, irregular wounds that can leave the plant susceptible to disease. Felled trees can also cause damage to buildings.

Cause: Freak weather conditions such as strong winds, lightning, heavy snowfalls and hail.

Plants affected: Many large trees, shrubs and conifers are vulnerable, and any plants with large, soft leaves.

Prevention and control: Usually none possible. Remove snow that settles on conifers to prevent a heavy build-up, which can break branches. On upright conifers, tie in branches if heavy snow is forecast. Avoid planting trees in exposed situations where they may be vulnerable to lightning strikes as well as strong winds. Cut back

Above: This viburnum leaf shows the effect of water damage.

damaged growth to create clean, rather than ragged, wounds. A large damaged tree may need the attentions of a qualified tree surgeon to restore balance to the tree.

WIND DAMAGE

How to identify: At worst, plants blow over and are flattened or can be ripped from the soil entirely. Branches can be ripped from mature trees. Top-heavy plants, such as standard roses, are particularly susceptible to being blown over by high winds. Cold, drying winds between autumn and early spring can cause conifer foliage to turn brown.

Above: Frost damage has caused blackening on *Crinum powellii*.

Damage: Plants are flattened or blown over. Wind can also dry out patches on plants (especially conifers and other evergreens), causing die-back.

Cause: Strong winds.

Plants affected: Mainly large, woody plants, but all tall plants are vulnerable.

Prevention and control: Severely damaged plants should be removed. Damage to large, mature trees is best treated by a

qualified tree surgeon to restore the plants' natural balance. Staking can limit wind damage on young woody plants. Affected conifers usually recover unaided, though applications of a foliar feed in the growing season can be beneficial. Protect young conifers with windbreaks made from netting stapled to stakes or canes.

Below: Severe winds can cause otherwise healthy trees to lean or even fall over.

Below: These pelargonium leaves have been damaged by a hailstorm.

Above: In dry weather, plants may wilt if not watered regularly.

CHRONIC LACK OF WATER

How to identify: Leaves turn yellow, red or brown and may be shed by the plant. Fruit and vegetables are small. Leafy crops run to seed.
Damage: In severe cases, plants can die; established ornamentals and fruit trees and bushes generally recover.
Cause: A prolonged hot, dry spell of weather.
Plants affected: All plants are vulnerable, especially seedlings, transplants, new plantings and very leafy plants.

Below: The dried-out brown leaves of this pelargonium show acute water deficiency.

Prevention and control: Keep plants well watered during periods of drought and mulch after watering. Prune back dead growth on evergreens.

ACUTE WATER DEFICIENCY (SUDDEN)

How to identify: Plants wilt.
Damage: Growth is temporarily checked. Plants can die if allowed to dry out repeatedly.
Cause: An unexpected hot, dry spell of weather.
Plants affected: All plants are vulnerable, especially young plants, new plantings and transplants and plants in containers (particularly those planted in peat-based composts/soil mixes).
Prevention and control: Keep plants watered at all times. Add water-retaining gels to the compost in containers to reduce the risk of it drying out.

LACK OF WATER AT CRITICAL TIMES

How to identify: Irregular supplies of moisture at the roots of fruit trees can cause fruits to crack. Grapes and other fruits can split.
Damage: Damage is localized, but affected fruits will be vulnerable to fungal infections.
Cause: Inadequate water supply.
Plants affected: New plantings, seedlings, transplants and fruiting trees and vines are particularly at risk, as well as crops that need regular supplies of water while in active growth and those grown in containers.
Prevention and control: Water thoroughly in drought, and mulch well. Remove split berries and grapes as soon as they are seen.

DROUGHT

How to identify: Plants stop growing. Leaves turn yellow or otherwise discolour and can be shed by the plant. Soft shoots die back. The bark of woody plants can crack, exposing tissue beneath. Fine roots can also die, though this effect naturally often goes undetected.
Damage: Plants perform poorly and run to seed prematurely. In cases of prolonged drought, plants can die. Stem tissue exposed by cracked bark can be vulnerable to disease.
Cause: A long hot, dry spell of weather coupled with inadequate irrigation.
Plants affected: Nearly all plants, apart from those that are specially adapted to drought, are vulnerable, particularly evergreen shrubs and trees, transplants, new plantings, seedlings and plants in containers.
Prevention and control: Keep susceptible plants well watered during dry periods and mulch well to conserve soil moisture.

Above: An irregular supply of water to the tree has caused this apple to crack and split.

Adding water-retaining gels to the compost (soil mix) in containers and hanging baskets can limit the risk of the growing medium drying out. Cracked bark often heals naturally, but any rotting tissue should be cut away.

SPORADIC WATER SUPPLY

How to identify: Plants fail to grow evenly. Flowering and fruiting can be impaired.
Damage: The garden display and cropping can be spoilt. In severe cases of uneven supply, plants can die.
Cause: Irregular water supplies.
Plants affected: All plants are potentially vulnerable, with the possible exception of those adapted to drought.
Prevention and control: Keep plants growing evenly through regular watering and the appropriate use of fertilizers.

Below: The curled leaf edges show the effects of sporadic watering on a chilli plant.

Above: Some of the leaves on this *Spathiphyllum* have turned brown, and will fall, indicating an overly dry atmosphere.

DRY ATMOSPHERE

How to identify: Growth slows down and leaves turn brown. Leaves and buds can be shed from plants. Dry atmosphere commonly causes problems on plants grown in the home or under glass during hot periods in summer.
Damage: In severe cases, plants can die.
Cause: High temperatures and a lack of humidity.
Plants affected: A range of greenhouse plants and houseplants, especially rainforest species.
Prevention and control: Mist vulnerable plants regularly in spring and summer (or all year round in centrally heated homes) to maintain the appropriate humidity level. Alternatively, stand containers on trays of expanded clay pellets that hold moisture and help to create a damp atmosphere around the plants.

MOIST ATMOSPHERE

see also Oedema (Dropsy)
How to identify: Too moist an atmosphere encourages fungal diseases. It can cause problems on plants outdoors and those grown under glass. Seedlings and cuttings in heated propagators are also at risk.
Damage: Fungal diseases take hold, killing plants and seedlings in extreme cases.
Cause: Excessive humidity. Outdoors, the cause can be a prolonged spell of wet or humid weather; indoors, it may be poor ventilation or excessive watering and spraying.
Plants affected: A range of plants, especially climbers in confined spaces whose growth has become congested. Under glass, vines, tomatoes, seedlings and cuttings are at risk.
Prevention and control: Outdoors, thin the growth of susceptible woody plants. Under glass, reduce humidity by opening vents. Mist plants in the morning rather than the evening, so that plants can dry out. Keep seedlings and cuttings in closed propagation units properly ventilated.

LOW TEMPERATURES

How to identify: Young leaves turn silver, white or yellow. Leaves curl and get distorted as they grow. Pink, purple or brown patches occur on young rose leaves. Weak and borderline hardy plants are vulnerable.
Damage: Growth is halted and damage may be visible for a long period.
Cause: An unexpected drop in temperature, especially following a warm, wet period.
Plants affected: All young plants, plants of borderline hardiness and evergreens.
Prevention and control: Protect vulnerable seedlings and small plants with floating mulches. Tent large plants with horticultural fleece. Remove protection once the cold spell has passed. Avoid planting vulnerable plants in frost pockets. Foliar feed can help restore vigour to affected roses.

WATERLOGGING

How to identify: Foliage discolours and plants die back. The bark of woody plants can become papery and begin to peel. Roots can also die back, in severe cases leading to the death

Above: Waterlogged ground resulting from poor drainage.

of the plant. Water collects on the soil surface. *Manganese deficiency* is an associated problem in some areas.
Damage: Plants suffer a check in growth; severely affected plants can die.
Cause: Excess water in the soil, caused by poor drainage or freak rainfall.
Plants affected: Nearly all plants can be affected, though drought-tolerant Mediterranean and succulent plants are the most vulnerable.
Prevention and control: Cut back affected plants and feed well to promote recovery. If waterlogging is an ongoing problem, consider laying a drainage system. Digging in grit and organic matter can improve drainage on heavy soils, but this should be done over a wide area if it is to be effective.

Below: Extensive brown areas where stems have died back show the effects of waterlogging on *Ceanothus* 'Pin Cushion'.

Below: Cold weather has changed the shape and colour of this forsythia's leaves.

Above: Cold has affected this variegated holly bush. The cream leaves lack chlorophyll.

Above: Frost has caused damage to this castor oil plant.

Above: Faded brown leaves show the effect of frost on an evergreen.

COLD

see also Frost damage and Low temperatures

How to identify: Soft stems wither and can die back. Leaves can discolour and can be shed by the plants. Emerging flowers and any developing fruits can be damaged.

Damage: Plants experience a check in growth. Young plants and seedlings can be killed outright. The flowering display and fruiting can be affected.

Cause: Sudden drops in temperature. The problem is common in late spring, when warm days are followed by frosty nights.

Plants affected: Potentially any plant, but especially seedlings, young plants, tender crops and evergreens of borderline hardiness. Early-flowering plants grown in a frost pocket are also susceptible to damage.

Prevention and control: Provide adequate protection, using a cloche, cold frame or floating mulch, when cold weather is forecast. Protect spring-flowering camellias and magnolias with horticultural fleece (or similar material) thrown over the plants at night.

FROST DAMAGE

How to identify: The petals of opening flowers turn brown at the edges. The bark of some fruit trees can crack. Developing fruits can be distorted, and russetting can appear on smooth-skinned apples (*see russetting*). Symptoms such as these can also indicate *faulty root action*.

Damage: The flowering display is spoilt. Damaged flowers are often shed by the plant. Crops of fruiting trees can be much diminished by frost damage at flowering time. Fruits distorted by frost will continue to grow unevenly. Tissue exposed by cracking bark is vulnerable to

disease. Leaves on damaged shoots are distorted and may be shed, and the shoots die back. Rhododendron bark can split. Most hardy plants generally recover, but various moulds can take a hold on frost-damaged tissue.

Cause: Sharp frosts, generally at flowering time or when sap is rising in spring.

Plants affected: A range of flowering ornamentals, especially rhododendrons (*Rhododendron*), camellias (*Camellia*) and magnolias (*Magnolia*); fruit trees such as apples, pears, cherries, plums, peaches, apricots and almonds. Evergreens with large, soft leaves, such as *Fatsia japonica*, are also vulnerable.

Prevention and control: Protect vulnerable plants by tenting them with horticultural fleece overnight when frost is forecast. Avoid planting in frost pockets. In frost-prone areas, choose late-flowering varieties and site them where the flowers will not be struck by early morning sun (a common cause of browning). Prune back any damaged growth and remove any distorted fruit. Bind split bark with grafting tape (this will be successful only if the treatment is immediate). Treat any secondary attacks of *grey mould* as appropriate.

Below: The flowers of spring-flowering magnolias may be turned brown by frost.

Below: The leaves on this grapevine have been discoloured by the cold.

Below: Tender plants such as this convolvulus are susceptible to cold.

Excessive water

Too much water or too sporadic a supply can have a detrimental effect on all garden plants, but whereas many ornamentals can recover from the damage caused in this way, crops of fruits, salads and vegetables may be lost completely.

CRACKED FRUITS

How to identify: Otherwise normally developing fruits show cracking of their skins.
Damage: Cropping is impaired.
Cause: Irregular water supply.
Plants affected: Apples, pears and tomatoes.
Prevention and control: Water and mulch the soil around fruit trees to prevent it drying out during periods of drought when the fruits are ripening. Water tomato plants regularly.

CRACKS (potatoes)

How to identify: Deep cracks appear in potato tubers. Holes can also be found in the middle of outwardly unaffected tubers.
Damage: Crops are spoilt, and fungal infections can attack the exposed flesh.
Cause: Excessive wet following a drought.
Plants affected: Potatoes.
Prevention and control: Water crops well during dry periods, ensuring that the soil is never allowed to dry out. Improve the soil by digging in organic matter prior to planting to improve moisture retention on free-draining soils.

Above: A deeply cracked potato.

CROWN ROT

How to identify: The crowns of plants become soft and slimy.
Damage: In severe cases, the plants die.
Cause: Excessive wet at the crown of the plant.
Plants affected: A range of succulent and drought-loving plants, such as sedums (*Sedum*) and lewisias (*Lewisia*).
Prevention and control: If the problem is localized, cut out affected plant tissue. Dig up plants that are severely affected. Add grit to improve drainage in heavy soils or replace with different species that are better adapted to the conditions.

TAN BARK (cherry trees)

How to identify: Small eruptions appear on year-old shoots (or trunks) of cherry trees, containing a tan powder.

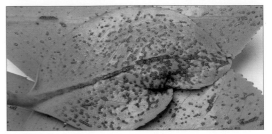

Damage: The outer bark layer peels off to reveal brown, dead cells. The damage to the tree is usually not serious.
Cause: The disorder commonly occurs on vigorously growing trees, but can also be an indication of *waterlogging*.
Plants affected: Cherry trees.
Prevention and control: None necessary, but if the ground is found to be waterlogged, preventive action may be necessary to improve the drainage around the trees.

OEDEMA (dropsy)

How to identify: Pimple-like growths appear on the undersides of leaves. These growths later turn corky.
Damage: The condition does

Below: This mature strawberry plant has been killed by crown rot as a result of overwatering.

Above: The undersides of these camellia leaves are peppered with the brown growths of oedema.

not threaten the health of the plant, provided steps are taken to improve its overall cultivation by reducing the moisture level surrounding it. The growths are, however, unsightly in the short term.
Cause: Overly wet soil and/or too moist an atmosphere.
Plants affected: A wide range, including camellias (*Camellia*), eucalyptus (*Eucalyptus*), ivy-leaved pelargoniums (*Pelargonium*) and peperomias (*Peperomia*).
Prevention and control: None possible. Removing affected leaves will result in other leaves developing the same symptoms. Improve cultivation, or replace affected plants. Under glass, keep plants well ventilated to prevent them being surrounded by too moist an atmosphere.

Below: As the growths of oedema develop, they turn corky, as shown on this pelargonium leaf.

Below: Cracks appear in tomatoes when watering is irregular.

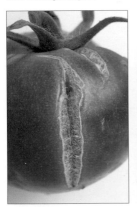

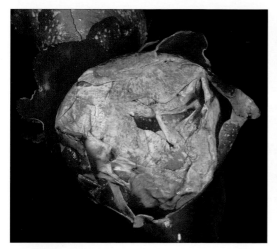

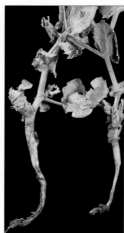

CAPPING (roses)

How to identify: Flower buds on roses swell but the flowers fail to open properly.
Damage: The flowering display is spoilt. Affected buds often attract *grey mould*.
Cause: Heavy rain or hail; other seasonal factors that check plant growth can also cause capping.
Plants affected: Roses (*Rosa*).
Prevention and control: Prevention is not possible. Cut off all affected buds to prevent grey mould taking hold. Spraying with a foliar feed can boost recovery.

Below: The bark on this *Acer griseum* is suffering from the effects of too much water.

Above: Grey mould has formed on this capped rose.

FAULTY ROOT ACTION

How to identify: A range of symptoms can indicate faulty root action, including discoloured or blackened leaves, and die-back of shoots. Sometimes, all the topgrowth can die back. Such symptoms can also be the effect of *frost damage* and/or *low temperatures*. Flower buds are shed

Above: Faulty root action has affected these peas.

prematurely or, in some cases, not produced at all.
Damage: Plants fail to thrive. In severe cases, plants can die.
Cause: Faulty root action can be caused by a variety of factors, including deficiency of any of a range of soil nutrients (see under specific nutrients), *waterlogging* or poor cultivation. Incorrect planting can also result in faulty root action.

Plants affected: A wide range of plants, especially woody plants.
Prevention and control: Check that the soil is not deficient in any of the trace elements important for plant growth, that it contains appropriate humus levels and that it is adequately drained. Feed plants as appropriate, water well in periods of drought and apply mulches to conserve moisture in the soil.

PAPERY BARK (apple trees and viburnums)

see also Faulty root action and Waterlogging
How to identify: Bark is thin and peels off the trunk.
Damage: Plant tissue beneath the bark is exposed and can rot; shoots can die back, especially if the plant has been girdled.
Cause: Waterlogging causes *faulty root action.*
Plants affected: Mainly apples, but also shrubs such as viburnums (*Viburnum*).
Prevention and control: Cut back all affected growth. Improve cultivation to prevent waterlogging of the soil.

Below: An example of root girdling.

Insufficient water

An inadequate water supply can have severe consequences for plants. How long a plant survives before reacting to lack of water is dependent on the species and the conditions in which it is grown.

DIE-BACK

How to identify: The tips of shoots blacken and wither. Leaves at the tips of stems wither and can be shed. Die-back can progress down the stem, in severe cases down to ground level.

Damage: Plants suffer a check in growth. In severe cases, plants can die.

Cause: A range of factors can cause die-back in plants: excessive or insufficient watering, sudden drops in temperature, inappropriate use of garden chemicals, lack of appropriate nutrients and poor planting. Some pests and diseases are also responsible for die-back.

Plants affected: Potentially all plants.

Prevention and control: Cut back affected growth, and improve cultivation. Use of a foliar feed can boost recovery. Water and mulch plants well, especially new plantings.

Above: The shoot tips of this conifer are suffering from die-back.

FAILURE TO SET FRUIT (runner beans)

How to identify: Plants flower normally but fail to set fruit.

Damage: Crops are reduced or are not produced at all.

Cause: A range of factors can result in crop failure: insufficient rain, inadequate watering or the activities of birds pecking at the flowers are common causes. Unseasonable cold at flowering time can inhibit the activities of pollinating insects.

Plants affected: Runner beans, especially red-flowered varieties.

Prevention and control: Grow

Below: The blackened and withered tips of the young shoots indicate that this rose has die-back.

in a sheltered area and space to promote cross-pollination. Keep plants adequately watered during the flowering period. Net susceptible crops against birds. Choose white- or pink-flowered varieties where this is a common problem.

FALSE SILVER LEAF (tree fruits)

How to identify: Foliage displays a silvery discoloration. The condition differs from *silver leaf* in that most of the plant is likely to be affected and *die-back* will not necessarily follow.

Damage: The appearance of the plant is spoilt by the discoloration.

Cause: An irregular water supply or a lack of soil fertility.

Plants affected: Tree fruits.

Prevention and control: Keep plants well fed and watered and mulch to conserve soil moisture. Cut back any shoots that show signs of die-back. If the problem occurs early in the season, apply a foliar feed to boost the plant's recovery.

SHANKING (vines)

How to identify: Stalks of individual grapes shrivel. Grapes fail to ripen normally or develop their natural colour.

Above: Some of the fruits on this runner bean plant have failed to set.

Damage: Cropping is impaired.

Cause: Inappropriate cultivation – usually leading to either *drought* or *waterlogging* – sometimes combined with a failure to thin the trusses of fruit correctly.

Plants affected: Outdoor vines.

Prevention and control: Cut out bunches of grapes that do not develop normally and spray the vine with a foliar feed to encourage vigour. Grapes should be thinned as a matter of routine. Bunches should be no closer than 30cm (12in), and the numbers of grapes within each bunch should be reduced to produce tapering clusters that ripen evenly.

Below: This capsicum plant has failed to set fruit.

Above: These *Parrotia* leaves display red and yellow discoloration that could have a number of causes.

DISCOLOURED LEAVES

How to identify: Leaves show a colour other than that typical of the plant – usually yellow, red, black or brown. The discoloration can appear as spots or patches, but sometimes whole leaves wither, prematurely on deciduous plants.

Damage: Discoloured leaves are usually shed by the plant, but are sometimes retained, especially on evergreens.

Cause: Drought and excessive sunlight are prime causes. Certain pests and diseases can also cause leaves to discolour.

Plants affected: Many plants, especially those with thin leaves.

Prevention and control: Ensure vulnerable plants are not exposed to excessive sunlight. Keep growing plants well watered, mulching them well in spring to conserve moisture.

Below: This peach stone has split in two, probably because of an irregular supply of water.

SPLIT STONE (peaches)

How to identify: Fruits have an abnormally deep cleft, possibly splitting at the stalk end. When cut, the stones (pits) are found to be split in two. This leads to rotting of the kernel (which may be absent).

Damage: Splits in the flesh of fruits allow insect pests to enter. Fruits do not ripen properly and are vulnerable to a range of rots and fungal diseases (*see* Fungal, bacterial and other diseases).

Cause: Can be caused by *poor pollination*, low lime levels, *malnutrition* or, most commonly, an *irregular water supply*.

Plants affected: Peaches.

Prevention and control: Ensure fruits are properly set by practising hand-pollination. Lime acid soils if necessary in autumn. Keep full-grown plants well fed to offset any mineral deficiency in the soil. Water the plants well in dry periods and mulch to conserve moisture.

BLINDNESS OF BULBS

How to identify: No flowers are produced, though leaves grow normally.

Damage: No long-term damage.

Cause: Congestion of the bulbs is the commonest cause. *Lack of water at critical times* can also cause blindness, especially of bulbs in containers. Storing dormant bulbs at too high a temperature can also affect flowering. (When buying bulbs, make sure they are of flowering

Above: These snowdrops have become congested, so no flowers are produced.

size. Immature bulbs will produce leaves only.)

Plants affected: Most bulbs.

Prevention and control: Divide established clumps of bulbs after flowering to relieve congestion. Keep bulbs in containers well watered when they are in growth. Feed bulbs after flowering but while still in active growth. Store dormant bulbs in cool but frost-free conditions.

SPLITTING OF ROOTS (root vegetables)

How to identify: Root vegetables are found to be split on harvesting.

Damage: Cropping is impaired.

Cause: A period of drought after a wet spell.

Plants affected: Root vegetables.

Prevention and control: Keep the soil in the vegetable plot well watered, and ensure it does not dry out. Digging organic matter in prior to planting root vegetables can reduce the risk of the problem occurring.

Below: Drought after a wet spell causes carrots to split.

Above: This cucumber has withered due to disease or an inadequate supply of water.

WITHERING OF CROP (cucumbers)

How to identify: Growth is uneven and fruits fail to develop properly.

Damage: Cropping is impaired.

Cause: Irregular watering, or diseases that affect the roots.

Plants affected: Cucumbers.

Prevention and control: Remove all fruits from an affected plant. Give the plant a foliar feed to promote further flowering and fruit set, then water it well.

BLOSSOM END ROT (tomatoes)

How to identify: There is a circular brown or greenish-black patch opposite the stalk.

Damage: Fruiting is impaired.

Cause: Usually lack of adequate water when the fruits are starting to form.

Plants affected: Tomatoes; a whole truss is often affected.

Prevention and control: Water plants regularly when the fruits are forming. If affected fruits are of the first crop only, remove these, then continue to water the plants well.

Below: Lack of water causes blossom end rot in tomatoes.

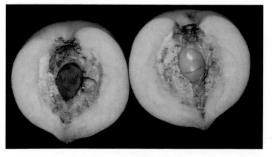

Frost

Sudden frosts can cause a range of problems, especially to young plants and others that are not fully hardy. The first frosts of autumn often strike without warning, and spring frosts can occur unexpectedly late in the growing season.

BLACK EYE (strawberries)

How to identify: The central parts of the flowers turn black (though the petals remain unharmed by the frost).
Damage: Flowers wither and fall; cropping is poor.
Cause: Frost.
Plants affected: Strawberries (when they are in flower).
Prevention and control: Protect plants with cloches or a floating mulch if frost is forecast during the flowering period.

Above: Withered and rolled leaf edges are a characteristic response of many plants to frost.

growing plants well and applying mulches to conserve soil moisture in spring.

CRINKLING OF LEAVES

How to identify: Leaves are crinkled. Flower buds may turn brown and fail to open.
Damage: The ornamental display is spoilt.
Cause: Dry soil or frost.
Plants affected: All bulbous plants.
Prevention and control: Unexpected frosts cannot be prevented, but guard against the soil drying out by watering

Below: Only the central parts of these strawberry flowers are affected by black eye.

SPLITTING OF STEMS

How to identify: Bark on young shoots of trees and shrubs splits. Sometimes the bark peels away in strips. Splitting can also occur towards the base of stems of herbaceous and other perennial plants.
Damage: The tissue beneath the bark or outer stem layer is exposed and is vulnerable to disease. Shoots can die back.
Cause: Frost (*see also* Frost damage). Heavy rainfall after a prolonged dry spell can also cause stems to split.
Plants affected: Trees and

shrubs planted in frost pockets, especially camellias (*Camellia*), border phlox (*Phlox*) and pelargoniums (*Pelargonium*).
Prevention and control: Cut back affected growth. On woody plants, it is sometimes possible to encourage recovery by binding split stems with grafting tape, which can be removed once the wound has healed. Mulch border perennials well to prevent the soil drying out excessively between bouts of rain, especially where the soil is free-draining.

Below: The stem of this forsythia has been enlarged and flattened, a phenomenon called fasciation.

Above: Fasciation in the ray florets of a sunflower (*Helianthus*).

FASCIATION

How to identify: Shoots are flattened and enlarged.
Damage: No serious damage is caused, and plants may continue to produce leaves and flowers normally.
Cause: A range of factors can cause fasciation, such as early injury to the growing tip (either mechanical or from frost), as well as attack by insects or slugs.

Below: Fasciation sometimes occurs in fruits, such as these pears, which also bear vestigial leaf growth.

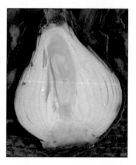

Above: This bulb has been frozen and the green part is soft.

Plants affected: Many plants. Susceptible perennials include delphiniums (*Delphinium*), euphorbias (*Euphorbia*) and primulas (*Primula*); woody plants include forsythia (*Forsythia*) and the Higan cherry (*Prunus x subhirtella* 'Autumnalis'). Prevention and control: None possible. On woody plants, any affected growth can be cut back, if necessary.

FROST DAMAGE TO STORED CORMS

How to identify: Corms in storage soften due to freezing.
Damage: Corms rot and develop a sweetish smell.

Below: This rose has produced buds through the centre of an open flower, an example of proliferation.

Cause: Any drops in temperature to below freezing.
Plants affected: Corms placed in storage while dormant, especially those of tender plants such as indoor cyclamen.
Prevention and control: Store corms in dry, frost-free conditions. Discard any affected corms.

PROLIFERATION (roses)

How to identify: Stems continue to grow through open flowers, producing a further flower or cluster of buds.
Damage: The flowering display is affected (though usually only a small number of flowers show proliferation).
Cause: Damage to the stems

Above: An apple with russetted patches on its skin.

while they are growing, usually as a result of a sudden frost.
Plants affected: Roses (*Rosa*). Some varieties are more susceptible than others.
Prevention and control: Not possible. Cut off and destroy affected flowers.

RUSSETTING (apples)

How to identify: Apples show rough (or "russetted") patches on the skin. Russetting is a natural condition of some apple varieties.
Damage: None, though the appearance of smooth-skinned apple varieties is affected. The

Below: The edges of these young Japanese maple leaves have been scorched by frost.

fruit under the skin remains palatable.
Cause: On smooth-skinned varieties, the appearance of russetting is generally due either to *frost damage* when the fruits are developing, or to *powdery mildew*, *chemical injuries* or *faulty root action*, caused by nutrient deficiencies in the soil.
Plants affected: Apples.
Prevention and control: None required, though it may be necessary to take preventive measures against *mildew* and improve the soil if the problem is recurrent.

SCORCH (maples and beech)

For damage to plants under glass, see Sun scorch under glass
How to identify: Leaves turn brown at the edges and curl.
Damage: In severe cases, the plant presents a generally scorched appearance.
Cause: Cold winds and frost when the leaves are young.
Plants affected: Mainly Japanese maples (*Acer japonicum* and *A. palmatum*). Young beech leaves are also susceptible.
Prevention and control: None possible. Affected leaves will not recover, but applying a foliar feed and improving cultivation generally in the growing season can boost the plant's health. Transfer vulnerable plants situated in frost pockets to more sheltered positions in the garden.

Temperature

Above and below certain temperatures, plants become dormant, and changes in temperature affect growth rates. If the changes are very sudden, therefore, they can have adverse effects on plant growth and the development of fruit and flowers.

BOLTING

How to identify: Crops grown for their leaves or stems flower and run to seed.

Damage: Reduction of crop, toughening of plant tissues and coarsening of flavour.

Plants affected: Celery, onions, leeks, beetroot (beet), spinach beet and all leafy vegetables.

Cause: Any combination of extremes of dryness at the roots, heat and day length. A check in growth, such as occurs when seedlings are planted out just before a cold snap or are thinned too late, can also cause plants to bolt.

Prevention and control: Make sure the soil does not dry out during prolonged dry spells. Remove any flower stalks as soon as they appear. If possible, make successive sowings of crops to counteract losses caused by sudden changes in the weather.

PEDICEL NECROSIS

How to identify: Flower stalks beneath flower buds turn black. Buds turn brown and do not open.

Damage: The flowering display is spoilt.

Below: This lettuce has bolted, sending up a flowering shoot from the centre, and is now inedible.

Above: The ripe tomatoes on this truss display the hard patches characteristic of greenback.

Cause: A range of environmental factors can cause pedicel necrosis, usually a lack of appropriate nutrients or drying out of the soil, both resulting in a lack of vigour.

Plants affected: Poppies (*Papaver*), pyrethrums (*Tanacetum coccineum*) and roses (*Rosa*).

Prevention and control: Remove affected buds. On roses, if the buds are those of the first crop of flowers, treating with a foliar feed can enable the plant to flower normally later in the season. To prevent the condition, feed roses with a rose fertilizer at the rate recommended by the manufacturer, water in dry periods and mulch to conserve soil moisture. Feed herbaceous perennials with a high-potassium fertilizer at the start of the next growing season.

GREENBACK (tomatoes)

How to identify: Hard green or yellow patches appear on the shoulders of fruits.

Damage: Crops are spoilt.

Cause: High temperatures and low potassium levels, coupled with excessive exposure to hot sun. *Blotchy ripening* is a similar

problem to greenback.

Plants affected: Tomatoes grown under glass without good shading.

Prevention and control: Provide good ventilation, and shade developing fruits from hot sun. Grow resistant varieties such as 'Alicante', 'Moneymaker', 'Golden Sunrise' or 'Tigerella'.

CRACKING OF BARK (conifers)

How to identify: Long, vertical cracks appear in the bark.

Damage: Exposure of tissue below the bark surface can allow rots to take hold.

Cause: Long periods of hot, dry weather.

Plants affected: Firs (*Abies*).

Prevention and control: Keep vulnerable trees well watered during dry summers and cover the surrounding soil with a mulch to conserve moisture in the soil. Cracks in the bark generally heal naturally, and treatment is not necessary. Inspect any deep cracks for signs of rotting tissue.

BUD DROP, Aborted Flowers

How to identify: Flower buds shrivel, fail to open and are shed by the plant.

Damage: The flowering display is impaired.

Cause: Bud drop is usually

Above: A long period of hot, dry weather has caused the bark of this fir tree to crack.

caused by excess dryness at the roots when the flower buds are forming (in autumn on spring-flowering camellias), or by a sudden cold spell just before the flowers open. Excessive watering can also cause flowers to be aborted.

Plants affected: Many ornamentals, especially pot plants under glass, camellias (*Camellia*) and sweet peas (*Lathyrus odoratus*).

Prevention and control: Make sure the soil or compost (soil mix) does not dry out when flower buds are forming. Mulching can be beneficial. Mist tropical pot plants such as gardenias (*Gardenia*) to maintain appropriate humidity.

Below: Camellias may suffer from bud drop if they are too dry. This flower is about to fall.

DUMPY BUD (roses)

How to identify: Buds either do not open or have shortened sepals and petals, giving the flower a flattened appearance.

Damage: The flowering display is spoilt.

Cause: A check in growth, such as may be caused by an unexpected cold spell or a period of *drought*.

Plants affected: Roses (*Rosa*).

Prevention and control: Keep plants well fed and watered when they are in active growth during spring. Cut off any affected buds. If the first crop of flowers is affected, remove all the damaged buds and apply a foliar feed, which should encourage further flowering later in the season.

FRUIT DROP (tree fruits)

How to identify: Fruits are dropped prematurely, before they ripen.

Damage: Cropping is reduced.

Cause: A variety of factors, including the action of certain pests and diseases. A common cause is *poor pollination*, generally due to a low population of pollinating insects during the flowering period (this is itself usually the result of *low temperatures*). Some trees shed a proportion of their fruits naturally in a process known as *June drop*.

Plants affected: A range of tree fruits.

Prevention and control: None possible. Consider hand-pollinating plants that regularly drop their fruits.

NON-ROOTING (hyacinth bulbs)

How to identify: Leaves do not develop at the normal rate, and as a result flower stems are stunted. Roots are either not present or very short.

Damage: Flowering is impaired.

Cause: A variety of factors can cause this problem in hyacinths: keeping the bulbs at too high a temperature during storage or when forcing, or lifting them too early can all make the condition more likely.

Plants affected: Hyacinths (*Hyacinthus*).

Prevention and control: None possible. The affected bulbs can be planted out in a sheltered place outdoors, where they may recover.

BLOTCHY RIPENING (tomatoes)

How to identify: Hard green or yellow patches on fruits. *Greenback* is a similar condition.

Damage: Fruits ripen unevenly and may be unpalatable.

Cause: High temperatures and low levels of potassium or nitrogen.

Plants affected: Tomatoes grown under glass.

Below: Hard patches on tomatoes indicate blotchy ripening.

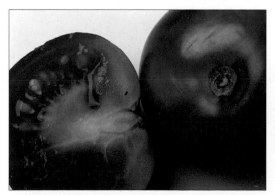

Above: Small tomatoes in a crop may indicate a case of chats.

Prevention and control: Keep growing plants well ventilated and shaded from hot sun. Maintain appropriate levels of potassium and nitrogen and water plants well.

CHATS (tomatoes)

How to identify: Tomatoes are small.

Damage: Crops are reduced.

Cause: Dry soil; *poor pollination* during unexpected cold weather or too dry an atmosphere can also cause chats.

Plants affected: Tomatoes.

Prevention and control: Mist flowering plants in the morning to encourage pollination; mist the plants again later in the day if the weather is hot. Keep plants well watered when the fruit is being set.

DRY SET (tomatoes)

How to identify: Fruits fail to swell properly and turn dry and brown.

Damage: Crops are disappointing.

Cause: *Poor pollination*, usually as a result of too hot and dry an atmosphere.

Plants affected: Tomatoes.

Below: A lack of atmospheric moisture has caused dry set in this tomato plant.

Above: A dry atmosphere has resulted in this scorched leaf tip.

Prevention and control: Mist flowering plants in the morning to encourage pollination, and also later in the day if the weather is dry and hot.

TIP SCORCH

How to identify: Leaf tips turn brown.

Damage: The plant's overall appearance is affected by the scorched tips.

Cause: Usually too hot and dry an atmosphere; *faulty root action* can also result in plants suffering from tip scorch.

Plants affected: A range of ornamentals grown in the home or under glass.

Prevention and control: Remove any affected leaves. Keep plants well watered when in growth, and create sufficient humidity by misting (either by hand or using an automated system). If faulty root action is to blame for the problem, repot the plants using fresh compost (soil mix) and use a foliar feed to boost recovery.

LACK OF POLLINATION

see also Poor pollination

How to identify: Fruits are absent.

Damage: Crops are non-existent.

Cause: Usually adverse weather conditions at flowering time that affect pollinating insects, or damage to flowers caused by pests or frost.

Plants affected: A range of fruiting plants.

Prevention and control: None possible.

Effects of sunlight

Whether outdoors or under glass, all plants need plenty of light to thrive, but too much or too little – or exposure to blisteringly hot sun after a period of frost or cold – can damage or weaken them or spoil their appearance.

SCALD (gooseberries)
How to identify: Soft fruits have depressed white patches.
Damage: Crops are spoilt. Affected fruits are susceptible to rotting.
Cause: Strong sunlight striking wet fruits. The problem is probably unavoidable if a hot spell immediately follows a heavy shower.
Plants affected: Gooseberries.
Prevention and control: Remove affected fruits. During hot weather, water gooseberry bushes in the evening rather than the morning.

RING PATTERN (African violets)
How to identify: Large yellow rings appear on leaves.
Damage: The general appearance of affected plants is spoilt.
Cause: Chilling of the leaves caused by overhead watering under direct light.
Plants affected: African violets (*Saintpaulia*).
Prevention and control: Cut off and dispose of affected leaves. Water plants during dull conditions or when the plants are in shade, and avoid splashing the leaves.

POOR LIGHT
How to identify: Stems and leaves are drawn and weak and pale green in colour as plants

Below: Sun scorch has caused the fronds of this fern to curl over and turn brown.

Above: Lack of light has made this cactus wilt.

attempt to reach the light. The problem is most likely to occur in winter where plants are grown under cover and light levels are naturally low.
Damage: Severely weakened plants become susceptible to disease and can die. Recovery is possible if plants are moved to better light in good time.
Cause: Low light levels.
Plants affected: A range of plants, especially seedlings, grown under cover.
Prevention and control: Make sure plants are not overcrowded. Thin seedlings as they grow. Move plants to well-lit positions in winter, when days are short, if necessary.

SCALD IN THE GREENHOUSE (grapes)
How to identify: Fruits show discoloured, sunken patches.
Damage: Affected fruits fail to ripen properly and can rot.
Cause: Strong sun striking wet fruit.
Plants affected: Grapes grown under glass.
Prevention and control: Cut affected fruits from the trusses. Ventilate the greenhouse to reduce humidity levels.

POOR POLLINATION
How to identify: Fruits fail to set or, where they are set, fail to develop normally.
Damage: Cropping is impaired.
Cause: Reduced activity of pollinating insects around flowering time. Low insect numbers may be seasonal, but are often the result of *low temperatures*.
Plants affected: A range of edible crops.
Prevention and control: None possible. In cold areas, plant cropping plants in a sheltered area and consider restricting choice to late-flowering varieties. Space plants at the

Below: Poor pollination has resulted in a reduced crop of grapes.

Above: This sweet corn has suffered poor pollination.

right distance to ensure adequate cross-pollination. Hand-pollination may be successful.

SUN SCORCH UNDER GLASS
How to identify: Areas of leaves turn a pale brown colour.
Damage: Leaves die, though the plant generally recovers if remedial action is taken.
Cause: Bright sunlight, sometimes intensified under glass, hitting wet leaves.
Plants affected: All plants under glass, especially houseplants with large, soft leaves.
Prevention and control: Shade plants in summer, and, where possible, turn them daily to maintain even growth. In greenhouses, where the temperature can rise sharply in summer, ventilate on hot days to lower humidity levels.

Below: Melons grown under plastic may suffer sun scorch.

Accidental damage

Incorrect pruning, inappropriate storage of bulbs or seeds, or garden chemical spillages can all weaken plants, leaving them susceptible to further damage caused by bacteria, fungi and invertebrate pests.

MECHANICAL INJURIES

How to identify: These are injuries inflicted unwittingly by gardeners, and include bad pruning cuts that snag the wood or crush growth buds, damage caused by plant ties that are too tight, indiscriminate hoeing, and lawnmower damage to plants at the edge of a lawn.

Damage: Wounded plants are susceptible to fungal diseases and can *die-back*.

Cause: Use of blunt, rusty tools; any garden procedure carried out without due care and attention can result in injury to plants.

Plants affected: Potentially all garden plants.

Prevention and control: Keep the blades of all garden tools clean and sharp so that they cut cleanly without tearing the bark of woody plants. When pruning, cut just above growth buds. Loosen all plant ties periodically to avoid chafing expanding stems. Cut back any accidentally damaged growth. Lay a mowing strip (typically a brick edging) around lawns adjacent to flower beds. Hoe with care to avoid damaging vulnerable plants.

Below: A bad pruning cut has damaged the trunk of this rhododendron.

Above: These *Daphne* leaves have been damaged by weedkiller.

CHEMICAL INJURIES

How to identify: A range of symptoms can be caused by inadvertent contact with garden chemicals. Growth will be stunted and leaves misshapen and/or discoloured.

Damage: Plant growth is checked. Severely affected plants will be susceptible to disease and can die.

Cause: Inappropriate or careless use of garden chemicals such as weedkillers, pesticides, fungicides and fertilizers.

Plants affected: Potentially all garden plants.

Prevention and control: Apply garden chemicals during dull, weather, when sun scorch is unlikely to occur. Choose a windless day so that the product cannot be blown on to neighbouring plants. If a product has to be diluted, follow the manufacturer's directions accurately: a common mistake is to make up solutions that are too strong. Remember that excess fertilizer can be toxic to plants. Dispose of any excess garden chemicals correctly, and do not water them indiscriminately on to beds or lawns.

HORMONE WEEDKILLER DAMAGE

How to identify: Leaves are distorted and may fall. Shoots and stems can be twisted.

Damage: There can be a check in growth, but plants usually recover and crop normally.

Cause: Misuse or inappropriate use of weedkillers.

Plants affected: Almost any plant, especially those with large, soft leaves, such as outdoor vines. Roses (*Rosa*) are particularly susceptible.

Prevention and control: Cut off any severely affected growth. Avoid mulching with grass clippings from a lawn that has recently been treated with weedkiller. Treat weeds on dull, still days, when the product is not likely to be blown on to neighbouring plants and will not cause sun scorch.

LOOSE BUD

(hyacinths)

How to identify: Stems below the flower buds break off.

Damage: The flowering display is spoilt.

Cause: Incorrect storage or forcing.

Plants affected: Hyacinths (*Hyacinthus*).

Prevention and control: None possible.

Above: Weedkiller spillage has damaged the leaves and spoilt the appearance of this plant.

CHALKINESS AND HARDNESS OF BULBS

How to identify: Dormant bulbs (including corms and tubers) harden. The problem affects bulbs in storage.

Damage: Affected bulbs fail to grow.

Cause: Lifting too early, before the leaves have died down fully, and incorrect storage.

Plants affected: Bulbs, typically tulips (*Tulipa*) and also dahlias (*Dahlia*).

Prevention and control: None possible. Discard affected bulbs.

Below: These bulbs have hardened while in storage because they were lifted too early.

Other causes

Some plant "problems" are natural occurences that are generally unavoidable, though their consequences can be minimalized by good husbandry; others may be caused by a combination of factors that are not always easy to identify.

COX'S SPOT

How to identify: Small, pale brown, round spots appear on leaves.
Damage: Depending on severity, growth can be checked and cropping affected.
Cause: Cox's spot can be caused by a range of factors. Magnesium deficiency may be a contributory factor, and the problem is likely to be worst on trees suffering from *faulty root action*, either as a result of *waterlogging* or *drought*.
Plants affected: Apples.
Prevention and control: Take action depending on the likely cause of the problem.

EXUDATION

How to identify: Small round droplets appear on leaves and stems, most noticeably on new growth in spring.
Damage: No immediate damage occurs, though the presence of droplets can be an indicator of excess humidity.
Cause: Exudation is a natural phenomenon and indicates that roots are growing strongly.
Plants affected: Crops grown under glass.
Prevention and control: None necessary, but maintain good ventilation to prevent too high a humidity level.

Below: Cox's spot on an apple leaf.

GLASSINESS OR WATER CORE

How to identify: The flesh of fruits is waterlogged and can develop an excessive sweetness to taste.
Damage: Fruit is inedible and can rot in storage. However, if fruits are only slightly affected, storing them in cool, well-ventilated conditions can cure the problem.
Cause: Unknown. Too high nitrogen levels in spring, excessive dryness at the roots during the growing season and wide fluctuations in temperature between day and night in late summer and autumn may be contributory factors. It is a particular problem of young trees.
Plants affected: Tree fruit.
Prevention and control: None possible. Keep trees (especially

Below: Blotchy rhododendron leaves.

Below: Exudation on parsley leaves.

newly planted ones) growing strongly by maintaining adequate water supplies and feeding appropriately. Mulch around the trees to conserve soil moisture.

LEAF BLOTCHES

How to identify: Irregular yellow, brown or black patches appear on leaves.
Damage: The problem is unsightly on ornamental plants. Affected leaves can also be shed from plants.
Cause: A number of factors can cause leaf blotches, including the action of various pests and diseases.
Plants affected: Most plants.
Prevention and control: Cut back affected growth. Improve cultivation around plants, keep them well watered and mulch to conserve soil moisture.

JUNE DROP

How to identify: Small fruits are shed by the plant in late spring to early summer.
Damage: None.
Cause: June drop is a natural phenomenon that does not affect the health of the tree or the quality of the crop. However, dropping of larger fruits later in summer can indicate the activity of pests, and fallen fruits should be cut open to see if there are any signs of infestation. *Faulty root action* can also cause fruits to drop prematurely.
Plants affected: Apples and pears.
Prevention and control: None necessary.

Below: June drop is a familiar sight around apple and pear trees in early summer.

own roots, especially after a wet summer.
Plants affected: Walnuts.
Prevention and control: Improve the drainage around fruiting trees. Grow grafted trees rather than seedlings.

SWEET PEA SCORCH

How to identify: Pale brown patches appear on leaves.
Damage: Leaves, and eventually whole plants, are killed.
Cause: Unknown.
Plants affected: Sweet peas (*Lathyrus odoratus*), especially where the plants are grown as cordons.
Prevention and control: Remove affected leaves and spray with a foliar feed to boost recovery. If sweet pea scorch occurs regularly, switch to growing them as bushes.

POOR FLOWERING

How to identify: Flowers are absent or present only in small numbers. Flower buds are small and hard and can be shed from the plant.
Damage: The flowers are disappointing.

Above: These walnuts show the characteristic holes of walnut soft shell, which allow rot to get in.

Cause: On woody plants, inappropriate pruning can result in the removal of flowering wood. Lack of sun, late frosts and dryness at the roots can also cause problems. Peonies planted too deep often fail to flower. *Potassium deficiency* can also be responsible for the problem.
Plants affected: Potentially all flowering plants may suffer poor flowering.
Prevention and control: Feed plants with a high-potassium fertilizer and/or ensure they have enough sun. Prune woody plants correctly.

Below: This hydrangea has disappointing flowers.

REPLANT DISORDER

How to identify: Plants sited where a similar plant was previously growing fail to grow or have stunted growth.
Damage: Replant disorder generally results in the death of the plant unless it is quickly moved to a new site.
Cause: Unknown, but may be

Below: This sickly rose has wilted and shows signs of distress due to replant disorder.

Above: This plant is showing signs of chemical and natural damage.

the result of the depletion of minerals in the soil. Replant disorder is most commonly a problem in neglected gardens, where old plants have not been regularly fed and watered and have thus exhausted the soil. (Where it affects roses, the condition is sometimes referred to as rose-sick soil.)
Plants affected: A minority of plants, including primroses (*Primula*), roses (*Rosa*), cherries and apples.
Prevention and control: If a susceptible plant needs to be replaced by another of the same genus, dig out the soil to a depth of 1m (1yd) and replace with fresh soil from a different part of the garden.

WALNUT SOFT SHELL

How to identify: Shells of nuts are thin and develop holes.
Damage: Fungi and other organisms enter holes in the shells, causing the kernels to rot.
Cause: Unknown. The problem is worst on trees grown on their

Plant nutrition

Most soils have an appropriate balance of minerals necessary for good plant growth, but an excess or deficiency can result in specific symptoms. Use a soil-testing kit to check the pH balance and mineral content of the soil.

Above: Despite looking healthy, these cucumbers may taste bitter.

BITTER CUCUMBERS

How to identify: The cucumbers have a bitter taste.
Damage: The crop is unpalatable.
Cause: Pollination of the fruit and/or excess nitrogen. Irregular growth (as a result of irregular watering) can also cause the fruits to become bitter.
Plants affected: Cucumbers.
Prevention and control: Remove male flowers to prevent pollination; alternatively, grow all-female varieties or those with a high proportion of female flowers. Water growing plants carefully to ensure even growth. Avoid excessive use of nitrogen-high fertilizers.

BITTER PIT (apples)

How to identify: Sunken pits appear on the skins of fruit. The flesh immediately beneath the pitting is brown and there are also brown areas throughout the fruit. Bitter pit usually occurs on fruits in storage, but can also sometimes be observed on fruits still on the tree.
Damage: Brown patches just beneath the skin can be removed by peeling, but fruits that have browning throughout the flesh are often inedible.
Cause: Lack of calcium, generally arising as a result of irregular watering; too high a level of potassium or magnesium also causes bitter pit in apples.
Plants affected: Apples.
Prevention and control: Keep trees well watered during times of drought when the fruit is developing. Spray with calcium nitrate throughout the summer.

BORON DEFICIENCY

How to identify: Lack of this trace element can produce a range of symptoms. *Pears:* Fruits are distorted and show brown patches within. The bark is also rough and pimpled. Leaves are often small and distorted, and shoots can die back. *Beetroot (beet) and spinach beet:* The inner tissues of the root are dry and turn brown. The outer tissues can rot and show cankers, and the crown can become sunken. Leaves die or are deformed and stunted. (Boron deficiency in these plants is often referred to as "heart rot".) *Swedes (rutabagas) and turnips:* No external symptoms are visible. However, if cut, affected roots show grey or brown rings. Once cooked, affected roots remain hard and are unpalatable. (Boron deficiency in these plants is often referred to as "brown heart".) *Celery:* Brown cracks appear on the stems. Growth is stunted and leaves turn yellow.
Damage: Plant growth is checked and cropping is impaired.
Cause: Lack of boron in the soil; alternatively, excessive liming of the soil can make the boron that is present unavailable to plants.
Plants affected: A range of plants, especially beetroot and spinach beet, swedes, turnips and pears.
Prevention and control: Spray pears with sodium tetraborate (borax) at petal fall. For other plants, fork borax into the soil prior to sowing.

Above: Bitter pit has spoilt the appearance of this apple and may have made it inedible.

CALCIUM DEFICIENCY

How to identify: Tomatoes suffer *blossom end rot*, apples suffer *bitter pit*.
Damage: Calcium deficiency is not normally a problem in plants grown in ordinary garden soil, but can occur in plants raised in peat-based growing bags, in which tomatoes and other annual crops are commonly grown.
Cause: Low levels of calcium.
Plants affected: Most plants are immune to calcium deficiency, and problems generally occur only on tomatoes and apples.
Prevention and control: Keep crops regularly watered so that they do not dry out, especially tomatoes in growing bags.

Below: Distorted fruits with brown patches indicate boron deficiency in these pears.

Above: Yellow leaves can be a symptom of manganese deficiency.

MANGANESE DEFICIENCY

How to identify: Leaves turn yellow (chlorosis), the oldest first, sometimes showing orange-brown or red tints before falling early.
Damage: Growth is checked and cropping can be disappointing.
Cause: Low levels of manganese, a trace element. The deficiency is likely to occur on peat, silt and clay soils, and on soils with a pH of over 7.5 where *iron deficiency* is an associated problem.
Plants affected: Potentially all plants, with peas and beets being especially vulnerable.
Prevention and control: Apply fertilizer containing manganese, or a solution of manganese sulphate, or spray on crops in dilute form.

Below and right: The marsh spots at the centre of these peas indicate a lack of manganese.

MARSH SPOT (peas)

See also Manganese deficiency.
How to identify: Pea pods develop normally, but the peas show a dark red spot or cavity at the centre. Yellowing between leaf veins can also occur.
Damage: Cropping is affected.
Cause: Lack of manganese, a trace element.
Plants affected: Peas.
Prevention and control: Where the soil is known to be deficient in manganese, spray developing plants with a solution of manganese sulphate; alternatively, fork an appropriate compound into the soil prior to sowing.

PHOSPHORUS DEFICIENCY

How to identify: Leaves turn dull bluish-green, with purplish or bronze tints. Purple or

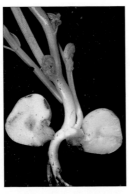

Above: These *Dipelta* leaves show the purplish spots that indicate phosphorus deficiency.

brown spots can appear on leaves. Fruits are soft and have an acid taste. They do not keep well.
Damage: Performance is poor and crops can be disappointing.
Cause: Lack of phosphorus, one of the three main plant nutrients, which promotes good root growth. The problem is most likely to occur on heavy soil in areas of high rainfall.
Plants affected: Potentially all plants, especially those grown for edible crops, annuals and bearded irises.
Prevention and control: Fork in a phosphorus-high fertilizer, such as bonemeal, around plants. Fruit trees benefit from applications of superphosphate every two or three years.

MALNUTRITION

See also separate entries for Boron, Iron, Magnesium, Manganese, Molybdenum, Nitrogen, Phosphorous and Potassium deficiencies, and Replant disorder.
How to identify: Plants generally fail to thrive.
Damage: Plants lack vigour and do not flower or fruit normally. In severe cases, plants can die.
Cause: Lack of appropriate plant nutrients.
Plants affected: Most plants can suffer malnutrition, with the possible exception of those adapted to very poor conditions, such as many coastal, Mediterranean and desert plants.
Prevention and control: Improve cultivation by working in organic matter prior to

planting; feed growing plants appropriately and mulch to conserve soil moisture. If many plants grown in proximity are failing to thrive, this may indicate a mineral deficiency. Consider testing the soil to establish the cause.

NITROGEN DEFICIENCY

How to identify: Growth is stunted, and plants have a spindly appearance. Leaves are initially yellow, later turning orange, red or purple. Edible crops crop poorly. The condition is most likely to occur on dry, light soils; pot-bound plants in containers also commonly show signs of nitrogen deficiency.
Damage: Plants perform poorly.
Cause: Lack of nitrogen, one of the three main plant nutrients, which promotes lush, green growth.
Plants affected: Potentially any plant.
Prevention and control: On poor soils, keep up nitrogen levels by digging in plenty of organic matter. Feed growing plants with a nitrogen-high fertilizer (but not after mid-summer). On a dedicated vegetable plot, consider sowing a green manure prior to planting crops to increase nitrogen levels.

Below: A lack of nitrogen has turned these camellia leaves yellow.

Above: Once cooked and drained, these potatoes begin to blacken.

Above: A small trickle of sticky resin mars the fruit on this plum tree.

Above: These blackberry leaves have turned yellow and look scorched as a result of iron deficiency.

BLACKENING (potatoes)

How to identify: Blackening of the flesh occurs after cooking (or sometimes before).
Damage: The crop is unpalatable.
Cause: Low potassium levels during the growing season; also storage of potatoes at too high a temperature, especially if bags are unventilated.
Plants affected: Potatoes.
Prevention and control: Maintain the potassium levels in the soil by use of an appropriate fertilizer; store potatoes in paper sacks in cool but frost-free conditions.

EXCESS NITROGEN

How to identify: Plants put on an excess of soft, leafy growth.
Damage: Plants can be susceptible to frost damage and disease. Flowering and

Below: An excess of nitrogen has killed this grass.

fruiting can be impaired.
Cause: Excess nitrogen, usually as a result of inappropriate use of fertilizers.
Plants affected: All plants can be affected.
Prevention and control: Use nitrogen-high fertilizers to boost growth in spring only. (Switch to potassium-high fertilizers to improve flowering and fruiting and to firm growth in late summer–autumn.) Where the soil is known to be rich in nitrogen, avoid adding nitrogen-high fertilizers or soil improvers such as chicken and pigeon manures, which are high in nitrogen.

GUMMING

How to identify: Stems or fruit exude beads of a sticky resin, which then turns hard. Trees lack vigour.
Damage: No permanent damage occurs: the gum often dries up on its own.
Cause: Usually a lack of nutrients or inappropriate soil conditions. (If the tree dies back, the problem is generally the result of the bacterial canker *Pseudomonas syringae*.)
Plants affected: Plums, peaches and cherries (including ornamentals).
Prevention and control: Cut off lumps of hardened resin, if necessary. Keep trees well fed and watered to encourage vigour, and mulch to conserve soil moisture.

IRON DEFICIENCY, Lime-induced Chlorosis

See also Manganese deficiency.
How to identify: Leaves turn yellow and can have a scorched appearance at the edges and tips, young growths being the most likely to be affected. The condition can be caused by a deficiency of manganese or magnesium, but on alkaline soils it is most likely due to low iron levels.
Damage: Plants fail to grow well, and flower and crop poorly.
Cause: Low levels of iron, a trace element. Lime in the soil prevents the take-up of iron and manganese by plants.
Plants affected: Acid-loving plants grown on alkaline soils (with a pH above 7). Ceanothus (*Ceanothus*), some japonicas (*Chaenomeles*), hydrangeas (*Hydrangea*), magnolias (*Magnolia*), wisterias (*Wisteria*), raspberries and

Below: This strawberry leaf shows the yellow colouring characteristic of iron deficiency.

peaches can also show symptoms. On rhododendrons, there may be some yellowing between the veins of the leaves on soils where the pH is higher than 5.5.
Prevention and control: Test the pH of the soil. If it is alkaline, apply an acidifying chemical such as flowers of sulphur to the soil at the rate of 125g per sq m (4oz per sq yd) or at the manufacturer's recommended rate for every point on the pH scale by which you wish the alkalinity to drop. (The application may not be effective immediately and will need to be repeated annually. Test the soil periodically to check the pH level.) Avoid using alkaline materials such as mushroom compost as a mulch or soil improver. Mulch annually with acidic materials such as bark or bracken. Alternatively, restock the area with plants that are alkaline-tolerant.

MAGNESIUM DEFICIENCY

How to identify: Leaves turn yellow (chlorosis), the oldest first, sometimes showing orange-brown or red tints (purple on some vines) before falling prematurely. Magnesium deficiency is most likely to be the cause of such a condition on acid soils.

Damage: Growth is checked and cropping can be disappointing.

Cause: Low levels of magnesium, a trace element, often caused by excess potassium in the soil. Magnesium can easily be washed through soils during prolonged, heavy rainfall.

Plants affected: Potentially all plants; tomatoes, chrysanthemums (*Chrysanthemum*) and all other

Below: Yellow and deep red blotches on these vine leaves denote magnesium deficiency.

Above: These yellowing tomato leaves are an indication of magnesium deficiency.

plants regularly fed with high-potassium fertilizers, such as roses (*Rosa*) (especially on sandy soils), are very vulnerable.

Prevention and control: Apply magnesium sulphate to the soil around plants or spray the topgrowth with a dilution. Repeated applications may be necessary; if this treatment is unsuccessful, the problem is most likely indicative of *manganese deficiency*. Affected roses should be fed with a fertilizer containing magnesium.

MOLYBDENUM DEFICIENCY, Whiptail

How to identify: Affected vegetable plants fail to develop normally. The condition affects certain brassicas.

Damage: Leaves are thinner than normal and are ruffled. Heads of cauliflowers and broccoli fail to develop.

Cause: Lack of molybdenum, a trace element, occasionally occurring on acid soils.

Plants affected: Vegetables belonging to the brassica family, mainly cauliflowers and broccoli.

Prevention and control: Where the soil is known to be lacking in this trace element, apply a proprietary product specially formulated to solve the problem prior to sowing or planting out.

POTASSIUM DEFICIENCY

How to identify: Leaves are bluish, with brown spots or brown tips and margins. They can also curl downwards.

Damage: Flowering and fruiting can be poor.

Cause: Lack of potassium, one of the three main plant nutrients, which promotes good flowering and fruiting.

Plants affected: Potentially all plants, especially potatoes, tomatoes, currants, beans, fruit, roses (*Rosa*) and flowering plants in containers and hanging baskets. The problem is most likely to occur on light, sandy, peat or chalk soils.

Prevention and control: Apply a high-potassium fertilizer, such as a rose or tomato fertilizer, in spring. Applications from

Above: The head of this cauliflower has failed to develop because of molybdenum deficiency.

midsummer can also help firm the growth (and thus improve the hardiness) of woody plants.

IRIS SCORCH

How to identify: Leaves turn red-brown and curl over. Roots also die.

Damage: In severe cases, plants can die.

Cause: Probably unsuitable soil conditions, such as excess wet in winter and/or drought in spring.

Plants affected: Rhizomatous irises (*Iris*).

Prevention and control: Remove affected leaves. Dig up rhizomes and cut off any affected roots. Firm rhizomes can be washed with a fungicide solution and replanted. Cultivate the soil to improve drainage, adding grit to very heavy soils.

Below: Potassium deficiency has caused these viburnum leaves to discolour and curl at the margins.

Index

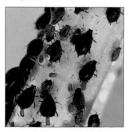

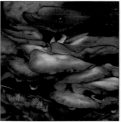

PICTURE ACKNOWLEDGEMENTS

Holt Studios: 4lc, 4rc, 4rbc, 5lab, 5rbc, 5rb, 5tr, 5rbc, 5rb, 13tc, 27c, 27bl, 32bl, 110–11, 112bl, 113t, 113b, 114bl, 114br, 115tl, 116tl, 116bcr, 117br, 118tr, 118bl, 118bc, 118br, 119tr, 119bl, 120bc, 120br, 121t, 121bl, 121bc, 122t, 123tl, 123tr, 124tl, 124bl, 1124bcr, 124br, 124tc, 124bcl, 125tl, 125b, 125tr, 126t, 126bl, 127bl, 127tcl, 127tcr, 127br, 128tr, 118tl, 128bl, 129tl, 129tr, 130tl, 130bl, 131bl, 131bc, 132tl, 132tr, 136tc 136b, 138tr, 138br, 139tr, 141tr, 141bl, 141bc 141br, 143t, 143br, 144br, 144bc, 144t, 145tl, 145tr, 145bl, 146t, 147tl, 148tl, 148tr, 148bl, 148bcl, 148bcr, 148br, 150bl, 150bc, 150br, 151bl, 152bl, 153tc, 153bl, 153bcl, 153bcr, 153br, 154br, 155tl, 155tr, 155bc, 156b, 157tr, 157bl, 157br, 158tl, 158tr, 158bc, 158br, 160tl, 161t, 161bcr, 161br, 162tl, 162tcr, 162bl, 162br, 163tl, 163br, 164tl, 165bl, 166tl, 166tr, 167tl, 167tr, 167bl, 167br, 168t, 168bl, 168br, 169tl, 169bl, 169br, 172bl, 172br, 173bc, 174tl, 174tc, 174tr, 174bl, 174br, 175tl, 175bl, 175bcl, 176t, 176bl, 176br, 177tr, 179tl, 179tcl, 179bcl, 180t, 180br, 181tl, 181tr, 181bl, 182t, 182bl, 183tr, 183bl, 183br, 184tl, 184tc, 184tr, 185tl, 185tr, 185b, 186tl, 186tr, 187tl, 187tr, 187bl, 187br, 188tl, 189br, 190tc, 190tr, 190bl, 191tl, 191tc, 191tr, 191b, 192tl, 192tcl, 192bcl, 192bl, 193tl, 193tr, 194tl, 195tl. 195br, 196bl, 197tr, 197br, 198br, 199tl, 199tcl, 199br, 200tl, 200br, 201t, 201bl, 201bc, 201br, 202t, 202bl, 202br, 203t, 203br, 203bl, 204bl, 205bl, 205bc, 205br, 206tr, 206tl, 207br, 207tr,
207bl, 207bc, 208tl,, 208tc, 208tr, 208bl, 209tc, 209tr, 210tl, 210tr, 210bc, 210br, 211t, 211bl, 211br, 212tl, 212tr, 212b, 214tr, 214bl, 214br, 215t, 215bl, 216tl, 216tr, 216b, 217tr, 219tr, 220br, 222tl, 222tr, 222bl, 222br, 223t, 223b, 224br, 225br, 226bl, 226br, 227tl, 227tcl, 227br, 230bl, 231tr, 233tc, 233tr, 234bc, 235tl, 235tr, 237bl, 238tr, 238bc, 238br, 239tl, 240tl, 240tr, 242tr, 242br, 243tr, 243bl, 243br, 244t, 244bl, 244br, 245tl, 245br, 246tl, 247tl, 247bl, 247bc, 248tl, 249tl, 249tr.
Premaphotos 22bc, 22br, 126bl, 138tl, 152tl, 165br.
DW Stock Images: 12bl, 13cr, 21bl, 22tl, 22tc, 22tr, 23t, 25t, 25bl, 112tr, 114tl, 115br, 117t, 119tl, 120bl, 120tr, 122bl, 123bc, 123bl, 131br, 132tc, 132b, 135bl, 137tl, 137tr, 137bl 139br, 140t, 142br, 145br, 147tr, 147b, 149tr, 149bl, 150t, 151bl, 153tr, 154t, 154br, 154bc, 155bl, 159br, 162tr, 163tr, 164bl, 164br, 165t, 166bl, 169tr, 181br, 186bl, 194tr, 196tl, 197cr, 199bl, 200bl, 204tr, 208bc, 208br, 213tl, 213tr, 213b, 214tl, 218tl, 225bl, 227tr,
Dave Bevan: 5tl, 10–11, 14br, 139bl, 179bl, 238bl.
Garden Matters: 122br, 190br, 200tr, 210br, 224bcr, 245tr.
Photos Horticultural: 115tr, 134br, 144br, 152tr, 205t, 221br, .

Key: t = top, b = bottom, c = centre, l = left, r = right.